Microcomputer Experimentation with the IBM PC

Lance A. Leventhal

Emulative Systems Company
San Diego, California

Microcomputer Experimentation with the IBM PC

HOLT, RINEHART AND WINSTON, INC.
NEW YORK   CHICAGO   SAN FRANCISCO
PHILADELPHIA   MONTREAL   TORONTO
LONDON   SYDNEY   TOKYO

8 9 0 1   039 9 8 7 6 5 4 3 2 1

Printed in the United States of America

ISBN 0-03-009542-5

Library of Congress Cataloging-in-Publication Data

Leventhal, Lance A., 1945-
    Microcomputer experimentation with the IBM PC.

    Bibliography: p.
    Includes index.
    1. IBM Personal Computer.   I.   Title.
QA76.8.I2594L446   1988   005.265   86-33629

Holt, Rinehart and Winston, Inc.
The Dryden Press
Saunders College Publishing

This book is dedicated to my wife, Donna, with all my love

preface

The purpose of this book is to provide experimental training on microcomputers for people in engineering, engineering technology, electronics, computer science, the physical sciences, and related fields. The emphasis is on peripheral interfacing and controller design. The experiments, examples, and problems were adapted from applications in instrumentation, test equipment, communications, computers and peripherals, industrial control, process control, business equipment, aerospace and military systems, and consumer electronics. The book shows how to use microcomputers and personal computers to do tasks that are essential in all these applications: responding to switches, controlling displays, encoding and decoding data, collecting and processing data, calculating arithmetic functions, interfacing simple handshaking peripherals (such as terminals and printers), timing and scheduling operations, and performing serial communications.

These same tasks are also the keys to more complex applications such as graphics, signal processing, CAD/CAM, image processing, and robotics. Current 16- and 32-bit microprocessors can play roles ranging from simple controllers to high-speed, complex computers. This book covers the basics of all these applications, as well as peripheral interfacing for personal computers.

First, the book explains how to operate the computer. It then introduces assembly language programming; shows how to do simple controller functions; discusses hardware/software tradeoffs; describes program design and development; presents alternative approaches to input/output and timing; explains the advantages and uses of programmable LSI devices; and describes serial communications. The last experiment gives a brief introduction to hardware design. The book includes many examples drawn from actual applications, but simplified to avoid the need for extensive background, special equipment, or long setup times. Because the book is self-contained, it is suitable for people with a variety of interests and backgrounds.

The book uses the popular IBM PC because of its low cost, wide availability, and extensive software support. To minimize cost and complexity, we use no software beyond the disk operating system (DOS) and the DEBUG program on the DOS Supplemental Programs disk. Thus the exercises should work on any PC, PC-compatible, generic PC, or other MS-DOS or PC-DOS machine. We do not require an assembler, editor, linker, or other software, although they make program development more convenient and allow larger projects.

We have added a parallel I/O port and an experiment board to the PC to provide external access. This hardware is inexpensive to build or buy and will not interfere with other uses of the computer. Parts for it are available from many suppliers, MetraByte Corporation (Taunton, MA) offers a low-cost parallel I/O board (model PIO-12).

The book emphasizes software control. This control is illustrated with simple examples using switches, single displays, and the PC's own keyboard and video display. Many complete working programs are included as starting points and references.

The standard format used in this book conforms with other textbooks, manuals, and reference materials. I have used the notation from IBM's macroassembler. I have tried to make all programs clear, simple, well structured, and well documented. I have avoided tricks even when they would make programs somewhat shorter and faster. Good programming practices are essential for microcomputer users, and I have tried to provide sound, fully tested examples. Besides, few things give people more pleasure than writing a program that is shorter, faster, and more ingenious than the one in the book. I must admit that no one has ever accused me of being a superprogrammer, anyway.

This book does not describe the 8088 microprocessor or the IBM PC in detail. Nor does it provide a complete introduction to 8088 assembly language programming. I have therefore included extensive references to textbooks, 8086 manuals, and 8086 and IBM PC programming books. However, none of the reference material is either required or essential. I have also compiled a large index for easy access to all discussions and examples.

Each experiment in the book is self-contained. Each includes a statement of purpose, a list of goals, definitions of new terms, references, descriptions of new instructions, list of required equipment (with diagrams), and a key point summary. Each experiment also contains many problems linked closely to the discussion. The problems illustrate key points, relate current material to previous experiments, and show examples from actual applications; there are no "make-work" problems or memory tests. I have checked all problems and have given sample data, hints, and discussions.

I have followed a few major precepts in writing this book. They are: (1) keep it short; (2) keep to the point; and (3) make it interesting. Microcomputers are a fascinating subject, and I see no reason to write a long-winded, dull book about them. Also I have not hesitated to express a few opinions and even to introduce a little humor. I suspect it's a bad sign if the author falls asleep while writing the book. At the same time, I have emphasized basic principles and modern trends in both programming and hardware design.

Many people contributed to this book. Irvin Stafford of Burroughs Corporation built the hardware, checked the examples and problems, and suggested many improvements and corrections. Rosemary Morrissey of IBM's Entry Systems Division provided manuals and the photograph of the IBM PC. George Alexy, Rich Bruns, Lance Belew, and Herb Chin of Intel answered questions and provided material and encouragement. Paul Becker, now Senior Acquisitions Editor at Prentice-Hall, got this continuing project started many years ago. My editor, Deborah Moore, and the reviewers (Professors Charles Nunnally of Virginia Polytechnic Institute and State University, Martin Kaliski of California State Polytechnic Institute/ San Luis Obispo, Fred Looft of Worcester Polytechnic Institute, Donald Gustafson of Texas Tech University, and Michael Lightner of University of Colorado, Boulder) helped keep me on track. All remaining errors are my fault (what else can I say?). Cheers!

San Diego, California   Lance A. Leventhal

contents

LABORATORY 8

Designing and Debugging Programs 145

LABORATORY 9

Arithmetic 172

Basic Operations

Purpose   To learn how to run and use the DEBUG monitor.

What You Should Learn
1. How to start the DEBUG monitor.
2. How to examine a memory location.
3. How to change a memory location.
4. How to enter and run a program.
5. How the 8088 computes memory addresses.
6. How to use segmented addresses in DEBUG commands.
7. How to prepare a bootable DEBUG disk.

Reference Materials
Comer, D. J. *Microprocessor-Based System Design*. New York: Holt, Rinehart and Winston, 1986, secs. 1.1 (number systems) and 3.5 (8086 storage organization and addressing).

Disk Operating System. Boca Raton, FL: International Business Machines Corporation, 1983, chap. 12 (DEBUG program).

Eccles, W. J. *Microprocessor Systems: A 16-Bit Approach*. Reading, MA: Addison-Wesley, 1985, chaps. 1 (the problem) and 2 (the microprocessor).

Goldstein, L. J., and M. Goldstein. *IBM PC: An Introduction to the Operating System, BASIC Programming, and Applications*. New York: Brady Books, 1984.

Gorsline, G. W. *16-Bit Modern Microcomputers*. Englewood Cliffs, NJ: Prentice-Hall, 1985, pp. 1-55 (classical microcomputer), 60-65 (memory segmentation).

Liu, Y. C., and G. A. Gibson. *Microcomputer Systems: The 8086/8088 Family* (2nd ed.). Englewood Cliffs, NJ: Prentice-Hall, 1986, pp. 1-24 (introduction), 26-31 (CPU architecture).

Norton, P. *MS-DOS and PC-DOS User's Guide.* New York: Brady Books, 1984, chap. 20 (DEBUG program).

Norton, P. *Programmer's Guide to the IBM PC.* Redmond, WA: Microsoft Press, 1985, chaps. 1–3 (anatomy of the PC, ins and outs, and ROM software).

Rector, R., and G. Alexy. *The 8086 Book.* Berkeley, CA: Osborne/McGraw-Hill, 1980, pp. 3-22 to 3-23 (segment registers), 3-30 to 3-31 (calculating segmented addresses).

Terms **Basic Input/Output System (BIOS):** the routines that enable an IBM Personal Computer (PC) or PC-compatible to use its keyboard, video display, disks, printer, and other I/O and storage devices.

Byte: a unit of 8 bits, may be described as consisting of two hexadecimal digits (the four most significant bits and the four least significant bits).

Central processing unit (CPU): the part of the computer that controls its operations and processes data.

Cursor: a marker that indicates the currently active position on a display.

DOS: see MS-DOS.

File: a collection of related information that is stored and retrieved as a unit.

Hexadecimal (or **hex**): number system with base 16. The digits are the numbers 0 through 9, followed by the letters A through F (see Table 0–1).

K (or **KB**): a unit of memory, 1 kilobyte or 2^{10} (1024) bytes.

M (or **MB**): a unit of memory, 1 megabyte or 2^{20} (1,048,576) bytes.

Microcomputer: a computer with a microprocessor CPU.

Microprocessor: a single-chip CPU. The IBM PC uses the Intel 8088; some PC-compatibles use related chips such as the Intel 8086, 80186, 80188, 80286, or 80386.

Monitor: a program that lets the operator enter programs and data, run programs, examine memory and registers, and use peripherals. Note that the term "monitor" also refers to a television-like device or video display.

MS-DOS: the most popular operating system for the IBM PC and PC-compatibles. It is a product of Microsoft Corporation (Redmond, WA). Often called PC-DOS or just DOS. It offers facilities for using peripherals (such as the video display, keyboard, printer, modem, and disk), moving programs and data to or from disk, managing disk files, developing programs, and adding I/O devices.

Nonvolatile memory: a memory that retains its contents when power is lost.

Offset (in 8088 addresses): the distance in bytes between an address and the base address of its segment, that is, the address within a segment.

Operating system: a program that controls a computer's overall operations and does such tasks as assigning places in memory to programs and data, running programs, and managing the I/O system.

Read-only memory (ROM): a memory that can be read but not changed in normal operation.

Read/write (random-access) memory (RAM): a memory that can be both read and changed (written) in normal operation.

Segment: a subdivision of memory. In 8088 terminology, a segment consists of up to 64K bytes starting at the address in a segment register (shifted left 4 bits). If, for example, the data segment register contains 1000_{16}, the current data segment starts at address 10000_{16} and could extend as far as address $1FFFF_{16}$.

Segmented address: an address consisting of a segment number or segment register designation and an offset. The standard convention is to put a colon between the two parts.

Segment number: base (starting address) of a segment divided by 16. For example, segment $C000_{16}$ starts at address $C0000_{16}$ and could extend as far as address $CFFFF_{16}$.

Segment register: a register containing a segment number.

Software interrupt (or trap): an instruction that forces a jump to a specific (CPU-dependent) address, often used to end a program or to indicate an error or special condition.

Volatile memory: a memory that loses its contents when power is removed.

Word: the basic group of bits that a computer can process at one time. The 8088 microprocessor has a 16-bit word internally but transfers data to or from memory 8 bits at a time.

8088
Instruction

INT 20H: software interrupt 20 hex; when DEBUG is running, INT 20H transfers control back to it, restoring its prompt.

Overview

The IBM PC (Figure 0-1) is currently the most widely used personal computer. This laboratory's references list three popular books about it: Goldstein's is a general introduction; and Norton's two books cover topics of interest to advanced users, programmers, and hardware and software developers. The PC has the following major components:

- An 8088 microprocessor, the central processing unit or "brain." This version of the 8086 microprocessor transfers data to or from memory 8 bits (rather than 16 bits) at a time; it is otherwise virtually identical to the 8086. Related chips (80188, 80186, 80286, and 80386) are used in PC-compatibles and advanced personal computers such as IBM's PC AT.
- Read-only memory (ROM). This permanent (nonvolatile) memory lets the computer get started, so it can then load external software from a disk. The ROM contains programs that allow the PC to use the keyboard, video display, disks, and other I/O and storage devices; these programs are called the *basic input/output system* (*BIOS*).
- Read/write memory (RAM). This is ordinary general-purpose memory used to hold programs and data. IBM PCs typically have between 256K and 640K of RAM, where 1K = 1024 (2^{10}) bytes. A byte, the basic unit of memory, consists of 8 bits.

Figure 0-1
The IBM Personal Computer (PC). (Photo courtesy of IBM Entry Systems Division, Boca Raton, FL).

- An 84-key typewriter-style keyboard. The standard typewriter keys are the light keys in the center. The dark keys surrounding them are extra command keys (such as "Ctrl," "Alt," and "Caps Lock"). There is also a numeric pad at the right and function keys at the left. The arrangement on your computer may differ slightly from this.
- A video display capable of showing 25 eighty-character lines. The computer generally reserves the bottom line for its own purposes.

Appendix 3 contains descriptions of the 8088 microprocessor and related chips. For those unfamiliar with the hexadecimal (base 16) number system, there are brief explanations in the textbooks by Comer and by Liu and Gibson, as well as in many other books. We will not emphasize this boring subject or assume great skill in hexadecimal (or hex) arithmetic. Hexadecimal notation is merely a convenience to avoid references to long binary numbers.

Starting DEBUG

To start the IBM PC, put the DOS disk in drive A (left-hand drive if your computer has two) and turn the computer on. It will ask for the date and time if these functions are not built-in. Answer the questions using the international 24-h clock for the time. The computer will then record when each new file is created, thus allowing you to recognize the latest versions.

When you see the A> prompt, remove the DOS disk and replace it with the DOS Supplemental Programs disk. Type

DEBUG

and press the "Enter" key. Fortunately, DOS does not care whether you type capital letters, lowercase letters, or some strange combination. This is a godsend, as the IBM PC does not indicate whether Caps Lock is on. So there is no way to tell which case will appear when you type a letter.

You should now see a line with a hyphen (DEBUG's prompt character) followed by a blinking underscore (the *cursor*). The IBM PC is executing DEBUG, a monitor that allows you to control the computer hardware in detail from the keyboard. You can place programs and data in memory, run programs, examine and change memory and internal CPU storage locations, and do other simple operations.

When you finish using DEBUG, press "Q" ("Quit" command) and Enter to return to DOS. This should restore the A> prompt. The last section of this Laboratory describes how to prepare a disk that loads DEBUG automatically from power-on.

Examining Memory

The IBM PC's memory is divided into units of up to 64K (2^{16}) bytes called *segments*. A byte, the basic unit of memory, consists of 8 bits; we often describe it as made up of two hexadecimal digits. Note that each location has a 16-bit address (four hexadecimal digits) within the current segment and contains one byte of data (two hexadecimal digits). Table 0-1 lists the hexadecimal digits and their binary and decimal equivalents. Use this table if you need help converting numbers between bases.

DEBUG automatically selects a segment (defined by its starting address divided by 16 or *segment number*) beginning just above the area of memory it occupies. We will assume generally that all addresses are in this segment. Its number depends on which model of computer and which options you have, so we will not refer to it by value. We will discuss segmentation briefly at the end of this Laboratory.

To avoid conflicts with DEBUG and to allow additions at either end of areas, we will use locations 200 through 2FF for programs and 340 through 4FF for data. This will suffice for short programs.

Table 0-1

**Hexadecimal to
Decimal
Conversion Table**

Hexadecimal Digit	Decimal Value	Binary Value
0	0	0000
1	1	0001
2	2	0010
3	3	0011
4	4	0100
5	5	0101
6	6	0110
7	7	0111
8	8	1000
9	9	1001
A	10	1010
B	11	1011
C	12	1100
D	13	1101
E	14	1110
F	15	1111

To examine memory, first press the E key (for the "Enter" command). Then type the address you want to examine, and finally press Enter. If the double use of "Enter" confuses you, think of the terminating key as "Return." Many computers have it marked that way, but not IBM's. Note that you can omit leading zeros from the address just as in normal usage. Remember that the digits are hexadecimal (see Table 0-1).

You will now see a line with the complete address at the far left, followed by its contents, a period, and the cursor. The complete address consists of the segment number, a colon, and the address within the segment (or *offset*).

For example, to examine location 200 hex, type E, 2, 0, 0, and press Enter. You can put spaces ahead of the address to make the command easier to read. Remember that the display is hexadecimal and that offsets (we will generally just call them addresses) are four digits long, whereas data entries are two digits long. If you have done everything correctly, you will see a line like the following:

$$08F1:0200 \qquad 09.$$

The cursor will be after the period. Remember that the segment number may be different on your computer.

Since address 200 is in RAM, its contents are arbitrary. RAM loses its contents when power is removed and could start in any state whatsoever. Such a memory is said to be *volatile*. Anything you put in it will be lost when you turn the computer off.

Thus you can examine a memory location as follows (starting from DEBUG's prompt):

1. Press E.
2. Enter its address as four hexadecimal digits starting with the most significant digit. You may omit leading zeros.
3. Press the Enter (or Return) key.

The contents of the location will appear, along with its complete address, on the next line of the display. If you enter the address incorrectly (and notice the error before pressing Enter), use the "Backspace" key to erase the erroneous digits. Backspace is the key with the thick left arrow in the top row of the keyboard; it is located above the Enter key and to the right of the "=" key. Don't confuse it with the left-arrow key in the numeric pad. To restore the DEBUG prompt, press the Enter key again.

Problem 0-1

Examine address 238 (hex).

Problem 0-2

Examine address 2000 (hex). What happens if you try to examine address 10000 (hex)?

After examining a memory address, you can move on to the next higher address by pressing the space bar. Try this and see what happens. The contents of the new address appear to the right of the previous display. After eight bytes, the computer starts a new line with a new address at the far left. A typical display is:

08F1:0200	09.	E8.	03.	01.	5B.	E8.	A5.	EF.
08F1:0208	E8.	A4.	F4.	E9.	88.	08.	8D.	1E.
08F1:0210	88.	09.	53.	E8.	DC.	00.	5B.	52.
08F1:0218	53.	EB.	03.	90.	32.	C0.	9F.	86.

Keep going to show the sequence of the hex digits. What happens if you start the display at an address that is not a multiple of 8 (say, 203)? To stop examining memory, press Enter.

You can also move back one location by pressing the hyphen (minus) key. This produces a complete new line with the current address at the left. Press the hyphen key several times to show the backward sequence.

Changing Memory

You can also change memory after examining it. Simply enter two new digits (more significant digit first) after the current contents appear. As usual, you need not enter a leading zero. For example, say you are examining location 0200. You can change it to 75 and proceed to 201 by typing 7 and 5 and then pressing the space bar. You can also press the hyphen key to back up one address or Enter to restore the DEBUG prompt. To verify the change, reexamine 200.

So you can change a memory location (after examining it) as follows:

4. Enter the data as two hex digits, starting with the more significant digit. A leading zero can be omitted.

If you enter the wrong data, simply press the Backspace key to erase it. What happens if you try to enter a third digit or an invalid digit such as R or Z?

Problem 0-3

Change address 2000 to A4 and verify the operation. (*Hint:* The easiest way to verify a value after entering it is to press the space bar, then the hyphen key.)

Problem 0-4

Enter the following data into 200 through 202:

Memory Address (Hex)	Memory Contents (Hex)
0200	B0
0201	6A
0202	CC

Verify the values after entering them.

Running a Program

To run a program (starting from the DEBUG prompt), type G ("Go" command) and =, enter the starting address, and press the Enter key. Be sure to press = and type the starting address correctly. If you make a mistake, the computer may freeze up completely, ignoring keyboard entries. The only way to recover is to turn the machine off, wait a few seconds, and turn it back on again. This is obviously disastrous if you have a lot of work in memory.

A simple example program consists of the single instruction INT 20H (SOFTWARE INTERRUPT 20 hex), which restores the DEBUG prompt. We can enter and run it as follows:

1. Press E to examine memory.
2. Press 2,0,0, Enter to examine address 200. We will start our program there. Note that we have omitted the leading zero. Do not type the commas.
3. Press C, D, space, 2, 0, and Enter to put CD in 200 and 20 in 201; then return to the monitor. CD is the hexadecimal version of INT; you can look it up in Table A1-3 of this book or in a listing such as the *ASM86 Macro Assembler Pocket Reference* (Intel Corporation, Santa Clara, CA, 1982). The interrupt number (20 hex) goes in the next byte.
4. Press G, =, 2, 0, 0, Enter to run the program, starting at address 200.

What happens?

All the computer does is restore the DEBUG prompt after printing the encouraging message, "Program terminated normally." Nothing much happens, but the ending is happy (or at least tolerable). We will present more impressive programs with actual results in Laboratory 1.

Problem 0-5

Enter and run INT 20H starting at location 22A.

Segmented Memory Addresses

We have described memory locations as having 16-bit addresses. This would give the PC access to only 64K (2^{16}) bytes of memory. In fact, it can access 1M (2^{20}) bytes. The obvious question is, "How does a 16-bit processor handle 20-bit addresses?"

The approach that Intel, the original manufacturer of the 8088 processor, takes is not straightforward, to say the least, but it works. The actual memory address consists of two 16-bit parts, as mentioned previously:

1. The offset. This is the address within a segment, a section of memory containing up to 64K bytes.
2. The segment number. This is the starting address of the segment divided by 16; it is contained in a segment register.

The 8088 calculates the actual memory address as follows:

1. It multiplies the segment number by 16. This is equivalent to shifting the number left 4 bits, and clearing the 4 least significant bits.
2. It adds the offset to the 20-bit product.

For example, suppose that the segment register contains E3A4 hex and the offset is D97E hex. The actual memory address is

$$
\begin{array}{r}
\text{E3A40} \\
+ \quad \underline{\text{D97E}} \\
\text{F13BE}
\end{array}
$$

Note that you can multiply a hex number by 16 by just putting 0 at the far right (after all, 16 is 10 hex). You can get help with hexadecimal addition from Table 0-1 (good), a hex calculator (better), or a visitor from a planet whose inhabitants have 16 fingers (best).

This approach probably seems strange. Both shifting the segment register by 4 bits and using two 16-bit numbers to get a 20-bit result are arbitrary and wasteful. However, they do let the processor form 20-bit addresses from two 16-bit numbers that it can handle easily.

To allow access to several segments at one time, the 8088 provides four segment registers. They are

CS, the code segment register, used primarily for instructions.

SS, the stack segment register, used primarily for the stack.

DS, the data segment register, used primarily for variable data.

ES, the extra (data) segment register, also used primarily for variable data.

Obviously, segment registers are easy to manage if the entire program and its data fall in one segment. Then we can simply load all segment registers with the segment number and refer to memory locations with 16-bit offsets. This is the case for all programs in this book. In fact, we will work only in the lowest segment of free memory (that is, the one just after the end of DEBUG itself). At startup, DEBUG automatically puts this segment's number in all segment registers. To simplify terminology, we will refer to offsets within this segment as *16-bit addresses*.

Thus we will not be concerned much with segment registers in this book. We will mention them occasionally, however, and you should read the reference material to learn more about their contents and uses. As you might expect, they are important to the writing of large programs.

We can use segmented addresses in DEBUG commands. All we must do is enter the segment number, a colon, and the offset. For example, the IBM PC has ROM to handle startup, basic input/output, and other functions in segment F000. To examine offset FFF7 in this segment, proceed as follows:

1. Type E.
2. Enter the segment number (F000).
3. Type a colon.
4. Enter the offset (FFF7).
5. Press the Enter key.

The contents should be 2F in any IBM PC. It is different, however, in PC-compatibles. What happens if you try to change the value? Change several successive addresses and then reexamine them with the hyphen key. Remember that these locations are in read-only memory.

To execute the power-on startup routine, proceed as follows. It begins at offset 0 in segment FFFF.

1. Type G.
2. Type =.
3. Enter the segment number (FFFF).
4. Type a colon.
5. Enter the offset (0).
6. Press the Enter key.

The computer should act as though you had turned the power off and then back on. There is a delay while the PC does a self-test.

Problem 0-6

What is the actual 20-bit address of the startup routine?

Problem 0-7

Examine addresses 000A through 000D in the current segment. Take the contents of 000A and 000B as an offset (more significant byte in 000B) and the contents of 000C and 000D as a segment number (more significant byte in 000D). What happens when you execute the routine starting at this segmented address? Do the same with addresses 000E through 0011 hex. What happens?

Problem 0-8

Try entering and executing the INT 20H program at addresses 0 and 1 of segment FFFF. What happens? Did the program ever actually get loaded into memory?

Preparing a Bootable DEBUG Disk

For convenience, you should make up a bootable disk with just DEBUG on it. A *bootable* disk can be loaded without loading DOS first; that is, you simply put it in drive A and turn the power on. It starts DEBUG automatically. You can produce such a disk as follows:

1. Format a blank disk with DOS on it (called a *system disk*).
2. Copy DEBUG onto the formatted disk.
3. Add an automatic startup file called AUTOEXEC.BAT.

Let us start by formatting a system disk. The following procedure assumes that your computer has two floppy disk drives. The process is a bit more awkward if it has only one floppy.

1. Put your DOS disk in drive A.
2. Put a blank disk in drive B.
3. Type FORMAT B:/S and press Enter.
4. When the message appears telling you to insert a new diskette, press Enter.
5. After the computer formats the disk (this takes about 45 s) and reports how much storage is available, it will ask you whether you want to format another. Press N and the A> prompt will reappear. Note that you do not have to press Enter.

To copy DEBUG onto the formatted disk, proceed as follows:

1. Put the DOS Supplemental Programs disk in drive A and the blank, formatted system disk in drive B.
2. Type COPY DEBUG.COM B: and press Enter.
3. When the copying is done, type DIR B: to verify that it worked.
4. Label the copy; include the date for reference purposes.

To add an automatic startup file, proceed as follows:

1. Put your bootable DEBUG disk in drive A.
2. Type COPY CON:AUTOEXEC.BAT and press Enter. AUTOEXEC.BAT is the name of DOS' automatic startup file.
3. Type the following, pressing the Enter key at the end of each line:

DATE
TIME
DEBUG

4. Press the F6 key. It is in the function key section at the far left or top of the keyboard. The characters ^Z will appear on the display. Then press Enter again.

You can now start DEBUG without using DOS. The computer will ask for the date and time, then load DEBUG immediately.

Key Point Summary

1. The IBM PC has a simple monitor called DEBUG on the DOS Supplemental Programs disk. DEBUG lets you control the computer from the keyboard, examine its memory and internal features, and enter and run programs.

2. The IBM PC has read/write memory (RAM) in its lowest addresses. It has read-only memory (ROM) in its highest addresses. The ROM is nonvolatile, and you cannot change it. The RAM is volatile (its contents are lost when the power goes off), and you can change it.

3. Some read/write memory is reserved, either by DEBUG or by the microprocessor. We will use addresses 200 through 2FF for programs and data and 340 through 4FF for data only. These addresses are all in the segment that starts just above DEBUG itself.

4. Each memory location has a 16-bit address (four hexadecimal digits) within the current segment; its contents are an 8-bit number (two hexadecimal digits).

5. You can examine a memory address by pressing the E key, typing the address, and pressing the Enter key. The contents of the address then appear on the next line. You can change them by entering two hexadecimal digits or proceed to the next higher or lower address by pressing the space bar or hyphen key, respectively. These procedures let you examine memory and put programs and data in it.

6. You can make DEBUG run a program by pressing G and =, typing its starting address, and then pressing the Enter key.

7. 8088 memory addresses are actually 20 bits long, giving the processor access to 1M of memory. It calculates 20-bit addresses from two 16-bit parts: the contents of a segment register (segment number), and an address within the segment (offset). The calculation involves multiplying the segment number by 16 (equivalent to shifting it left four bits and clearing the four least significant bits) and adding the offset.

8. The IBM PC's user memory is located in the lowest numbered segments (0000 through 9000). The ROM containing the fundamental I/O software (the BIOS) is located in segment F000.

9. You can use segmented addresses in DEBUG commands. All you must do is enter the segment number, type a colon, and then enter the offset.

Writing and Running Simple Programs

Purpose To learn how to write, load, and run simple programs.

What You Should Learn
1. How to load programs into memory.
2. How to enter data for programs and examine their results.
3. How to make the 8088 do simple arithmetic and logic.
4. How to examine registers.
5. How to change registers.
6. How to get printed output.
7. How to transfer programs to and from disk.

Reference Materials

Comer, D. J. *Microprocessor-Based System Design.* New York: Holt, Rinehart and Winston, 1986, secs. 3.4A (8086 CPU) and 3.7 (8086 instruction set).

Eccles, W. J. *Microprocessor Systems: A 16-Bit Approach.* Reading, MA: Addison-Wesley, 1985, secs. 4.1 (iAPX 86/10 characteristics) and 4.2 (sequence examples).

Gorsline, G. W. *16-Bit Modern Microcomputers.* Englewood Cliffs, NJ: Prentice-Hall, 1985, chaps. 2–4.

Liu, Y. C., and G. A. Gibson. *Microcomputer Systems: The 8086/8088 Family* (2nd ed.). Englewood Cliffs, NJ: Prentice-Hall, 1986, chaps. 2 (8086 architecture) and 3 (assembler language programming).

Norton, P. *MS-DOS and PC-DOS User's Guide.* New York: Brady Books, 1984, chap. 7 (DOS editing keys), chap. 20 (DEBUG program), sec. 21.3 (DEBUG commands).

Terms **Accumulator:** a register that holds one operand and, subsequently, the result in most arithmetic and logical operations.

Addressing modes: ways to specify the addresses used in executing an instruction. Common addressing modes are *direct, immediate, indexed,* and *relative.*

Assembler: a program that converts assembly language programs into a form (*machine language*) that a computer can execute directly. The assembler translates mnemonic operation codes and names into their numerical equivalents and assigns places in memory to data and instructions.

Assembly language: a computer language that allows the programmer to use mnemonic operation codes, labels, and names to refer to their numerical equivalents.

Comment: part of a program that has no purpose other than documentation. Comments are neither translated nor executed; they are simply copied into the program listing.

Direct addressing: an addressing mode in which the instruction contains the actual address required to execute it.

Disassembler: a program that converts machine language programs back into assembly language (the opposite of an assembler). IBM refers to this conversion as *unassembly.*

Instruction pointer: a register that contains the address of the next instruction byte to be executed. Often called the *program counter.*

Logical shift: a shift that fills vacated bit positions with zeros.

Machine language: the programming language that the computer can execute directly.

Mnemonic: name that suggests something's purpose or function.

Object code: the program that is the output of a translator program such as an assembler. Usually a machine language program ready for execution.

Operation code (op code): part of an instruction that tells what operation it performs.

Program counter: *see* **Instruction pointer.**

Register: a storage location inside the CPU.

Reset: a signal that puts the computer in a known initial state.

Source code: a computer program written in a form requiring translation, such as assembly language.

8088 **AND: logical AND.**
Instructions

INT 3: software interrupt 3; when DEBUG is running, INT 3 returns control to it after displaying all the registers.

MOV: move data. MOV op1,op2 moves data from operand 2 to operand 1; this does not affect the source (operand 2).

OR: logical (INCLUSIVE) OR.

SHL: logical shift left; shift a register or a memory location left, and clear the least significant bits (see Figure 1-1 for an example of a 1-bit shift).

SHR: logical shift right; shift a register or a memory location right and clear the most significant bits (see Figure 1-1 for an example of a 1-bit shift).

XOR: logical EXCLUSIVE OR.

Figure 1-1

8088 instructions SHL and SHR in their 1-bit forms.

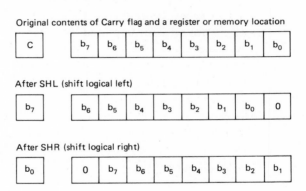

Original contents of Carry flag and a register or memory location

| C | b_7 | b_6 | b_5 | b_4 | b_3 | b_2 | b_1 | b_0 |

After SHL (shift logical left)

| b_7 | b_6 | b_5 | b_4 | b_3 | b_2 | b_1 | b_0 | 0 |

After SHR (shift logical right)

| b_0 | 0 | b_7 | b_6 | b_5 | b_4 | b_3 | b_2 | b_1 |

Data Transfer Program

Our first program simply moves the contents of memory location 400 (hex) to 401.

```
MOV   AL,[400H]        ;GET DATA
MOV   [401H],AL        ;MOVE DATA
INT   20H              ;RETURN TO DEBUG
```

We are using the format of the IBM (or Microsoft) Macro Assembler as described briefly in Figure 1-2. H after a number means *hexadecimal* and brackets around a number or expression indicate that it is an address, not data. The comments (preceded by semicolons) act only as documentation and do not affect the program. Figure 1-3 shows the 8088's registers; note that some (AX, BX, CX, and DX) consist of two 8-bit registers (AH and AL, BH and BL, CH and CL, and DH and DL).

Figure 1-2

Format for the IBM Macro Assembler.

After a number:

B —binary

D (or no designation)—decimal

H—hexadecimal

The default case (that is, unmarked) is decimal.

Other symbols:

: —after a label associated with an instruction statement, or between segment register designations or segment numbers and offsets

; —before a comment

' —around characters (before and after a string)

[ ]—around a memory address

Figure 1-3

Programming model of the 8088 microprocessor.

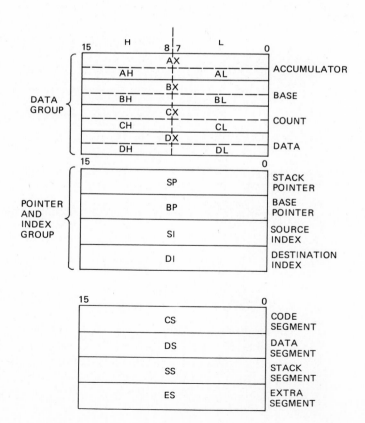

Let us now examine each instruction in detail:

1. MOV AL,[400H] loads register AL (the 8-bit accumulator) with the contents of memory location 400. The H means hexadecimal, and the brackets indicate an address. Remember, the address is four hexadecimal digits (16 bits) long but the data stored there is two digits (8 bits) long. We know this is an 8-bit transfer because it involves the 8-bit register AL.
2. MOV [401H],AL stores register AL in location 401. Here again, the address is four digits long, whereas the data is two digits.
3. INT 20H returns control to DEBUG. You should put it at the end of every program.

We first write the program in a form in which we can refer to the instructions by name. This form is called *assembly language*. The short instruction names are called *mnemonics* (memory joggers), although they are unique to a particular microprocessor and often are quite difficult to remember.

However, the 8088 does not understand mnemonics directly; it can execute only their numerical equivalents (a form called *machine language*). We therefore need a way to translate assembly language into machine language. We refer to the original program as *source code* and to the translated form as *object code*.

Manual translation (or hand assembly) is one approach. It involves looking up each instruction in a table (such as Table A1-3) or on a programming card. It is tedious and error-prone because the 8088 has a large, complex instruction set. Hand assembly makes sense only for patching a few instructions into an almost completed program.

Fortunately, DEBUG itself contains a simple assembler (the A command). While this assembler is not as powerful as the IBM or Microsoft assemblers, it is convenient for short programs. Besides, it comes free with DOS. We will use it throughout this book, but we will present all programs in generalized assembly language as well. Another inexpensive approach is CHASM, the public domain "cheap assembler." It is available from most user's groups and sources of public domain programs.

To assemble a program with DEBUG, proceed as follows:

1. Press A.
2. Type the starting address (usually 200).
3. Press the Enter or Return key.

Now just type the program lines, pressing Enter at the end of each one. You can include the comments. DEBUG will ignore them just as an assembler does. When you finish, press Enter one last time and the prompt will reappear.

To see the object code, disassemble the program with the U ("Unassemble") command. U translates machine language back into assembly language. Although this may sound like making orange juice into oranges, it is useful for verifying programs and documenting changes. To produce a disassembly, type U, enter the starting address, a space, and the ending address (the address where INT 20H begins). Then press Enter. You can now check your program.

Program 1-1 is the DEBUG version of the transfer program starting at address 200, along with the object code. Note the following:

1. DEBUG assumes all entries are hexadecimal, so you must omit the assembler's H designations.
2. Square brackets around numbers indicate that they are addresses, rather than data. Be sure to put brackets around addresses when you want to refer to their contents, not their values.
3. Both MOV instructions occupy three bytes of memory, one for the operation code and two for the address.
4. Addresses are stored upside down, with the less significant byte first.
5. Both MOVs use *direct addressing*, in which the instruction contains the address that it needs. The address follows the operation code in memory.

Most instructions have different operation (op) codes for different addressing modes. We will explain the modes as we use them. They provide a variety of ways for instructions to access memory addresses. You may compare them to different sets of directions to places or reference materials. Note the difference between a memory address and its contents. They are related in the same way as a building and its street address or a book and its library catalog number.

Run Program 1-1 with 6C in 400. The result should be 6C in 401. Clear 401 before running the program to prove that the computer is actually doing something.

PROGRAM 1-1		
Memory Address (Hex)	Memory Contents (Hex)	Instruction (DEBUG Form)
0200	A0	MOV AL,[400]
0201	00	
0202	04	
0203	A2	MOV [401],AL
0204	01	
0205	04	
0206	CD	INT 20
0207	20	

Entering and Running the Data Transfer Program

To enter Program 1-1 and the test data, then run the program, proceed as follows:

Enter Program

1. Start DEBUG if necessary.
2. Begin assembly at 200 by pressing

> A
> space (optional)
> 2
> 0
> 0
> Enter

3. Enter the assembly language program in DEBUG form as follows, pressing Enter at the end of each line.

> MOV   AL,[400]
> MOV   [401],AL
> INT   20

Remember to drop the Hs (for hex). Note that DEBUG moves the address display ahead automatically after each line.
4. Press Enter one last time to restore the DEBUG prompt.
5. To check your program, disassemble it by pressing

> U
> space (optional)
> 2
> 0
> 0
> space
> 2
> 0
> 6
> Enter

The ending address is 206 (the address of the first byte of INT 20H), even though DEBUG proceeds to 208 before quitting. The disassembly shows complete addresses with leading zeros.

Enter Data

1. Examine 400 by pressing

> E
> space (optional)
> 4
> 0
> 0
> Enter

2. Enter the data (6C) and clear 401 by pressing

> 6
> C
> space
> 0
> Enter

Note that you must enter the test data into memory in the same way that you enter the program.

Run Program

You can now run the program by pressing

> G
> =
> 2
> 0
> 0
> Enter

Remember, the program starts in 200. The final Enter transfers control to it; control returns to DEBUG with the "Program terminated normally" message when the computer executes INT 20H.

Examine Results

Finally, you can examine the data and the result (after running the program) by pressing

E
4
0
0
Enter

400 and 401 should now both contain 6C. The computer does not tell you the result (regardless of what some fiction writers think). It simply runs the program and returns control to DEBUG (since you put INT 20H at the end).

By the way, like DOS, DEBUG does not care whether you type capital or lowercase letters. All programs, instructions, and hexadecimal data appear in capitals in this book, mainly because the author misspent his youth working on antique keypunches and teletypewriters.

Problem 1-1

Run Program 1-1 with the following data in location 400:

  a. F0
  b. 28

Problem 1-2

Make Program 1-1 do the following:

  a. Store the data in 402.
  b. Move the contents of 401 to 400.

Problem 1-3

Revise Program 1-1 to use register BL instead of AL. How would you make it use CL? Does the program's length change?

Problem 1-4

Write and run a program that moves the contents of location 400 to 402 and the contents of 401 to 403. Use register AX to move 16 bits (two bytes) at once; AX consists of AH (more significant byte) and AL (less significant byte).

SAMPLE PROBLEM (the brackets around a memory address mean "contents of"):

DATA: [0400] = C6
     [0401] = 5E

RESULT: [0402] = C6
       [0403] = 5E

Processing Data

Of course, we usually want to process data rather than just move it. For example, the following program shifts each data bit left one position and clears the least significant bit before storing the result in 401. The computer here mimics an 8-bit shift register. The program is

```
MOV    AL,[400H]      ;GET DATA
SHL    AL,1           ;SHIFT DATA LEFT
MOV    [401H],AL      ;SAVE RESULT
INT    20H            ;RETURN TO DEBUG
```

The only new instruction is SHL AL,1, which shifts register AL left one bit and clears the least significant bit. Note that SHL AL,1 is a two-byte instruction; it does not need an address, as the data is in AL.

Run this program (Program 1-2 is the DEBUG version) with the data 01 (00000001 binary) in 400. The answer should be 02 (00000010 binary) in 401. Why? Use Table 0-1 to convert hexadecimal numbers to binary, and vice versa.

PROGRAM 1-2		
Memory Address (Hex)	Memory Contents (Hex)	Instruction (DEBUG Form)
0200	A0	MOV AL,[400]
0201	00	
0202	04	
0203	D0	SHL AL,1
0204	E0	
0205	A2	MOV [401],AL
0206	01	
0207	04	
0208	CD	INT 20
0209	20	

Problem 1-5

Run Program 1-2 with the following data in location 400:

a. 40. The answer in 401 should be 80.

b. C7. The answer in 401 should be 8E. What happens to the 1 that is originally at the far left?

Problem 1-6

Make Program 1-2 shift the data right instead of left.
(*Hint*: Replace SHL with SHR.)

SAMPLE PROBLEMS:

a. [0400] = 02
Result: [0401] = 01
b. [0400] = C7
Result: [0401] = 63

What happens to the 1 that is originally at the far right?

Problem 1-7

Revise Program 1-2 to shift the contents of two successive locations and store the results in the next two locations. That is, the new program should store the shifted version of 400 in 402 and the shifted version of 401 in 403.

SAMPLE PROBLEM:

[0400] = 01
[0401] = 08

RESULT:

[0402] = 02
[0403] = 10

Logically ANDing Two Values

We can easily convert the left shift program into a logical AND program. The task now is to logically AND 400 and 401 and put the result in 402. Here the computer mimics eight 2-input AND gates. The program is

```
MOV   AL,[400H]      ;GET FIRST OPERAND
AND   AL,[401H]      ;LOGICALLY AND SECOND OPERAND
MOV   [402H],AL      ;SAVE RESULT
INT   20H
```

Program 1-3 is the DEBUG version. We have started at 210 to preserve Program 1-2. AND works as follows on each bit:

Bit n of Operand 1	Bit n of Operand 2	Bit n of Operand 1 AND Operand 2
0	0	0
0	1	0
1	0	0
1	1	1

Note that the AND instruction occupies four bytes, two for the operation code and two for the memory address.

PROGRAM 1-3		
Memory Address (Hex)	Memory Contents (Hex)	Instruction (DEBUG Form)
0210	A0	MOV AL,[400]
0211	00	
0212	04	
0213	22	AND AL,[401]
0214	06	
0215	01	
0216	04	
0217	A2	MOV [402],AL
0218	02	
0219	04	
021A	CD	INT 20
021B	20	

Enter Program 1-3 into memory and run it for the following sample cases. Remember to start at 210, *not* at 200. Use Table 0-1 to convert hexadecimal values into binary to check your results.

a. Data: [0400] = 23
          [0401] = 34
   Result: [0402] = 20

b. Data: [0400] = F0
          [0401] = 3B
   Result: [0402] = 30

c. Data: [0400] = 0C
          [0401] = 77
   Result: [0402] = 04

Problem 1-8

Make Program 1-3 logically OR two locations and save the result. How would you get a logical EXCLUSIVE OR? Refer to Table 3-3 if you cannot remember how logical functions work.

SAMPLE PROBLEM:

DATA: [0400] = 23
         [0401] = 34

RESULT: [0402] = 37 for logical OR
             = 17 for logical EXCLUSIVE OR

Examining Registers

One way to see what a program is doing is to examine the processor's registers. In DEBUG, you can do this with the R ("Register") command. Pressing R and Enter displays the values of all registers as well as the next instruction to be executed. Figure 1-4 shows a typical result. You can display a single 16-bit register by typing its name after R (a space is optional), then pressing Enter. The valid register names are

AX	BP	SS
BX	SI	CS
CX	DI	IP
DX	DS	PC
SP	ES	F

After the display appears, press Enter to restore the DEBUG prompt.

Figure 1-4
Typical DEBUG
register display.

```
AX = 0000  BX = 0000  CX = 0000  DX = 0000  SP = FFEE  BP = 0000  SI = 0000  DI = 0000
DS = 08F1  ES = 08F1  SS  = 08F1  CS  = 08F1  IP = 0100    NV UP DI PL NZ NA PO NC
08F1 : 0100   0000                ADD        [BX+SI],AL              DS : 0000 = CD
```

Note that you can display only 16-bit registers, not 8-bit registers. For example, to examine register AL, display register AX. The contents of AL are the two rightmost digits.

We have not yet discussed some registers. We will describe the flags in Laboratory 2 and the stack pointer in Laboratory A. The instruction pointer (IP, also called the program counter or PC) contains the address of the next instruction byte. Each time the CPU executes a byte, it adds one to the pointer's contents. Thus the computer executes instructions sequentially unless specifically told to do otherwise. We described the segment registers (CS, DS, SS, and ES) briefly at the end of Laboratory 0.

You can get a register display automatically after a program runs. Just end it with INT 3 instead of INT 20H. INT 3 is useful because it is a one-byte instruction (CC hex). You can, for example, stop a program and display the registers at any point by replacing the first byte of the next instruction with INT 3. Laboratory 8 explores this technique further. In general, we will end programs with INT 3 when we want a register display afterward and with INT 20H otherwise. Be careful; INT 20H does not preserve the registers.

Changing Registers

After displaying a single register, you can change its contents by entering hexadecimal digits, then pressing Enter to save the new value. As usual, you can omit leading zeros. Note that you cannot change just half of register AX, BX, CX, or DX; that is, you cannot enter data into just AL, AH, and the like.

For example, the following sequence puts 4CF2 in register DX:

1. Starting from the prompt, press R, space, DX, and Enter to display register DX's current contents. The computer skips down to the next line automatically and prints a broken vertical line character, then the flashing cursor.
2. Enter the new data by pressing 4, C, F, 2.
3. Save the new data in the register and return to DEBUG by pressing Enter. To verify the change, repeat the R DX command, then press Enter again to exit.

Replace INT 20H at the end of Program 1-2 (location 208) with INT 3, then run the program with [0400] = C7. What are the final contents of register AL and the instruction pointer? Does it matter if you clear AL initially by putting 0 in AX?

Problem 1-9

Put INT 3 at the end of Program 1-3 (location 21A), then run it with [0400] = 23 and [0401] = 34. What are the final contents of register AL and the instruction pointer? Does it matter if you clear register AL initially?

Obtaining Printed Output

To make DEBUG produce printed output (program listings, register displays, and the like), press Ctrl-P. That is, hold down the Ctrl key (just left of A) and press P. Nothing seems to happen, but DEBUG will subsequently print as well as display everything, including its prompts and results and your commands. The printing starts as soon as you complete a command by pressing the Enter key. To turn the printing off, press Ctrl-P again. Be sure your printer is on-line and has its paper adjusted properly before using this feature.

Transferring Programs to and from Disk

Entering, assembling, and correcting programs with DEBUG often takes a long time. Furthermore, computers have perverse traits such as a love of overwriting completed programs. Users (including the author) have also been known to do clever things such as pressing Q ("Quit") and Enter instead of the intended A ("Assemble") and Enter. A few sessions will surely convince you of the need to save completed or nearly completed programs. Besides, such programs often serve as good starting points for later work.

Fortunately, DEBUG lets you save assembled programs (and data) on disk and load them back into memory. To save a program, proceed as follows:

1. Put a formatted disk in a floppy drive. Use drive B if you have a dual-floppy system and keep DEBUG in drive A.
2. Assign the program a file name with the N ("Name") command. We suggest a convention such as the following:

   a. Start program file names with the letter P, problem file names with PR, and data file names with DP or DPR.

   b. Continue names with the laboratory number (0 through F), a dash (−), and a two-digit program or problem number (e.g., 02 for Program 1-2, 14 for Problem 3-14). The leading zero in front of a single digit makes names appear in the proper order in a directory.
   c. End program and problem file names with .OBJ (i.e., object code), data files with .DAT. Be sure to type OBJ with the letter O, not the number 0.

Typical Name commands using this convention are:

   a. N P1-03.OBJ to save Program 1-3.
   b. N PR1-04.OBJ to save the answer to Problem 1-4.
   c. N DP1-02.DAT to save the data associated with Program 1-2.

If you are using drive B for your files, put B: ahead of all names.

   3. Put the number of bytes to be saved in registers BX and CX (more significant digits in BX). That is, put 0 in BX using the R BX command and the number of bytes in CX using the R CX command. For example, to save Program 1-3, you would put 0 in BX and A (10 decimal) in CX. Be sure to enter the length in hex, not decimal.
   4. Save the program or data on disk by typing W ("Write"), entering the starting address, and pressing Enter. For example, to save Program 1-3, type W, 2, 1, 0, Enter.

Loading a program from disk is even easier than saving one. All you must do is name the file with an N command, then load it by typing L ("Load"), entering the starting address, and pressing Enter. You do not have to specify the file's length. For example, to reload Program 1-3 into memory starting at address 210, you would press L, 2, 1, 0, and Enter. If you mistype the file name, the computer will report "File not found." Unfortunately, the only way to get a directory is to exit from DEBUG and type DIR. Note that you can obtain a printed directory from DOS with the command

$$DIR > PRN$$

This redirects the screen output to the printer.
   Take the following precautions when saving or loading programs:

   1. Always name the file with an N command first.
   2. Be sure to specify the file's length correctly when saving it. Note, for example, that locations 200 through 208 contain nine bytes (count them!), not eight. Watch that register BX is always 0, and that the entry in CX is in hex.
   3. Check that you have the correct disk. Remember that blank disks must be formatted.

4. Put B: before the file name if you are using drive B for your files.
5. Always label and date all disks. Make backups occasionally to avoid depending on a single copy.
6. Handle disks carefully. You don't have to treat them like precious jewels, but you should keep them upright, clean, and "dressed" in their sleeves and jackets.

Although saving object code on disk is helpful, it does not provide any way to easily change or correct programs. This requires saving either source code or DEBUG commands. Laboratory 8 describes both approaches.

Key Point Summary

1. Most simple 8088 programs use the accumulator (either the 16-bit register AX or the 8-bit register AL) as the center of operations. They begin by loading the accumulator from memory and end by storing the result (from the accumulator) in memory.
2. The simplest addressing mode is direct addressing, in which the instruction contains the address it needs. This address follows the operation code in memory.
3. To make the computer do useful work, you must enter the program and data into memory, run the program, and examine the results. Before entering the program, you must convert the assembly language version into the simplified form that DEBUG's A command accepts. DEBUG will then convert that form (source code) into the machine language (object code) that the computer can actually execute.
4. You can examine all 8088 registers with the R command. You can also examine a particular 16-bit register by typing its name after R. You can then change the register by entering a hexadecimal number or exit by pressing the Enter key immediately. INT 3 at the end of a program makes it return control to DEBUG and display all the registers.
5. To obtain printed output from DEBUG, press Ctrl-P. To return to the usual displayed output only, press Ctrl-P again.
6. To transfer programs or data to or from disk, you must first name the file with the N (Name) command. You can then save it by placing its length in bytes in registers BX and CX (more significant digits in BX) and doing a W (Write) command from a specific starting address. You can load a file by doing an L (Load) command to a specific starting address.

Simple Input

Purpose To learn how to use the computer's input ports.

Parts Required Eight switches attached to port A of the 8255 device on the add-on I/O board as shown in Figure 2-1. Table 2-1 lists the pin assignments for the 60 pin connector used to attach the I/O board to the external experiment board. Figure 2-2 contains a schematic of the I/O board that goes in a slot inside the IBM PC. We will refer to its 8255 device as P1 for short. For more details about the experimental setup, see Appendix 4.

What You Should Learn
1. How the 8088 identifies I/O ports and reads data from them.
2. How to determine whether a switch is open or closed.
3. Which bit positions can be assessed most easily.
4. How to examine and change the flags.
5. How to handle a series of switch closures.
6. How to recognize a starting (synchronization) character.
7. Common operating errors and how to avoid them or minimize their effects.
8. How to stop runaway commands and programs.

Table 2-1

I/O Connector Pin
Assignments for
Port P1A

Assignment	Pin
Bit 0	1
Bit 1	2
Bit 2	3
Bit 3	4
Bit 4	5
Bit 5	6
Bit 6	7
Bit 7	8

Reference
Materials

Comer, D. J. *Microprocessor-Based System Design.* New York: Holt, Rinehart and Winston, 1986, sec. 3.6 (I/O operations).

Gorsline, G. W. *16-Bit Modern Microcomputers.* Englewood Cliffs, NJ: Prentice-Hall, 1985, chap. 5 (input/output).

Liu, Y. C., and G. A. Gibson. *Microcomputer Systems: The 8086/8088 Family* (2nd ed.). Englewood Cliffs, NJ: Prentice-Hall, 1986, chap. 6 (I/O programming).

Figure 2-1

Attachment of
switches to port A
of the add-on 8255
device (device P1).

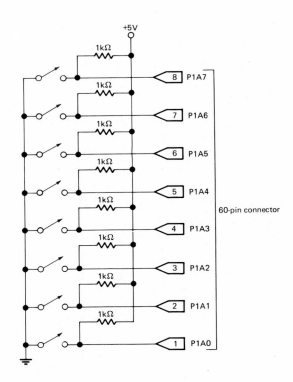

Figure 2-2

Schematic for the
add-on I/O board.

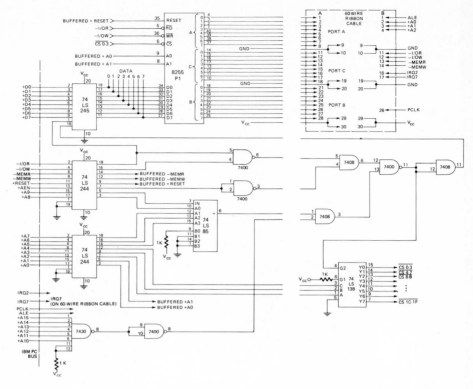

Terms **Branch Instruction:** *see* **Jump instruction.**

Carry flag: a flag that is 1 if the last operation generated a carry or borrow from the most significant bit and 0 if it did not.

Flag: a bit that indicates a condition inside the computer, often used to choose between alternative instruction sequences.

Flag register: a register that contains bits (flags) describing the computer's current state.

Immediate addressing: an addressing method in which the instruction contains the data it needs, usually immediately after the operation code in memory.

Isolated input/output: assigning I/O ports their own addresses, rather than giving them memory addresses.

Jump instruction (or **branch instruction**): an instruction that replaces the program counter (instruction pointer in the 8088), thus departing from the normal one-step incrementing. A conditional jump replaces the instruction pointer only if a condition holds.

Label: a name attached to an instruction or statement in a program. Its value is the starting address in memory of the resulting machine language or assignment.

Masking: isolating one or more bits from a group of bits.

Memory-mapped input/output: assigning I/O ports to memory addresses, rather than giving them their own addresses.

Port: the basic addressable unit of the computer's I/O section.

Relative addressing: an addressing method in which the instruction contains the offset from a base address.

Relative offset: the difference between the address used in an instruction and the current value of the program counter (instruction pointer in the 8088).

Relocatable: can reside anywhere in memory without changes; that is, can occupy any set of consecutive memory addresses.

Sign flag: a flag that contains the most significant bit of the result of the previous operation.

Status register: *see* **Flag register**.

Synchronization (or **sync**) **character:**   a character used only to synchronize the transmitter and the receiver. It does not contain any actual information.

Zero flag: a flag that is 1 if the last operation produced a zero result and 0 if it did not.

8088
Instructions

ADD: add. ADD op1,op2 adds its operands and stores the sum in place of operand 1.

CMP: compare; subtract one operand from the other but do not save the result. This instruction affects only the flags. CMP op1,op2 sets the flags from op1 – op2.

IN accumulator,DX: load the accumulator (either AL or AX) from the port whose address is in register DX.

The following conditional jump instructions all skip over the specified number of memory locations (bytes) if the specified condition is true; otherwise, they proceed to the next instruction in sequence. Note that some of them have alternative mnemonics.

JC (or JB): jump if Carry = 1 (or jump if below).

JNC (or JAE): jump if Carry = 0 (or jump if above or equal).

JNS: jump if Sign = 0.

JNZ (or JNE): jump if not equal to zero (Zero flag = 0).

JS: jump if Sign = 1.

JZ (or JE): jump if equal to zero (Zero flag = 1).

OUT DX,accumulator: output; store the accumulator (either AL or AX) in the port whose address is in register DX.

TEST: bit test; logically AND the operands but do not save the result. This instruction affects only the flags.

8088 Input/Output Instructions

The 8088 has the following common I/O instructions:

- IN AL,DX loads register AL with a byte of data from the port whose address is in DX.
- OUT DX,AL stores a byte of data from register AL in the port whose address is in DX.

These instructions always use an accumulator (AL or AX) and DX; they do not work with other registers. Note that port addresses are distinct from memory addresses. For example, port address FF00 is not the same as memory address FF00. We call this approach *isolated input/output*, as opposed to *memory-mapped input/output* in which I/O ports occupy memory addresses. Note also that port addresses are 16-bit numbers; they are not segmented as memory addresses are.

Simple Input

To begin, we will use two I/O ports attached to the 8255 device on the add-on I/O board. Their addresses are FF00 (called P1 port A) and FF01 (called P1 port B). Throughout this book, we will use port A for input and port B for output. Don't confuse the A and B here with port addresses. Starting from power-on, the following program loads accumulator AL from P1 port A:

```
MOV    DX,0FF00H
IN     AL,DX
INT    3
```

If your computer has different port addresses, all you must change is the operand in MOV DX. The 0 in front of FF00 simply tells the assembler that what follows is a number rather than a name. It has no effect on the object code. A leading zero is necessary in front of any hexadecimal number that starts with a letter.

Program 2-1 is the DEBUG version. It does not need a zero in front of FF00 because the A command accepts only hex numbers anyway. Open all switches attached to P1 port A and run the program. What is in AL afterward?

Close the switch attached to bit 5 and run Program 2-1 again. Now what does AL contain?

PROGRAM 2-1		
Memory Address (Hex)	Memory Contents (Hex)	Instruction (DEBUG Form)
0200	BA	MOV DX,FF00
0201	00	
0202	FF	
0203	EC	IN AL,DX
0204	CC	INT 3

Problem 2-1

The computer reads an open switch as ——— and a closed switch as ——— if the connections are as shown in Figure 2-1.

Problem 2-2

Determine what value Program 2-1 puts in AL if:

a. The switch attached to bit 2 of P1 port A is closed.

b. Switches attached to bits 2 and 5 are closed.

c. Switches attached to bits 0, 6, and 7 are closed.

Leave all other switches open.

Problem 2-3

What happens if you replace MOV DX,0FF00H with MOV DX,0FF01H? Does opening or closing switches affect the input? Explain the result.

Remember the following:

1. The standard in the computer industry is to number bits starting with zero at the far right. Thus the bits in a byte are numbered 0 through 7 from right to left; bit 0 is least significant and bit 7 most significant. Figure 2-3 shows an example of the standard numbering for a word (bits 0 through 15 from right to left). Be careful—switches, other I/O devices, and integrated circuits often use other conventions (for example, 1 to 8 or left to right).

2. We must put the port address is register DX before using IN AL,DX. MOV DX,0FF00H puts the 16-bit number FF00 in DX. Note that there are no brackets around FF00. We call this method of specifying constants *immediate addressing*, as the data comes immediately after the operation code in memory. Note that FF00 appears upside down in locations 201 and 202.

Flags and Conditional Jumps

To have the computer determine whether a switch is open or closed, we must use the flags and conditional jump instructions. Instructions that process data (for example, arithmetic, logical, and shift instructions, as opposed to those that merely move data or change the instruction pointer) also affect the flags. A conditional jump lets the computer use a flag to choose between alternative paths through a program.

The major 8088 flags are:

S (Sign): 1 if the result of the last arithmetic or logical instruction had a 1 in its most significant bit, 0 if it did not. Note that the most significant bit is bit 7 for 8-bit operations, but bit 15 for 16-bit operations.

Z (Zero): 1 if the last arithmetic or logical instruction produced a zero result, 0 if it did not.

C (Carry): 1 if the last arithmetic or shift instruction produced a carry or borrow, 0 if it did not.

The flags are simply flip-flops inside the 8088 processor.

Conditional jumps replace the instruction pointer if the specified condition holds. Otherwise, they do nothing, and the processor simply continues its normal sequence. These instructions make a computer "smart," that is, capable of making decisions based on current information. The computer thus becomes an intelligent controller. Table 2-2 lists the 8088's major conditional jump instructions.

Table 2-2

8086 Major
Conditional Jump
Instructions

Instruction	Flag Used*	Value on Which Jump Occurs
JNC (JAE)	Carry	0
JC (JB)	Carry	1
JNE (JNZ)	Zero	0
JE (JZ)	Zero	1
JNS	Sign	0
JS	Sign	1

*If the specified flag does not have the specified value, no jump occurs.

Waiting for a Switch to Close

Let us now focus on the switch attached to bit 5 of port A (switch 5, for short). The following program waits for you to close switch 5; it then returns control to DEBUG. Remember that an open switch is 1 and a closed switch is 0 (see Figure 2-1). Program 2-2 is the DEBUG version.

```
        MOV   DX,0FF00H      ;GET PORT NUMBER
WAITC:  IN    AL,DX          ;GET INPUT DATA
        AND   AL,00100000B   ;IS SWITCH 5 CLOSED?
        JNZ   WAITC          ;NO, WAIT
        INT   20H            ;YES, EXIT
```

Let us now look at each instruction:

1. MOV DX,0FF00H puts the port address in register DX. This is a 16-bit operation, as DX is a 16-bit register.
2. IN AL,DX loads the accumulator from port A. WAITC is our name for the memory address containing IN AL,DX. Such a name is called a *label*; its sole purpose is to make the program easier for a reader to follow. However, since DEBUG does not accept labels, we must replace them with the actual addresses to which they refer. For example, if Program 2-2 starts at 200, WAITC is 203 and JNE WAITC must produce a conditional jump to 203.

The name WAITC is arbitrary; we chose it because it suggests *wait*ing for a *c*losure.

3. AND AL,00100000B logically ANDs AL with the binary number 00100000. B means "binary." Note that the data (00100000B or 20 hex) appears in the byte immediately after the operation code. The result is 0 if the switch is closed and 00100000 if it is open. (Verify this!) The AND thus singles out bit 5 (an operation called *masking*).

4. JNZ WAITC makes the processor execute the instruction in address WAITC next if the Zero flag is 0. Otherwise, the processor continues sequentially (to INT 20H in this case). Remember that the Zero flag is 0 if the latest result *was not zero*.

PROGRAM 2-2			
Memory Address (Hex)	Memory Contents (Hex)		Instruction (DEBUG Form)
0200	BA		MOV DX,FF00
0201	00		
0202	FF		
0203	EC	WAITC:	IN AL,DX
0204	24		AND AL,20
0205	20		
0206	75		JNZ 203
0207	FB		
0208	CD		INT 20
0209	20		

Note the following features of Program 2-2:

1. IN AL,DX requires a port address in register DX. MOV DX,0FF00H puts the address of P1 port A there.

2. AND AL,00100000B uses immediate addressing. The data (00100000 binary = 20 hex) follows the operation code. An instruction with immediate addressing contains the actual data, not its address.

   Although we have written the data in binary to clarify its effect, we must enter it in hexadecimal. To convert, we split the binary value down the middle and use Table 0-1 to convert the halves: 0010 is 2 hex and 0000 is 0 hex.

3. JNZ requires an 8-bit relative offset following the operation code. This offset tells the computer how many bytes to skip over from the end of the instruction (address 208 here). A positive value (most significant bit = 0) is added to the final address (for example, a value of 02 would be added to 208 to make the destination 20A); the maximum positive value is 7F or +127 decimal. A negative value (most significant bit = 1) tells the computer how many locations down to go (down one is FF, down two is FE, and so on). You can compute the offset by subtracting the final address from the destination; in Program 2-2, the difference is

$$
\begin{array}{ll}
\ 0203 & \text{(destination)} \\
-\ \underline{0208} & \text{(address immediately following JNZ)} \\
\ \text{FFFB}
\end{array}
$$

Only the FB is significant; the most negative value is 80 hex or −128 decimal.

Hexadecimal subtraction is a nuisance unless you have either a hexadecimal calculator or 16 fingers. Fortunately, DEBUG will compute relative offsets for you. All you must do is enter the destination as the jump instruction's operand. DEBUG will then compute the distance to that address.

But what if you don't know where the destination is? If the branch goes backward, you can locate the destination when you pass it during program entry. But if the branch goes forward, you must figure the address using the instruction lengths in Table A1-3. Of course, you can always guess and correct the value later after you reach the actual address.

You can check or correct offsets (or simply satisfy an uncontrollable urge to do hexadecimal arithmetic) with DEBUG's H ("Hexarithmetic") command. H computes the sum and difference of two hexadecimal numbers. All you must do is type H followed by the two values with a space in between. DEBUG responds with the sum and difference (left value minus right value) from left to right.

Open switch 5 and run Program 2-2. What happens if you leave switch 5 open? What happens if you close other switches?

Problem 2-4

Make Program 2-2 wait for you to close switch 4 (that is, the switch attached to bit 4 of P1 port A). Next try switch 2 and then switch 6. How difficult would it be to make these changes in hardware?

Problem 2-5

Make Program 2-2 start at address 210. A program that you can put anywhere in memory without changes is called *relocatable*. Is Program 2-2 relocatable? Explain why the relative offset in JNZ is important. Would the program be relocatable if JNZ contained the actual destination address? Why would you want a program to be relocatable?

DEBUG lets you examine an input port without running a program. To do this, use the I ("Input") command. You must enter the port address (say, FF00) and press the Enter key to display the port's current contents. You can use I to show the effects of opening and closing switches and to verify an input value. However, you cannot use I to change the input port.

Special Bit Positions

Some instructions and flags make certain bit positions more accessible than others. For example:

1. SHL AL,1 (see Figure 1-1) shifts each bit of AL left one position. Bit 7 ends up in the Carry flag, where it can be used as a condition by JC or JNC.
2. SHR AL,1 (see Figure 1-2) similarly moves bit 0 to the Carry.
3. 8-bit arithmetic and logical instructions put the final value of bit 7 in the Sign flag; it can then be used by JS or JNS. 16-bit instructions similarly put the final value of bit 15 in the Sign flag.

The following program thus waits for you to close switch 7:

```
        MOV   DX,0FF00H
WAITC:  IN    AL,DX       ;GET INPUT DATA
        SHL   AL,1        ;MOVE BIT 7 TO CARRY
        JC    WAITC       ;WAIT UNTIL SWITCH 7 IS CLOSED
        INT   20H
```

No AND is necessary. Program 2-3 is the DEBUG version.

Problem 2-6

Write two programs that wait for you to close switch 0, one using AND and one using SHR AL,1. Which version is shorter? Which takes less time to examine the switch and jump? You can look up the execution times in Table A1-3.

Problem 2-7

The TEST instruction does a logical AND but does not save the result. Both operands therefore remain available for later use. Revise Program 2-2 to use TEST instead of AND. What is the final value in AL if all switches except 5 are open? Remember to replace INT 20H with INT 3.

	PROGRAM 2-3		
Memory Address (Hex)	Memory Contents (Hex)		Instruction (DEBUG Form)
0200	BA		MOV DX,FF00
0201	00		
0202	FF		
0203	EC	WAITC:	IN AL,DX
0204	D0		SHL AL,1
0205	E0		
0206	72		JC 203
0207	FB		
0208	CD		INT 20
0209	20		

If you have only one or two switches (or other serial inputs) to attach to a port, which bit positions should you use, and why? If you have many switches, where should you attach the ones that are read most frequently?

Examining Flags

The register display shows the current flag values at the right end of the second line (see Figure 1-4). You can also display the flags by themselves with the R F command. The order is determined by the physical order in the flag register (see Figure 2-3). Rather than show 0's and 1's, DEBUG codes the values as listed in Table 2-3. This makes it easy to find a particular flag's value.

We will consider only the Sign, Zero, and Carry flags for now. The Sign is either NG (1) or PL (0), the Zero flag either ZR (1) or NZ (0), and the Carry either CY (1) or NC (0).

Table 2-3

DEBUG Flag Designations (Left to Right)

Flag Name	Set (1)	Clear (0)
Overflow (yes/no)	OV	NV
Direction (autodecrement/ autoincrement)	DN	UP
Interrupt (enable/disable)	EI	DI
Sign (negative/positive)	NG	PL
Zero (yes/no)	ZR	NZ
Auxiliary (half) carry (yes/no)	AC	NA
Parity (even/odd)	PE	PO
Carry (yes/no)	CY	NC

Figure 2-3

Organization of the 8088 flag (F or FL) register.

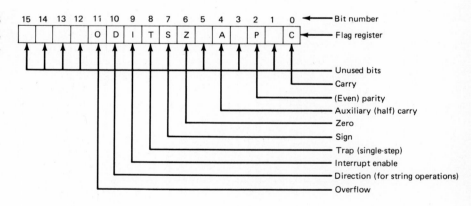

You can see how an instruction affects the flags by loading the F register and the operands, letting the computer execute the instruction, and then examining F afterward. The result depends on the instruction and the operands.

To load F, examine it with the R F command and enter the opposite codes for any settings you want to change. The order does not matter. For example, suppose the flag register appears as

OV DN EI NG ZR AC PE CY

To clear the Sign, Zero, and Carry flags, type PL, NZ, and NC in any order with spaces in between, then press Enter. You can verify the changes with another R F command.

If, for example, we start with [AL] = 80 hex and the Sign, Zero, and Carry flags all 0 (that is, values PL, NZ, and NC, respectively), executing ADD AL,AL (add AL to itself) gives the flags the following values:

$$
\begin{array}{lll}
\text{Sign} & = & 0 \quad (\text{PL}) \\
\text{Zero} & = & 1 \quad (\text{ZR}) \\
\text{Carry} & = & 1 \quad (\text{CY})
\end{array}
$$

The result of adding 80 hex (10000000 binary) to itself is zero plus a carry. Thus the instruction sets the Zero flag, clears the Sign flag, and sets the Carry flag.

Problem 2-8

What are AL and the Sign, Zero, and Carry flags after the processor executes ADD AL,AL for the following initial conditions?

a. [AL] = 80
   Sign, Zero, and Carry flags all 1 (NG, ZR, and CY).
b. [AL] = 7F
   Sign, Zero, and Carry flags all 0 (PL, NZ, and NC).
c. [AL] = 7F
   Sign, Zero, and Carry flags all 1 (NG, ZR, and CY).

HINT: Use the program

```
ADD   AL,AL
INT   3
```

Do the final flag values depend on the initial values?

Note that many 8088 instructions (for example, jumps and MOV) do not affect any flags. Others, such as shifts, affect only one or a few flags. The only way to determine how an instruction affects the flags is by looking it up in Table A1-1.

Waiting for Two Closures

We can easily extend Program 2-2 to wait for two closures. The following program waits for switches 2 and 5 to be closed in that order, assuming that all switches are open initially.

```
            MOV  DX,0FF00H       ;GET INPUT PORT ADDRESS
WAIT2:      IN   AL,DX           ;GET INPUT DATA
            AND  AL,00000100B    ;IS SWITCH 2 CLOSED?
            JNZ  WAIT2           ;NO, WAIT
WAIT5:      IN   AL,DX           ;GET INPUT DATA
            AND  AL,00100000B    ;IS SWITCH 5 CLOSED?
            JNZ  WAIT5           ;NO, WAIT
            INT  20H
```

		PROGRAM 2-4		

Memory Address (Hex)	Memory Contents (Hex)		Instruction (DEBUG Form)	
0200	BA		MOV	DX,FF00
0201	00			
0202	FF			
0203	EC	WAIT2:	IN	AL,DX
0204	24		AND	AL,4
0205	04			
0206	75		JNZ	203
0207	FB			
0208	EC	WAIT5:	IN	AL,DX
0209	24		AND	AL,20
020A	20			
020B	75		JNZ	208
020C	FB			
020D	CD		INT	20
020E	20			

Enter and run this program; the DEBUG version is Program 2-4. What happens if you close switch 2 and then switch 5? What happens if you reverse the order? Explain the result. Does it change if you allow only one switch to be closed at a time?

Problem 2-9

Make Program 2-4 wait for you to close switch 3 followed by switch 1. What happens if you leave one switch closed all the time?

Write a program that waits for a particular sequence of switch closures, then ask someone to guess at what you chose. What happens if the other person simply closes all the switches? You can defeat this strategy by using CMP instead of AND. CMP (Compare) affects the flags as if it had subtracted the operands. Thus CMP sets the Zero flag only if its operands are equal. Because the outcome depends on all eight switches, a subsequent JNZ forces a jump unless they are all set correctly.

For example, after

```
IN    AL,DX          ;GET INPUT DATA
CMP   AL,11011111B
```

the Zero flag is 1 (ZR) only if all eight switches are in the positions given by CMP's operand (0 = closed, 1 = open). Note that CMP AL,11011111B computes AL − 11011111B, not the other way around. Note also that CMP's mask is the inverse of the one we used with AND, since we want to match bits, not clear or test them.

Problem 2-10

Write a program that waits for you to close switch 0 and then switch 7. Write one version that ignores the other switches and one that works only if all other switches are open. What happens in the second version if you reverse the order (that is, close switch 7 first and then switch 0) or leave either switch 0 or switch 7 closed all the time?

Problem 2-11

Write a program that waits for you to close switches 2 and 5 at the same time and then switches 0 and 7 at the same time.

Problem 2-12

Write a program that waits for you to close either switch 2 followed by switch 5 or switch 5 followed by switch 2. Allow only one switch to be closed at a time.

Both IBM's assembler and DEBUG's A command accept two sets of mnemonics for conditional jumps (see Table 2-2). One set (JB—jump if below; JNB—jump if not below; JE—jump if equal; and JNE—jump if not equal) makes sense after a comparison, as its names indicate which relationship between the operands causes a jump. Of course, to use JB and JNB, you must remember what is being subtracted from what. The other set (JC, JNC, JZ, and JNZ) makes sense after other instructions, such as AND, SHR, SHL, and TEST. The object code does not depend on which set of mnemonics you use. DEBUG always uses the second set when displaying instructions during disassembly.

Searching for a Starting Character

In communications applications, the input data is the latest character received. But, if the transmitter is off, that character will be noise. How do we tell noise from actual data? One common method is for the transmitter to start each message with a synchronization, or sync, character. This is a special character that is not part of the actual information.

Problem 2-13

Write a program that waits for the synchronization character 7F to appear at port FF00. An easy way to produce 7F is first to open all switches (producing FF), then close switch 7.

If the input data is random noise, how often will the computer think it has found a message? That is, what is the probability of a random value being 7F? How often would the computer find a message erroneously if the synchronizing pattern were two 7F characters? How about three 7F characters?

Clearly, a longer synchronizing pattern results in fewer false messages. On the other hand, noise could cause a 7F to be received incorrectly, and the computer would then miss a real message.

Problem 2-14

Write a program that accepts the input as 7F even if bit 2 is 0. That is, it accepts either 7F or 7B as a synchronization character. How often will this program find a message erroneously, that is, what is its probability of finding a 7F in random data?

Common Operating Errors

By now, you have undoubtedly discovered the following common errors that plague the DEBUG user:

1. Forgetting to press the Enter key to complete a command. If you press the next command key instead, you will get a letter entry. Remember that a command is not complete until you press Enter.

   Henceforth, we will assume that you press Enter after all commands; we will therefore often not mention it. In particular, be sure to press Enter after an A command; don't just start typing your program or you will get an error message.
2. Forgetting to enter a starting address after an A, G, or U command. A or U alone makes the computer proceed from wherever it stopped the last time you used the command. G alone makes the computer start execution at the instruction pointer's current value. Omitting the ending address after U makes the computer disassemble as many instructions as fit (at least partially) in the next 20 (hexadecimal) bytes.
3. Pressing a key twice, producing a double entry. Watch the display carefully to avoid this. Also don't hold a key down too long (more than half a second), or it will repeat.
4. Forgetting to press R to display or change a register. You will get an error message if you simply type the register's name.
5. Misinterpreting data as instructions. For example, you may press G, 4, 0, 0, Enter instead of G, 2, 0, 0, Enter. This mistake causes the computer to execute the data as though it consisted of instructions. The way to avoid this is to keep programs and data clearly separated at all times.
6. Forgetting to run the program. That is, entering the program and the data and waiting for something to happen. This is like entering data into a calculator and waiting for it to give a result. Neither a computer nor a calculator will do anything until you make it run a program.

7. Starting program execution at the wrong address. The computer will execute whatever it finds. This is particularly likely to happen if you have several programs in memory. Be sure to mark the starting address on each program.
8. Entering numbers in decimal rather than in hex. All DEBUG entries must be in hex.

Stopping Runaway Commands and Programs

If the computer gets stuck in a long DEBUG command, such as displaying thousands of locations or saving all of memory on disk (forgot to clear BX, didn't you?), try pressing

1. Ctrl-Break. Break (or Scroll Lock) is in the top, right-hand corner of the entire keyboard. This will usually restore the prompt. Ctrl-C is equivalent.
2. Ctrl-Alt-Del. Alt is left of the space bar, Del is in the bottom, right-hand corner of the numeric pad. This is a reset, so you must restart DEBUG.

Programming errors may make the PC lose its way and never return to DEBUG. Generally speaking, sad to say, the only solution is to turn the computer off, wait a while, and turn it back on again. You must then restart DEBUG. Aren't you glad you saved your program on disk? Good thing you aren't a procrastinator like me; I was intending to save my program just before this happened (sure I was!). To avoid wear and tear on the power switch, connect the computer to a switched outlet box and turn it on and off from there.

While lost programs are impossible to avoid, the following hint can help preserve your sanity. Before running a program, use the R F command to change the Interrupt (I) flag to EI (rather than DI). You can then escape from most erroneous programs by pressing Ctrl-Alt-Del. Unfortunately, although this saves you from having to turn the computer on and off, you must still reload DEBUG and your program (and reset the I flag) afterward. EI simply allows keystrokes entries to get through, as the keyboard works via an interrupt (see Laboratory C).

Key Point Summary

1. The IN AL,DX instruction loads accumulator AL with the contents of the port address in register DX. 8088 port addresses are distinct from memory addresses, a method called isolated input/output.

2. Our IBM PC add-on I/O board has two free ports in 8255 device P1. We will use port A (address FF00) for input and port B (address FF01) for output.

3. The 8088 has three major flags (Sign, Zero, and Carry) that are set from the result of the latest arithmetic, logical, or shift instruction. Other instructions (for example, MOV and jumps) do not affect the flags. DEBUG's register display shows the flag values in coded form (NG or PL for the Sign flag, ZR or NZ for the Zero flag, and CY or NC for the Carry flag).

4. A conditional jump instruction replaces the instruction pointer if the specified condition is true. But if the condition is false, the processor continues its normal sequence. Conditional jumps are the key to computer decision making.

5. The processor can determine the value of a bit in a register or memory location by logically ANDing the contents with a mask. The mask has a 1 in the specified bit position and 0's elsewhere. The result is zero if, and only if, the bit is zero. Bit positions at either end of a byte or word can be handled by using the Sign or Carry flag and the shift or test instructions.

6. The processor can determine whether a register or memory location contains a specified value by subtracting the value from the contents. The result is zero only if the register or memory location contains the value.

7. The processor does logical operations (AND, OR, EXCLUSIVE OR, NOT) bit by bit, 8 or 16 bits at a time. However, arithmetic operations (addition and subtraction) involve carries or borrows, so the bit positions are not independent.

8. Common errors in using DEBUG include failing to press the Enter key to end a command; forgetting to press the R key to display or change a register; pressing keys more than once or holding them down too long (and thus getting double entries); failing to enter a starting or ending address; misinterpreting data as instructions; forgetting to run the program; starting program execution at the wrong address; and entering numbers in decimal rather than in hexadecimal.

9. Pressing Ctrl-Break will stop an erroneous DEBUG command, but only turning the computer off will generally stop a runaway user program. However, if you change the I flag to EI before running a program, you will be able to exit from it and DEBUG by pressing Ctrl-Alt-Del.

Simple Output

Purpose   To learn how to use the computer's output ports.

Parts Required   Eight LEDs (light-emitting diodes) attached to port B of 8255 device P1 (on the add-on I/O board), as shown in Figure 3-1. Table 3-1 contains the pin assignments.

Figure 3-1
Attachment of
LEDs to port B of
8255 device P1.

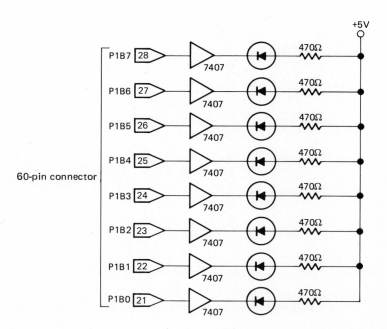

***What You
Should Learn***

1. How to make 8255 I/O ports into inputs or outputs.
2. How to turn LEDs on and off.
3. How to make the computer wait between operations.
4. How to manipulate single bits of data.
5. How to operate LED displays at a specific duty cycle.

Table 3-1

I/O Connector Pin
Assignments for
Port P1B

Assignment	Pin
Bit 0	21
Bit 1	22
Bit 2	23
Bit 3	24
Bit 4	25
Bit 5	26
Bit 6	27
Bit 7	28

***Reference
Materials***

Gorsline, G. W. *16-Bit Modern Microcomputers*. Englewood Cliffs, NJ: Prentice-Hall, 1985, chap. 5 (input/output).

Liu, Y. C., and G. A. Gibson. *Microcomputer Systems: The 8086/8088 Family* (2nd ed.). Englewood Cliffs, NJ: Prentice-Hall, 1986, chap. 6 (I/O programming).

Terms

Anode: positive terminal.
Cathode: negative terminal.
Complement: *see* **One's complement.**
Control register: a register whose contents determine a device's operating mode.
Duty cycle: the ratio of the length of time a device is active to its overall operating time.
Light-emitting diode (LED): a semiconductor device that emits light when its cathode is sufficiently more negative than its anode.
Nesting: constructing programs hierarchically with one level contained inside another.
One's complement: bit-by-bit inversion, replacing each 0 with a 1 and each 1 with a 0.
Software delay: a program that does nothing except waste time.

8088 *Instructions*	**DEC: decrement; subtract 1 from a register or memory location.** **NOT: logical NOT (one's complement); invert the bits in a register or memory location.**

LED Connections

Attach eight LEDs to port B of 8255 device P1, as described in Table 3-1 and Figure 3-1. An LED lights when its cathode is sufficiently more negative than its anode. The computer can therefore light an LED either by grounding its cathode or by applying +5V to its anode. Since we have connected the output port to the cathodes, a 0 from the computer lights an LED.

Assigning Directions to 8255 I/O Ports

In Laboratory 2, we used an 8255 port for input. In fact, you can make each 8255 port either input or output by placing either a 1 (input) or a 0 (output) in a specific bit of the device's control register. These bits determine which way data flows, much like arrows or semaphores on a highway or railroad. The control register itself occupies an I/O address; the one in device P1 is at address FF03 (see Table 3-2).

Table 3-2

I/O Addresses for
the Ports in 8255
Device P1

Address(Hex)	Function
FF00	Port A
FF01	Port B
FF02	Port C
FF03	Control register

To assign directions to ports A and B, we must set bit 7 of the control register to 1. Then bit 1 makes port B input (1) or output (0), and bit 4 does the same for port A. Examples of assigning directions are

1. Storing 10010010 binary in port FF03 makes ports A and B both inputs. This is also the condition after power-on or reset.

```
MOV   DX,0FF03H      ;GET CONTROL REGISTER ADDRESS
MOV   AL,10010010B   ;PORTS A AND B BOTH INPUT
OUT   DX,AL
```

2. Storing 10010000 binary in port FF03 makes port A input and port B output. We will use this setup throughout our experiments.

```
MOV   DX,0FF03H        ;GET CONTROL REGISTER ADDRESS
MOV   AL,10010000B     ;PORT A INPUT, PORT B OUTPUT
OUT   DX,AL
```

Of course, specifying the control register in binary makes it easier to see which ports are inputs and which outputs. A hex value is difficult to interpret, since only individual bits matter. Note that bit 7 is 1 to assign directions in both examples.

The 8255 device has the following key features:

1. Power-on and reset make all ports input. This is why we could ignore the control register in Laboratory 2, as long as we started from power-on. Note that you cannot check the control register's contents, as it is write-only.
2. You can only make an entire port input or output. You cannot control individual I/O lines.
3. In an application, the initialization routine (starting from power-on) must make ports input or output. The main program rarely changes the assignments.

Problem 3-1

Write and run a program that makes port A of 8255 device P1 input and port B output. How would you test this program? What happens when you run it after power-on? What happens if you then run a program that makes port B input?

Problem 3-2

Write a program that makes port A output and port B input. What is the result of reading port A (address FF00) with the I command? Does moving the switches have any effect?

Lighting an LED

The following program lights the LED attached to bit 3 of port B of 8255 device P1 (LED 3, for short).

```
MOV   DX,0FF03H        ;GET CONTROL REGISTER ADDRESS
MOV   AL,10010000B     ;PORT A INPUT, PORT B OUTPUT
OUT   DX,AL
```

```
MOV    DX,0FF01H      ;GET PORT B ADDRESS
MOV    AL,11110111B   ;LIGHT LED 3
OUT    DX,AL
INT    20H
```

Because the port is connected to the cathodes, 0 turns an LED on, and 1 turns it off. We must make B an output port before any LEDs will light. Program 3-1 is the DEBUG version; enter and run it. What happens if you then make port B input?

PROGRAM 3-1		
Memory Address (Hex)	Memory Contents (Hex)	Instruction (DEBUG Form)
0200	BA	MOV DX,FF03
0201	03	
0202	FF	
0203	B0	MOV AL,90
0204	90	
0205	EE	OUT DX,AL
0206	BA	MOV DX,FF01
0207	01	
0208	FF	
0209	B0	MOV AL,F7
020A	F7	
020B	EE	OUT DX,AL
020C	CD	INT 20
020D	20	

Problem 3-3

Change Program 3-1 to light only LED 4. How would you make it light only LEDs 2 and 5?

Problem 3-4

Write a program that shows the data from port A on the LEDs attached to port B. Does a switch have to be open or closed for the corresponding LED to light?

DEBUG's O (output) command lets you send data to an output port without running a program. You must type the port address (say, FF01), a space, and the data. For example, the command

O FF01 FF

turns all the LEDs attached to port B off, whereas

O FF01 0

lights them all. You can use O to show how values look on the LEDs, to produce test outputs, and to load control registers.

Be careful when using O. It only works on output ports, so you may have to load the control register first. This problem seldom occurs with the I (input) command, since power-on makes the 8255 ports into inputs.

Software Delay

Of course, real applications do not leave outputs on or off forever. Instead, they typically turn them on or off for specific amounts of time. The microprocessor can waste time between operations with steps such as

1. Load a register with a value.
2. Keep subtracting 1 from the register until it contains zero.

The program to waste time using register CX is

```
          MOV   CX,COUNT
DLY:      DEC   CX
          JNZ   DLY
```

This works like a countdown before a missile launch or a dynamite blast. We call it a *software delay*.

We can determine how much time the delay wastes from the following information:

Instruction	Number of Times Executed	Clock Cycles per Execution
MOV CX,COUNT	1	4
DEC CX	COUNT	2
JNZ DLY	COUNT	4 if no jump, 16 if a jump occurs

Table A1-3 contains execution times for 8086 (*not* 8088) instructions. The 8088 takes longer, because it must fetch instructions from memory 8 bits at a time, whereas the 8086 fetches 16 bits at once. JNZ's execution time depends on whether a jump occurs; it takes 16 cycles if the Zero flag is 0 and the program jumps, and four cycles otherwise.

The delay's execution time is

$$[4 + 22 \times (COUNT - 1) + 6] \times t_C$$

where t_C is the IBM PC's clock period. The constants are: 4 for the initial MOV CX,COUNT; 18 for DEC CX (2) and JNZ with a jump (16); 4 as an estimate of the 8088's extra fetch time; and 6 for the last DEC, JNZ sequence in which no jump ocurs and hence JNZ takes only four cycles. The 8088 penalty does not apply to 8086-based PC-compatibles such as the AT&T 6300. The entire timing analysis differs for 80286 or 80386-based computers. Arithmetic simplifies the expression to

$$(22 \times COUNT - 16) \times t_C$$

A complicating factor is that the PC uses 5 of every 72 clock cycles for refresh. Refresh is the rewriting of memory contents before they "leak away." As the processor is inactive during refresh, we must multiply all execution times by

$$72/(72-5) = 1.075$$

Because the standard IBM PC has a 4.77 MHz clock, $t_C = 0.210\,\mu s$. $t_C \times 1.075 = 0.225\,\mu s$. If, for example, COUNT = 10 (decimal), the time wasted is

$$(22 \times 10 - 16) \times 0.225\,\mu s = 46\,\mu s$$

Be sure to change the period if your computer has a higher clock rate. The most time the program can waste is

$$(22 \times 65,536 - 16) \times 0.225\,\mu s = 324,400\,\mu s$$
$$\text{or } 0.324 \text{ s}$$

What value of COUNT gives the longest delay? Note that the program subtracts 1 from CX before jumping.

You can add a delay to Program 3-1 as follows:

```
MOV    DX,0FF03H      ;GET CONTROL REGISTER ADDRESS
MOV    AL,10010000B   ;PORT A INPUT, PORT B OUTPUT
OUT    DX,AL
```

```
        MOV    DX,0FF01H      ;GET PORT B ADDRESS
        MOV    AL,11110111B   ;LIGHT LED 3
        OUT    DX,AL
        MOV    CX,COUNT
DLY:    DEC    CX
        JNZ    DLY
        MOV    AL,11111111B   ;TURN OFF LED 3
        OUT    DX,AL
        INT    20H
```

Program 3-2 is the DEBUG version. The first six instructions are the same as in Program 3-1.

When entering Program 3-2, you must replace COUNT with a number. Be sure to enter it in hex, not decimal.

A good initial value for COUNT is 0, as it gives the longest delay. (Why?) You will have about one-third of a second to see the LED light. If you reduce the delay time, put a dark background behind the LED. To get the clearest view, first type G=200. Then put a finger on the Enter key and stare directly at the LED. Finally, press the Enter key. Be careful not to hypnotize yourself during this intellectually challenging exercise.

	PROGRAM 3-2		
Memory Address (Hex)	Memory Contents (Hex)		Instruction (DEBUG Form)
0200	BA		MOV DX,FF03
0201	03		
0202	FF		
0203	B0		MOV AL,90
0204	90		
0205	EE		OUT DX,AL
0206	BA		MOV DX,FF01
0207	01		
0208	FF		
0209	B0		MOV AL,F7
020A	F7		
020B	EE		OUT DX,AL
020C	B9		MOV CX,COUNT
020D	00		
020E	00		
020F	49	DLY:	DEC CX
0210	75		JNZ 20F
0211	FD		

PROGRAM 3-2 (continued)		
Memory Address (Hex)	Memory Contents (Hex)	Instruction (DEBUG Form)
0212	B0	MOV AL,FF
0213	FF	
0214	EE	OUT DX,AL
0215	CD	INT 20
0216	20	

Problem 3-5

Run Program 3-2 repeatedly, dividing COUNT's more significant byte (address 20E) in half after each execution; use the sequence 0, 80, 40, 20, 10, 8, 4, 2, 1. What is the smallest value of COUNT for which you can see the LED light? If you have sharp eyes, you will need to make 20E 0 and apply the sequence to address 20D.

Lengthening the Delay

You can lengthen the delay by placing one time-wasting routine inside another (called *nesting*); that is,

```
        MOV   BX,CT1   ;SET MULTIPLYING FACTOR
DLY1:   MOV   CX,CT2   ;SET DELAY FACTOR
DLY2:   DEC   CX
        JNZ   DLY2
        DEC   BX
        JNZ   DLY1
```

CT1 controls how many times the CT2 loop is executed. Program 3-3 is a revision of Program 3-2 with a nested delay. Run it with CT1 = CT2 = 400 hex; the delay should be about 5.2 seconds. Don't use CT1 = CT2 = 0, as it will take about 354 minutes or 6 hours.

	PROGRAM 3-3		

Memory Address (Hex)	Memory Contents (Hex)	Instruction (DEBUG Form)	
0200	BA	MOV	DX,FF03
0201	03		
0202	FF		
0203	B0	MOV	AL,90
0204	90		
0205	EE	OUT	DX,AL
0206	BA	MOV	DX,FF01
0207	01		
0208	FF		
0209	B0	MOV	AL,F7
020A	F7		
020B	EE	OUT	DX,AL
020C	BB	MOV	BX,CT1
020D	CT1 − LSB		
020E	CT1 − MSB		
020F	B9	DLY1: MOV	CX,CT2
0210	CT2 − LSB		
0211	CT2 − MSB		
0212	49	DLY2: DEC	CX
0213	75	JNZ	212
0214	FD		
0215	4B	DEC	BX
0216	75	JNZ	20F
0217	F7		
0218	B0	MOV	AL,FF
0219	FF		
021A	EE	OUT	DX,AL
021B	CD	INT	20
021C	20		

Problem 3-6

If you set CT1 (20D and 20E) to 1000 (3E8 hex), what value of CT2 (210 and 211) gives a 1-s delay? What value gives a 10-s delay?

Bit Manipulation

Often we want to change one LED without altering others attached to the same port. We can do this by using the following effects of the logical functions (see Table 3-3):

1. Logically ANDing a bit with 0 clears it, whereas logically ANDing it with 1 leaves it unchanged.
2. Logically ORing a bit with 1 sets it (to 1), whereas logically ORing it with 0 leaves it unchanged.
3. Logically EXCLUSIVE ORing a bit with 1 complements (inverts) it, whereas logically EXCLUSIVE ORing it with 0 leaves it unchanged.

Thus you can change a bit of AL (bit 5, for example) as follows:

1. Make it 1 with OR AL,00100000B.
2. Make it 0 with AND AL,11011111B.
3. Complement (invert) it with XOR AL,00100000B.

In Program 3-2, for example, we could set bit 3 of AL and thus affect only LED 3 by using OR AL,00001000B instead of MOV AL,11111111B; that is,

```
0212    0C    OR    AL,8
0213    08
```

Make this change and run the revised program. Make a similar change in Program 3-3.

Table 3-3
Effects of Logical Instructions

Original Value	Mask Value	AND	OR	Exclusive OR
0	0	0	0	0
0	1	0	1	1
1	0	0	1	1
1	1	1	1	0

We can change several bits at once with the appropriate pattern, or *mask*. For example, AND AL,11101011B clears bits 2 and 4 of AL. NOT AL complements (inverts) the entire accumulator.

Problem 3-7

Write a program that turns LED 4 off, waits for a while, and then turns LED 4 on without altering any other displays.

Problem 3-8

Write a program that obtains the data for the LEDs from 400, turns LEDs 2 and 5 on, waits for a while, turns LED 5 off, waits again, and finally turns LED 2 off and LED 5 on without affecting any other displays. Put C3 (11000011 binary) in 400 initially for testing.

Problem 3-9

Write a program that displays the contents of 400 on the LEDs attached to port B of 8255 device P1. Make the data appear in the form an observer would expect, that is, 1's should light LEDs and 0's should turn them off.

Duty Cycle

The computer can operate an LED at a specific duty cycle by simply turning it on and then off for periods of time. The following program uses two delay routines to run the LED for 40 (28 hex) iterations.

```
        MOV    DX,0FF03H     ;GET CONTROL REGISTER
                             ;  ADDRESS
        MOV    AL,10010000B  ;PORT A INPUT, PORT B
                             ;  OUTPUT
        OUT    DX,AL
        MOV    BX,40         ;COUNT = 40 ITERATIONS
        MOV    DX,0FF01H     ;GET PORT B ADDRESS
CYCLE:  MOV    AL,11110111B  ;LIGHT LED 3
        OUT    DX,AL
        MOV    CX,CT1        ;DELAY WHILE LED IS ON
DLY1:   DEC    CX
        JNZ    DLY1
        MOV    AL,11111111B  ;TURN OFF LED 3
        OUT    DX,AL
        MOV    CX,CT2        ;DELAY WHILE LED IS OFF
```

```
DLY2:    DEC    CX
         JNZ    DLY2
         DEC    BX                    ;COUNT ITERATIONS
         JNZ    CYCLE
         INT    20H
```

Program 3-4 is the DEBUG version. Run it with CT1 = CT2 = 8000. You can reduce the overall execution time by having fewer iterations (location 207).

	PROGRAM 3-4			

Memory Address (Hex)	Memory Contents (Hex)		Instruction (DEBUG Form)	
0200	BA		MOV	DX,FF03
0201	03			
0202	FF			
0203	B0		MOV	AL,90
0204	90			
0205	EE		OUT	DX,AL
0206	BB		MOV	BX,28
0207	28			
0208	00			
0209	BA		MOV	DX,FF01
020A	01			
020B	FF			
020C	B0	CYCLE:	MOV	AL,F7
020D	F7			
020E	EE		OUT	DX,AL
020F	B9		MOV	CX,CT1
0210	CT1 − LSB			
0211	CT1 − MSB			
0212	49	DLY1:		
0213	75		JNZ	212
0214	FD			
0215	B0		MOV	AL,FF
0216	FF			
0217	EE		OUT	DX,AL
0218	B9		MOV	CX,CT2
0219	CT2 − LSB			
021A	CT2 − MSB			
021B	49	DLY2:	DEC	CX
021C	75		JNZ	21B
021D	FD			
021E	4B		DEC	BX
021F	75		JNZ	20C

	PROGRAM 3-4 (continued)	
Memory Address (Hex)	Memory Contents (Hex)	Instruction (DEBUG Form)
0220	*EB*	
0221	*CD*	*INT 20*
0222	*20*	

Problem 3-10

Try the following sequence of hex values for the more significant bytes of CT1 and CT2 (locations 211 and 21A, respectively) in Program 3-4: 80, 40, 20, 10, 8, 4, 2, 1. What is the smallest value for which you can see the LED flicker? How many times per second is the LED being turned on and off at this value?

Problem 3-11

Run Program 3-4 with CT1 = CT2 = 2000 hex. Then try the following hex values for the more significant bytes of CT1 and CT2 (locations 211 and 21A): (*a*) CT1 = 38, CT2 = 08; (*b*) CT1 = 30, CT2 = 10; (*c*) CT1 = 10, CT2 = 30; and (*d*) CT1 = 08, CT2 = 38. Describe how different values affect the LED's brightness and continuity. Compare the effects to those you saw in Problem 3-10.

Problem 3-12

In Program 3-4, set CT1 = CT2 = 2000 hex. What initial value in register BX flashes the LED on and off for 5 s?

Key Point Summary

1. The I/O ports in an 8255 device can be either inputs or outputs. Each port is given a direction by storing a value (1 for input, 0 for output) in a specified bit position of the control register. The control register itself occupies an I/O port address. The user must remember, however, that it is actually located inside the 8255 device and is not connected to peripherals.

2. By storing the proper value in the control register, the user can make ports input or output for different applications. In most applications, the initialization routine assigns the directions, and the rest of the program simply uses the ports.

3. The computer can wait by counting down the contents of a register. The length of the wait depends on the number of instructions in the countdown program and their execution times. Nested delay programs can produce longer waits.

4. A bit can be cleared, set, or complemented by means of logical operations with appropriate masks. The NOT instruction inverts an entire register or memory location.

5. The computer can establish a duty cycle by waiting after turning a peripheral on and off.

6. You can easily change a peripheral's timing in software. Replacing a few numbers can change the operating speed or duty cycle.

Processing Data Inputs

Purpose   To learn how to process data inputs.

What You Should Learn
1. How to wait for any of a set of switches to open or close.
2. How to debounce a switch.
3. How to count switch closures.
4. How to find the bit position of a switch closure.
5. How to read data from the computer's keyboard.
6. How to make simple hardware/software tradeoffs.

Reference Materials
Comer, D. J. *Microprocessor-Based System Design*. New York: Holt, Rinehart and Winston, 1986, sec. 5.6G (keyboard interface).

Gorsline, G. W. *16-Bit Modern Microcomputers*. Englewood Cliffs, NJ: Prentice-Hall, 1985, chap. 5 (input/output).

Liu, Y. C., and G. A. Gibson. *Microcomputer Systems: The 8086/8088 Family* (2nd ed.). Englewood Cliffs, NJ: Prentice-Hall, 1986, chap. 6 (I/O programming).

Norton, P. *Programmer's Guide to the IBM PC*. Redmond, WA: Microsoft Press, 1985, chaps. 6 (keyboard basics) and 11 (ROM-BIOS keyboard services).

Terms   **ASCII:**   American Standard Code for Information Interchange, a 7-bit character code widely used in computers and communications. Table A2-1 contains a list of ASCII characters.

Bounce: move back and forth between states before settling down.

Character: one of a set of elementary symbols, usually including controls and delimiters as well as representations of letters, digits, punctuation marks, and other symbols.

Cross-coupled: describing two devices each of which has its output fed back into the other's input.

Debounce: convert the output from a contact with bounce into a clean transition.

Enable: allow an activity to proceed or a device to produce data outputs.

Encoder: a device that produces coded outputs from unencoded inputs. A *keyboard encoder* produces a unique code for each key closure.

Scan code: a code generated by pressing or releasing a key on a keyboard. Tables A2-2 and A2-3 contain the IBM PC's keyboard scan codes.

8088
Instructions

INC: increment; add 1 to a register or memory location.

INT 16H: software interrupt 16 hex. INT 16H makes the IBM PC do a keyboard operation. The value in register AH selects the operation as follows:

0 — Read next keyboard character.

1 — Report whether a character is ready.

2 — Get shift status.

JMP: jump unconditionally.

SUB reg,reg: clear a register by subtracting its contents from themselves. For example, SUB AX,AX clears accumulator AX. XOR reg,reg is equivalent (see Table 3-3).

Handling More Complex Inputs

We generally want a microprocessor to do more than just determine whether a binary input is 0 or 1. Rather, it must deal with a series of inputs and do such tasks as smoothing data and handling system timing. These tasks can be done entirely in software or partly in hardware. Designers must make tradeoffs based on per-unit cost, development time and cost, reliability, compatibility with other applications, power dissipation, board space, and availability of parts for specific functions.

Waiting for Any Switch to Close

Table 4-1 lists the inputs produced by closing just one of the eight switches attached to P1 port A. If all eight are open, the input is all 1's (FF hex). The following program waits for you to close any switch:

```
                  MOV   DX,0FF00H      ;GET PORT A ADDRESS
       WAITC:     IN    AL,DX          ;GET INPUT DATA
                  CMP   AL,0FFH        ;ARE ANY SWITCHES CLOSED?
                  JE    WAITC          ;NO, WAIT
                  INT   3              ;YES, EXIT AND DISPLAY
                                       ;  REGISTERS
```

Table 4-1

Inputs Resulting
From the Closure
of Individual
Switches

Bit Position of Closed Switch	Input	
	Binary	Hex
0	11111110	FE
1	11111101	FD
2	11111011	FB
3	11110111	F7
4	11101111	EF
5	11011111	DF
6	10111111	BF
7	01111111	7F

Program 4-1 is the DEBUG version. CMP AL,0FFH subtracts FF from register AL and sets the flags but does not save the result. Thus AL still contains the data from port A afterward.

Enter and run Program 4-1. Show that it exits if you close any switch. What happens if you close several switches at once? What happens if you close switches before running the program? Note the final contents of AL in each case.

	PROGRAM 4-1			
Memory Address (Hex)	Memory Contents (Hex)		Instruction (DEBUG Form)	
0200	BA		MOV	DX,FF00
0201	00			
0202	FF			
0203	EC	WAITC:	IN	AL,DX
0204	3C		CMP	AL,FF
0205	FF			
0206	74		JE	203
0207	FB			
0208	CC		INT	3

We can easily add a section that waits until all switches are open again. The jump here uses the opposite condition.

```
WAITO:  IN   AL,DX      ;GET INPUT DATA
        CMP  AL,0FFH    ;ARE ANY SWITCHES CLOSED?
        JNE  WAITO      ;YES, WAIT
        INT  20H        ;NO, EXIT
```

Program 4-2 is the DEBUG form of the added instructions. Enter it and run the combined program several times. Does it always wait for you to open the switch?

PROGRAM 4-2				
Memory Address (Hex)	Memory Contents (Hex)		Instruction (DEBUG Form)	
0208	EC	*WAITO:*	IN	AL,DX
0209	3C		CMP	AL,FF
020A	FF			
020B	75		JNE	208
020C	FB			
020D	CD		INT	20
020E	20			

Problem 4-1

Write a program that waits for you to close and open switch 5, regardless of the other switches' positions.

Problem 4-2

Write a program that waits for you to close switch 5, open it, and then close it again, regardless of the other switches' positions.

Debouncing a Switch

In practice, Programs 4-1 and 4-2 will often exit before you open the switch. This happens because a mechanical switch does not open or close cleanly. Instead, it bounces for a while before settling into its final position. Thus opening or closing a switch typically causes several transitions, just as though it had been opened and closed repeatedly.

We can eliminate the extra transitions by debouncing the switch. This can be done in hardware with cross-coupled NAND gates (see Figure 4-1) or in software with a delay that waits until the switch stops bouncing. If the bounce lasts less than 1 ms, the following program will do the job:

```
        MOV   DX,0FF00H        ;GET PORT A ADDRESS
WAITC:  IN    AL,DX            ;GET INPUT DATA
        CMP   AL,0FFH          ;ARE ANY SWITCHES CLOSED?
        JE    WAITC            ;NO, WAIT
        MOV   CX,0CBH          ;DELAY 1 MS TO DEBOUNCE
DLY:    DEC   CX
        JNZ   DLY
WAITO:  IN    AL,DX            ;GET INPUT DATA
        CMP   AL,0FFH          ;ARE ANY SWITCHES CLOSED?
        JNE   WAITO            ;YES, WAIT
        INT   20H
```

Figure 4-1

Debouncing a switch with cross-coupled NAND gates.

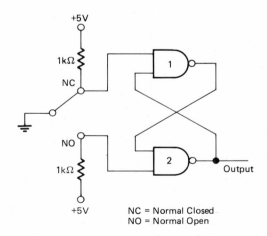

Program 4-3 is the DEBUG version of the extension to Program 4-1. We obtained CB hex (203 decimal) from the timing equation in Laboratory 3. Many switches require a larger value, such as 0FC9 (20 ms).

	PROGRAM 4-3			
Memory Address (Hex)	Memory Contents (Hex)		Instruction (DEBUG Form)	
0208	B9		MOV	CX,CB
0209	CB			
020A	00			
020B	49	DLY:	DEC	CX
020C	75		JNZ	20B
020D	FD			
020E	EC	WAITO:	IN	AL,DX
020F	3C		CMP	AL,FF
0210	FF			
0211	75		JNE	20E
0212	FB			
0213	CD		INT	20
0214	20			

Debouncing allows a tradeoff between hardware and software. The software delay costs very little, as the program is simple and takes only six bytes of memory. But it also ties up the processor, keeping it from doing other work. On the other hand, hardware debouncing frees the processor but requires an extra part.

Counting Closures

We can keep a running count in register BX of the number of switches closed as follows, assuming that we close only one at a time:

1. Add the instructions

```
        INC   BX        ;ADD 1 TO NUMBER OF CLOSURES
        MOV   CX,0CBH    ;DELAY 1 MS TO DEBOUNCE OPENING
DLY1:   DEC   CX
        JNZ   DLY1
        CMP   BX,5       ;COUNT CLOSURES UP TO 5
        JB    WAITC
        INT   20H
```

to the end of Program 4-3, as shown in Program 4-4. This sequence stops after five closures.

2. Clear register BX before running the program. If you forget, it will stop after the first closure unless BX is less than 5.

If the count is erratic, lengthen the debouncing delay by increasing CX's initial value. Remember to debounce both the opening and the closing of the switch.

				PROGRAM 4-4		

Memory Address (Hex)	Memory Contents (Hex)		Instruction (DEBUG Form)	
0213	43		INC	BX
0214	B9		MOV	CX,CB
0215	CB			
0216	00			
0217	49	DLY1:	DEC	CX
0218	75		JNZ	217
0219	FD			
021A	83		CMP	BX,5
021B	FB			
021C	05			
021D	72		JB	203
021E	E4			
021F	CD		INT	20
0220	20			

Problem 4-3

Write a program that stops after counting the number of switch closures in memory location 400. Assume that only one switch is ever closed at a time. Run the program with [400] = 5.

Problem 4-4

Write a program that counts closures of switch 6 (up to a maximum of five closures). Keep the count in register BX.

Problem 4-5

Write a program that counts closures of switches 2 and 6. Keep the count for switch 2 in BH and that for switch 6 in BL. Assume that only one switch is ever closed at a time. Make the maximum 4 for both counts.

Identifying the Switch

In Table 4-1, the bit that is 0 shows which switch is closed. That is, bit 0 is 0 if switch 0 is closed, bit 1 is 0 if switch 1 is closed, and so forth. A simple way to find the zero bit is the following (see Figure 4-2 for a flowchart):

Step 1.   SWITCH NUMBER = 0
             DATA = input from switches
Step 2.   Shift DATA right 1 bit. If Carry = 0, the program is done.
Step 3.   SWITCH NUMBER = SWITCH NUMBER + 1
             Return to step 2.

A program that does this is

```
          SUB    BX,BX      ;SWITCH NUMBER = ZERO
SRCHS:    SHR    AL,1       ;IS NEXT SWITCH CLOSED?
          JNC    DONE       ;YES, DONE
          INC    BX         ;NO, ADD 1 TO SWITCH NUMBER
          JMP    SRCHS
DONE:     INT    20H
```

The switch number ends up in register BX. SUB reg,reg is a fast way to clear a register. The result is its contents minus themselves, which is surely zero. If you have a devious nature, you might prefer the less obvious XOR reg,reg; it has the same effect (see Table 3-3).

A different initial value in BX lets us eliminate one jump as follows:

```
          MOV    BX,-1      ;SWITCH NUMBER = -1
SRCHS:    INC    BX         ;ADD 1 TO SWITCH NUMBER
          SHR    AL, 1      ;IS NEXT SWITCH CLOSED?
          JC     SRCHS      ;NO, KEEP LOOKING
          INT    20H
```

Which version do you prefer, and why?

An identification program must do the following:

1. Wait for a switch to be closed.
2. Wait 1 ms to debounce the switch.
3. Identify the switch by shifting the input and counting until Carry becomes 0.

Figure 4-2
Flowchart for
switch
identification.

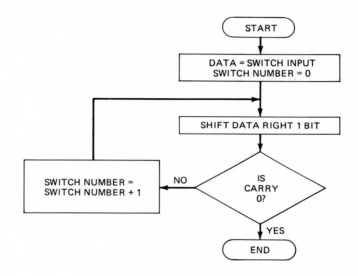

A complete assembly language program is

```
            MOV   DX,0FF00H   ;GET PORT A ADDRESS
WAITC:      IN    AL,DX       ;GET INPUT DATA
            CMP   AL,0FFH      ;ARE ANY SWITCHES CLOSED?
            JE    WAITC        ;NO, WAIT
            MOV   CX,0CBH      ;DELAY 1 MS TO DEBOUNCE
DLY:        DEC   CX
            JNZ   DLY
            MOV   BX,-1        ;SWITCH NUMBER = -1
SRCHS:      INC   BX           ;ADD 1 TO SWITCH NUMBER
            SHR   AL,1         ;IS NEXT SWITCH CLOSED?
            JC    SRCHS        ;NO, KEEP LOOKING
            MOV   [400H],BX    ;YES, SAVE SWITCH NUMBER
            INT   20H
```

The switch number ends up in location 400. Program 4-5 is a DEBUG version; the first seven instructions (addresses 200 through 20D) are the same as in Programs 4-1 and 4-3. Note that −1 appears in the object code as the 16-bit number FFFF hex.

Enter Program 4-5 into memory, and test it on each switch. What happens if you close several switches before running the program? Which closure does it find? Why?

PROGRAM 4-5				
Memory Address (Hex)	Memory Contents (Hex)		Instruction (DEBUG Form)	
0200	BA		MOV	DX,FF00
0201	00			
0202	FF			
0203	EC	WAITC:	IN	AL,DX
0204	3C		CMP	AL,FF
0205	FF			
0206	74		JE	203
0207	FB			
0208	B9		MOV	CX,CB
0209	CB			
020A	00			
020B	49	DLY:	DEC	CX
020C	75		JNZ	20B
020D	FD			
020E	BB		MOV	BX,−1
020F	FF			
0210	FF			
0211	43	SRCHS:	INC	BX
0212	D0		SHR	AL,1
0213	E8			
0214	72		JC	211
0215	FB			
0216	89		MOV	[400],BX
0217	1E			
0218	00			
0219	04			
021A	CD		INT	20
021B	20			

Problem 4-6

Write a program that always finds the highest numbered switch that is closed. (*Hint:* Shift the data left and decrement BX, but be sure to initialize BX correctly.)

Problem 4-7

a. Revise Program 4-5 to check the switches only once. If all are open, have it put FFFF in 400 and 401. What happens if this program checks the switches while one is bouncing? How could you solve this problem? (*Hint:* If the program finds all switches open, have it wait 1 ms and examine them again.)

b. Write a general program that accepts the input from the switches only if it remains the same after a 1-ms delay. That is, the program should keep checking the switches until two readings taken 1 ms apart are the same.

Reading Data from an Encoded Keyboard

The IBM PC's keyboard consists of a set of switches much like the one attached to the 8255 device. Of course, the keyboard is large and would require many ports if each key were attached directly to the computer. Instead, it has circuitry (called an *encoder* for obvious reasons) that converts each closure into a unique code. For standard typewriter characters (such as letters, numbers, and punctuation marks), the code is ASCII, the American Standard Code for Information Interchange. Table A2-1 is a list of ASCII characters.

The PC also has built-in keyboard software. It is part of the Basic Input/Output System (BIOS) mentioned in Laboratory 0. To access BIOS routines, we use special instructions called traps or software interrupts. We have already used two traps (INT 20H and INT 3) to return control to DEBUG. INT 16H makes the computer do a keyboard operation (or service). The value in register AH selects the service as follows:

0 — Read next character.

1 — Report whether a character is ready.

2 — Get shift status.

For example, the next program (Program 4-6 is the DEBUG version) waits for you to press a key. It uses service 1 which clears the Zero flag if a character is ready and sets it otherwise. Be careful—the logic here may seem backward; the Zero flag is cleared (0) if a character is ready and set (1) if not. A JZ instruction afterward thus jumps if no key has been pressed. If this discussion gives you a headache, just try the jump you think is correct. Fortunately, there are only two choices.

```
WTKEY:  MOV   AH,1       ;EXAMINE KEYBOARD
        INT   16H        ;IS CHARACTER READY?
        JZ    WTKEY      ;NO, WAIT
        INT   3          ;YES, EXIT AND DISPLAY
                         ;  REGISTERS
```

	PROGRAM 4-6		
Memory Address (Hex)	Memory Contents (Hex)		Instruction (DEBUG Form)
0200	B4	WTKEY:	MOV AH,1
0201	01		
0202	CD		INT 16
0203	16		
0204	74		JZ 200
0205	FA		
0206	CC		INT 3

There is another complication here. The keyboard program entered via INT 16H changes register AH, so you must reload it each time. Never count on traps preserving registers.

Enter and run Program 4-6. Test a random selection of keys. The program responds to most special keys (for example, function keys, arrow keys, and control keys such as Enter and Backspace) as well as to the standard typewriter keys. Note the final contents of AX in each case.

Problem 4-8

Write a program that sets location 400 to 0 if a key is being pressed and to FF otherwise. Put a delay ahead of the program to give yourself time to press a key.

Problem 4-9

Write a program that shows the data from port A of 8255 device P1 on the LEDs attached to port B. Make the program run continuously until you press a key. Many PC programs use this kind of delay to give the user time to observe results; load or change disks; check whether a printer is on-line; or decide whether to proceed with some drastic action, such as erasing an entire disk or exiting from a program without saving work-in-progress.

Program 4-6 does not respond to the Caps Lock or Num Lock key. However, it returns different codes depending on whether the locks are active. Try a few letter keys with Caps Lock on and off. What effect does the lock have on AH and AL?

The Shift, Alt (Alternate) and Ctrl (Control) keys work only in conjunction with other keys. What do AH and AL contain if you press Ctrl-N, Ctrl-R, Alt-N, or Alt-R? What happens if you press Ctrl-C? To make sure a combination registers properly, hold down the control key (Shift, Alt, or Ctrl), then press and release the other key.

Some combinations such as Ctrl-Del, Alt-Tab (Tab is the key with arrows pointing in both directions; it is just left of Q), and Alt-] are invalid. That is, Program 4-6 will not respond to them. Try to find other invalid combinations by experimenting.

One drawback to keyboard service 1 is that it leaves the key closure active. DEBUG therefore responds to the key as soon as it regains control. To avoid this, execute keyboard service 0 before exiting, that is, put

```
SUB    AH,AH      ;YES, READ KEY CLOSURE
INT    16H
```

after JZ WTKEY. Now what happens when you press Ctrl-C?

Let us focus for a while on the number keys. Pressing one gives an ASCII value between 30 and 39 hex (see Table A2-1). As you might expect, the codes are in numerical order; thus ASCII 0 is 30 hex, ASCII 1 is 31 hex, and so on. The next program (Program 4-7 is the DEBUG version) reads an ASCII digit from the keyboard and stores its decimal value in location 400. Here we use service 0 which waits for the next keyboard input and returns its ASCII value in register AL.

```
SUB    AH,AH       ;GET KEYBOARD INPUT
INT    16H
SUB    AL, '0'      ;CONVERT ASCII TO DECIMAL
MOV    [400H],AL    ;SAVE DECIMAL DIGIT
INT    20H
```

Note that the assembler accepts ASCII characters enclosed in apostrophes. As usual, DEBUG wants values in hex.

PROGRAM 4-7

Memory Address (Hex)	Memory Contents (Hex)	Instruction (DEBUG Form)
0200	28	SUB AH,AH
0201	E4	
0202	CD	INT 16

Memory Address (Hex)	Memory Contents (Hex)	Instruction (DEBUG Form)
	PROGRAM 4-7 (continued)	
0203	16	
0204	2C	*SUB AL,30*
0205	30	
0206	A2	*MOV [400],AL*
0207	00	
0208	04	
0209	CD	*INT 20*
020A	20	

Problem 4-10

Write a program that waits for you to press the 5 key. Modify it to wait for you to press the 5 key four times. Be careful—do not assume that INT 16H preserves any registers.

Problem 4-11

a. Write a program that waits for you to press a digit key (ASCII characters 30 through 39). Make it store the decimal digit in location 400.

b. How would you modify your program to accept and convert hex digits (ASCII characters 30 through 39 and 41 through 46)? This is more difficult because of the gap between ASCII 9 (39 hex) and ASCII A (41 hex). Be sure to enter letter digits as capitals when running the modified program; otherwise, you must allow for codes 61(a) through 66(f).

There are no ASCII characters for special PC keys such as the function and arrow keys or for many combinations involving the Alt or Ctrl keys. If you press one of these, keyboard service 0 returns 0 in AL and a so-called auxiliary byte value, or *scan code*, in AH. Table A2-2 contains the code values for special keys and combinations. The following program (Program 4-8 is the DEBUG version) waits for you to press any of these keys.

```
WTSPEC:  SUB   AH,AH    ;GET KEYBOARD INPUT
         INT   16H
         TEST  AL,AL    ;IS INPUT A SPECIAL KEY?
```

```
JNZ     WTSPEC      ;NO, KEEP LOOKING
INT     3           ;YES, EXIT AND DISPLAY
                    ;   REGISTERS
```

\ PROGRAM 4-8				
Memory Address (Hex)	Memory Contents (Hex)		Instruction (DEBUG Form)	
0200	28	WTSPEC:	SUB	AH,AH
0201	E4			
0202	CDNT			16
0203	16			
0204	84		TEST	AL,AL
0205	C0			
0206	75		JNZ	200
0207	F8			
0208	CC		INT	3

Use Program 4-8 to verify some values in Table A2-2. Many IBM PC programs use special keys and combinations for commands and control functions, thus leaving the typewriter keys available for normal data entry.

Problem 4-12

Write a program that waits for you to press the Home key (auxiliary byte value 47 hex). Be sure Num Lock is off when you run the program.

Problem 4-13

a. Write a program that accepts Alt-F1 (auxiliary byte value 68 hex) as a "jump to location 230" command. Put INT 3 in location 230 for testing.

b. Extend your program to make Alt-F2 (auxiliary byte value 69 hex) mean "load register AL from location 400." Your test program should ignore all other keyboard inputs.

An encoded keyboard simplifies software since the program need not identify each key closure directly. On the other hand, the encoding electronics increases costs, parts count, and power consumption. The IBM PC's keyboard actually has its own microprocessor and control program. In low-volume applications, you can surely afford extra hardware if it simplifies the software. In high-volume, cost-sensitive applications, you must minimize hardware, because it adds to the cost of each system produced.

Key Point Summary

1. A mechanical switch requires a relatively long time to settle into a new position. You can either introduce a delay during which the processor does not examine the switch, or you can add hardware that smooths the transition. Mechanical components generally change state far slower than electrical components. Either hardware or software must account for this difference.

2. Inputs must usually be converted into a convenient form before being processed. Either hardware or software can do the conversion.

3. Timing and code conversion are common tasks that either hardware or software can do. Extra hardware can result in simpler, faster programs. This usually makes system development easier, particularly if the designer is more familiar with hardware than with software. Doing everything in software reduces parts count, saves board space, and increases reliability.

4. Many factors affect tradeoffs between software and hardware. Among these are the cost and availability of parts, designer experience, product volume, amount of memory available, amount of board space, and performance requirements. Remember the following:

   a. Software costs are incurred only once, whereas hardware costs are repeated for each system produced. Thus, high-volume products should have more software and less hardware than low-volume products should.

   b. A single processor can do many tasks in software, particularly if they involve slow mechanical components. External hardware, on the other hand, is more difficult to share, even among similar tasks.

   c. Certain tasks, such as switch and keyboard encoding, display decoding, and serial/parallel interfacing, are so common that inexpensive circuits are readily available to do them. Circuits for similar but less common tasks are generally far more expensive. The obvious reason is that manufacturers must recover their design and development costs over fewer units.

LABORATORY 5

Processing Data Outputs

Purpose   To learn how to process data outputs.

What You Should Learn
1. How to send data to the video display.
2. How to convert decimal and hexadecimal digits to ASCII.
3. How to use lookup tables for code conversion.
4. How indexed addressing works and how it is used.
5. How to count on the video display.
6. The advantages and disadvantages of lookup tables.

Reference Materials
Comer, D. J. *Microprocessor-Based System Design*. New York: Holt, Rinehart and Winston, 1986, sec. 6.3B (design example).

Gorsline, G. W. *16-Bit Modern Microcomputers*. Englewood Cliffs, NJ: Prentice-Hall, 1985, pp. 70–74 (calculation of the operand address), 102–104 (word and data byte movement).

Liu, Y. C., and G. A. Gibson. *Microcomputer Systems: The 8086/8088 Family* (2nd ed.). Englewood Cliffs, NJ: Prentice-Hall, 1986, pp. 35–39 (addressing modes), 100–107 (directives and operators), 220–226 (table translation and number format conversions).

Norton, P. *Programmer's Guide to the IBM PC.* Redmond, WA: Microsoft Press, 1985, chap. 9 (ROM-BIOS video services).

Terms   **Base address** (or **base**):   memory address at which a table begins.
Based addressing: an addressing method in which the effective address is the sum of a base register and displacement in the instruction. *See also* **Indexed addressing.**

Displacement: an offset that is added to a base value to form an effective address.

Effective address: actual address used by an instruction to do its overall function.

Endless loop (or **jump-to-self**) **instruction:** an instruction that transfers control to itself.

Index: data item used to select an element from a set.

Indexed addressing: addressing method in which the address in the instruction is modified by an index register to compute the effective address. 8088 references also call this method *register-offset, register-relative,* or *based addressing.*

Index register: register that can be used to modify memory addresses.

Lookup table: set of data organized so that a result may be obtained merely by selecting the correct entry (without any calculations).

8088
Instructions

INT 10H: software interrupt 10 hex. INT 10H makes the IBM PC do a video display operation. The value in register AH selects which one according to Table 5-1.

XLAT: translate; load register AL from the address that is the sum of registers BX and AL. XLAT does a simple 8-bit table lookup using a base address in BX and an index in AL. AL's original value is lost, but BX is unchanged.

Table 5-1

IBM PC Video Display Operations (Interrupt 10 Hex)

Operation (Service) Number (in register AH)		Description
Decimal	Hex	
0	0	Set video mode
1	1	Set cursor size
2	2	Set cursor position
3	3	Read cursor position
4	4	Read light-pen position
5	5	Set active display page
6	6	Scroll window up
7	7	Scroll window down
8	8	Read character and attribute
9	9	Write character and attribute
10	A	Write character
11	B	Set color palette

**Table 5-1
(continued)**

**IBM PC Video
Display Operations
(Interrupt 10 Hex)**

Operation (Service) Number (in register AH)		Description
Decimal	Hex	
12	C	Write pixel dot
13	D	Read pixel dot
14	E	Write character and advance cursor
15	F	Get current video mode
19	13	Write character string

Handling More Complex Outputs

In real applications, the microprocessor must do more than merely turn a bit on or off. Rather, it must produce a sequence of outputs and convert the data into the forms peripherals require. The processor should also time the outputs properly.

As with inputs, either hardware or software can process outputs. The designer must make tradeoffs suited to an application. Furthermore, he or she may be able to make tradeoffs between execution time and memory usage. One way to do a calculation is with a table containing all possible results. Now the program must simply select an entry. It's like looking up a tax rate, a postage charge, or a delivery zone number in a printed list. This method (called *table lookup*) is fast and easy to program but usually requires more memory than an explicit calculation.

Using the Video Display

The IBM PC's video display is an output device that requires parallel data, timing, and code conversion. The display is complex, but fortunately we need not write programs for it. Instead, we can simply use the BIOS routines much as we did with the keyboard in Laboratory 4.

INT 10H makes the PC do a video display operation (or service). The value in register AH selects which one according to Table 5-1. The main ones we will use are 2 (set cursor position) and 14 (write character and advance cursor).

Writing on the video display requires the following steps:

1. Clear the display.
2. Move the cursor to its starting position.
3. Write the characters.

Let us now examine each step in detail.

The PC has no explicit "Clear display" command. However, it clears the display automatically whenever a new video mode is set. The mode decides the numbers of rows and columns, color selection, and other characteristics. To avoid configuration dependence, we will simply set the mode to its current value. Fortunately, the computer is not smart and acts just as it would if the mode had changed.

We can, therefore, clear the display as follows:

1. Determine the current mode with service 15 (0F hex) of interrupt 10H. The mode number ends up in register AL.
2. Set the mode (from register AL) with service 0 of interrupt 10H.

The assembly language version is

```
MOV    AH,0FH        ;GET CURRENT MODE (IN AL)
INT    10H
SUB    AH,AH         ;SET SAME MODE (FROM AL)
INT    10H
```

To move the cursor, we use service 2 of interrupt 10H. Here the row number (usually 0 to 24 with 0 at the top) must be in register DH, and the column number (usually 0 to 79 with 0 at the far left) must be in register DL. Register BH must be 0. For example, the following lines put the cursor near the center of the screen (column 35 of row 12):

```
MOV    DH,12         ;ROW 12
MOV    DL,35         ;COLUMN 35
SUB    BH,BH
MOV    AH,2          ;MOVE CURSOR
INT    10H
```

To actually write a character (from location 400 hex), we use service 14 (0E hex) of interrupt 10. AL must contain the ASCII data (see Table A2-1). The following lines display one character.

```
MOV    AL,[400H]     ;GET ASCII CHARACTER
MOV    AH,0EH        ;WRITE CHARACTER
INT    10H
```

The next program (Program 5-1 is the DEBUG version) combines the three steps. It clears the screen, moves the cursor, and writes the character.

```
MOV    AH,0FH          ;CLEAR SCREEN BY GETTING AND
INT    10H             ;   SETTING VIDEO MODE
SUB    AH,AH
INT    10H
MOV    DH,12           ;ROW 12
MOV    DL,35           ;COLUMN 35
SUB    BH,BH
MOV    AH,2            ;POSITION CURSOR
INT    10H
MOV    AL,[400H]       ;GET ASCII CHARACTER
MOV    AH,0EH          ;WRITE CHARACTER
INT    10H
INT    20H
```

PROGRAM 5-1

Memory Address (Hex)	Memory Contents (Hex)	Instruction (DEBUG Form)	
0200	B4	MOV	AH,F
0201	0F		
0202	CD	INT	10
0203	10		
0204	28	SUB	AH,AH
0205	E4		
0206	CD	INT	10
0207	10		
0208	B6	MOV	DH,C
0209	0C		
020A	B2	MOV	DL,23
020B	23		
020C	28	SUB	BH,BH
020D	FF		
020E	B4	MOV	AH,2
020F	02		
0210	CD	INT	10
0211	10		
0212	A0	MOV	AL,[400]
0213	00		
0214	04		
0215	B4	MOV	AH,E
0216	0E		
0217	CD	INT	10
0218	10		
0219	CD	INT	20
021A	20		

Enter and run Program 5-1 with [400] = 35 (ASCII 5). What happens? The problem is that DEBUG writes its reassuring "Program terminated normally" message as soon as the processor executes INT 20H. You can separate DEBUG's message from the program's output by moving the cursor. For example, you could put the following instructions after the last INT 10H:

```
SUB    DX,DX        ;MOVE CURSOR TO TOP, LEFT-HAND
SUB    BH,BH        ;   CORNER BEFORE EXITING
MOV    AH,2
INT    10H
INT    20H
```

0219	CD	INT	20
021A	20		
021B	28	SUB	BH,BH
021C	FF		
021D	B4	MOV	AH,2
021E	02		
021F	CD	INT	10
0220	10		
0221	CD	INT	20
0222	20		

Problem 5-1

Make Program 5-1 write the character in the bottom, right-hand corner of the display.

Problem 5-2

Write a program that puts the number 88 near the center of the display. Note that INT 10H changes AH but not AL.

Putting a delay routine at the end of Program 5-1 and then clearing the screen again makes the character appear only briefly. The added instructions are

```
            MOV   CX,COUNT        ;WAIT A WHILE
DLY:        DEC   CX
            JNZ   DLY
            MOV   AH,0FH          ;CLEAR SCREEN AGAIN
            INT   10H
            SUB   AH,AH
            INT   10H
            INT   20H
```

Program 5-2 is the DEBUG extension of Program 5-1 with COUNT = 0.

	PROGRAM 5-2		
Memory Address (Hex)	Memory Contents (Hex)		Instruction (DEBUG Form)
0219	B9		MOV CX,0
021A	00		
021B	00		
021C	49	DLY:	DEC CX
021D	75		JNZ 21C
021E	FD		
021F	B4		MOV AH,F
0220	0F		
0221	CD		INT 10
0222	10		
0223	28		SUB AH,AH
0224	E4		
0225	CD		INT 10
0226	10		
0227	CD		INT 20
0228	20		

Problem 5-3

Change Program 5-2 to show the word "On" briefly near the center of the screen.

Code Conversion

We can easily convert a decimal digit to ASCII. As noted in Laboratory 4, ASCII digits form a sequence from 30 through 39 hex. So the conversion simply involves adding 30 hex (ASCII 0). The following program (Program 5-3 is the DEBUG version) converts a decimal digit in location 400 to an ASCII digit in 401. Run it with [400] = 07.

```
MOV    AL,[400H]      ;GET DECIMAL DIGIT
ADD    AL,'0'         ;CONVERT TO ASCII
MOV    [401H],AL      ;SAVE ASCII DIGIT
INT    20H
```

	PROGRAM 5-3	
Memory Address (Hex)	Memory Contents (Hex)	Instruction (DEBUG Form)
0200	A0	MOV AL,[400]
0201	00	
0202	04	
0203	04	ADD AL,30
0204	30	
0205	A2	MOV [401],AL
0206	01	
0207	04	
0208	CD	INT 20
0209	20	

Problem 5-4

Write a program that takes two decimal digits from locations 400 and 401 and displays them near the center of the screen. Run it with [400] = 06 and [401] = 02.

Problem 5-5

Combine Programs 4-5 and 5-3 to make the computer wait for a switch closure at port A of 8255 device P1 and report its number near the center of the screen.

The conversion is more complex for hex digits. Now we must add 30 hex to numbers, but 37 hex to letters. The difference is the result of A not following immediately after 9 in ASCII (see Table A2-1). Instead, there is a gap with codes for the semicolon, colon, and other symbols. So we need the following program (Program 5-4 is the DEBUG version) to convert a hex digit in location 400 to an ASCII digit in 401.

```
          MOV    AL,[400H]      ;GET HEXADECIMAL DIGIT
          CMP    AL,9           ;IS DIGIT A LETTER?
          JBE    ADDZ           ;NO, JUMP
          ADD    AL,7           ;YES, ADD EXTRA OFFSET FOR
                                ;  LETTERS ('A'-'9'-1)
ADDZ:     ADD    AL,'0'         ;CONVERT TO ASCII
          MOV    [401H],AL      ;SAVE ASCII DIGIT
          INT    20H
```

		PROGRAM 5-4	

Memory Address (Hex)	Memory Contents (Hex)		Instruction (DEBUG Form)
0200	A0		MOV AL,[400]
0201	00		
0202	04		
0203	3C		CMP AL,9
0204	09		
0205	76		JBE 209
0206	02		
0207	04		ADD AL,7
0208	07		
0209	04	ADDZ:	ADD AL,30
020A	30		
020B	A2		MOV [401],AL
020C	01		
020D	04		
020E	CD		INT 20
020F	20		

Run Program 5-4 for the following cases:

a. Data = [400] = 07
   Result = [401] = 37 (ASCII 7)
b. Data = [400] = 0C
   Result = [401] = 43 (ASCII C)

Problem 5-6

Write a program that takes two hexadecimal digits from locations 400 and 401 and displays them near the center of the screen. Run it with [400] = 0B and [401] = 0E.

An alternative conversion method uses a list of ASCII characters as a lookup table. This general approach applies to any conversion, no matter how the codes are arranged. The program must do the following:

1. Compute the address of the desired code by adding the starting (or *base*) address of the table to the element number (or *index*).
2. Get the code by loading it from the computed address.

Table 5-2

Hexadecimal-to-ASCII Conversion Table

ADD
38°4

Hexadecimal Digit	ASCII Character (Hex)
0	30
1	31
2	32
3	33
4	34
5	35
6	36
7	37
8	38
9	39
A	41
B	42
C	43
D	44
E	45
F	46

Our first idea might be to use an ADD instruction followed by a MOV. However, the 8088 lets us combine the steps by using indexed addressing (sometimes called *register-offset, register relative,* or *based addressing* in Intel manuals). Here the processor adds a register to a *displacement* contained in the instruction. It then uses the sum as the address needed to execute the instruction. We refer to the offset as the *base address*, the register's contents as the *index*, and the sum (the actual address used to do the overall operation) as the *effective address*. The effective address in indexed addressing is exactly what we need to select a code from our lookup table.

The following program uses indexed addressing to convert a hex digit in location 400 into an ASCII digit in 401. Note that we must extend the digit to 16 bits by clearing register BH. This is because the processor uses BX, not just BL, in its address calculation; we cannot assume that BH contains zero just because we have not used it. The 8088 can employ registers BP, BX, DI, or SI as base addresses for indexing.

```
MOV    BL,[400H]         ;GET HEXADECIMAL DIGIT
SUB    BH,BH             ;EXTEND DIGIT TO 16 BITS
MOV    AL,[BX+380H]      ;GET ASCII DIGIT FROM TABLE
MOV    [401H],AL         ;SAVE ASCII DIGIT IN MEMORY
INT    20H
```

This program assumes an ASCII table in locations 380 through 38F. The table is thus outside our program and data areas. Note that you must enter both Program 5-5 (starting at address 200) and Table 5-2 (starting at address 380) into memory. The indexed instruction takes four bytes and 18 clock cycles (see Table A1-3), as it involves a 16-bit displacement and an address calculation.

PROGRAM 5-5

Memory Address (Hex)	Memory Contents (Hex)	Instruction (DEBUG Form)
0200	8A	MOV BL,[400]
0201	1E	
0202	00	
0203	04	
0204	28	SUB BH,BH
0205	FF	
0206	8A	MOV AL,[BX+380]
0207	87	
0208	80	
0209	03	
020A	A2	MOV [401],AL
020B	01	
020C	04	
020D	CD	INT 20
020E	20	

Program 5-5 works as follows (assuming that location 400 contains 0D):

1. MOV BL,[400H] loads the data (0D) into register BL. SUB BH,BH then clears register BH, extending the data to 16 bits (000D).
2. MOV AL,[BX+380H] first computes the effective address by adding 380 (the table's base address) to register BX (the index). The sum is 380 + 0D = 38D. The processor then loads AL from address 38D, which contains 44, an ASCII D.

You can use the E command to enter the entire table at one time. Just follow E with the starting address, then the data items with spaces in between. The command to load Table 5-2 into memory starting at address 380 is

E 380 30 31 32 33 34 35 36 37 38 39 40 41 42 43 44 45 46

To see the entire table at once, use the D ("Dump") command. It requires starting and ending addresses separated by a space. For example, to examine locations 380 through 38F, enter

D 380 38F

The display shows all 16 bytes of data on one line with a hyphen between the eighth and ninth bytes. The ASCII versions are at the far right; nonprinting characters appear as periods. The D command thus lets you scan an entire section of memory, but you cannot make changes as you can with the E command.

Problem 5-7

XLAT (translate) is a special instruction for table lookup. It loads AL from the address obtained by adding AL and BX. Revise Program 5-5 to use XLAT; it does not need a 16-bit index but it is, of course, limited to tables with 8-bit indexes and values.

Problem 5-8

Revise Program 5-5 or Table 5-2 to make letter digits appear in lowercase.

Counting on the Display

We can use Table 5-2 to count in hexadecimal on the video display. The following program counts up. Note that INT 10H does not affect register DI or SI, so we can use either freely as a counter.

```
          MOV    AH,0FH          ;CLEAR SCREEN BY GETTING AND
          INT    10H             ;   SETTING VIDEO MODE
          SUB    AH,AH
          INT    10H
          SUB    SI,SI           ;CLEAR COUNT INITIALLY
DSPLY:    MOV    DH,12           ;ROW 12
          MOV    DL,35           ;COLUMN 35
          SUB    BH,BH
          MOV    AH,2            ;MOVE CURSOR
          INT    10H
          MOV    AL,[SI+380H]    ;CONVERT COUNT TO ASCII
          MOV    AH,0EH          ;WRITE CHARACTER
          INT    10H
          MOV    CX,0            ;WASTE SOME TIME
DLY:      DEC    CX
          JNZ    DLY
          INC    SI
          CMP    SI,10H          ;IS COUNT COMPLETED?
          JNE    DSPLY           ;NO, CONTINUE
          INT    20H
```

Program 5-6 is the DEBUG version. Remember to put Table 5-2 in locations 380 through 38F. Note that CMP's operand must be 10 hex (not 0F), as the program increments register SI before the comparison.

PROGRAM 5-6

Memory Address (Hex)	Memory Contents (Hex)	Instruction (DEBUG Form)		
0200	B4		MOV	AH,F
0201	0F			
0202	CD		INT	10
0203	10			
0204	28		SUB	AH,AH
0205	E4			
0206	CD		INT	10
0207	10			
0208	29		SUB	SI,SI
0209	F6			
020A	B6	DSPLY:	MOV	DH,C
020B	0C			
020C	B2		MOV	DL,23
020D	23			

	PROGRAM 5-6 (continued)		
Memory Address (Hex)	Memory Contents (Hex)		Instruction (DEBUG Form)
020E	28		SUB BH,BH
020F	FF		
0210	B4		MOV AH,2
0211	02		
0212	CD		INT 10
0213	10		
0214	8A		MOV AL,[SI+380]
0215	84		
0216	80		
0217	03		
0218	B4		MOV AH,E
0219	0E		
021A	CD		INT 10
021B	10		
021C	B9		MOV CX,0
021D	00		
021E	00		
021F	49	DLY:	DEC CX
0220	75		JNZ 21F
0221	FD		
0222	46		INC SI
0223	83		CMP SI,10
0224	FE		
0225	10		
0226	75		JNE 20A
0227	E2		
0228	CD		INT 20
0229	20		

Problem 5-9

a. Make Program 5-6 count in the bottom, left-hand corner.

b. Revise Program 5-6 to fetch the row number (assumed to be between 0 and 24 inclusive) from location 402 and the column number (assumed to be between 0 and 79 inclusive) from location 403.

Problem 5-10

Make Program 5-6 repeat the count a number of times given by the contents of register DI, starting over at zero after it reaches F. Run the program with [DI] = 5.

Problem 5-11

Make Program 5-6 start at F and count down to zero.

Problem 5-12

Revise Program 5-6 to stop counting immediately if the switch attached to bit 0 of port A of 8255 device P1 is closed.

Problem 5-13

Make Program 5-6 use the following nonstandard hexadecimal digits for 11 through 15. This set's advantages are that its digits are easy to tell apart, can be read upside-down, and can be formed on seven-segment displays without using any lowercase letters. For example, Hewlett-Packard uses it in the HP5001 Signature Analyzer, a piece of test equipment that detects faults in microprocessor-based systems.

Normal Hexadecimal Digit	HP5001 Hexadecimal Digit
B	C
C	F
D	H
E	P
F	U

Problem 5-14

Revise Program 5-6 to send the display a backspace character (08 hex) after showing each digit. This makes it unnecessary to move the cursor each time.

Advantages and Disadvantages of Lookup Tables

By now, you have seen many advantages and disadvantages of lookup tables. Among the advantages are that

- No computation is necessary, and so tables are usually faster than calculations.
- No programming is required beyond the basic lookup routine. Lookup tables are thus easy to implement.
- The same lookup routine can access many different tables. Changes and extensions are simple, and new tables require little or no programming.

- Table entries are available for other purposes (such as counting) in a convenient order.
- The table-lookup procedure is the same for all values. There are no boundary problems or differences in execution time.

Among the disadvantages of tables are that

- They take extra memory, particularly if the range of input values is large or the output values have many digits.
- They may be difficult to organize unless the input data is simple.
- The table-lookup procedure cannot distinguish common or simple cases that might be handled easily.
- Programs that use tables may be difficult to understand, as they do no explicit calculations.

Key Point Summary

1. Most output devices (and observers) require data to be available for a long time, by processor standards. The processor must not change the data too often.
2. Outputs must usually be converted into the forms required by peripherals.
3. Lookup tables often simplify code conversions. Such tables simply contain all the codes, organized in a convenient manner. They are easy and quick to use but may take a large amount of memory.
4. In indexed addressing, the processor calculates the actual (effective) address to be used in executing the instruction. The calculation adds an index or base register to the displacement in the instruction. Indexed addressing lets the programmer access lookup tables.
5. Changes in index registers also change the effective addresses of indexed instructions. Those instructions can therefore refer to different effective addresses at different times.
6. A microprocessor can usually update operator displays while doing other tasks, as the displays change slowly.

Processing Data Arrays

Purpose   To learn how to process data arrays.

What You Should Learn
1. What identifies elements of an array.
2. The best way to process arrays with the 8088.
3. How to do a summation.
4. How to use a terminator.
5. How to determine whether numbers are within limits.
6. How to display a message.

Reference Materials

Eccles, W. J. *Microprocessor Systems: A 16-Bit Approach.* Reading, MA: Addison-Wesley, 1985, pp. 107–109 (programs with loops), 119–122, 133–137, 187–190, 311–323 (program examples).

Gorsline, G. W. *16-Bit Modern Microcomputers.* Englewood Cliffs, NJ: Prentice-Hall, 1985, pp. 80–88 (comparisons and flow of control), 88–93 (loop control), 106–107 (string data movement).

Liu, Y. C., and G. A. Gibson. *Microcomputer Systems: The 8086/8088 Family* (2nd ed.). Englewood Cliffs, NJ: Prentice-Hall, 1986, pp. 35–37 (addressing modes), 47–50 (instruction execution timing), 65–69 (binary arithmetic), 86–90 (LOOP instruction), 207–212 (string instructions).

Norton, P. *Programmer's Guide to the IBM PC.* Redmond, WA: Microsoft Press, 1985, chap. 9 (ROM-BIOS video services).

Terms **Array:**   set of related data items.

Autodecrement: decreasing a pointer or index automatically while executing an instruction.

Autoincrement: increasing a pointer or index automatically while executing an instruction.

Borrow: bit that is set (1) if the result of a subtraction is negative and cleared (0) if it is positive or zero. Borrows are used to subtract numbers that are too long for a single operation.

Checksum: logical sum used to guard against errors.

Indirect address: address that contains the data's address, as opposed to a direct address that contains the actual data.

Indirect addressing: an addressing method in which the instruction refers to a storage location containing the effective address.

Limit checking: determining if data is within limits, that is, below an upper threshold and above a lower threshold. This procedure can be used to reject invalid data resulting from operator or communications errors. Typical examples of such data are a transaction dated February 30 and a room temperature setting of 70°C (instead of °F).

Logical sum: binary sum with no carries between bit positions.

Pointer: register or memory location that contains an address rather than data.

Register indirect addressing: indirect addressing in which the effective address is in a register.

String: an array of characters (8-bit elements).

String instruction: an instruction that performs one step in a string operation. The step usually involves updating indexes, counters, or pointers as well as doing a basic task. String instructions are also called *string primitives*, as they serve as building blocks for complex string operations.

Terminator: item that marks the end of an array.

8088 Instructions

CLD: clear direction (D) flag; make the direction flag 0, thus causing subsequent string instructions to increment their pointers.

JA (or JNBE): jump if above (not below or equal); jump if carry clear (0) and result not zero (Zero flag = 0).

JBE (or JNA): jump if below or equal (not above); jump if carry set (1) or result is zero (Zero flag = 1).

LODSB: load byte string; load register AL from the location whose address is in register SI, then either increment or decrement SI by 1 depending on whether the D flag is 0 (increment) or 1 (decrement).

LOOP: subtract 1 from register CX and jump to the specified address if CX is not zero.

STD: set direction (D) flag; make the direction flag 1, thus causing subsequent string instructions to decrement their pointers.

Data Arrays

Most computer tasks involve applying instructions to sets of related data, or *arrays*. Typical array operations are calculating averages and other statistics, finding the largest element for scaling, organizing data for storage on tape or disk, editing, sorting, arranging sequences of operations, and searching for commands or entries.

The elements of arrays are usually stored in consecutive memory addresses. Two items are needed to reach an element:

1. The array's starting (*base*) address.
2. The element's number, or *index*.

We often refer mathematically to an element as A_i, where A identifies the entire array (that is, base address), and i identifies the particular element (that is, index).

Flexible addressing modes are the keys to processing arrays. One sequence of instructions should be able to process any element. Otherwise, minor changes in the arrays' locations or lengths will require major revisions in the program. A flexible addressing mode, such as indexed or indirect addressing, allows an instruction to use different effective addresses at different times.

Problem 6-1

Which of these instructions could handle any element of an array? Why?

   a. MOV AL,[400H]
   b. MOV BX,3E0H
   c. MOV AL,[BX+380H]
   d. AND AL,[400H]

Which instruction can load data from different memory locations at different times even if the program is in read-only memory?

Problem 6-2

If an array starts at address BASE and each element occupies one byte, where is the second element? Assume that BASE contains the zeroth element. Where is the jth element?

Problem 6-3

How do the answers to Problem 6-2 change if each element occupies two bytes? What if each element occupies k bytes?

Problem 6-4

We can store a two-dimensional array either by row or by column. For example, we can store an array A with m rows and n columns by row, starting at row 1, column 1. Denoting the element in row i and column j as A_{ij}, the order in memory is: $A_{11}, A_{12}, A_{13}, \ldots, A_{1n}, A_{21}, A_{22}, A_{23}, \ldots, A_{m1}, A_{m2}, A_{m3}, \ldots, A_{mn}$. If A_{11} is in address B, where is A_{23}? Where is A_{ij}? What is the lowest address occupied by A_{ij} if each element occupies k bytes? Note that we are starting the indexes at 1 here, *not* at 0.

Problem 6-5

Assume that an array contains the angles at which a vehicle should move (0 to 359 deg) and the number of minutes (0 to 59) for which it should travel at each angle. Each entry consists of 3 bytes; the first two contain the angle and the third, the travel time at that angle. If the first angle is in addresses BASE and BASE + 1, where will you find:

a. the third angle?
b. the travel time at the fifth angle?
c. the sixth angle?

Processing Arrays with the 8088 Microprocessor

The fastest and simplest way to process arrays with the 8088 is as follows (see Figure 6-1 for a flowchart):

1. Put the array's base address in an index or base register. You can use BX, SI (source index register), or DI (destination index register). These registers serve as *pointers*, as they contain addresses rather than data. We will generally use SI or DI, leaving BX for 8-bit operations. Note that BX is byte-addressable (the bytes are BH and BL), whereas SI and DI are not.

2. Refer indirectly to an element of the array, that is, as [BX], [SI], or [DI]. This is just like indexing, except with no displacement. We call this mode *register indirect addressing.*
3. Move the pointer to the next element with INC SI or INC DI (or to the previous element with DEC SI or DEC DI).
4. Access an arbitrary element by using its offset as a displacement in indexed addressing. For example, ADD AL,[SI+5] will add to AL an element located five bytes ahead of where SI is currently pointing.

The key point here is that only step 1 (initialization) depends on where the array is located.

Figure 6-1

Flowchart for array processing with the 8088 microprocessor.

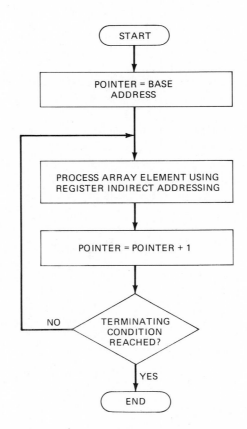

Problem 6-6

Write a program that logically ANDs AL with the memory location three bytes ahead of the one addressed by SI. It should store the result in the location one byte before the address in SI.

EXAMPLE:

$$[SI] = 0440$$

RESULT:

$$[043F] = [0440] \text{ AND } [0443]$$

Remember that the brackets mean "contents of."
Note that the 8088 has a short form for signed 8-bit displacements (between −128 and +127). As in conditional jumps, it represents −1 as FF, −2 as FE, and so forth. Positive values (most significant bit = 0) are taken literally.

Sum of Data

A simple example of array processing is summing the elements. This is an essential step in computing averages, variances, or numerical integrals. The following program assumes an array of four elements in 420 through 423 (see Figure 6-2 for a flowchart). The pointer is in register SI.

Figure 6-2
Flowchart for summation program.

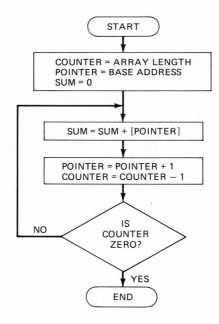

```
MOV   CX,4        ;COUNT = 4
MOV   SI,420H     ;POINT TO START OF ARRAY
SUB   AL,AL       ;SUM = ZERO INITIALLY
```

```
ADDELM:  ADD    AL,[SI]         ;ADD ELEMENT TO SUM
         INC    SI
         DEC    CX              ;COUNT ELEMENTS
         JNZ    ADDELM
         MOV    [400H],AL       ;SAVE SUM
         INT    20H
```

	PROGRAM 6-1	

Memory Address (Hex)	Memory Contents (Hex)	Instruction (DEBUG Form)
0200	B9	MOV CX,4
0201	04	
0202	00	
0203	BE	MOV SI,420
0204	20	
0205	04	
0206	28	SUB AL,AL
0207	C0	
0208	02	ADDELM: ADD AL,[SI]
0209	04	
020A	46	INC SI
020B	49	DEC CX
020C	75	JNZ 208
020D	FA	
020E	A2	MOV [400],AL
020F	00	
0210	04	
0211	CD	INT 20
0212	20	

Program 6-1 is the DEBUG version. Run it with the following data:

$$[0420] = 07$$
$$[0421] = 23$$
$$[0422] = 31$$
$$[0423] = 20$$

RESULT:

$$[0400] = 7B$$

Remember that the data is hexadecimal. You can use the command

E 420 7 23 31 20

to enter it. Change 422 to F1 and run the program again. What is the result, and why?

Problem 6-7

Write a program that sums six elements starting at 420.

SAMPLE PROBLEM:

[0420] = 07
[0421] = 23
[0422] = 31
[0423] = 20
[0424] = 16
[0425] = 38

RESULT:

[0400] = C9

Problem 6-8

Make Program 6-1 EXCLUSIVE OR the elements instead of adding them. The result, called a *logical sum* or *checksum*, is often used to detect errors in tape or disk records.

SAMPLE PROBLEM: (four elements, starting at 420, result in 400)

[0420] = 07
[0421] = 23
[0422] = 31
[0423] = 20

RESULT:

[0400] = 35

Problem 6-9

Extend Program 6-1 to save the carries and store the 16-bit sum in 400 and 401 (more significant byte in 401).

SAMPLE PROBLEM:

$$[0420] = F7$$
$$[0421] = 23$$
$$[0422] = 31$$
$$[0423] = 20$$
$$[0424] = 16$$

RESULT:

$$[0400] = 81 \text{ (less significant byte of sum)}$$
$$[0401] = 01 \text{ (more significant byte of sum)}$$

The 8088 has a LOOP instruction that replaces the common countdown sequence

```
DEC   CX
JNZ   BEGLOOP
```

LOOP uses CX automatically. For example, in Program 6-1, we can replace the DEC CX, JNZ ADDELM sequence with LOOP ADDELM. The savings are one byte of memory and one clock cycle. Like JNZ, LOOP requires an 8-bit relative offset. The end of the program (locations 20B on) is now

Memory Address (Hex)	Memory Contents (Hex)	Instruction (DEBUG Form)	
020B	E2	LOOP	208
020C	FB		
020D	A2	MOV	[400],AL
020E	00		
020F	04		
0210	CD	INT	20
0211	20		

The D command has a form for displaying arrays of known length. In it, you follow D with:

1. Starting address
2. L
3. Number of bytes.

For example, you can display the data and result from Problem 6-9 with the commands

D 420 L 5 (display five bytes starting at 420)
D 400 L 2 (display two bytes starting at 400)

Note that the L option works with the D command but not with E.

Using a Terminator

If you are not sure how long the array is (or do not want to count the elements), you can follow the data with a special marker, or *terminator*. It must have a value that cannot be a real data item. In a summation, zero is a good choice because it does not affect the sum. The program using zero as a terminator is (see Fig. 6-3 for a flowchart)

```
            MOV   SI,420H        ;POINT TO START OF ARRAY
            SUB   BL,BL          ;SUM = ZERO INITIALLY
ADDELM:     MOV   AL,[SI]        ;GET NEXT ELEMENT
            TEST  AL,AL          ;IS IT TERMINATOR (ZERO)?
            JZ    DONE           ;YES, DONE
            ADD   BL,AL          ;NO, ADD ELEMENT TO SUM
            INC   SI
            JMP   ADDELM
DONE:       MOV   [400H],BL      ;SAVE SUM
            INT   20H
```

TEST AL,AL sets the flags from AL's contents. Remember that MOV (as well as IN, OUT, and other data movement instructions) does not affect the flags. ANDing or ORing a register with itself does nothing except set the flags (see Table 3-3). Thus AND reg,reg, OR reg,reg, and TEST reg,reg all set the flags from a register. We chose TEST only to emphasize that the register does not change. A good way to confuse readers is to select among the three at random.

Figure 6-3
Flowchart for
summation program
with a terminator.

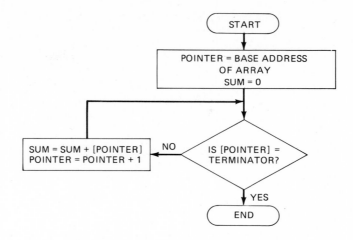

PROGRAM 6-2			
Memory Address (Hex)	Memory Contents (Hex)		Instruction (DEBUG Form)
0200	BE		MOV SI,420
0201	20		
0202	04		
0203	28		SUB BL,BL
0204	DB		
0205	8A	ADDELM:	MOV AL,[SI]
0206	04		
0207	84		TEST AL,AL
0208	C0		
0209	74		JZ 210
020A	05		
020B	00		ADD BL,AL
020C	C3		
020D	46		INC SI
020E	EB		JMP 205
020F	F5		
0210	88	DONE:	MOV [400],BL
0211	1E		
0212	00		
0213	04		
0214	CD		INT 20H
0215	20		

Program 6-2 is the DEBUG version. Run it with the following data:

$$[0420] = 07$$
$$[0421] = 23$$
$$[0422] = 31$$
$$[0423] = 20$$
$$[0424] = 16$$
$$[0425] = 38$$
$$[0426] = 00$$

RESULT:

$$[0400] = C9$$

What happens if you set $[0423] = 00$? What are the pros and cons of using a terminator, as compared with counting the elements? Which approach gives faster programs? Which makes data entry simpler?

Problem 6-10

If zero is an acceptable data value, you must use a different terminator. Revise Program 6-2 to use FF as a terminator. Run the revision with the original sample data except set $[0426] = FF$. Which terminator should you use if the data values are the numbers of characters received from a 30-cps (characters per second) teletypewriter in 1 s?

Like the countdown sequence, the sequence

```
MOV   AL,[SI]
INC   SI
```

has a single-instruction equivalent called LODSB. In fact, LODSB may either increment or decrement SI, depending on whether the D (direction) flag is 0 (increment) or 1 (decrement). The next program (Program 6-3 is the DEBUG version) is a revision of Program 6-2 to use LODSB. Note that we clear the D flag initially with CLD (the alternative is to set it with STD). In the flag register display, D appears as DN (1) or UP (0).

We call instructions like LODSB *string instructions*, as they handle arrays or strings of data elements. We call the automatic increase or decrease of SI an *autoincrement* or *autodecrement*, respectively. Note that LODSB always uses AL and SI.

```
            MOV     SI,420H      ;POINT TO START OF ARRAY
            SUB     BL,BL        ;SUM = ZERO INITIALLY
            CLD                  ;SELECT AUTOINCREMENTING
ADDELM:     LODSB                ;GET NEXT ELEMENT
            TEST    AL,AL        ;IS IT TERMINATOR (ZERO)?
            JZ      DONE         ;YES, DONE
            ADD     BL,AL        ;NO, ADD ELEMENT TO SUM
            JMP     ADDELM
DONE:       MOV     [400H],BL    ;SAVE SUM
            INT     20H
```

	PROGRAM 6-3			
Memory Address (Hex)	Memory Contents (Hex)		Instruction (DEBUG Form)	
0200	BE		MOV	SI,420
0201	20			
0202	04			
0203	28		SUB	BL,BL
0204	DB			
0205	FC		CLD	
0206	AC	ADDELM:	LODSB	
0207	84		TEST	AL,AL
0208	C0			
0209	74		JZ	20F
020A	05			
020B	00		ADD	BL,AL
020C	C3			
020D	EB		JMP	206
020E	F7			
020F	88	DONE:	MOV	[400],BL
0210	1E			
0211	00			
0212	04			
0213	CD		INT	20
0214	20			

Limit Checking

We often want a computer to check whether data is valid, that is, whether it is within certain limits, below a threshold, or has an allowed value. Determining whether data is within limits is called *limit checking*. The key instruction here is a comparison that subtracts a data value from a limit (or vice versa). If the operands are treated as unsigned, the Carry flag indicates which is larger. CMP op1,op2 sets the Carry as follows:

$$\text{Carry} = 0 \text{ if op1} \geq \text{op2}$$
$$\text{Carry} = 1 \text{ if op1} < \text{op2}$$

Carry is thus a *borrow*; that is, it is set if the difference is negative.

We can follow CMP with any of the following jump instructions:

JA (or JNBE): jump if above (Carry = 0 and Zero = 0).

JAE (JNB or JNC): jump if above or equal (Carry = 0).

JBE (or JNA): jump if below or equal (Carry = 1 or Zero = 1).

JB (JC or JNAE): jump if below (Carry = 1).

In general, after CMP op1,op2, the condition in the jump refers to how op1 compares to op2 (for example, is op1 "above" op2 ?). The alternative mnemonics simply make the sequence easier to understand.

The following program sums six elements but ignores ones that are 80 hex or above (that is, have a most significant bit of 1).

```
            MOV   CX,6          ;COUNT = NUMBER OF ELEMENTS
            MOV   SI,420H       ;POINT TO START OF ARRAY
            SUB   BL,BL         ;CLEAR SUM INITIALLY
            CLD                 ;SELECT AUTOINCREMENTING
ADDELM:     LODSB               ;COMPARE ELEMENT TO
                                ;   THRESHOLD
            CMP   AL,80H
            JAE   COUNT         ;BRANCH IF ABOVE OR AT
                                ;   THRESHOLD
            ADD   BL,AL         ;ELSE ADD ELEMENT TO SUM
COUNT:      LOOP  ADDELM        ;COUNT ELEMENTS
            MOV   [400H],AL     ;SAVE SUM
            INT   20H
```

Remember that LODSB increments SI automatically and LOOP decrements CX automatically.

Program 6-4 is the DEBUG version; run it with the following data:

$$[0420] = 07$$
$$[0421] = 20$$
$$[0422] = F1$$

$$[0423] = 3C$$
$$[0424] = 80$$
$$[0425] = 73$$

RESULT:

$$[0400] = D6$$

To make the threshold itself valid (that is, ignore elements that are above 80 hex, instead of 80 hex or above), simply replace JAE COUNT with JA COUNT.

Problem 6-11

Make Program 6-4 ignore elements that are 80 hex or above or 20 hex or below.

SAMPLE PROBLEM:

$$[0420] = 07$$
$$[0421] = 20$$
$$[0422] = F1$$
$$[0423] = 3C$$
$$[0424] = 80$$
$$[0425] = 73$$

RESULT:

$$[0400] = AF$$

PROGRAM 6-4		
Memory Address (Hex)	Memory Contents (Hex)	Instruction (DEBUG Form)
0200	B9	MOV CX,6
0201	06	
0202	00	
0203	BE	MOV SI,420
0204	20	
0205	04	

PROGRAM 6-4 (continued)			

Memory Address (Hex)	Memory Contents (Hex)		Instruction (DEBUG Form)
0206	28		SUB BL,BL
0207	DB		
0208	FC		CLD
0209	AC	ADDELM:	LODSB
020A	3C		CMP AL,80
020B	80		
020C	73		JAE 210
020D	02		
020E	00		ADD BL,AL
020F	C3		
0210	E2	COUNT:	LOOP 209
0211	F7		
0212	88		MOV [400],BL
0213	1E		
0214	00		
0215	04		
0216	CD		INT 20
0217	20		

Limit checking is often used to reject measurements that are far removed from the majority (and therefore suspect). Many data analysis routines discard the highest and lowest values before computing statistics to eliminate readings caused by noise, equipment malfunction, or human error. Limit checking also guards against obviously incorrect entries, such as a time of 8:80 instead of the intended 8:00 or an automobile speed of 1000 km/hr instead of the intended 100 km/hr.

Displaying a Message

The next program (see Figure 6-4 for a flowchart and Program 6-5 for a DEBUG version) prints a message on the video display. It takes the message from locations starting at 420. Note that the delay loop uses register AX here.

```
MOV    AH,0FH    ;CLEAR THE DISPLAY
INT    10H
SUB    AH,AH
```

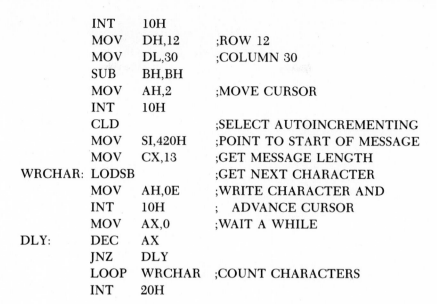

```
            INT     10H
            MOV     DH,12       ;ROW 12
            MOV     DL,30       ;COLUMN 30
            SUB     BH,BH
            MOV     AH,2        ;MOVE CURSOR
            INT     10H
            CLD                 ;SELECT AUTOINCREMENTING
            MOV     SI,420H     ;POINT TO START OF MESSAGE
            MOV     CX,13       ;GET MESSAGE LENGTH
WRCHAR:     LODSB               ;GET NEXT CHARACTER
            MOV     AH,0E       ;WRITE CHARACTER AND
            INT     10H         ;   ADVANCE CURSOR
            MOV     AX,0        ;WAIT A WHILE
DLY:        DEC     AX
            JNZ     DLY
            LOOP    WRCHAR      ;COUNT CHARACTERS
            INT     20H
```

Figure 6-4
Flowchart for displaying a message.

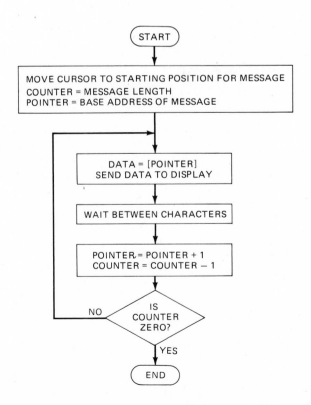

PROGRAM 6-5

Memory Address (Hex)	Memory Contents (Hex)		Instruction (DEBUG Form)	
0200	B4		MOV	AH,F
0201	0F			
0202	CD		INT	10
0203	10			
0204	28		SUB	AH,AH
0205	E4			
0206	CD		INT	10
0207	10			
0208	B6		MOV	DH,C
0209	0C			
020A	B2		MOV	DL,1E
020B	1E			
020C	28		SUB	BH,BH
020D	FF			
020E	B4		MOV	AH,2
020F	02			
0210	CD		INT	10
0211	10			
0212	FC		CLD	
0213	BE		MOV	SI,420
0214	20			
0215	04			
0216	B9		MOV	CX,D
0217	0D			
0218	00			
0219	AC	WRCHAR:	LODSB	
021A	B4		MOV	AH,E
021B	0E			
021C	CD		INT	10
021D	10			
021E	B8		MOV	AX,0
021F	00			
0220	00			
0221	48	DLY:	DEC	AX
0222	75		JNZ	221
0223	FD			
0224	E2		LOOP	219
0225	F3			
0226	CD		INT	20
0227	20			

Run Program 6-5 with the following data:

[0420] = 41
[0421] = 42
[0422] = 41
[0423] = 4E
[0424] = 44
[0425] = 4F
[0426] = 4E
[0427] = 20
[0428] = 53
[0429] = 48
[042A] = 49
[042B] = 50
[042C] = 21

You can use the E command to enter ASCII characters into memory. Just put quotation marks around them. For example, to put THE COMPUTER IS DEAD! in locations 420 through 434, type

E 420 "THE COMPUTER IS DEAD!"

You can also use the F (fill) command with the L option to fill memory with specific values or characters. For example, the following command clears locations 420 through 42F:

F 420 L 10 0

The order is: starting address, L, length in bytes, and fill value. The following command puts ASCII spaces in locations 420 through 44F:

F 420 L 30 " "

You can replace " " with 20 (an ASCII space).

Problem 6-12

Reduce the more significant byte of the delay count (location 220) according to the following sequence: 80, 40, 20, 10, 8, 4, 2, 1. Explain what happens.

Problem 6-13

Write a program that creates a "newspanel" or "Times Square" display in which the message appears to move from right to left. Your program should:

1. Start by clearing the entire display.
2. After a delay, put the first character of the message in the rightmost position.
3. Continue this process until the message has moved all the way across the display. Then start over.

Your data should consist of a set of blanks, the message, and another set of blanks. Both sets of blanks should be the same length as the message. Save an overall counter in register BP and a starting pointer in DI. The counter's initial value should be twice the message length plus 1 to allow for the leading blanks. The pointer should always contain the base address of the display data for the current iteration. Try the following message (13 characters long):

[0420]–[042C] = "   " (blanks)
[042D]–[0439] = "ABANDON SHIP!"
[043A]–[0446] = "   " (blanks)

One problem here is the static caused by the moving cursor. To get rid of it, blank the cursor by putting the following sequence ahead of your program:

```
MOV    AH,3              ;GET CURSOR CHARACTERISTICS
INT    10H
OR     CH,00100000B      ;BLANK CURSOR
MOV    AH,1
INT    10H
```

Then put the following sequence at the end to restore the cursor:

```
MOV    AH,3              ;GET CURSOR CHARACTERISTICS
INT    10H
AND    CH,11011111B      ;UNBLANK CURSOR
MOV    AH,1
INT    10H
```

If you forget to restore the cursor or accidentally return to DEBUG or DOS without it, enter and run the unblanking sequence. While DEBUG is tolerable without a cursor, your word processor will become very difficult to use (guess how I discovered this!).

Occasionally, for reasons that are beyond my comprehension, the cursor may end up as a solid block. If this happens, run the following program to get the underscore:

```
MOV   AH,3              ;GET CURSOR CHARACTERISTICS
INT   10H
AND   CH,00000111H     ;MAKE CURSOR ONE COLUMN HIGH
MOV   CH,CL
DEC   CH
MOV   AH,1
INT   10H
INT   3
```

As Table A2-4 shows, the IBM PC's video display can form many symbols besides standard typewriter characters. Among them are card suit symbols, graphics characters (parts of lines, circles, and solid figures), modified letters used in foreign languages such as French and German, mathematical symbols, and Greek letters. For example, you can use the following command to enter a cheerful message for Program 6-5:

E 420 1 "HAVE A NICE DAY!" 1

The message is 20 characters (14 hex) long, including the spaces. What happens if you replace the 1's with 2's?

Problem 6-14

Use Program 6-5 and the graphics characters DC through DF to draw a thick-sided box near the center of the screen. Use the line feed (0A), backspace (08), and space (20) characters to move the cursor.

Key Point Summary

1. Arrays are sets of elements with similar meanings or purposes. Each element is characterized by its number or index, and the entire array is characterized by its base address. Thus, to reach a particular element of an array, you must know the base address and the index.

2. The keys to processing arrays are:

   - A pointer that holds the address of the element being processed.
   - A flexible addressing mode that allows a single set of instructions to handle any element.
   - A counter or terminator that can be used to determine the length of the array.

3. To process arrays with the 8088, you can use an index register or base register to hold the pointer, register indirect addressing to reach the data in memory, and a data register to hold the counter or terminator.

4. The 8088 has special instructions for loop control and array or string operations. These instructions automatically perform overhead functions such as decrementing counters and incrementing or decrementing pointers. They apply only to specific registers.

5. Comparison instructions can determine whether an element is within limits. If the operands are unsigned, the Carry flag indicates which is larger.

6. Loops inside loops (that is, nested loops) and variable pointers and counters can handle multidimensional arrays and provide greater flexibility.

Forming Data Arrays

Purpose   To learn how to form data arrays.

What You Should Learn
1. How to use pointers and counters to form arrays.
2. How to fill an area of memory.
3. How to enter input data into an array.
4. How to access a specific element of an array.
5. How to keep counts or running totals in an array.
6. How to differentiate between logical and physical devices.

Reference Mateials

Eccles, W. J. *Microprocessor Systems: A 16-Bit Approach.* Reading, MA: Addison-Wesley, 1985, pp. 307–323 (characters and strings).

Gorsline, G. W. *16-Bit Modern Microcomputers.* Englewood Cliffs, NJ: Prentice-Hall, 1985, pp. 72–74 (addressing methods), 106–107 (string data movement), 111–113 (arithmetic shift), 124–125 (direction flag).

Liu, Y. C., and G. A. Gibson. *Microcomputer Systems: The 8086/8088 Family,* (2nd ed.). Englewood Cliffs, NJ: Prentice-Hall, 1986, pp. 57–58 and 107 (PTR operator), 97–100 (shift instructions), 208–212 (string instructions), 212–214 (REP prefix).

Terms   **Arithmetic shift:** a shift that preserves the sign (most significant) bit. A right arithmetic shift copies the sign bit into the positions to the right (called *sign extension*).

Clear: set to zero.

Driver: *see* **I/O driver.**

I/O device table: a table that assigns actual (physical) devices or I/O drivers to the device numbers (logical devices) to which programs refer.

I/O driver: a program that transfers data to or from an I/O device.

Logical device: the I/O device to which a program refers. The physical device is determined from an I/O device table.

Physical device: an actual I/O device, as opposed to a logical device.

Rotate: a shift that works as if the data were arranged in a circle, that is, as if its most significant and least significant bits were connected.

Two's complement: a binary number that, when added to the original number, produces a zero result.

Two's complement representation: a method of representing signed numbers in which the most significant bit is the sign, a positive number is represented by its binary value, and a negative number is represented by the two's complement of its absolute value.

8088 Instructions

MOVSB: move byte string; move a byte from the address in register SI to the address in register DI, then either increment or decrement both DI and SI by 1, depending on whether the D flag is 0 (increment) or 1 (decrement).

REP: repeat; repeat the following steps:

1. Test register CX and exit if it is 0.
2. Subtract 1 from CX.
3. Do the subsequent string instruction.

Since the processor tests CX first, nothing happens if it contains 0 initially.

ROL(R): rotate left (right); shift a register or a memory location left (right) as if its most significant and least significant bits were connected directly (see Figure 7-1).

SAR: arithmetic shift right; shift a register or memory location right, preserving the most significant bit (see Figure 7-2).

STOSB(W): store byte (word) string; store register AL (AX) at the address in register DI, then either increment or decrement DI by 1 (2), depending on the D flag's value. D = 0 for autoincrement or 1 for autodecrement.

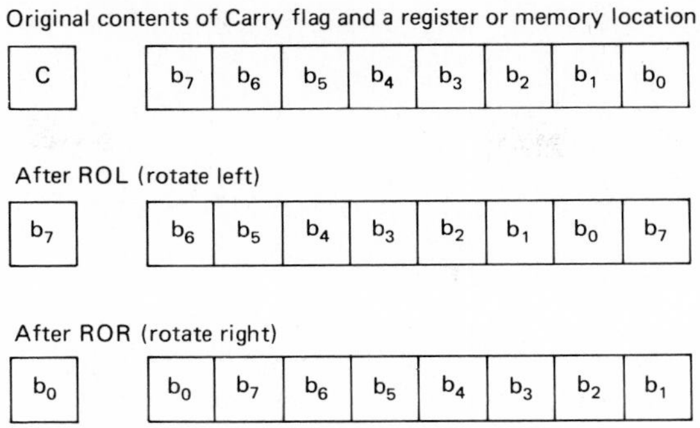

Figure 7-1

8088 instructions
ROL and ROR in
their 1-bit forms.

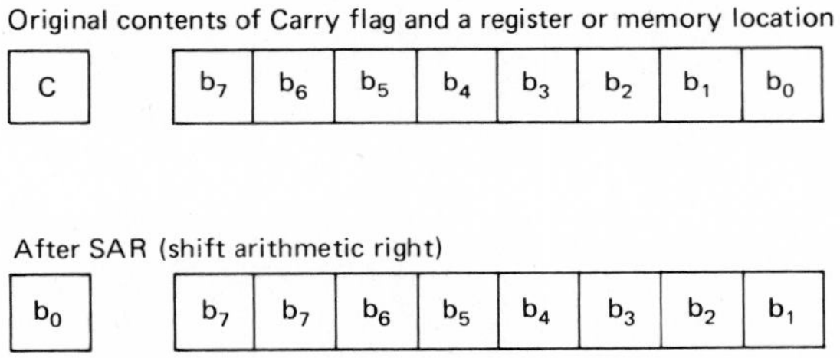

Original contents of Carry flag and a register or memory location

| C | | b_7 | b_6 | b_5 | b_4 | b_3 | b_2 | b_1 | b_0 |

After ROL (rotate left)

| b_7 | | b_6 | b_5 | b_4 | b_3 | b_2 | b_1 | b_0 | b_7 |

After ROR (rotate right)

| b_0 | | b_0 | b_7 | b_6 | b_5 | b_4 | b_3 | b_2 | b_1 |

Figure 7-2

8088 instruction
SAR in its 1-bit
form.

Original contents of Carry flag and a register or memory location

| C | | b_7 | b_6 | b_5 | b_4 | b_3 | b_2 | b_1 | b_0 |

After SAR (shift arithmetic right)

| b_0 | | b_7 | b_7 | b_6 | b_5 | b_4 | b_3 | b_2 | b_1 |

Standard Procedure for Forming Arrays

The arrays in Laboratory 6 do not, of course, appear magically in the computer's memory. In applications, the program must form the array before processing it; as with processing, this requires a pointer and a counter.

The standard procedure for forming an array of 8-bit elements is as follows (see Figure 7-3):

1. Initialization.

> POINTER = BASE ADDRESS OF ARRAY
> COUNTER = 0
> LENGTH   = LENGTH OF ARRAY (if known)

2. Entering an element.

> [POINTER] = DATA
> POINTER   = POINTER + 1
> COUNTER   = COUNTER + 1

The data may be a constant, the result of a calculation, or an external input.

3. Conclusion.

    a. Maximum length.

        If COUNTER = LENGTH, then DONE; otherwise, return to step 2.

    b. Terminator.

        If DATA = TERMINATOR, then DONE; otherwise, return to step 2.

Figure 7-3

Flowchart for array formation.

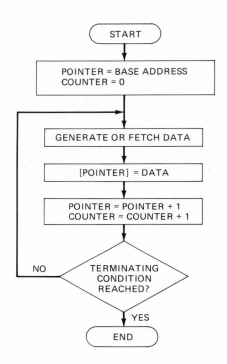

Clearing an Array

A simple way to initialize an array is to clear its elements. This is a natural starting point for accumulating counts, totals, or test results. Never assume that an unused RAM location contains zero; it could take any value whatsoever when power is applied.

The following program (Program 7-1 is the DEBUG version) clears 340 through 347. Like LODSB, STOSB both moves data and updates a pointer. It stores AL at the address in DI, then increments or decrements DI. Note that STOSB uses DI, whereas LODSB uses SI.

```
SUB    AL,AL       ;DATA = ZERO
MOV    CX,8        ;NUMBER OF BYTES = 8
MOV    DI,340H     ;POINT TO BASE OF ARRAY
```

```
        CLD                    ;SELECT AUTOINCREMENTING
CLRBYT: STOSB                  ;CLEAR A BYTE
        LOOP   CLRBYT          ;COUNT BYTES
        INT    20H
```

Remember that you can use the E or F command to load a block of memory for testing and the D command to display it.

	PROGRAM 7-1			
Memory Address (Hex)	Memory Contents (Hex)		Instruction (DEBUG Form)	
0200	28		SUB	AL,AL
0201	C0			
0202	B9		MOV	CX,8
0203	08			
0204	00			
0205	BF		MOV	DI,340
0206	40			
0207	03			
0208	FC		CLD	
0209	AA	CLRBYT:	STOSB	
020A	E2		LOOP	209
020B	FD			
020C	CD		INT	20
020D	20			

Problem 7-1

Make Program 7-1 clear 350 through 35F. Revise the answer to use STOSW, the word version of STOSB. Yes, these are supposedly mnemonics, not the names of obscure Polish towns! STOSW stores a word from register AX, then increases or decreases DI by 2 to reach the next word.

Problem 7-2

Make Program 7-1 place [0400] in 340 through a number of locations given by [0401]. Does your program work properly if [0401] = 00?

EXAMPLE:

$$[0400] = 3F \quad \text{(value)}$$
$$[0401] = 03 \quad \text{(number of locations)}$$

RESULT:

$$[0340] = 3F$$
$$[0341] = 3F$$
$$[0342] = 3F$$

The program should do nothing if $[0401] = 00$.

We can make Program 7-1 shorter and faster by using the REP prefix instead of LOOP. REP makes the processor do the following:

1. Check whether CX is 0 and exit if it is.
2. Otherwise, subtract 1 from CX, execute the subsequent string instruction, and return to step 1.

REP followed by a string instruction thus forms a tight loop. It even automatically handles the case in which CX is originally zero. Loops using REP run much faster than ones using LOOP or conditional jumps.

The following program (Program 7-2 is the DEBUG version) uses REP to clear an area. Note that REP works only with string instructions, not with MOV, shifts, or arithmetic and logical operations. Be careful when using REP—you can easily forget that it forms an implicit loop. The execution time depends on CX's initial value; for example, a repeated STOSB takes 10 cycles per iteration plus 9 cycles overhead (see Table A1-3).

```
SUB    AL,AL     ;DATA = ZERO
MOV    CX,8      ;NUMBER OF BYTES = 8
MOV    DI,340H   ;POINT TO BASE OF AREA
CLD              ;SELECT AUTOINCREMENTING
REP              ;CLEAR AREA
STOSB
INT    20H
```

	PROGRAM 7-2		
Memory Address (Hex)	Memory Contents (Hex)	Instruction (DEBUG Form)	
0200	28	*SUB*	*AL,AL*
0201	C0		
0202	B9	*MOV*	*CX,8*
0203	08		
0204	00		
0205	BF	*MOV*	*DI,340*
0206	40		
0207	03		
0208	FC	*CLD*	
0209	F3	*REP*	
020A	AA	*STOSB*	
020B	CD	*INT*	*20*
020C	20		

Problem 7-3

Write a program that uses REP and MOVSB to copy an array. MOVSB moves a byte from the address in SI to the one in DI, then either increments or decrements both SI and DI. Assume that the length of the arrays is in 400, the original array starts at 340, and the destination area starts at 360.

EXAMPLE:

$$[0400] = 03 \quad (\text{length of array})$$

$$[0340] = 4F \quad (\text{original array})$$
$$[0341] = 55$$
$$[0342] = 54$$

RESULT:

$$[0360] = 4F \quad (\text{copy of array})$$
$$[0361] = 55$$
$$[0362] = 54$$

Placing Values in an Array

The next step is to place different values in different elements. The following program puts the element numbers (1 through 8) in the corresponding positions (see Figure 7-4 for a flowchart). Program 7-3 is the DEBUG version.

```
        MOV    CX,8       ;NUMBER OF BYTES = 8
        MOV    DI,340H    ;POINT TO BASE OF ARRAY
        MOV    AL,1       ;ELEMENT NUMBER = 1
        CLD               ;SELECT AUTOINCREMENTING
LDNUM:  STOSB             ;ELEMENT = ELEMENT NUMBER
        INC    AL         ;ADD 1 TO ELEMENT NUMBER
        LOOP   LDNUM
        INT    20H
```

Enter and run Program 7-3. It has practical value, as it creates an array of identification numbers. For example, you may have a set of pressure readings taken at different points in a chemical process. You could sort the set into descending order and use the identification numbers to keep track of where the readings were taken. The top line of the result would show the highest value and where it occurred. For instance, you could start with

Position	Pressure
1	40
2	27
3	66
4	59

and end with the pressures arranged in descending order as

Position	Pressure
3	66
4	59
1	40
2	27

Without the identification numbers, we would not know where the highest pressure occurred.

PROGRAM 7-3

Memory Address (Hex)	Memory Contents (Hex)		Instruction (DEBUG Form)	
0200	B9		MOV	CX,8
0201	08			
0202	00			
0203	BF		MOV	DI,340
0204	40			
0205	03			
0206	B0		MOV	AL,1
0207	01			
0208	FC		CLD	
0209	AA	LDNUM:	STOSB	
020A	FE		INC	AL
020B	C0			
020C	E2		LOOP	209
020D	FB			
020E	CD		INT	20
020F	20			

Figure 7-4
Flowchart for placing element numbers in an array.

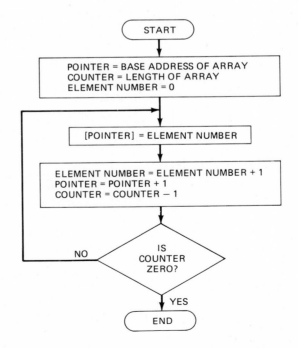

Problem 7-4

Start with 1, then double each element to get the next one; that is,

$$[0340] = 01$$
$$[0341] = 02$$
$$[0342] = 04$$
$$[0343] = 08$$
$$[0344] = 10$$
$$[0345] = 20$$
$$[0346] = 40$$
$$[0347] = 80$$

Problem 7-5

Create the following sequence:

$$[0340] = 80 \quad (10000000B)$$
$$[0341] = C0 \quad (11000000B)$$
$$[0342] = E0 \quad (11100000B)$$
$$[0343] = F0 \quad (11110000B)$$
$$[0344] = F8 \quad (11111000B)$$
$$[0345] = FC \quad (11111100B)$$
$$[0346] = FE \quad (11111110B)$$
$$[0347] = FF \quad (11111111B)$$

What are the values of these numbers if they are in the two's complement representation? To get the next element, use a right *arithmetic shift,* which preserves the sign (most significant) bit.

Entering Input Data into an Array

The next task is to form an array from data entered on the switches attached to port A of 8255 device P1. The steps are (see Figure 7-5):

1. Initialize the pointer and counter.

$$\text{POINTER} = \text{BASE ADDRESS}$$
$$\text{COUNTER} = \text{LENGTH OF ARRAY (4)}$$

2. Wait for a switch to be closed.
3. Debounce the switch closure.

Figure 7-5
Flowchart for
forming an array
from switch inputs.

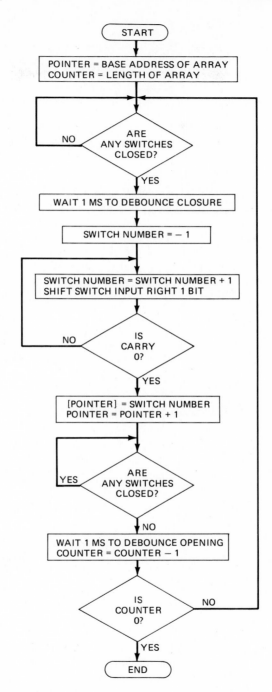

4. Identify the switch.
5. Put the switch number in the array.

$$[POINTER] = SWITCH\ NUMBER$$

6. Update the pointer and counter for the next entry.

$$POINTER = POINTER + 1$$
$$COUNTER = COUNTER - 1$$

7. Wait for all switches to be open.
8. Debounce the switch opening.
9. If COUNTER is not zero, return to step 2.

The following program forms an array starting in 340 from four switch closures (all switches must be opened between closures).

```
;
;   SET UP 8255 DEVICE P1 PORT A FOR INPUT
;
           MOV    DX,0FF03H        ;GET CONTROL REGISTER
                                   ;  ADDRESS
           MOV    AL,10010000B     ;PORT A INPUT, PORT B OUTPUT
           OUT    DX,AL
;
;   INITIALIZE SWITCH ARRAY
;
           MOV    DI,340H          ;POINT TO BASE OF ARRAY
           MOV    CX,4             ;COUNT = ARRAY LENGTH
           CLD                     ;SELECT AUTOINCREMENTING
;
;   WAIT FOR A SWITCH TO BE CLOSED
;
           MOV    DX,0FF00H        ;GET PORT A ADDRESS
WAITC:     IN     AL,DX            ;GET INPUT DATA
           CMP    AL,0FFH          ;ARE ANY SWITCHES CLOSED?
           JE     WAITC            ;NO, WAIT
;
;   DEBOUNCE SWITCH CLOSURE WITH 1 MS DELAY
;
           MOV    SI,0CBH          ;DELAY 1 MS AFTER CLOSURE
DLYC:      DEC    SI
           JNZ    DLYC
```

```
;
;   IDENTIFY SWITCH BY SHIFTING INPUT
;
          MOV    BX,-1         ;SWITCH NUMBER = -1
SRCHS:    INC    BX            ;ADD 1 TO SWITCH NUMBER
          SHR    AL,1          ;IS NEXT SWITCH CLOSED?
          JC     SRCHS         ;NO, KEEP LOOKING

;
;   ENTER SWITCH NUMBER INTO ARRAY
;
          MOV    AL,BL
          STOSB                ;PUT SWITCH NUMBER IN
                               ;  ARRAY

;
;   WAIT FOR ALL SWITCHES TO OPEN
;
WAITO:    IN     AL,DX         ;READ DATA FROM SWITCHES
          CMP    AL,0FFH       ;ARE ANY SWITCHES CLOSED?
          JNE    WAITO         ;YES, WAIT

;
;   DEBOUNCE SWITCH OPENING WITH 1 MS DELAY
;
          MOV    SI,0CBH       ;DELAY 1 MS AFTER OPENING
DLYO:     DEC    SI
          JNZ    DLYO

;
;   COUNT SWITCH CLOSURES
;
          LOOP   WAITC
          INT    20H
```

Program 7-4 is the DEBUG version; enter and run it. Use the following sequence of switch closures: 5, 7, 0, 3. Remember to reopen each switch before closing any others. The result should be:

$$[0340] = 05$$
$$[0341] = 07$$
$$[0342] = 00$$
$$[0343] = 03$$

	PROGRAM 7-4			
Memory Address (Hex)	Memory Contents (Hex)		Instruction (DEBUG Form)	
0200	BA		MOV	DX,FF03
0201	03			
0202	FF			
0203	B0		MOV	AL,90
0204	90			
0205	EE		OUT	DX,AL
0206	BF		MOV	DI,340
0207	40			
0208	03			
0209	B9		MOV	CX,4
020A	04			
020B	00			
020C	FC		CLD	
020D	BA		MOV	DX,FF00
020E	00			
020F	FF			
0210	EC	WAITC:	IN	AL,DX
0211	3C		CMP	AL,FF
0212	FF			
0213	74		JE	210
0214	FB			
0215	BE		MOV	SI,CB
0216	CB			
0217	00			
0218	4E	DLYC:	DEC	SI
0219	75		JNZ	218
021A	FD			
021B	BB		MOV	BX,FFFF
021C	FF			
021D	FF			
021E	43	SRCHS:	INC	BX
021F	D0		SHR	AL,1
0220	E8			
0221	72		JC	21E
0222	FB			
0223	88		MOV	AL,BL
0224	D8			
0225	AA		STOSB	
0226	EC	WAITO:	IN	AL,DX
0227	3C		CMP	AL,FF
0228	FF			
0229	75		JNE	226
022A	FB			

PROGRAM 7-4 (continued)				
Memory Address (Hex)	Memory Contents (Hex)		Instruction (DEBUG Form)	
022B	BE		MOV	SI,CB
022C	CB			
022D	00			
022E	4E	DLYO:	DEC	SI
022F	75		JNZ	22E
0230	FD			
0231	E2		LOOP	210
0232	DD			
0233	CD		INT	20
0234	20			

Problem 7-6

Revise Program 7-4 to exit when you close switch 0. Can you ever get a data entry of zero?

Problem 7-7

Extend Program 7-4 to combine the four entries in 340 through 343 into two two-digit numbers in 360 and 361. Load 360 from 340 (4 MSBs) and 341 (4 LSBs); load 361 from 342 (4 MSBs) and 343 (4 LSBs).

EXAMPLE:

Switches closed are 7, 3, 4, and 2, so Program 7-4 produces

$$[0340] = 07$$
$$[0341] = 03$$
$$[0342] = 04$$
$$[0343] = 02$$

RESULT:

$$[0360] = 73$$
$$[0361] = 42$$

Note how similar this process is to the entry of a four-digit hex data value or address from the keyboard. Remember that the keys are just binary switches.

Accessing Specific Elements

Still another problem is how to reach a specific element of an array. This is essential when a program must count events (number of transactions of a particular type or number of activations of a particular sensor) or must accumulate data properly (for example, the total for a particular account, test point, or station). The next program clears one element of an array starting at 340. The element number is in 400.

Program 7-5 is the DEBUG version. Enter it and run the following two examples:

1. Data: [0400] = 02
    Result: [0340 + [0400]] = [0342] = 00
2. Data: [0400] = 07
    Result: [0340 + [0400]] = [0347] = 00

```
MOV    BL,[400H]              ;GET INDEX
SUB    BH,BH                  ;EXTEND INDEX TO 16 BITS
SUB    AL,AL                  ;GET DATA
MOV    [BX+340H],AL           ;CLEAR INDEXED ELEMENT
INT    20H
```

PROGRAM 7-5		
Memory Address (Hex)	Memory Contents (Hex)	Instruction (DEBUG Form)
0200	8A	*MOV BL,[400]*
0201	1E	
0202	00	
0203	04	
0204	28	*SUB BH,BH*
0205	FF	
0206	28	*SUB AL,AL*
0207	C0	
0208	88	*MOV [BX+340],AL*
0209	87	
020A	40	
020B	03	
020C	CD	*INT 20*
020D	20	

A shorter version of Program 7-5 uses MOV to store a constant directly into memory. That is, we can replace

```
SUB    AL,AL
MOV    [BX+340H],AL
```

with

```
MOV   BYTE PTR [BX+340H],0
```

BYTE PTR indicates an 8-bit operation (WORD PTR would indicate a 16-bit operation). Because the instruction does not use a register, the assembler cannot tell how many bits are involved without an indicator. Note that you must use either BYTE PTR or WORD PTR in ambiguous instructions; there is no default. DEBUG's A command allows the abbreviations BY for BYTE PTR and WO for WORD PTR.

The instruction

```
MOV   BYTE PTR [BX+340H],0
```

is long and time-consuming. It requires five bytes of memory: one for the operation code, one for addressing information, two for the displacement, and one for the value to be stored. The execution time is 19 clock cycles.

Problem 7-8

Revise Program 7-5 to add 1 to the element.

EXAMPLE:

$$[0400] = 04 \quad \text{(index)}$$
$$[0344] = CF \quad \text{(original value)}$$

RESULT:

$$[0340 + 2 \times [0400]] = [0344] = [0344] + 1 = D0$$

Problem 7-9

Revise Program 7-5 to put [0401] in the element.

EXAMPLE:

$$[0400] = 06 \quad (\text{index})$$
$$[0401] = 3F \quad (\text{value})$$

RESULT:

$$[0340 + [0400]] = [0346] = [0401] = 3F$$

How can you make your program replace the old value only if [0401] is larger? Assume unsigned values. This procedure is necessary if the elements are the worst cases for a set of tests or scaling values for a set of plots.

Problem 7-10

Revise Program 7-5 to clear a two-byte element.

EXAMPLE:

$$[0400] = 03$$

RESULT:

$$[0340 + 2 \times [0400]] \quad = [0346] = 00$$
$$[0340 + 2 \times [0400] + 1] = [0347] = 00$$

(*Hint*: Use SHL BX,1 to double the element number.)

Counting Switch Closures

Problem 7-11

Write a program that counts how many times each switch attached to port A of 8255 device P1 is closed. Assume that only one switch is ever closed at a time. Allow a total of five closures. The steps required are (see Figure 7-6):

Figure 7-6
Flowchart for cumulative counts program.

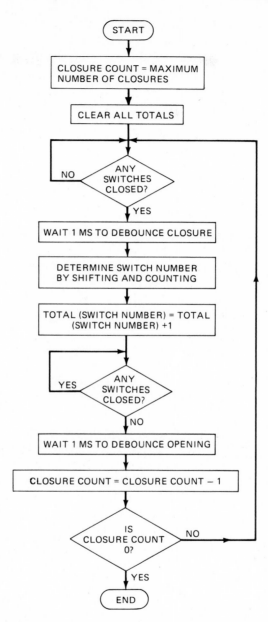

1. Initialize the array of counts by clearing all elements.
2. Wait until a switch is closed.
3. Debounce the switch closure.
4. Identify the switch.
5. Add 1 to the count for that switch.

6. Wait until all switches are open.
7. Debounce the switch opening.
8. Subtract 1 from the overall closure count and return to step 2 if it is not zero.

Put the array in locations 340 through 347.

Arrays of Addresses

Arrays may contain addresses instead of data. This allows programs to select from a set of storage addresses or entry points.

For example, we can use an array to assign device numbers to the starting addresses of I/O routines *(I/O drivers)* for a particular system. The programmer can then refer to I/O devices by number (for example, "Print on device 2" or "Read data from device 3"). An *I/O device table* contains the addresses of the I/O drivers corresponding to the numbers. We call the device number to which programs refer a *logical device*, and the actual I/O device a *physical device*.

The advantages of maintaining this distinction are

1. Programmers need not deal with actual I/O addresses. They can refer to devices by number without worrying about differences resulting from updates, model changes, or optional equipment.
2. Programs written using device numbers can be made to work on a particular system by creating an I/O device table. Such programs can be changed easily to work on computers with different peripherals.
3. A programmer can change the actual I/O addresses by revising the device table. For example, you might want the results of a test run or a minor change shown on a CRT display rather than printed. Similarly, you could make a terminal simulate I/O devices that are unavailable or malfunctioning. Implementing these changes is much like switching the output of a stereo system from the front speaker to the rear speaker.

The following program sends data to either device 0 (the LEDs attached to port B of 8255 device P1) or device 1 (the video display). The device table in addresses 450 through 453 contains the starting addresses of the I/O drivers. Location 400 contains the device number, and 401 contains the data.

```
MOV    DX,0FF03H       ;GET CONTROL REGISTER
                       ;  ADDRESS
MOV    AL,10010000B    ;PORT A INPUT, PORT B OUTPUT
```

```
OUT     DX,AL
MOV     AH,0FH              ;CLEAR VIDEO DISPLAY
INT     10H
SUB     AH,AH
INT     10H
MOV     DH,12               ;MOVE CURSOR TO ROW 12
MOV     DL,35               ;   COLUMN 35
SUB     BH,BH
MOV     AH,2
INT     10H
MOV     BL,[400H]           ;GET DEVICE NUMBER
SUB     BH,BH               ;EXTEND NUMBER TO 16 BITS
SHL     BX,1                ;DOUBLE DEVICE NUMBER TO
                            ;   INDEX TABLE OF ADDRESSES
MOV     AL,[401H]           ;GET DATA FOR DRIVER
JMP     [BX+450H]           ;JUMP TO DRIVER VIA DEVICE
                            ;   TABLE


STARTING AT 240H

MOV     DX,0F01H            ;SEND DATA TO LEDS
OUT     DX,AL
INT     20H


STARTING AT 260H

MOV     AH,0EH              ;WRITE DATA ON VIDEO DISPLAY
INT     10H
INT     20H
```

Program 7-6 is the DEBUG version of the main program and the I/O drivers; it also shows the I/O device table. Note that JMP can use indexed addressing just like other instructions. Watch the gaps in the memory addresses; we have separated the three routines to avoid overlap and simplify the device table. If you save the program on disk, make it one big file including the gaps (that is, save locations 200 through 265).

Before running Program 7-6, load the device table into memory with the command

                    E 450 40 2 60 2

Run the program with [400] = 00 and [401] = 3F. What happens if you change [400] to 01 and run the program again? 3F forms a "?" on the video display and lights only LEDs 6 and 7 at port B of 8255 device P1. Remember that 0 outputs light the LEDs.

Problem 7-12

Change Program 7-6 to make both drivers obtain the number of bytes to transmit from location 401 and the base address of the data area from locations 402 and 403. Put a software delay between outputs so you can see the different values.

EXAMPLE:

[0401] = 04   (number of data bytes)
[0402] = 40   (base address of data area)
[0403] = 03

[0340] = 40   (ASCII @, 01000000B)
[0341] = 41   (ASCII A, 01000001B)
[0342] = 42   (ASCII B, 01000010B)
[0343] = 44   (ASCII D, 01000100B)

RESULT:

The data will appear as characters on the video display if [0400] = 01 and in inverted binary form on the LEDs if [0400] = 00. On the LEDs, bit 6 will be off throughout. All other bits will be on initially, then bit 0 will go off and the dark bit will later move left one position each time a new data value appears.

PROGRAM 7-6

Memory Address (Hex)	Memory Contents (Hex)	Instruction (DEBUG Form)
0200	BA	MOV DX,FF03
0201	03	
0202	FF	
0203	B0	MOV AL,90
0204	90	
0205	EE	OUT DX,AL
0206	B4	MOV AH,F
0207	0F	
0208	CD	INT 10
0209	10	

PROGRAM 7-6 (continued)		
Memory Address (Hex)	Memory Contents (Hex)	Instruction (DEBUG Form)
020A	28	SUB AH,AH
020B	E4	
020C	CD	INT 10
020D	10	
020E	B6	MOV DH,C
020F	0C	
0210	B2	MOV DL,23
0211	23	
0212	28	SUB BH,BH
0213	FF	
0214	B4	MOV AH,2
0215	02	
0216	CD	INT 10
0217	10	
0218	8A	MOV BL,[400]
0219	1E	
021A	00	
021B	04	
021C	28	SUB BH,BH
021D	FF	
021E	D1	SHL BX,1
021F	E3	
0220	A0	MOV AL,[401]
0221	01	
0222	04	
0223	FF	JMP [BX+450]
0224	A7	
0225	50	
0226	04	
0240	BA	MOV DX,FF01
0241	01	
0242	FF	
0243	EE	OUT DX,AL
0244	CD	INT 20
0245	20	
0260	B4	MOV AH,E
0261	0E	
0262	CD	INT 10
0263	10	
0264	CD	INT 20
0265	20	

		PROGRAM 7-6 (continued)	

Memory Address (Hex)	Memory Contents (Hex)	Instruction (DEBUG Form)
0450	*40*	*STARTING ADDRESS OF DRIVER FOR*
0451	*02*	*DEVICE 0 (LEDS AT PORT FF01)*
0452	*60*	*STARTING ADDRESS OF DRIVER FOR*
0453	*02*	*DEVICE 1 (VIDEO DISPLAY)*

Key Point Summary

1. An array can be formed by using a pointer to hold the address of the next element and a counter to hold the element number. Either a maximum length or a terminator can conclude the formation.
2. On the 8088, an index or base register can hold the pointer. Then you can use register indirect addressing to access the element.
3. To reach an element, you must know the array's base address and the element's index. Indexed addressing then allows the computer to access the element easily.
4. You can handle an array with multibyte elements by multiplying the index by the size of an element and adding the product to the base address. An arithmetic left shift is equivalent to multiplication by 2.
5. Indexed addressing allows the processor to select from a set of indirect addresses to use in transferring data. It can be used to convert the logical device numbers to which a program refers into the I/O drivers for a particular computer.
6. Using logical I/O devices lets you write programs that can run on many computers. To tailor them to a particular machine, you must create an I/O device table that converts logical device numbers into I/O driver addresses. Changing the table lets the programmer vary I/O addresses without changing the program. This makes it easy to direct test results to a console; choose whether outputs should be displayed only or printed for permanent records; or switch between local and remote control.

LABORATORY 8

Designing and Debugging Programs

Purpose	To learn the basic approaches to program design and debugging.

What You Should Learn	1. The stages of software development.
	2. The standard flowcharting symbols.
	3. How to use flowcharts to design programs.
	4. The common debugging tools.
	5. How to insert and use breakpoints.
	6. How to trace and single-step a program.
	7. How to debug simple programs systematically.
	8. Common errors in 8088 assembly language programs.

Reference Materials	Comer, D. J. *Microprocessor-Based System Design.* New York: Holt, Rinehart and Winston, 1986, chap. 4 (programming a microprocessor system).
	Dale, N., and D. Orshalick. *Introduction to PASCAL and Structured Design.* Lexington, MA: D. C. Heath, 1985.
	Eccles, W. J. *Microprocessor Systems: A 16-Bit Approach.* Reading, MA: Addison-Wesley, 1985, pp. 122–127, 175–182, 349–352.

Terms	**Breakpoint:** a stopping condition specified by the user as a debugging tool. We refer to specifying conditions as *setting breakpoints,* and to removing (deactivating) them as *clearing breakpoints.*
	Coding: writing computer instructions.

Command file: a file containing commands for a program. It can be used to automate command entry, thus avoiding repetitive typing and minor errors. Sometimes called a *procedure file* or *batch file*.

Debugger: a program that helps find and correct program errors.

Debugging: finding and correcting program errors.

Dump: a facility that displays the contents of a section of memory.

Editor: a program that lets a user enter, correct, revise, save, and recall text material.

Flowchart: a graphic representation of a computer program.

Modular programming: a programming method that divides the overall program into logically separate sections, or modules.

Murphy's law: the maxim "Whatever can go wrong, will." No one has ever doubted that it applies to computer programming.

No-op (or **no operation**):   an instruction that does nothing except increase the program counter (instruction pointer on the 8088).

Problem definition: the determination of exactly what requirements a system must meet.

Program design: the design of a computer program to meet the requirements of the problem definition.

Redirection: making a program obtain input from or send output to a device other than the one normally assumed.

Single step: a facility that executes a program one step at a time.

Structured programming: a programming method that bases all programs on a few logical forms or structures, each of which has a single entry and a single exit.

Testing: ensuring that a system meets its requirements.

Text file: a file containing characters rather than numbers (a *data file*) or computer instructions (a *program file*).

Top-down design: a design method that starts with the program's overall framework or outline and later defines its components in more detail.

Trace: a facility that displays a program's status (that is, the contents of registers, flags, and memory locations) while it is running.

Unsigned number: a number in which all bits represent magnitude.

8088
Instructions

NOP: no operation; do nothing except add 1 to the instruction pointer.

SCASB: scan byte string; compare the byte at the address in DI with the contents of AL, and then either increment or decrement DI by 1, depending on the D flag (0 = increment, 1 = decrement). The flags are set as if the computer had calculated [AL] − [[DI]].

Stages of Software Development

So far, our programs have been short, and we have started with initial versions. But programming real applications is, of course, more difficult. We cannot deal with all its aspects here, but we will discuss the design and debugging of small and moderate-size programs.

Software development consists of a series of stages:

1. *Problem definition*, in which you specify the requirements the program must meet.
2. *Program design*, in which you create a "blueprint" for the program.
3. *Coding*, in which you convert the design into computer instructions. Note that writing instructions is only one of many stages.
4. *Debugging*, in which you find and correct errors in the program.
5. *Testing*, in which you ensure that the program meets its requirements.
6. *Documentation*, in which you describe the program for later use, maintenance, and extension.
7. *Maintenance*, in which you correct and upgrade the program to handle problems found in field use.
8. *Extension* and *redesign*, in which you upgrade the program to handle new requirements or new tasks.

A computer program thus goes through the same stages as a hardware project. Definition, design, debugging, testing, documentation, and maintenance typically require far more time and effort than does coding (or the building of a hardware prototype). As with any project, you must allow an adequate amount of time for definition and design and proceed cautiously and systematically through debugging and testing.

In practice, programmers spend much of their time debugging. Errors are often irreproducible, incredibly elusive, and amazingly obvious once uncovered. There are many books about writing programs but only a few about debugging them. This is because debugging is poorly understood and highly dependent on one's specific problem and tools.

Finding errors in programs requires persistence, organization, imagination, and luck. A touch of insanity may help as well.

We shall concentrate here on simple problems in which

1. The requirements have already been determined.
2. The program can be designed with a flowchart.
3. Debugging and testing are virtually the same.
4. The later stages (for example, documentation and maintenance) can be ignored. This is certainly not the case in practice; maintenance is often the costliest and most time-consuming stage of all.

Flowcharting

Flowcharting is the traditional method for program design. Its advantages are its graphic form, set of standard symbols (see Figure 8-1), and wide recognition and acceptance.

Figure 8-1
Standard flowchart symbols.

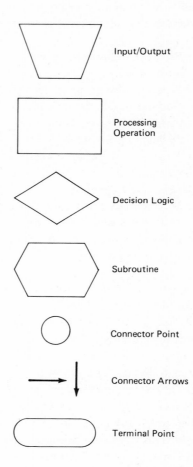

Input/Output

Processing Operation

Decision Logic

Subroutine

Connector Point

Connector Arrows

Terminal Point

We strongly recommend the following approach to flowcharting:

1. First draw a rough flowchart. Don't worry about how it looks or how complete it is.
2. Check the flowchart for obvious errors and improvements. Be sure that all branches lead somewhere, all variables are initialized or derived, and all decisions make sense.
3. Next, revise the flowchart. Again, do not worry about details or appearance. It is now time to write an initial program.

4. When you finish coding, debugging, and testing the program, draw a current flowchart as part of the final documentation.

Don't let the flowchart become a burden. There is no systematic way to debug a flowchart or to code from it. You might as well work on the actual program as keep revising the flowchart. If the program logic is complex, flowcharting alone is not an adequate design method. You must then consider such methods as modular programming, structured programming, and top-down design.

Flowcharting Example 1: Counting Zeros

PURPOSE:
Count the number of zeros in 340 through 347 and put the result in 400.

SAMPLE CASE:

$$
\begin{aligned}
[0340] &= 37 \\
[0341] &= 40 \\
[0342] &= 00 \\
[0343] &= 5E \\
[0344] &= 00 \\
[0345] &= D1 \\
[0346] &= 39 \\
[0347] &= 00
\end{aligned}
$$

RESULT:
[0400] = 03, since 342, 344, and 347 contain zeros.

Our initial flowchart is Figure 8-2. A hand check shows that we forgot to initialize NZERO and that we reversed the logic after testing the memory location for zero. Figure 8-3 shows the revised flowchart. We have not checked it in detail; we will describe how to debug the actual program later.

Problem 8-0 (No Answer)

Change the search value to 2B. Now we can pose the issue as "2B or not 2B, that is the question." Sorry, but I thought of this and had to put it somewhere. My apologies to W. Shakespeare and the State of Denmark.

Figure 8-2
Initial flowchart for
the zero counting
program.

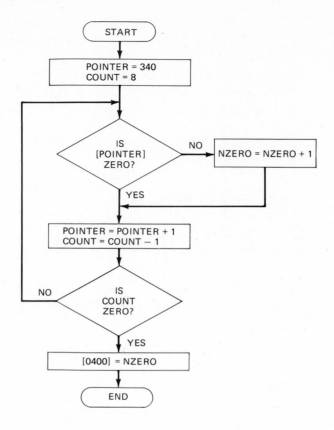

Problem 8-1

Draw a flowchart for a program that counts the number of 8-bit unsigned values
in 340 through 347 that exceed [0401]. Put the result in 400.

EXAMPLE:

$$
\begin{aligned}
[0401] &= 67 &&\text{(threshold)}\\
[0340] &= 35 &&\text{(first value)}\\
[0341] &= 4A\\
[0342] &= A9\\
[0343] &= 67\\
[0344] &= B3\\
[0345] &= 69\\
[0346] &= 14\\
[0347] &= 33 &&\text{(last value)}
\end{aligned}
$$

RESULT:
[0400] = 03, since 342, 344, and 345 contain values larger than [0401].

Figure 8-3
Revised flowchart
for the zero
counting program.

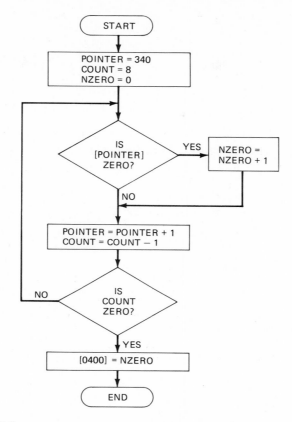

Problem 8-2

Draw a flowchart for a program that searches 340 through 347 for a nonzero value. If it finds one, it stops the search, puts the value in 401, and clears the location. If all values are zero, the program clears 401.

EXAMPLE 1:

$$[0340] = 00$$
$$[0341] = 04$$
$$[0342] = 12$$
$$[0343] = 00$$
$$[0344] = 13$$
$$[0345] = 06$$
$$[0346] = 00$$
$$[0347] = 00$$

RESULT:

$[0401] = 04$, the first nonzero value encountered. $[0341] = 00$, since the nonzero element is then cleared.

EXAMPLE 2:

[0340] through [0347] = 00

RESULT:
[0401] = 00, since all elements are zero.

Flowcharting Example 2: Maximum Value

PURPOSE:
Find the largest unsigned 8-bit number in 340 through 347 and put it in 400.

SAMPLE CASE:

[0340] = 37
[0341] = 40
[0342] = 88
[0343] = 5E
[0344] = 2B
[0345] = D1
[0346] = 39
[0347] = AE

RESULT:

[0400] = D1

Our initial flowchart is Figure 8-4. A simple hand check shows that we did not initialize MAX or save the new maximum. In fact, as you should see if you write the program, the revised flowchart of Figure 8-5 is still far from optimal.

Problem 8-3

Draw a flowchart for a simple sort that puts the unsigned numbers in 340 through 347 in ascending order. Use the "bubble sort" that compares each pair of consecutive numbers, exchanges them if necessary, and continues until a pass through the entire array causes no exchanges. For more details on this method, see Y. Langsam *et al.*, *Data Structures for Personal Computers*, Englewood Cliffs, NJ: Prentice-Hall, 1985, pp. 427–430.

Figure 8-4
Initial flowchart for
the maximum
program.

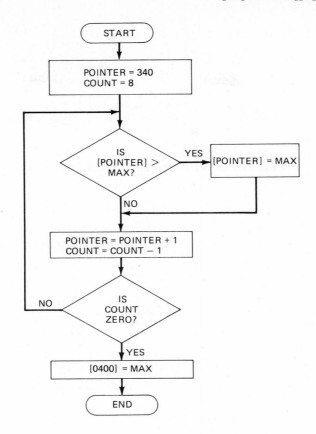

EXAMPLE:

$$[\,0340\,] = 40$$
$$[\,0341\,] = 88$$
$$[\,0342\,] = 5E$$
$$[\,0343\,] = 2B$$
$$[\,0344\,] = D1$$
$$[\,0345\,] = 39$$
$$[\,0346\,] = AE$$
$$[\,0347\,] = A6$$

RESULT:

$$[\,0340\,] = 2B$$
$$[\,0341\,] = 37$$
$$[\,0342\,] = 39$$
$$[\,0343\,] = 40$$

[0344] = 5E
[0345] = 88
[0346] = AE
[0347] = D1

Flowcharting Example 3: Variable Delay

PURPOSE:

A switch attached to bit 7 of port A of 8255 device P1 causes a delay. When it is closed, the processor waits for the number of seconds (between 0 and 63) specified by the switches attached to bits 0 through 5 of port A.

Figure 8-5
Revised flowchart for the maximum program.

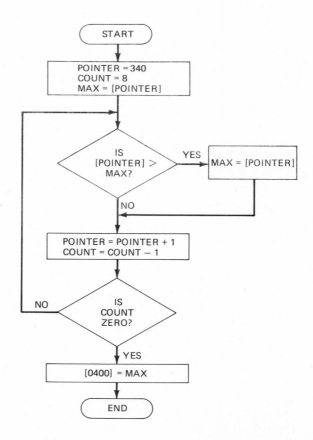

SAMPLE CASE:

The switches attached to bits 0 through 5 give a reading of 011110 (1 = open, 0 = closed). When switch 7 is closed, the processor waits for 30 s (011110B = 1E hex = 30 decimal). Figure 8-6 is the initial flowchart. A check shows that it is wrong if the delay has zero length. (Why?) Figure 8-7 is the revised flowchart.

Problem 8-4

Draw a flowchart for an extension that uses switch 6 to decide whether the delay is in seconds (switch open) or milliseconds (switch closed).

Figure 8-6
Initial flowchart for
variable delay
program.

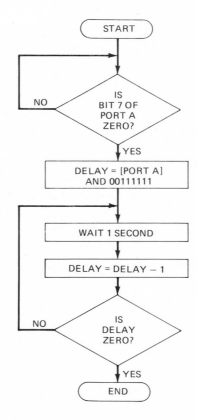

Figure 8-7
Revised flowchart
for variable delay
program.

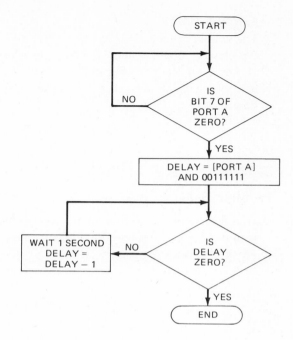

Debugging Tools

DEBUG has the following major debugging tools:

1. *Breakpoints*, which let the user stop the program and examine its status. Breakpoints help you localize an error within a section of a program and pass quickly through sections that you know are correct.
2. A *single-step* facility, which lets the user run the program one instruction at a time. A single-step mode helps you pinpoint an error.
3. A *trace*, which displays registers and memory locations while the program is running. Traces show a program's behavior in detail. In fact, DEBUG's single-step mode is just a special case of its general tracing capability.
4. A *dump*, which displays an entire section of memory. This is the D command introduced in Laboratory 5.

Breakpoints

To run a program with breakpoints, put their addresses after the starting address in the G command. For example,

$$G=200\ 210\ 21C$$

puts breakpoints in addresses 210 and 21C. Execution begins in 200.

The computer will stop and display all the registers if it reaches a breakpoint. DEBUG simply puts INT 3 (CC hex) in each breakpoint address. The advantage over doing this by hand is that DEBUG automatically saves the original instructions and restores them if the program reaches a breakpoint. Be careful—if the program ends without reaching a breakpoint, the instructions are not restored. You can resume the program at the breakpoint by simply pressing G and Enter. Of course, the breakpoint is gone, and you must reenter it to use it again.

The bottom line of the register display is helpful in debugging. Its contents are, starting at the far left:

1. The address of the next instruction to be executed. Be careful—this isn't the instruction the computer has just done, which would be much more useful.
2. The object and source code for the next instruction.
3. The next instruction's effective address and that address' contents.

The register display thus tells you a great deal about where the program is heading, but nothing (except the register contents) about where it has been. You can see the future, but the past is a mystery.

Take the following precautions with breakpoints:

1. Never put one anywhere except in the first byte of an instruction. This applies whether DEBUG inserts them or you enter them by hand.
2. Remember that the instructions you replaced are no longer in the program. The results reflect only the previous instructions, *not* including the one you see disassembled on the screen.
3. Do not let the computer return to a program in the middle of an instruction.
4. Be sure to put = in front of the starting address. Otherwise, the computer will treat the address as a breakpoint, and will start execution at the instruction pointer's current value.
5. After using breakpoints, verify your program with the U command. You may find INT 3 instructions left over because of incorrect addresses or runs that ended without reaching a breakpoint. Of course, you can always reload your program from disk (you did save it, didn't you?).
6. Do not replace a repeated string instruction with a breakpoint. The computer will resume the program properly, but will only execute the instruction once. It will not change CX at all. That is, it acts as though the REP were not there. The correct way to handle the situation is to treat REP and the string instruction as a unit. You can replace REP with a breakpoint; if you do, the register display will show both REP (it appears as REPZ) and the string instruction as the next instruction to be executed.

Another way to find leftover INT 3 instructions is with the S (search) command. The typical form is

S starting address   ending address   search value

The result is a list of addresses containing the value. For example, to look for INT 3 (CC hex) in locations 200 through 219, enter

S 200 219 CC

Of course, this could find data that happened to be CC.

Microcomputer development systems usually have far more extensive breakpointing facilities than DEBUG has. Useful features include the ability to retain breakpoints, clear all or single breakpoints, and set breakpoints on such conditions as:

1. Whenever a particular operation code is executed. The usual ones selected are IN or OUT.
2. Whenever a particular memory address or I/O port is accessed.
3. Whenever a particular sequence of instructions is executed.
4. Whenever a particular signal or combination of signals occurs. This is strictly a hardware breakpoint.
5. Whenever the processor executes the instruction at a particular ROM address. Obviously, neither you nor DEBUG can replace an instruction in ROM. For example, you cannot put an ordinary breakpoint in a ROM-BIOS routine.

More advanced facilities combine simpler features and count occurrences. Setting breakpoints thus becomes similar to specifying triggering events on an oscilloscope.

Traces

To activate DEBUG's trace, enter

1. T
2. =
3. Starting address;
4. A space and the number of instructions to execute. 1 is the default, so T alone is a single-step mode.

Tracing produces a register display after each instruction executes. You may continue a trace by entering T without a starting address. Remember to enter the number of instructions in hex; for example, 10 traces the next 16 instructions. Do not forget the = in front of the starting address; otherwise, the computer will think it is the number of instructions to execute.

Do not trace ROM-BIOS routines. In the first place, they are often quite long. Besides, the trace output may interfere with them, and the computer may get completely lost. Use breakpoints instead to debug sections containing INT instructions. If you accidentally start tracing a BIOS routine, be sure to restore the code segment (CS) register's original value before proceeding. Otherwise, you will be working in a DOS segment.

You can trace a REP prefix. The computer will repeat the string instruction and display the registers after each iteration. This shows exactly how REP works.

The main drawbacks of traces become obvious after you run a few. They are slow and often produce a lot of useless, repetitive output. After all, most instructions change only one or two registers, and many registers and flags are seldom used. In practice, you should not trace sequences longer than about ten instructions. Furthermore, you should always write down the key values you plan to check. Otherwise, register displays may streak by on the screen before you can interpret them.

A useful hint: To freeze the screen display temporarily, hold down Ctrl and press Num Lock (above the 7 and 8 keys in the numeric pad). This works much better than trying to peer above the top of the display for a line that has just disappeared. To resume the program and display, press the space bar. To stop a runaway trace (perhaps the result of entering T 200 instead of T=200), press Ctrl-Break or Ctrl-C.

Debugging Example: Counting Zeros

From the flowchart in Figure 8-3, we write the following program for counting zeros:

```
            MOV    CX,[8]
            MOV    DI,[340H]
            SUB    AX,AX
CNTZ:       MOV    AX,BX
            CMP    AL,[DI]
            JE     CHCNT
            INC    BX
CHCNT:      INC    DI
            LOOP   CNTZ
            MOV    BL,[400H]
            INT    20H
```

Program 8-1 is the DEBUG version.

	PROGRAM 8-1		
Memory Address (Hex)	Memory Contents (Hex)		Instruction (DEBUG Form)
0200	8B		MOV CX,[8]
0201	0E		
0202	08		
0203	00		
0204	8B		MOV DI,[340]
0205	3E		
0206	40		
0207	03		
0208	29		SUB AX,AX
0209	C0		
020A	89	CNTZ:	MOV AX,BX
020B	D8		
020C	3A		CMP AL,[DI]
020D	05		
020E	74		JE 213
020F	03		
0210	43		INC BX
0211	47	CHCNT:	INC DI
0212	E2		LOOP 20A
0213	F6		
0214	8A		MOV BL,[400]
0215	1E		
0216	00		
0217	04		
0218	CD		INT 20
0219	20		

Enter Program 8-1 but *don't run it*. (*Important rule*: Never just let a program run the first time. It may (and probably will, since Murphy's Law applies) write over itself or destroy its data. Expect errors and plan for them. This is also a good time to save the program on disk in case of a major catastrophe. The most successful programmers are born pessimists; the rest become pessimistic with experience.)

Let us first run the program with a breakpoint after the initialization (that is, in address 20C). The required command is

G=200 20C

The results at the breakpoint should be

$$[AX] = 0000$$
$$[BX] = 0000 \quad \text{(number of zeros found)}$$
$$[CX] = 0008 \quad \text{(counter)}$$
$$[DI\ ] = 0340 \quad \text{(base address of array)}$$

Our results are

$$[AX] = 0000$$
$$[BX] = 0000 \quad \text{(number of zeros found)}$$
$$[CX] = F01D \quad \text{(counter)}$$
$$[DI\ ] = 0000 \quad \text{(base address of array)}$$

Your results may be different, as the program is far from correct.

The breakpoint tells us that something is wrong. To pinpoint the error, use the Trace command. From the prompt, enter

$$T=200\ 3$$

Don't forget the = after T. This makes the computer execute the first three instructions, displaying the registers and the next instruction after each one. Note that we never see the first instruction at all.

MOV CX,[8] should give

$$[CX] = 0008$$

Instead, we get

$$[CX] = F01D$$

Obviously, we have the wrong instruction. Note that we cannot watch it execute—all we see are the results. The only way to get more information is to use an instrument or control panel that monitors the processor's external signals.

What instruction should we have? The obvious alternative is MOV CX,8. This is, in fact, the one we want, as our aim is to load CX with the number 8, not the contents of addresses 0008 and 0009. Always be careful to distinguish between data and addresses. Address 8 could contain anything; it does not necessarily contain 8.

So we must replace the four-byte instruction MOV CX,[8] with the three-byte instruction MOV CX,8. But what happens to the extra byte? The simplest solution is to put a NOP in location 200. NOP is a space filler that does nothing except add 1 to the instruction pointer. Later we can compact the program by eliminating all NOPs. For now, just start at 201 to avoid stepping through the NOP each time.

The second instruction should give the result

$$[DI] = 0340 \qquad \text{(base address of array)}$$

The actual display, however, shows

$$[DI] = 0000$$

We immediately suspect the same mistake as before; we want MOV DI immediate, not MOV DI direct. We can correct this error by entering NOP followed by MOV DI,340 at address 204. Making the change and repeating the trace (use T=201 4) gives the correct results:

$$[CX] = 0008 \qquad \text{(number of elements)}$$
$$[DI] = 0340 \qquad \text{(base address of array)}$$

The next two instructions should clear AX and BX. However, as they already contain zero, we cannot tell whether anything is happening. So, before continuing the trace, use R commands to change AX to 1234 and BX to 5678. Always be sure that you can tell whether the program works. Remember, good programmers are pessimists; they are the kind of people who carry umbrellas on sunny days and ask Santa Claus for identification before inviting him in on Christmas Eve.

Now enter T 2 to trace SUB AX,AX and MOV AX,BX. SUB AX,AX correctly sets AX to 0000. MOV AX,BX, however gives

$$[AX] = 5678$$

Here the move is going the wrong way. What we want is MOV BX,AX. This is probably the single most common error in 8088 assembly language programs. One naturally expects MOV op1,op2 to move op1 to op2, not the other way around.

Note the key points of this debugging exercise:

1. A breakpoint can tell you whether an entire section of a program is correct.
2. A trace that displays the registers after each instruction can show you precisely what is wrong with a program.
3. Unnecessary program bytes can be replaced by NOP instructions. Clearly, it is much easier to remove instructions than to add them.

4. Always be sure that you can tell whether the program is correct. Beware of situations where the result is already in a register or memory location (perhaps left over from a previous test run).
5. Most programmers make the same mistakes consistently. Knowing your own favorites will help you debug programs. Obviously, it is easier to list one's favorite errors than to change one's habits.

Debugging a Loop

Now that we know the initialization instructions are correct, we are ready to debug the loop. The simplest approach is to put a breakpoint at the beginning, then trace a few iterations.

To proceed, we need some data. Let us try

$$[0340] = 00$$
$$[0341] = 01$$

That is, type

E 340 0 1

This gives us one element that is zero and another that is not.

To reach the loop, run the program with a breakpoint in 20C just as before (remember to use G, not T). When the program reaches the breakpoint, press T. The instruction pointer already has the proper value, so just press Enter immediately to execute one instruction. Note that location 20C contains its original value (3A), as DEBUG has replaced the breakpoint. Do a second T command to execute the conditional jump.

Something is surely wrong here. First, the program jumps when it shouldn't (location 340 does contain zero). Second, the jump sends the processor to address 213, which does not even contain an instruction. You know it doesn't, since the op code appears as "???" in the register display. We can correct the first error by replacing JE (JZ) with JNE (JNZ) and the second one by changing the destination from 213 to 211. Here we have managed to make two common errors—inverting decision logic and misdirecting a forward jump. Always check all forward jumps before running a program entered with DEBUG's A command.

Let us now start over. That is, start the program at 200 and set a breakpoint in 212. The results are

[AX] = 0000
[BX] = 0001
[CX] = 0008   (since LOOP has not yet been executed)
[DI] = 0341

These are all correct. If your results differ, verify the program with the U 200 219 command. You may find leftover INT 3 instructions.

We can now try the next iteration. Press G, set a breakpoint in location 211, and press the Enter key. When the computer reaches the breakpoint, the results should be

$$[AX] = 0000$$
$$[BX] = 0001 \quad \text{(one zero element has been found)}$$
$$[CX] = 0007 \quad \text{(count has not yet been decremented)}$$
$$[DI] = 0341 \quad \text{(pointer has not yet been incremented)}$$

The actual results are:

$$[AX] = 0000$$
$$[BX] = 0000$$
$$[CX] = 0007$$
$$[DI] = 0341$$

The program is forgetting the zero it has already counted. A trace of the next two instructions shows that label CNTZ is misplaced. It should be one instruction later (that is, attached to CMP AX,[DI]) to keep the program from clearing BX each time. We need LOOP 20C instead of LOOP 20A in the DEBUG version. This is a particularly annoying type of error, doing an entire series of operations correctly and then overwriting the result.

Now try the program on some test data, such as:

1. [0340] through [0347] = 00.
2. Same as (1) except [0340] = 01.
3. Same as (1) except [0347] = 01.

The final version is

```
        NOP
        MOV    CX,8          ;NUMBER OF ELEMENTS = 8
        NOP
        MOV    DI,340H        ;POINT TO START OF ARRAY
        SUB    AX,AX          ;GET ZERO FOR COMPARISON
        MOV    BX,AX          ;NUMBER OF ZEROS FOUND = 0
CNTZ:   CMP    AL,[DI]        ;IS NEXT ELEMENT 0?
        JNE    CHCNT
        INC    BX             ;YES, INCREMENT NUMBER OF
                              ;   ZEROS
```

```
CHCNT:  INC    DI
        LOOP   CNTZ          ;COUNT ELEMENTS
        MOV    BL,[400H]     ;SAVE NUMBER OF ZEROS FOUND
        INT    20H
```

Program 8-2 is a DEBUG version with the corrections.

Note the following key points from this part of the example:

1. Breakpoints help you pass quickly through a section that you know is correct.
2. Different debugging tools are complementary rather than competitive. Breakpoints help restrict a search to a small section of a program, whereas a trace shows the details that usually let you spot the error.
3. Debugging tools cannot correct programs by themselves. All they do is provide information; you must figure out what it means. Debugging is not a simple or routine job; it requires organization, caution, patience, common sense, experience, and insight.

Problem 8-5

a. What errors still remain in Program 8-2? Correct them and run the final version for the three test cases we just described.
b. Revise the program to use the instruction SCASB (scan string). SCASB is a string operation like LODSB and STOSB; it compares AL to the byte at the address in DI, then increments or decrements DI by 1, depending on the D flag.

PROGRAM 8-2		
Memory Address (Hex)	Memory Contents (Hex)	Instruction (DEBUG Form)
0200	*90*	*NOP*
0201	*B9*	*MOV CX,8*
0202	*08*	
0203	*00*	
0204	*90*	*NOP*
0205	*BF*	*MOV DI,340*
0206	*40*	

	PROGRAM 8-2 (continued)			

Memory Address (Hex)	Memory Contents (Hex)		Instruction (DEBUG Form)	
0207	03			
0208	29		SUB	AX,AX
0209	C0			
020A	89		MOV	BX,AX
020B	C3			
020C	3A	CNTZ:	CMP	AL,[DI]
020D	05			
020E	75		JNE	211
020F	01			
0210	43		INC	BX
0211	47	CHCNT:	INC	DI
0212	E2		LOOP	20C
0213	F8			
0214	8A		MOV	BL,[400]
0215	1E			
0216	00			
0217	04			
0218	CD		INT	20
0219	20			

Problem 8-6

Revise Program 8-2 to count the number of positive 8-bit elements in 340 through 347. An element is positive if its most significant bit (bit 7) is zero, but its value is not zero.

EXAMPLE:

$$[0340] = 01$$
$$[0341] = 80$$
$$[0342] = 7F$$
$$[0343] = FF$$
$$[0344] = 00$$
$$[0345] = 00$$
$$[0346] = 00$$
$$[0347] = 00$$

RESULT:

[0400] = 02, since 340 and 342 contain positive numbers.

Problem 8-7

Code, debug, and test Flowcharting Example 2, the maximum-value program.

Problem 8-8

Code, debug, and test Flowcharting Example 3, the variable delay. The following routine (see Problem 3-6) uses registers BX and CX to wait for 1 s:

```
        MOV   BX,0CAH     ;WAIT 1 SECOND
DLY1:   MOV   CX,3E8H
DLY2:   DEC   CX
        JNZ   DLY2
        DEC   BX
        JNZ   DLY1
```

You should verify the delay constants.

Moving Programs

As a last step in the debugging process, let us compact Program 8-2 by removing the NOPs. To do this, we will use DEBUG's M (Move) command, which moves a block of memory. M takes three addresses:

• The base of the source area (the lowest address to be moved).
• The end of the source area (the highest address to be moved).
• The base of the destination area.

The source comes first, as you would expect.

We will first use M to delete the NOP from 200. We must move locations 201 through 219 to new addresses starting at 200. The required command is:

M 201 219 200

Be sure that the source area includes the second byte of INT 20H.

Now use the U command to verify the move. Note that the addresses in JNZ and LOOP change automatically, since the relative offsets stay the same. Clearly, moving a program is much easier and faster than reentering it. For practice, use M to delete the second NOP from location 203.

Features like the M command solve many problems. If, for example, you accidentally omit a line near the beginning of a program, you can use M to avoid a complete reentry. Of course, Murphy's Law guarantees that omissions always occur near the beginning of a program, rather than near the end.

However, the M command still requires the programmer to keep track of memory addresses and the lengths of programs. A better approach is to enter the source code using an *editor* that lets you insert, delete, correct, and move text. Except for the format, this is just like using word processing to write a letter or report. The editor lets you save the completed program as a *text file* which you can then assemble. If you find errors during assembly or execution, you can correct them by returning to the editor, revising the text file, and reassembling.

DEBUG Command Files

There is a middle ground between DEBUG's A command and a full-fledged editor and assembler. It involves using an editor to create command files which you then submit to DEBUG via input redirection. Professor Charles Nunnally of Virginia Tech suggested it to me in a review and was kind enough to explain it in detail over the telephone. A letter by Richard Ranson in *PC World* (January 1985, pp. 230–231) also describes the technique.

The idea here is to save the commands one would normally enter to assemble and run a program with DEBUG. You can then correct or change them with an editor, rather than having to retype them all each time. Of course, DEBUG does not know (or care) that the commands are actually coming from a file rather than directly from the keyboard.

Let us see how this works in an example. Using an editor (perhaps EDLIN on the DOS disk or WordStar in its nondocument mode), create the following file of commands for assembling and running Program 1-1 and call it P1-01.DEB:

```
A 200
MOV AL,[400]
MOV [401],AL
INT 20

U 200 206
E 400
6C 0
G=200
E 401

Q
```

This works just as though we were leading someone through the procedure for using DEBUG. That is,

1. Line 1 is the A command starting at location 200.
2. Lines 2-4 are the simplified assembly language entries for Program 1-1. You can put comments on these lines preceded by semicolons.
3. Line 5 is the extra Enter that ends the A command.
4. Line 6 produces a disassembly.
5. Lines 7 and 8 enter the data into location 400 and clear location 401.
6. Line 9 executes the program, starting at location 200.
7. Lines 10 and 11 display the result. The extra Enter ends the E command.
8. Line 12 exits from DEBUG.

Once we have created the file, all we must do to run it is type

DEBUG<P1-01.DEB

"<," the input redirection symbol, makes DEBUG get its inputs from file P1-01.DEB rather than from the keyboard.

Executing the command file is like watching someone follow a list of written orders. DEBUG responds to the commands, just as though you were entering them from the keyboard. The effect is a bit eerie, even though the logic is straightforward.

One problem with this approach is that you must enter the commands exactly as you would type them at the keyboard. For example, don't forget the extra Enters that end such commands as A and E. The computer follows your orders precisely, regardless of whether they make sense. Of course, you can correct any errors with the editor. Remember the Q command at the end to exit DEBUG and return control to DOS.

To ensure that Ctrl-Alt-Del is active, insert the lines

R F
EI

ahead of the G command. This is the sequence from Laboratory 2 to admit keyboard entries.

Common Programming Errors

Watch for the following common errors in 8088 assembly language programs:

1. Confusing data and addresses. Remember the difference between immediate and direct addressing; immediate addressing means that the instruc-

tion contains the data, whereas direct addressing means that it contains the data's address. Remember also that the value in a memory location is not related to the direct address, effective address, base address, or index.

2. Inverting the logic of conditional jumps (for example, using JC instead of JNC or JNZ instead of JZ). Be particularly careful after a comparison.

3. Jumping to the wrong address. This often results in repeating or omitting initialization instructions or instructions that update counters or pointers.

4. Reversing the operands in a MOV or CMP instruction. Remember that MOV op1,op2 loads op1 from op2, not the other way around. Similarly, CMP op1,op2 sets the flags according to op1-op2.

5. Confusing 8-bit and 16-bit registers and operations. Remember the difference between the 8-bit accumulator AL and the 16-bit accumulator AX.

6. Inverting the order of the bytes in 16-bit addresses or data. Remember that the 8088 expects the less significant byte first.

Other common errors are

7. Failing to initialize counters and pointers. Be especially careful with instructions such as LOOP, LODS, and STOS that use certain registers implicitly. Also be sure to initialize the D flag when using string instructions.

8. Jumping incorrectly when operands are equal. Note that comparing equal values *clears* the Carry flag.

9. Overlooking trivial cases or boundary conditions such as zero or one element in an array or table, no inputs, and so on.

10. Using the flags incorrectly. Typical examples are using a flag that an instruction does not affect and overlooking changes caused by intervening instructions. The only way to learn how an instruction affects the flags is to look it up in Table A1-1 (Appendix 1). Instructions that often cause problems are moves (they do not affect any flags), logicals (they clear the Carry flag), and increment and decrement (they do not affect the Carry flag).

11. Using a register for several purposes without saving and restoring the values.

12. Using the wrong base address or index. Be particularly careful of the first and last elements in an array. If the base address is BASE and the array contains N byte-length elements, the first element is at address BASE (not BASE + 1) and the last element is at address BASE + N − 1 (not BASE + N).

You will undoubtedly make errors not mentioned here (or even imagined anywhere in the civilized world), but these lists should suggest some possibilities. Unfortunately, debugging computer programs is more of an art than a science.

Key Point Summary

1. Writing software, like building hardware, consists of many stages. Writing the actual computer instructions (coding) is one of the easiest stages.
2. Flowcharting is a simple graphic technique for designing and documenting programs. A set of standard flowchart symbols is in widespread use.
3. A flowchart is a good starting place for writing a program, but it should not become a burden in and of itself.
4. Breakpoints are stopping places in programs. You can use them to determine whether sections contain errors and to pass through sections that you know are correct.
5. The T (Trace) command makes the IBM PC display its registers and the next instruction after it executes each of a specified number of instructions. You can use a trace to pinpoint an error after using breakpoints to narrow the search to a short section.
6. Common programming errors include confusing data and addresses; inverting logic or reversing the direction of operations; failing to initialize variables or save results; omitting operands; forgetting how instructions affect flags; ignoring trivial cases; and branching incorrectly.
7. Program debugging is a difficult, time-consuming job. You must know which tools to use and when to use them, what to look for, and which errors are likely. Debugging requires caution, organization, and imagination; in fact, it requires the same skills needed to work a crossword puzzle, play chess or bridge, or solve a maze, riddle, or murder mystery.

LABORATORY 9

Arithmetic

Purpose   To learn how to do arithmetic with the 8088 microprocessor.

**What You
Should Learn**
1. The standard BCD representation.
2. How to add and subtract decimal numbers.
3. How to add and subtract 16-bit numbers.
4. How to add and subtract multiple-precision numbers.
5. How to do arithmetic with lookup tables.

**Reference
Materials**
Andrews, M. "Mathematical Microprocessor Software: A Square Root
   Comparison," *IEEE Micro*, May 1982, pp. 63–79.
Eccles, W. J. *Microprocessor Systems: A 16-Bit Approach*. Reading, MA: Ad-
   dison-Wesley, 1985, pp. 92–95, 297–307, 324–326.
Gorsline, G. W. *16-Bit Modern Microcomputers*. Englewood Cliffs, NJ:
   Prentice-Hall, 1985, pp. 113–124 (arithmetic instructions), 124–125
   (status flag instructions).
Hwang, K. *Computer Arithmetic*. New York: John Wiley, 1979.
Kulisch, U. W., and W. L. Mirankar. *Computer Arithmetic in Theory and
   Practice*. Orlando, FL: Academic Press, 1980.
Liu, Y. C., and G. A. Gibson, *Microcomputer Systems: The 8086/8088
   Family* (2nd ed.). Englewood Cliffs, NJ: Prentice-Hall, 1986, pp.
   63–78 (arithmetic instructions).
"Binary Floating-Point Arithmetic, Standard for (IEEE Std 754-1985)." IEEE,
   Piscataway, NJ, 1985.

Terms   **Auxiliary carry:**   *see* **Half carry.**
BCD (binary-coded-decimal):   a representation of decimal numbers in
   which each digit is coded separately in binary.

Carry: a bit that is 1 if an addition overflows into the succeeding digit position.

Half carry (or **auxiliary carry**): the carry from the less significant 4 bits in an 8-bit operation.

Interpolation: estimating a function at points between those at which its values are known.

Linearization: approximating a function by a straight line between two points at which its values are known.

Pseudo-operation: an assembly language operation code that directs the assembler to do something but does not generate a machine language instruction. Also called a *directive* or *pseudo-instruction*.

8088 Instructions

ADC: add with carry. ADC op1,op2 produces the result op1 = op1 + op2 + Carry.

CLC: clear Carry flag (make it 0).

DAA: decimal adjust for addition; convert a binary sum in register AL to a BCD sum. DAA works only after an ADC AL or ADD AL instruction.

DAS: decimal adjust for subtraction; convert a binary difference in register AL to a BCD difference. DAS works only after an SBB AL or SUB AL instruction.

SBB: subtract with borrow. SBB op1,op2 produces the result op1 = op1 − op2 − Carry.

STC: set Carry flag to 1.

SUB: subtract. SUB op1,op2 produces the result op1 = op1 − op2.

8088 Assembler Pseudo-Operations

DB: define byte-length data; place 8-bit data items (separated by commas) in the next available memory locations. DB loads memory with fixed data (such as tables, messages, and numerical constants) needed for program execution.

DW: define word-length data; place 16-bit data items (separated by commas) in the next available memory locations. DW loads memory with 16-bit fixed data or addresses stored in the usual 8088 format (that is, less significant byte first).

ORG: set origin; place the object code generated from the subsequent statements in memory addresses, starting with the one specified. ORG lets the programmer determine where programs and data are placed in memory.

Applications of Arithmetic

Data processing almost always involves arithmetic. Typical operations are averaging, scaling, linearizing inputs, computing numerical integrals and derivatives, determining frequency responses, doing statistical analysis, and preparing plots. Simple applications require only binary or decimal addition and subtraction. Decimal arithmetic is necessary in calculators, business equipment, terminals, instruments, appliances, and games.

This laboratory starts with 8-bit binary arithmetic programs from Laboratory 6. It then covers decimal arithmetic, multibyte arithmetic, and the use of lookup tables.

8-Bit Binary Sum

The following program adds 8-bit unsigned binary numbers from 340 and 341 and puts the sum in 400.

```
MOV   AL,[340H]     ;GET FIRST NUMBER
ADD   AL,[341H]     ;ADD SECOND NUMBER
MOV   [400H],AL     ;SAVE SUM
INT   3             ;EXIT AND DISPLAY REGISTERS
```

Program 9-1 is the DEBUG version; we have inserted a NOP to allow for BCD operands later.

PROGRAM 9-1		
Memory Address (Hex)	Memory Contents (Hex)	Instruction (DEBUG Form)
0200	A0	*MOV AL,[340]*
0201	40	
0202	03	
0203	02	*ADD AL,[341]*
0204	06	

PROGRAM 9-1 (continued)		
Memory Address (Hex)	Memory Contents (Hex)	Instruction (DEBUG Form)
0205	41	
0206	03	
0207	90	NOP
0208	A2	MOV [400],AL
0209	00	
020A	04	
020B	CC	INT 3

Run Program 9-1 for the following cases:

1. [0340] = 32
    [0341] = 25
    Result: [0400] = 57
2. [0340] = 38
    [0341] = 25
    Result: [0400] = 5D

You can use the H (hexarithmetic) command to check the sums.

Problem 9-1

Make Program 9-1 subtract instead of add. Try the following cases:

a. [0340] = 32
    [0341] = 25
    Result: [0400] = 0D
b. [0340] = 32
    [0341] = 58
    Result: [0400] = DA

Problem 9-2

Make Program 9-1 save the carry in 401. Try the following cases:

a. [0340] = 38
    [0341] = 25
    Result: [0400] = 5D
            [0401] = 00

b. [0340] = 98
[0341] = 89
Result: [0400] = 21
[0401] = 01

(*Hint:* Use ADC AH,0 to add the Carry to AH.)

Binary-Coded-Decimal (BCD) Representation

A BCD code is the simplest way to represent decimal numbers in a computer, because it does not require multiplications or divisions by 10. In the standard BCD code (Table 9-1), 0 through 9 are the same as in binary. However, numbers above 9 are different (see Table 9-2 for examples). Note the following:

1. Each decimal digit is encoded separately in BCD. This is not true in binary, since 10 is not an integral power of 2. When computers take over the world, they will force people to have either 8 or 16 fingers.
2. The BCD representation takes more memory than the binary representation. For example, 8 bits can represent a binary number as large as 255 but only 99 in BCD. The number 999 requires three BCD digits (12 bits) but only 10 bits in binary (because $2^{10} = 1024$).
3. Some binary numbers are invalid in BCD. In standard BCD, no digit can exceed 9.

Table 9-1
Standard BCD Representation

Decimal Digit	BCD Representation
0	0000
1	0001
2	0010
3	0011
4	0100
5	0101
6	0110
7	0111
8	1000
9	1001

Table 9-2
Standard BCD
Representations of
Some Decimal
Numbers

Decimal Number	BCD Representation	Binary Representation
10	0001 0000	00001010
11	0001 0001	00001011
12	0001 0010	00001100
13	0001 0011	00001101
16	0001 0110	00010000
25	0010 0101	00011001
50	0101 0000	00110010
66	0110 0110	01000010
83	1000 0011	01010011

BCD numbers are difficult to process in binary arithmetic units. The reason is that BCD 10 (00010000) is not one larger than BCD 9 (00001001); it is, in fact, seven larger. (Try subtracting!) Thus, to get a BCD sum from a binary adder, you must add an extra 6 whenever the sum of two digits exceeds 9. Subtraction works similarly: You must subtract an extra 6 whenever the difference between two digits is negative.

EXAMPLE 1:

$$
\begin{array}{r}
33 \ (\text{BCD}) = 00110011 \\
+ \quad 25 \ (\text{BCD}) = \underline{00100101} \\
01011000 = 58 \ (\text{BCD})
\end{array}
$$

There is no problem here, as neither digit exceeds 9.

EXAMPLE 2:

$$
\begin{array}{r}
38 \ (\text{BCD}) = 00111000 \\
+ \quad 25 \ (\text{BCD}) = \underline{00100101} \\
01011101 = 5D
\end{array}
$$

Here we need an extra 6 in the lower digit position, as 8 + 5 produces a decimal carry.

$$
\begin{array}{r}
5D \\
+ \quad \underline{06} \\
63
\end{array}
$$

EXAMPLE 3:

$$98 \ (BCD) = 10011000$$
$$+ \quad 25 \ (BCD) = \underline{00100101}$$
$$10111101 = BD$$

Here we need an extra 6 in both digit positions.

$$BD$$
$$+ \quad \underline{66}$$
$$123$$

Obviously, a program that decides when to add or subtract 6 is not easy to write, as it must check each digit. Because decimal arithmetic is essential to many common applications, most processors have special instructions for it. The 8088 has DAA (decimal adjust for addition), and DAS (decimal adjust for subtraction). They convert a binary sum or difference in AL (the result of an ADC AL, ADD AL, SBB AL, or SUB AL instruction) to a decimal sum or difference; that is, DAA adds 6 and DAS subtracts 6 wherever necessary.

8-Bit Decimal Sum

The following program adds BCD numbers from 340 and 341 and saves the sum in 400.

```
MOV   AL,[340H]     ;GET FIRST NUMBER
ADD   AL,[341H]     ;ADD SECOND NUMBER
DAA
MOV   [400H],AL     ;SAVE SUM
INT   3
```

The only change from Program 9-1 is DAA instead of NOP.

Run the BCD version of Program 9-1 with the following data:

1. [0340] = 32
   [0341] = 25
   Result: [0400] = 57
2. [0340] = 38
   [0341] = 25
   Result: [0400] = 63

The second sum differs from the binary result.

Problem 9-3

In Program 9-1, what do register AL, the Auxiliary Carry flag, and the Carry flag contain after ADD AL,[341H] for the following examples:

a. [0340] = 38
   [0341] = 25
b. [0340] = 98
   [0341] = 25
c. [0340] = 98
   [0341] = 89
d. [0340] = 90
   [0341] = 91

To display the registers and flags, put a breakpoint in location 207. Note (see Table 2-3) that DEBUG displays the Auxiliary Carry as AC (1) or NA (0). Why is the Auxiliary Carry necessary? (*Hint:* Examine the results of examples *c* and *d* above.)

Problem 9-4

Write a decimal subtraction program and try it on the examples in Problem 9-3. What is Carry at the end of each example? What does Carry mean at the end?

Problem 9-5

Extend the decimal addition program to show the sum near the center of the screen.

Decimal Summation

The following revision of Program 6-1 adds an array of unsigned 8-bit binary numbers, starting at 340; it puts the sum in 400. The length of the array is in 401. Program 9-2 is the DEBUG version.

```
        MOV   CL,[401H]    ;COUNT = ARRAY LENGTH
        SUB   CH,CH        ;EXTEND COUNT TO 16 BITS
        MOV   SI,340H       ;POINT TO BASE OF ARRAY
        SUB   AL,AL        ;SUM = ZERO INITIALLY
ADDELM: ADD   AL,[SI]      ;ADD ELEMENT TO SUM
        NOP
```

```
        INC    SI              ;CONTINUE THROUGH ALL
                               ;  ELEMENTS
        LOOP   ADDELM
        MOV    [400H],AL       ;SAVE SUM
        INT    20H
```

		PROGRAM 9-2	

Memory Address (Hex)	Memory Contents (Hex)		Instruction (DEBUG Form)
0200	8A		MOV CL,[401]
0201	0E		
0202	01		
0203	04		
0204	28		SUB CH,CH
0205	ED		
0206	BE		MOV SI,340
0207	40		
0208	03		
0209	28		SUB AL,AL
020A	C0		
020B	02	ADDELM:	ADD AL,[SI]
020C	04		
020D	90		NOP
020E	46		INC SI
020F	E2		LOOP 20B
0210	FA		
0211	A2		MOV [400],AL
0212	00		
0213	04		
0214	CD		INT 20
0215	20		

We have again inserted a NOP to allow a BCD version. Run Program 9-2 with the following data:

```
[0401] = 03    (number of elements)
[0340] = 35    (elements)
[0341] = 47
[0342] = 28
```

RESULT:

```
[0400] = A4
```

Change the program to make the summation decimal (BCD) rather than binary. Run the revision with the same data. The answer should be

[0400] = 10

16-Bit Arithmetic

We can easily extend Program 9-2 to handle 16-bit numbers. The only changes are the use of AX instead of AL and two increments of SI instead of one. Of course, the sum now occupies two bytes of memory. The revised program is as follows (Program 9-3 is the DEBUG version):

```
        MOV   CL,[402H]      ;COUNT = ARRAY LENGTH
        SUB   CH,CH          ;EXTEND COUNT TO 16 BITS
        MOV   SI,340H        ;POINT TO BASE OF ARRAY
        SUB   AX,AX          ;SUM = ZERO INITIALLY
ADDELM: ADD   AX,[SI]        ;ADD ELEMENT TO SUM
        INC   SI
        INC   SI
        LOOP  ADDELM
        MOV   [400H],AX      ;SAVE SUM
        INT   20H
```

Run Program 9-3 with the following data:

[0402] = 02   (number of 16-bit elements)
[0340] = 3E   (LSBs of first element)
[0341] = 47   (MSBs of first element)
[0342] = F5   (LSBs of second element)
[0343] = 2A   (MSBs of second element)

RESULT:

[0400] = 33   (LSBs of sum)
[0401] = 72   (MSBs of sum)

that is,

```
      473E
  +   2AF5
      7233
```

		PROGRAM 9-3	
Memory Address (Hex)	Memory Contents (Hex)		Instruction (DEBUG Form)
0200	8A		MOV CL,[402]
0201	0E		
0202	02		
0203	04		
0204	28		SUB CH,CH
0205	ED		
0206	BE		MOV SI,340
0207	40		
0208	03		
0209	29		SUB AX,AX
020A	C0		
020B	03	ADDELM:	ADD AX,[SI]
020C	04		
020D	46		INC SI
020E	46		INC SI
020F	E2		LOOP 20B
0210	FA		
0211	A3		MOV [400],AX
0212	00		
0213	04		
0214	CD		INT 20
0215	20		

A decimal version is complicated by the fact that DAA and DAS work only on bytes in AL. The program thus must handle the data a byte at a time. However, it must also deal with carries between bytes. Here ADC (add with Carry) is useful, as its result is

$$\text{Operand 1} = \text{Operand 1} + \text{Operand 2} + \text{Carry}$$

The way to do 16-bit decimal addition is, therefore,

1. Add the less significant bytes using ADD and DAA.
2. Add the more significant bytes using ADC and DAA.

The following program adds an array of 16-bit decimal numbers, starting at 340; it puts the sum in 400 and 401. Each number occupies two memory locations, with the less significant byte first. The length of the array (how many 16-bit numbers there are) is in 402.

```
            MOV   CL,[402H]    ;COUNT = ARRAY LENGTH
            SUB   CH,CH        ;EXTEND COUNT TO 16 BITS
            MOV   SI,340H      ;POINT TO BASE OF ARRAY
            SUB   BX,BX        ;SUM = ZERO INITIALLY
            CLD                ;SELECT AUTOINCREMENTING
ADDELM:     LODSW              ;GET NEXT 16-BIT ELEMENT
            ADD   AL,BL        ;ADD LESS SIGNIFICANT BYTES
            DAA                ;MAKE SUM DECIMAL
            MOV   BL,AL
            MOV   AL,AH        ;ADD MORE SIGNIFICANT BYTES
            ADC   AL,BH
            DAA                ;MAKE SUM DECIMAL
            MOV   BH,AL
            LOOP  ADDELM
            MOV   [400H],BX    ;SAVE SUM
            INT   20H
```

Program 9-4 is the DEBUG version. Run it with the following data:

```
[0402] = 02   (number of four-digit elements)

[0340] = 36   (LSDs of first element)
[0341] = 21   (MSDs of first element)
[0342] = 97   (LSDs of second element)
[0343] = 18   (MSDs of second element)
```

RESULT:

```
[0400] = 33   (LSDs of sum)
[0401] = 40   (MSDs of sum)
```

that is,

$$
\begin{array}{r}
2136 \\
+\ \underline{1897} \\
4033
\end{array}
$$

PROGRAM 9-4				
Memory Address (Hex)	Memory Contents (Hex)		Instruction (DEBUG Form)	
0200	8A		MOV	CL,[402]
0201	0E			
0202	02			
0203	04			
0204	28		SUB	CH,CH
0205	ED			
0206	BE		MOV	SI,340
0207	40			
0208	03			
0209	29		SUB	BX,BX
020A	DB			
020B	FC		CLD	
020C	AD	ADDELM:	LODSW	
020D	00		ADD	AL,BL
020E	D8			
020F	27		DAA	
0210	88		MOV	BL,AL
0211	C3			
0212	88		MOV	AL,AH
0213	E0			
0214	10		ADC	AL,BH
0215	F8			
0216	27		DAA	
0217	88		MOV	BH,AL
0218	C7			
0219	E2		LOOP	20C
021A	F1			
021B	89		MOV	[400],BX
021C	1E			
021D	00			
021E	04			
021F	CD		INT	20
0220	20			

Problem 9-6

Extend Program 9-4 to place the carries in 402. Use 403 for the number of elements. Try the following example:

[0403] = 02   (number of four-digit elements)

[0340] = 36   (LSDs of first element)
[0341] = 21   (MSDs of first element)
[0342] = 97   (LSDs of second element)
[0343] = 98   (MSDs of second element)

RESULT:

[0400] = 33   (LSDs of sum)
[0401] = 20   (middle digits of sum)
[0402] = 01   (MSDs of sum = carries)

that is,

$$
\begin{array}{r}
2136 \\
+\quad 9897 \\
\hline
12033
\end{array}
$$

Be sure to keep the carries as a decimal number. That is, do not simply use INC to add a Carry to the most significant digits.

Multiple-Precision Arithmetic

We can extend Programs 9-1 through 9-4 to handle numbers of any length. The procedure (see Figure 9-1) is as follows:

1. Initialization.

COUNT   = LENGTH OF NUMBERS (IN BYTES)
POINTER 1 = BASE ADDRESS OF NUMBER 1
POINTER 2 = BASE ADDRESS OF NUMBER 2
CARRY   = 0, as there is never a Carry into the least significant bytes.

2. Add bytes.

[POINTER 1] = [POINTER 1] + [POINTER 2] + CARRY

This step generates a new CARRY.

Figure 9-1
Flowchart for
multiple-precision
addition.

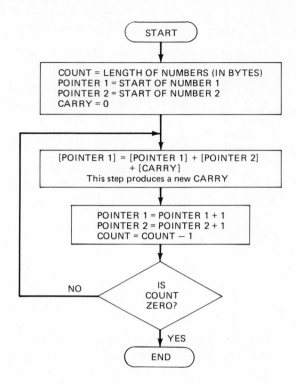

3. Update counter and pointers.

$$POINTER \ 1 \ = \ POINTER \ 1 + 1$$
$$POINTER \ 2 \ = \ POINTER \ 2 + 1$$
$$COUNT \qquad = \ COUNT - 1$$

If COUNT is not 0, return to Step 2.

The numbers are in the usual 8088 format with their least significant bytes at the lowest addresses.

If the length of the numbers is in 400, the numbers start in 340 and 360, and the sum replaces the number starting in 340, the program is

```
MOV    CL,[400H]      ;GET LENGTH OF NUMBERS IN
                      ;  BYTES
SUB    CH,CH          ;EXTEND LENGTH TO 16 BITS
MOV    DI,340H        ;POINT TO BASE OF FIRST
                      ;  NUMBER
```

```
          MOV     SI,360H          ;POINT TO BASE OF SECOND
                                   ;  NUMBER
          CLD                      ;SELECT AUTOINCREMENTING
          CLC                      ;CLEAR CARRY INITIALLY
ADBYTE:   LODSB                    ;GET BYTE OF SECOND
                                   ;  NUMBER
          ADC     AL,[DI]          ;ADD BYTE OF FIRST NUMBER
          STOSB                    ;STORE SUM AS FIRST NUMBER
          LOOP    ADBYTE
          INT     20H
```

Program 9-5 is the DEBUG version. A key factor is that LODSB, STOSB, and LOOP do not affect Carry, so its value is available for the next ADC. INC and DEC do not affect the Carry either. Thus they can also be used in loops that depend on Carry to save a bit for the next iteration.

PROGRAM 9-5		
Memory Address (Hex)	Memory Contents (Hex)	Instruction (DEBUG Form)
0200	8A	MOV CL,[400]
0201	0E	
0202	00	
0203	04	
0204	28	SUB CH,CH
0205	ED	
0206	BF	MOV DI,340
0207	40	
0208	03	
0209	BE	MOV SI,360
020A	60	
020B	03	
020C	FC	CLD
020D	F8	CLC
020E	AC	ADBYTE: LODSB
020F	12	ADC AL,[DI]
0210	05	
0211	AA	STOSB
0212	E2	LOOP 20E
0213	FA	
0214	CD	INT 20
0215	20	

Try Program 9-5 on the following example:

[0400] = 06   (length of numbers in bytes)

[0340] = C7   (LSBs of first number)
[0341] = 59
[0342] = F0
[0343] = AB   (MSBs of first number)

[0360] = EA   (LSBs of second number)
[0361] = 93
[0362] = A1
[0363] = 28   (MSBs of second number)

RESULT:

[0340] = B1   (LSBs of sum)
[0341] = ED
[0342] = 91
[0343] = D4   (MSBs of sum)

that is,

```
   ABF059C7
+  28A193EA
   D491EDB1
```

Problem 9-7

Write a program that adds decimal numbers of arbitrary length. Assume the same conditions as in Program 9-5. Try the following sample case:

[0400] = 04   (length of numbers in bytes)

[0340] = 60   (LSDs of first number)
[0341] = 71
[0342] = 34
[0343] = 29   (MSDs of first number)

[0360] = 28   (LSDs of second number)
[0361] = 81
[0362] = 93
[0363] = 15   (MSDs of second number)

RESULT:

[0340] = 88   (LSDs of sum)
[0341] = 52
[0342] = 28
[0343] = 45   (MSDs of sum)

that is,

```
  29347160
+ 15938128
  45285288
```

Problem 9-8

Write a program that subtracts decimal numbers of arbitrary length. Assume the same conditions as in Program 9-5. Subtract the number starting at 360 from the one starting at 340. Try the following example:

[0400] = 04   (length of numbers in bytes)

[0340] = 60   (LSDs of minuend)
[0341] = 71
[0342] = 34
[0343] = 29   (MSDs of minuend)

[0360] = 81   (LSDs of subtrahend)
[0361] = 28
[0362] = 60
[0363] = 19   (MSDs of subtrahend)

RESULT:

[0340] = 79   (LSDs of difference)
[0341] = 42
[0342] = 74
[0343] = 09   (MSDs of difference)

that is,

```
  29347160
- 19602881
  09744279
```

Arithmetic with Lookup Tables

One way to do arithmetic is by using lookup tables that contain all possible results. The program must then locate the one we want, just as in the code conversion of Program 5-5.

For example, suppose we form a table of the squares of the decimal digits. The following program uses it to square the digit in 400, placing the square in 401.

```
MOV    AL,[400H]      ;GET DATA
MOV    BX,380H        ;GET BASE ADDRESS OF TABLE
XLAT                  ;GET SQUARE FROM TABLE
MOV    [401H],AL      ;SAVE SQUARE
INT    20H

ORG    380H           ;SQUARES OF DECIMAL DIGITS
DB     0,1,4,9,16,25,36,49,64,81
```

ORG (Set Origin) is an assembler directive (called a *pseudo-operation*); it indicates where the object code generated from subsequent statements is to be placed in memory. The directive DB (Define Byte-Length Data) places a list of 8-bit data items in the next available locations.

Program 9-6 is the DEBUG version. Remember that the table entries are in hex (in case you are wondering why $4^2 = 10$!). You can use DB and DW (Define Word-Length Data) in DEBUG programs; both take commas between operands and ASCII characters inside quotation marks. However, because DEBUG does not allow ORG, you must exit from the current A command and start another at the new address to simulate its effect.

PROGRAM 9-6

Memory Address (Hex)	Memory Contents (Hex)	Instruction (DEBUG Form)
0200	A0	MOV AL,[400]
0201	00	
0202	04	
0203	BB	MOV BX,380
0204	80	
0205	03	
0206	D7	XLAT
0207	A2	MOV [401],AL
0208	01	

PROGRAM 9-6 (continued)		
Memory Address (Hex)	Memory Contents (Hex)	Instruction (DEBUG Form)
0209	04	
020A	CD	INT 20
020B	20	
0380	00	DB 0,
0381	01	1,
0382	04	4,
0383	09	9,
0384	10	10,
0385	19	19,
0386	24	24,
0387	31	31,
0388	40	40,
0389	51	51

Run Program 9-6 for the following examples:

1. [0400] = 04
   Result: [0401] = 10 hex = 16 decimal
2. [0400] = 07
   Result: [0401] = 31 hex = 49 decimal

The table lookup saves time, even though the 8088 has a multiply (MUL) instruction. XLAT takes only 11 cycles, whereas MUL takes 70 to 77 cycles for an 8-bit operation.

Problem 9-9

Write a program that uses the table in Program 9-6 to add the squares of 400 and 401. Put the sum in 402.

EXAMPLE:

[0400] = 03
[0401] = 06

RESULT:

[0402] = 2D (hex), as 2D = 09 (3^2) + 24 (6^2). In decimal, this is
45 = 9 + 36.

Problem 9-10

Write a program that uses a table to cube a decimal digit. Allow two bytes for
each entry, as some cubes exceed 256. Assume that the data is in 400 and put
the result in 401 and 402 (MSBs in 402).

EXAMPLES:

1. [0400] = 03
     Result: [0401] = 1B
             [0402] = 00
2. [0400] = 07
     Result: [0401] = 57
             [0402] = 01

The results are hexadecimal numbers.

Problem 9-11

Write a program that takes the four-digit square root of a decimal digit. The
digit is in 400 and the square root ends up in 401 and 402 (more significant
digits in 402). Use the following table starting at 380; enter it with a DW
pseudo-operation.

Value	Square Root
0	00.00
1	01.00
2	01.41
3	01.73
4	02.00
5	02.24
6	02.45
7	02.65
8	02.83
9	03.00

EXAMPLES:

1. [0400] = 03
     Result: [0401] = 73
              [0402] = 01
2. [0400] = 07
     Result: [0401] = 65
              [0402] = 02

Problem 9-12

Extend the answer to Problem 9-11 to produce a six-digit square root in 401, 402, and 403 (most significant digits in 403). Use the following table:

Value	Square Root
0	00.0000
1	01.0000
2	01.4142
3	01.7321
4	02.0000
5	02.2361
6	02.4495
7	02.6458
8	02.8284
9	03.0000

EXAMPLES:

1. [0400] = 02
     Result: [0401] = 42
              [0402] = 41
              [0403] = 01
2. [0400] = 06
     Result: [0401] = 95
              [0402] = 44
              [0403] = 02

If the table is long, one option is to keep only some entries in memory. You could, for example, keep every tenth entry and interpolate to get intermediate values.

Key Point Summary

1. BCD is a convenient way to represent decimal numbers, as each digit is coded separately. However, BCD requires more memory and processing instructions than the binary representation.
2. The 8088 processor has special decimal arithmetic instructions. DAA converts a byte-length binary sum to decimal, and DAS does the same to a byte-length binary difference. Both operate only on register AL; DAA works only after an ADC AL or ADD AL instruction, whereas DAS works only after an SBB AL or SUB AL instruction.
3. Multiple-precision arithmetic requires a series of 8-bit or 16-bit operations. The Carry flag transfers carries or borrows between them. Decimal operations must be done one byte at a time.
4. Lookup tables provide a simple way to do complex arithmetic. The lookup procedure depends only on the organization of the table and the length of the elements; it does not depend on the data values or the function involved.

Subroutines and the Stack

Purpose To learn how to write and use subroutines.

What You Should Learn
1. Why subroutines are useful.
2. How the processor's RAM stack works.
3. How to transfer control to and from subroutines.
4. How to use the stack for data storage.
5. How to use I/O routines as subroutines.
6. How to make subroutines more general and easier to use.
7. How to transfer control to one of a set of subroutines.

Reference Materials

Eccles, W. J. *Microprocessor Systems: A 16-Bit Approach*. Reading, MA: Addison-Wesley, 1985, pp. 175–182, 187–190, 208–211.

Gorsline, G. W. *16-Bit Modern Microcomputers*. Englewood Cliffs, NJ: Prentice-Hall, 1985, pp. 16–25 (program flow-of-control instructions), 93–99 (subprocedures), 245–246 (procedures), 255–256 (targets of jump and call instructions).

Liu, Y. C., and G. A. Gibson. *Microcomputer Systems: The 8086/8088 Family* (2nd ed.). Englewood Cliffs, NJ: Prentice-Hall, 1986, pp. 151–155 (stacks), 155–169 (procedures).

An Introduction to ASM86, Santa Clara, CA: Intel Corporation, pp. 55–59 (the PL/M procedural interface).

Terms   **Call:**   *see* **Subroutine call.**

Indexed jump: jump to an indexed address.

Overflow (of a stack):   exceeding the amount of memory allocated to a stack

Parameter: an item that a subroutine needs to execute properly.

Passing parameters: making parameters available to a subroutine.

Pop: remove an operand from a stack.

Push: store an operand in a stack.

Stack: a section of memory accessed in a last-in, first-out manner. That is, data is added to or removed from it through its top; new data is placed above the old data, and removing a data item makes the one below it the new top.

Stack pointer: a register that contains the address of the top of a stack.

Subroutine: a subprogram that another program can call.

Subroutine call: the process in which a computer transfers control to a subroutine, while retaining the information required to resume its current program.

Subroutine linkage: the mechanism that allows a computer to resume its current program after executing a subroutine.

Underflow (of a stack):   attempting to remove more data from a stack than has been entered into it.

8088
Instructions   **CALL: call subroutine; subtract 2 from the stack pointer, save the instruction pointer (the value after fetching the CALL) at the top of the stack, and jump to the specified address.**

POP: load register or memory from stack; load a 16-bit register or pair of memory locations from the top of the stack, then add 2 to the stack pointer.

POPF: load flags from stack; load the flags from the top of the stack, then add 2 to the stack pointer.

PUSH: store register or memory in stack; subtract 2 from the stack pointer, then store a 16-bit register or pair of memory locations at the top of the stack.

PUSHF: store flags in stack; subtract 2 from the stack pointer, then store the flags at the top of the stack.

RET: return from subroutine; load the instruction pointer from the top of the stack, then add 2 to the stack pointer.

Rationale and Terminology

Most tasks we have described occur repeatedly in real applications. Actual programs often, for example, perform many time delays, code conversions, and arithmetic functions. Clearly, repeating sequences of instructions would waste memory and programming time. We would prefer to use one copy of each common sequence.

To do this, the processor must suspend its current program, execute a sequence, and resume the current program where it left off. Then the processor can access the same sequence from many different places. The sequence could even be part of the operating system. In that case, the programmer would not have to code it or load it into memory.

We use the following terms to describe such common sequences of instructions:

- The sequence is a *subroutine*, as it is subordinate to the calling program.
- The process of transferring control to it is a *subroutine call*.
- A data item or an address that it needs is a *parameter*.
- The process of providing it with parameters is *passing parameters*.
- The method by which the computer transfers control to it and back to the calling program is a *subroutine linkage*.

Call and Return Instructions

The CALL and RET instructions are essential to using subroutines; they work as follows:

- CALL (jump to subroutine) saves the instruction pointer in the stack, then jumps. CALL is just a JMP that remembers its origin.
- RET (return from subroutine) loads the instruction pointer from the top of the stack.

A CALL in the main program thus jumps to a subroutine. An RET at the end of the subroutine jumps back to the main program just after the CALL. The subroutine linkage is in the stack; CALL saves the return address there and RET retrieves it. Note that both CALL and RET update the stack pointer automatically.

8088 Stack and Stack Pointer

To explain CALL and RET in more detail, we must describe how the 8088 moves data to and from its stack. It does this as follows (see Figures A-1 and A-2):

1. To save data (called a *push*), it first subtracts 2 from the stack pointer and then stores the data at the top of the stack.
2. To remove data (called a *pop*), it first loads the data from the top of the stack and then adds 2 to the stack pointer.

The stack pointer must always contain an even value; the effects of its having an odd value are too awful to describe in a family-oriented book.

Figure A-1

Entering data into the stack (*a push*).

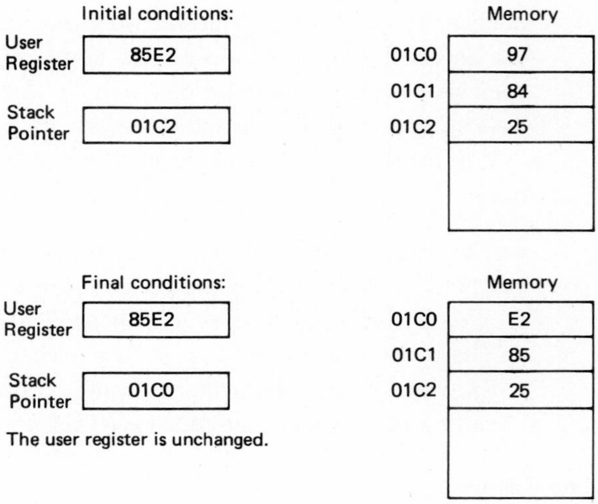

Initial conditions:

| User Register | 85E2 |
| Stack Pointer | 01C2 |

Memory	
01C0	97
01C1	84
01C2	25

Final conditions:

| User Register | 85E2 |
| Stack Pointer | 01C0 |

The user register is unchanged.

Memory	
01C0	E2
01C1	85
01C2	25

Figure A-2

Removing data from the stack (*a pop* or pull).

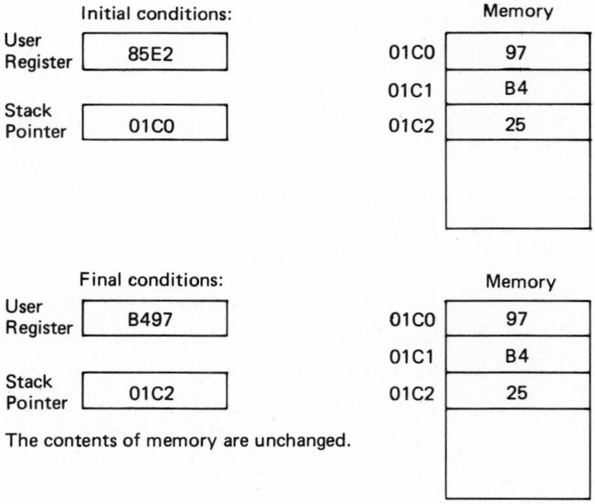

Initial conditions:

| User Register | 85E2 |
| Stack Pointer | 01C0 |

Memory	
01C0	97
01C1	B4
01C2	25

Final conditions:

| User Register | B497 |
| Stack Pointer | 01C2 |

The contents of memory are unchanged.

Memory	
01C0	97
01C1	B4
01C2	25

Note the following:

1. The stack is just an ordinary area of memory. The processor moves its top up or down by decreasing or increasing the stack pointer (examine Figures A-1 and A-2 carefully).

2. The programmer (or the monitor program) selects where the stack begins by initializing the stack pointer. Since DEBUG puts its stack near the end of its default segment, we will start ours at 180 to avoid confusion and still not impinge on our standard program and data areas. Programs seldom change the stack pointer explicitly after it has been initialized. Later we will often not even load the stack pointer, thus leaving the stack wherever DEBUG puts it.

3. The stack grows down (that is, toward lower addresses). If this makes you uneasy, stand on your head, and everything will be all right.

4. The stack pointer always contains the lowest address actually occupied by the stack. The next available word is at [SP]-2. This means you must start the stack pointer at a value two larger than the stack's highest word address.

5. CALL, RET, PUSH, and POP all transfer 16 bits to or from the stack. As usual, the less significant byte always ends up at the lower address.

EXAMPLES:

a. [SP]   = 016E
   [IP]   = 021C
   [021C] = E8   (operation code for CALL with relative addressing)
   [021D] = 19   (16-bit relative offset)
   [021E] = 00

After the processor executes CALL 238H (occupying addresses 21C through 21E),

[SP] = [SP] − 2 = 016C, as a two-byte address has been saved in the stack.

[IP] = 021F + 0019 = 0238, the starting address of the subroutine.

[016C] = 1F, the low byte of the address immediately after the CALL.

[016D] = 02, the high byte of the address immediately after the CALL.

Note that CALL requires a 16-bit relative offset. There is no short (8-bit) form as there is with jumps.

b. [SP]   = 017C
   [IP]   = 0245
   [017C] = 28
   [017D] = 02

After the processor executes RET,

[SP] = [SP] + 2 = 017E, as a two-byte address has been removed from the stack.

[IP] = [017D][017C] = 0228

The old instruction pointer is lost, just as in a jump instruction. In fact, RET is simply a jump to the address obtained by popping the stack.

6. POP (load register or pair of memory locations from stack) and POPF

(load flags from stack) remove a word of data from the top of the stack. PUSH (store register or pair of memory locations in stack) and PUSHF (store flags in stack) insert a word of data at the top of the stack. All these instructions update the stack pointer automatically.

EXAMPLES:

a. [SP] = 0166
[AX] = E1F2

After the processor executes PUSH AX,
[SP] = [SP] − 2 = 0164
[0164] = [AL] = F2
[0165] = [AH] = E1

Register AX does not change. Note that PUSH decrements the stack pointer before storing AX.

b. [SP]   = 016E
[016E] = 3B
[016F] = 59
After the processor executes POP CX,
[CL] = [016E] = 3B
[CH] = [016F] = 59
[SP] = [SP] + 2 = 0170

Locations 16E and 16F do not change, but they are no longer part of the stack. The stack expands and contracts like ocean waves that regularly cover and then uncover parts of the shoreline. Note that POP increments the stack pointer after loading CX.

Guidelines for Stack Management

Most beginners find the stack confusing and even a little frightening. However, it is easy to manage if you follow these guidelines:

1. Load the stack pointer during system initialization (from reset or power-on). Start the pointer at the highest available RAM address plus 1. For example, if that address is 017F, start the stack pointer at 0180. Be sure the pointer is even.
2. Always pair stack operations. Pair each CALL with an RET and each PUSH or PUSHF with a POP or POPF. This is like pairing left and right parentheses in arithmetic or opening and closing quotation marks in sentences. The added constraint is that each path through a program must have the same effect on the stack.

3. Don't be fancy. Leave the stack and stack pointer alone, except for CALL, RET, PUSH, and POP instructions. Simple programs rarely need more than 20 bytes for the stack. Leave lots of room so the stack never overflows. Also be sure it never underflows; that is, never try to take more out of the stack than you have put into it. Both overflow and underflow may become problems in programs with many branches. A single erroneous path can cause a malignancy if it adds or removes extra stack items.

Note that the stack pointer must contain a RAM address. Occasionally on the IBM PC, executing incorrect instructions will place a ROM or unassigned address in the stack pointer. Then neither the G nor the T command will work properly, as both use the stack. You can solve this problem by using the R command to reload registers SS (set it to the value in DS) and SP (set it to FFEE).

Subroutine Linkages in the Stack

Let us see how CALL and RET work in a simple situation. Enter the following program into memory.

STARTING AT 200H

```
MOV    SP,180H        ;INITIALIZE USER STACK POINTER
CALL   260H           ;GO TO SUBROUTINE
INT    3              ;EXIT AND DISPLAY REGISTERS
```

STARTING AT 260H

```
MOV    [400H],SP       ;SAVE STACK POINTER
INT    3               ;EXIT AND DISPLAY REGISTERS
```

Program A-1 is the DEBUG version.

PROGRAM A-1		
Memory Address (Hex)	Memory Contents (Hex)	Instruction (DEBUG Form)
0200	BC	*MOV SP,180*
0201	80	
0202	01	
0203	E8	*CALL 260*
0204	5A	

PROGRAM A-1 (continued)		
Memory Address (Hex)	Memory Contents (Hex)	Instruction (DEBUG Form)
0205	00	
0206	CC	INT 3
0260	89	MOV [400],SP
0261	26	
0262	00	
0263	04	
0264	CC	INT 3

Note the 16-bit relative offset (260–206) immediately after the operation code for CALL.

Problem A-1

What is in the stack pointer and in locations 17E, 17F, 400, and 401 after you run Program A-1? What happens to the stack pointer if you reset the computer by pressing Ctrl-Alt-Del? Do 17E and 17F change? What happens if you exit DEBUG with the Q command, then reload it?

Problem A-2

What do the stack pointer and locations 17E and 17F contain at the end if you replace the INT 3 in 264 with RET? Explain the changes.

Problem A-3

What are the final values of the stack pointer and locations 17C through 17F if you put the following instructions in memory? Remember to run the main program starting at 200. You can examine 17C through 17F with the command D 17C L 4.

0260	89	MOV [400],SP
0261	26	
0262	00	
0263	04	
0264	E8	CALL 280
0265	19	

0266	00		
0267	CC	INT	3
0280	89	MOV	[402],SP
0281	26		
0282	02		
0283	04		
0284	CC	INT	3

What do you find in 400 through 403? What happens if you revise the program as follows?

0260	89	MOV	[400],SP
0261	26		
0262	00		
0263	04		
0264	E8	CALL	280
0265	19		
0266	00		
0267	89	MOV	[404],SP
0268	26		
0269	04		
026A	04		
026B	CC	INT	3
0280	89	MOV	[402],SP
0281	26		
0282	02		
0283	04		
0284	C3	RET	

Saving Registers in the Stack

If you save registers in the stack before a call, you need not worry about whether the subroutine affects them. Remember the following:

1. You can save and restore any 16-bit register with PUSH and POP. The only way to save and restore an 8-bit register is as part of a 16-bit register.
2. You can save and restore the flags (Figure 2-3) with PUSHF and POPF.

3. You can save and restore memory locations directly using PUSH and POP without going through registers.
4. You must restore registers in the opposite of the order in which you saved them. For example, if you saved them with

```
PUSH    AX
PUSH    BX
PUSH    CX
PUSH    DI
PUSH    DX
PUSH    SI
PUSHF
```

you must restore them with

```
POPF
POP     SI
POP     DX
POP     DI
POP     CX
POP     BX
POP     AX
```

Remember that the last item placed in the stack is the first one retrieved.

Delay Subroutine

The following subroutine derived from Program 4-3 gives a 1-ms delay:

```
DLYMS:  MOV     CX,0CBH      ;DELAY 1 MS
DLY:    DEC     CX
        JNZ     DLY
        RET
```

We can use it in a main program as follows:

```
        MOV     SP,180H      ;INITIALIZE USER STACK POINTER
        CALL    DLYMS        ;DELAY 1 MS
        INT     20H
```

Program A-2 is the DEBUG version of the main program and subroutine.

	PROGRAM A-2			
Memory Address (Hex)	Memory Contents (Hex)		Instruction (DEBUG Form)	
0200	BC		MOV	SP,180
0201	80			
0202	01			
0203	E8		CALL	260
0204	5A			
0205	00			
0206	CD		INT	20
0207	20			
0260	B9	DLYMS:	MOV	CX,CB
0261	CB			
0262	00			
0263	49	DLY:	DEC	CX
0264	75		JNZ	263
0265	FD			
0266	C3		RET	

Problem A-4

Make the subroutine preserve the flags and register CX. How much do the new instructions add to the execution time? Change the initial count in the revision to make the delay 1 ms.

Problem A-5

Revise the subroutine to produce a delay in seconds instead of milliseconds. The subroutine should preserve all registers and flags. Use register AX for the count in seconds and use the 1-s delay program from Problem 8-8.

EXAMPLE:

[AX] = 0005 gives a delay of 5 s.

Input Subroutine

The following subroutine (derived from Program 4-5) encodes a switch closure. It assumes that register AL contains the data from an input port attached to eight switches.

```
IDSW:   MOV   BX,-1     ;SWITCH NUMBER = -1
SRCHS:  INC   BX        ;ADD 1 TO SWITCH NUMBER
        SHR   AL,1      ;IS NEXT SWITCH CLOSED?
        JC    SRCHS     ;NO, KEEP LOOKING
        MOV   AL,BL     ;RETURN SWITCH NUMBER IN AL
        RET
```

Program A-3 is the DEBUG version. We started it at 270 to avoid a conflict with the 1-ms delay (Program A-2). The following program waits until a switch is closed at port A of 8255 device P1 and then uses Program A-3 to identify it.

PROGRAM A-3			
Memory Address (Hex)	Memory Contents (Hex)		Instruction (DEBUG Form)
0270	BB	IDSW:	MOV BX,-1
0271	FF		
0272	FF		
0273	43	SRCHS:	INC BX
0274	D0		SHR AL,1
0275	E8		
0276	72		JC 273
0277	FB		
0278	88		MOV AL,BL
0279	D8		
027A	C3		RET

```
        MOV   SP,180H      ;INITIALIZE USER STACK POINTER
        MOV   DX,0FF00H    ;SET INPUT DATA PORT
WAITC:  IN    AL,DX        ;GET DATA FROM SWITCHES
        CMP   AL,0FFH      ;ARE ANY SWITCHES CLOSED?
        JE    WAITC        ;NO, WAIT
        CALL  IDSW         ;YES, IDENTIFY CLOSED SWITCH
        MOV   [400H],AL    ;SAVE SWITCH NUMBER
        INT   20H
```

Program A-4 is the DEBUG version of the main program. Enter and run it. Note that we use register AL for both the input parameter and the result; standardized parameter passing methods like this make subroutines easier to use, although somewhat longer and slower.

	PROGRAM A-4			
Memory Address (Hex)	Memory Contents (Hex)		Instruction (DEBUG Form)	
0200	BC		MOV	SP,180
0201	80			
0202	01			
0203	BA		MOV	DX,FF00
0204	00			
0205	FF			
0206	EC	WAITC:	IN	AL,DX
0207	3C		CMP	AL,FF
0208	FF			
0209	74		JE	206
020A	FB			
020B	E8		CALL	270
020C	62			
020D	00			
020E	A2		MOV	[400],AL
020F	00			
0210	04			
0211	CD		INT	20
0212	20			

Problem A-6

How could you make Program A-4 examine the switches once and end with either the switch number or FF (if no switches are closed) in 400?

Problem A-7

Make Program A-4 wait for the number of switch closures specified in 402 and save the entries starting at 340. Use subroutine DLYMS to provide a 1-ms delay for debouncing. You may want to modify DLYMS and IDSW so they do not affect any registers (see Problem A-4).

EXAMPLE:

If [0402] = 03 and you close switches 0, 6, and 5 in that order, the result should be

$$[0340] = 00$$
$$[0341] = 06$$
$$[0342] = 05$$

Assume that you have only one switch closed at a time.

Output Subroutine

The next subroutine (derived from Programs 5-1 and 5-3) converts a decimal digit in register AL to an ASCII character, and shows it near the center of the screen. Program A-5 is the DEBUG version. The screen is blank if AL does not contain a decimal digit.

```
DSP1:     PUSH   AX          ;SAVE DATA
          MOV    AH,0FH      ;CLEAR SCREEN
          INT    10H
          SUB    AH,AH
          INT    10H
          MOV    DH,12       ;ROW 12
          MOV    DL,35       ;COLUMN 35
          SUB    BH,BH
          MOV    AH,2
          INT    10H         ;POSITION CURSOR
          POP    AX          ;RESTORE DATA
          CMP    AL,10       ;IS DATA A DECIMAL DIGIT?
          JAE    EXITDS      ;NO, NO CONVERSION
                             ;  NECESSARY
          ADD    AL,'0'      ;YES, CONVERT TO ASCII
                             ;  DIGIT
          MOV    AH,0EH      ;WRITE CHARACTER
          INT    10H
EXITDS:   RET
```

PROGRAM A-5			
Memory Address (Hex)	Memory Contents (Hex)		Instruction (DEBUG Form)
02A0	50	DSP1:	PUSH AX
02A1	B4		MOV AH,F
02A2	0F		
02A3	CD		INT 10
02A4	10		
02A5	28		SUB AH,AH
02A6	E4		
02A7	CD		INT 10
02A8	10		
02A9	B6		MOV DH,C
02AA	0C		
02AB	B2		MOV DL,23
02AC	23		
02AD	28		SUB BH,BH
02AE	FF		
02AF	B4		MOV AH,2
02B0	02		
02B1	CD		INT 10
02B2	10		
02B3	58		POP AX
02B4	3C		CMP AL,A
02B5	0A		
02B6	73		JAE 2BE
02B7	06		
02B8	04		ADD AL,30
02B9	30		
02BA	B4		MOV AH,E
02BB	0E		
02BC	CD		INT 10
02BD	10		
02BE	C3	EXITDS:	RET

Problem A-8

Write a main program that uses Program A-5 and the 1-s delay routine (Problem 8-8) to show [400] near the center of the screen for 1 s. Run it with [400] = 05.

Problem A-9

Make Program A-5 accept the row number (0 through 24) in register DH and the column number (0 through 79) in register DL.

EXAMPLE:

$$[AL] = 03 \text{ (data)}$$
$$[DH] = 04 \text{ (row number)}$$
$$[DL] = 40 \text{ (column number, 64 decimal)}$$

RESULT:

3 appears in column 64 of row 4 (near the top, right-hand corner).

Calling Variable Addresses

Some applications require subroutine calls with variable addresses. For example, many interactive systems ask the operator what to do next (such as continue, start over, change parameters, repeat the latest operation, report results, or stop). Many systems also have function keys that the operator uses for common tasks, such as mathematical or statistical functions, loading programs or data, or graphics operations. In either case, the system does not know which subroutine to execute until the operator selects one.

Assume that we have a table of starting addresses. For example, in a calculator, they might be entry points for the sine, cosine, exponential, logarithm, reciprocal, and other mathematical routines. In a piece of test equipment, they might be entry points for the self-test, initial condition setting, parameter selection, data analysis, and reporting routines. To transfer control to a particular routine, all we need is the table's base address and the entry number.

The following subroutine uses an indexed JMP to jump to an address stored in memory. It must double the index before jumping. Program A-6 is the DEBUG version. We have assumed that the table of addresses starts at 340.

```
JCALC:  MOV   BL,AL        ;GET ENTRY NUMBER
        SUB   BH,BH        ;EXTEND ENTRY NUMBER TO 16 BITS
        SHL   BX,1         ;DOUBLE IT FOR TWO-BYTE ENTRIES
        JMP   [BX+340H]    ;TRANSFER CONTROL TO ENTRY
```

Subroutine JCALC requires an address table and an INT 3 instruction at each destination for testing. For example, if the table is

```
ORG   340H
DW    260H, 280H, 2A0H, 2C0H
```

we must put INT 3 in 260, 280, 2A0, and 2C0.

Enter and run Program A-6 with this four-entry table. Test it for [AL] = 0, 1, 2, and 3.

PROGRAM A-6			
Memory Address (Hex)	Memory Contents (Hex)		Instruction (DEBUG Form)
0240	88	*JCALC:*	*MOV BL,AL*
0241	C3		
0242	28		*SUB BH,BH*
0243	FF		
0244	D1		*SHL BX,1*
0245	E3		
0246	FF		*JMP [BX+340]*
0247	A7		
0248	40		
0249	03		
0260	CC		*INT 3*
0280	CC		*INT 3*
02A0	CC		*INT 3*
02C0	CC		*INT 3*
0340	60		*DW 260,*
0341	02		
0342	80		*280,*
0343	02		
0344	A0		*2A0,*
0345	02		
0346	C0		*2C0*
0347	02		

Problem A-10

Write a main program that sets the stack pointer to 180, loads the data from location 400, and then calls Program A-6. What are the final contents of the stack pointer and locations 17E and 17F if [400] = 0? What happens if you replace the INT 3's in 260, 280, 2A0, and 2C0 with RETs?

Problem A-11

Revise Program A-6 to exit immediately if AL's contents are invalid (that is, larger than 3). Another approach to error handling is to end the table with an error exit, then replace any invalid entry with the table's length. Revise Program A-6 to do this. (*Hint:* For example, in the abovementioned case, we would put an error exit in 348 and 349. The program would replace any entry above 4 with 4, thus causing a jump to the error exit.)

Key Point Summary

1. You can make a sequence of instructions available from any-where in a program by coding it as a subroutine. We refer to the transfer of control to it as a subroutine call, and to the items it needs as parameters.
2. On the 8088, a CALL instruction in the calling program saves the instruction pointer in the stack before jumping to a subroutine. An RET instruction at the end of the subroutine returns control to the calling program by loading the instruction pointer from the top of the stack.
3. The stack is just an ordinary area of read/write memory. The stack pointer contains the lowest filled address. All that happens as the stack expands or contracts is that the stack pointer decreases or increases. The stack grows down (that is, toward lower addresses).
4. The programmer must initialize the stack pointer before calling subroutines or using the stack.
5. You can use the stack for temporary storage. This is convenient, as the stack is ordered and easy to expand.
6. Standard parameter-passing methods and saving and restoring registers make subroutines easier to use. These approaches make it unnecessary to know exactly how each subroutine works. But they also make subroutines longer and slower because of the extra overhead.
7. A program can choose among subroutines with an indexed jump or call. But because the addresses are 16 bits long, the program must double the index before jumping.

Handshake Input / Output

Purpose   To learn how to perform I/O using handshake status and control signals.

What You
Should Learn
1. How synchronous and asynchronous I/O work.
2. How to manage handshake status inputs and control outputs in software.
3. The features of an 8255 Programmable Peripheral Interface (PPI).
4. How to select a PPI's operating mode.
5. How to handshake with a PPI.
6. The advantages and disadvantages of programmable I/O devices.

Parts Required
- Two switches attached to bits 2 and 4 of port C of 8255 device P1 as shown in Figure B-1. Table B-1 contains the pin assignments. These switches should be debounced with cross-coupled NAND gates.
- Four LEDs attached to bits 0, 1, 3, and 5 of port C of 8255 device P1 as shown in Figure B-2. Table B-1 contains the pin assignments. The LEDs should be attached by their cathodes.

Table B-1
I/O Connector Pin
Assignments for
Port P1C

Assignment	Pin
Bit 0	11
Bit 1	12
Bit 2	13
Bit 3	14
Bit 4	15
Bit 5	16
Bit 6	17
Bit 7	18

Figure B-1

Attachment of switches to bits 2 and 4 of port C of 8255 device P1.

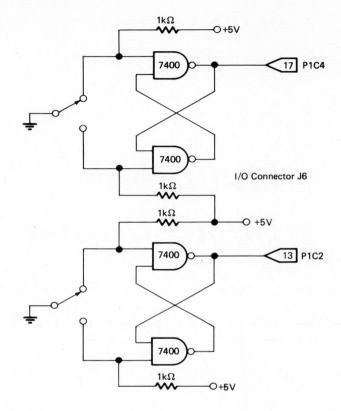

Figure B-2

Attachment of LEDs to bits 0, 1, 3, and 5 of port C of 8255 device P1.

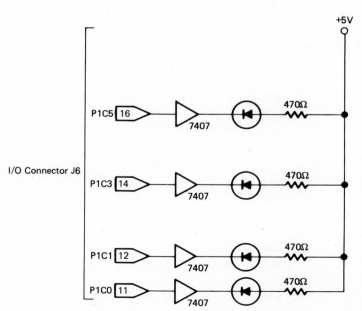

Reference Materials
Comer, D. J. *Microprocessor-Based System Design*. New York: Holt, Rinehart and Winston, 1986, secs. 5.3 (general I/O interface), 5.4A (programmed I/O), 5.6C (parallel I/O chips).

Gorsline, G. W. *16-Bit Modern Microcomputers*. Englewood Cliffs, NJ: Prentice-Hall, 1985, pp. 142–156 (I/O protocols).

Liu, Y. C., and G. A. Gibson. *Microcomputer Systems: The 8086/8088 Family*, (2nd ed.). Englewood Cliffs, NJ: Prentice-Hall, 1986, pp. 229–240 (I/O programming), 369–377 (parallel communication).

Microsystem Components Handbook: Microprocessors and Peripherals, Volume II. Santa Clara, CA: Intel Corporation, 1985, pp. 5-273 to 5-293 (8255A Programmable Peripheral Interface).

Terms
Acknowledgment: a signal indicating the successful completion of the latest operation.

Asynchronous: operating without a clock, that is, at irregular intervals.

Clock: a regular series of pulses that controls transitions in a system.

Control (or **command**) **register:** a register that determines how a device operates.

Control signal: a signal that directs an I/O transfer.

Data accepted: a signal indicating that the latest data has been transferred successfully.

Data ready: a signal indicating that new data is available. *Same as* **Valid data**.

Handshake: the exchange of signals by sender and receiver to manage a data transfer.

Latch: a storage device that holds its current contents until they are explicitly changed.

Peripheral ready: a signal indicating that a peripheral can accept more data.

Polling: determining which I/O devices are ready by examining the status of one at a time.

Programmable I/O device: an I/O device whose operating mode is determined by a program.

Ready for data: a signal indicating that the receiver can accept more data.

Status register: a register that indicates the state of a transfer or the operating mode of a device.

Status signal: a signal that indicates the state of a device or an operation.

Strobe: a signal that identifies or describes another set of signals, often used to control a register or buffer.

Synchronous: operating from a clock, that is, at regular intervals.

Valid data: a signal indicating that new data is available.

Synchronous and Asynchronous I/O

So far we have dealt only with simple, slow I/O devices, such as switches and displays. Our main problems have been ignoring meaningless changes in inputs and making outputs last long enough for a peripheral to accept or a person to see. Factors that we have not considered include

1. Whether the peripheral is ready.
2. Whether new data is available.
3. Whether the data has been transferred successfully.

These become key issues with medium-speed peripherals, such as terminals, printers, modems, plotters, mice (mouses?), and card readers.

A successful data transfer requires the following conditions:

1. The receiver must be ready.
2. The data must be available (or *valid*).
3. The receiver must accept the data before it changes.

The sender thus must know whether the receiver is ready and whether it has accepted the data. And the receiver must know whether new data is available.

One approach is to operate from a clock (that is, a regular series of pulses). The receiver must then be ready, and the data must be available and accepted at specific points in the clock cycle (for example, 100 ms after a pulse's rising edge). This method, called *synchronous transfer*, forces the receiver and transmitter to synchronize with the clock.

The major problem with this approach is its rigidity. The only way to change the data rate is by changing the clock. Thus synchronous transfer cannot easily handle peripherals that operate at varying data rates or that send data irregularly. Nor does it allow for simple upgrading or replacement of peripherals (for example, adding a faster printer or modem or substituting a plotter for a printer).

An alternative is to use status and control signals to manage the transfer. Typical signals are

READY FOR DATA: active when the receiver can accept more data.

VALID DATA: active when new data is available.

DATA ACCEPTED: active when the receiver has accepted the latest data.

The sender must provide VALID DATA; the receiver must provide READY FOR DATA and DATA ACCEPTED. This method, called *asynchronous transfer*, needs no clock and allows any data rate.

The asynchronous approach is flexible (because the participants determine the timing) and simple (no clock or synchronization is necessary). Its drawbacks are the extra signals and lower maximum data rates (because the signals must overlap properly).

We commonly use the terms polling and handshaking to describe asynchronous transfers. *Polling* is examining each peripheral's status individually to determine whether it is ready for a data transfer. *Handshaking* is exchanging status and control signals to manage a data transfer; the handshake validates the transfer much as a human handshake indicates that both parties have accepted a contract.

Using Data Inputs for Status

One way to handle status and control signals is to treat them as data. They then act like the binary inputs and outputs considered in Laboratories 2 and 3. In our examples, we will use bit 4 of port C of 8255 device P1 as a status input and bit 3 of port C as a control output.

To use port C, we must know how to configure and address it. The 8255's control register contains bits that govern the upper and lower halves of port C (that is, bits 4 to 7 and 0 to 3). Bit 3 makes the upper half input (1) or output (0); bit 0 does the same for the lower half. On the add-on I/O board, port C is at address FF02 (see Table B-2).

Table B-2

Port Addresses in 8255 Device P1 (on the Add-on I/O Board)

Port Designation	Port Address
P1A	FF00
P1B	FF01
P1C	FF02
P1 Control Register	FF03

The following program (Program B-1 is the DEBUG version) assigns directions to 8255 device P1's ports and turns off the LEDs. We will use it for initialization in the next series of examples.

```
MOV   DX,0FF03H        ;GET CONTROL REGISTER ADDRESS
MOV   AL,10011000B     ;MAKE PORT A INPUT, PORT B OUTPUT
OUT   DX,AL            ;  PORT C—UPPER HALF INPUT, LOWER
                       ;  HALF OUTPUT
```

```
MOV   DX,0FF01H       ;GET PORT B ADDRESS
MOV   AL,0FFH         ;TURN OFF THE LEDS
OUT   DX,AL
```

PROGRAM B-1		
Memory Address (Hex)	Memory Contents (Hex)	Instruction (DEBUG Form)
0200	BA	MOV DX,FF03
0201	03	
0202	FF	
0203	B0	MOV AL,98
0204	98	
0205	EE	OUT DX,AL
0206	BA	MOV DX,FF01
0207	01	
0208	FF	
0209	B0	MOV AL,FF
020A	FF	
020B	EE	OUT DX,AL

Let us now use bit 4 of port C for status. During input, a status signal (often called a *strobe*) may show whether new data is available (for example, whether an operator has pressed a key on a keyboard). The following program waits for the status switch to close. It then reads the data from port A, inverts it (because the LED interface uses negative logic), and displays it on the LEDs at port B. Program B-2 is the DEBUG version.

```
        MOV    DX,0FF02H      ;ACCESS STATUS/CONTROL PORT
WAITR:  IN     AL,DX          ;IS DATA READY?
        TEST   AL,00010000B
        JNZ    WAITR          ;NO, WAIT
        MOV    DX,0FF00H      ;YES, READ DATA
        IN     AL,DX
        MOV    DX,0FF01H      ;GET PORT B ADDRESS
        NOT    AL             ;INVERT DATA
        OUT    DX,AL          ;SHOW INVERTED DATA ON LEDS
        INT    20H
```

Open the status switch and run Program B-2. What happens? Does opening or closing other switches (at port A or C) have any effect? Open all other switches, and then close the status switch. What happens? The processor accepts only the data that is present when the status signal becomes active. Changes that occur while the status signal is inactive are ignored.

	PROGRAM B-2		
Memory Address (Hex)	Memory Contents (Hex)		Instruction (DEBUG Form)
020C	BA		MOV DX,FF02
020D	02		
020E	FF		
020F	EC	WAITR:	IN AL,DX
0210	A8		TEST AL,10
0211	10		
0212	75		JNZ 20F
0213	FB		
0214	BA		MOV DX,FF00
0215	00		
0216	FF		
0217	EC		IN AL,DX
0218	BA		MOV DX,FF01
0219	01		
021A	FF		
021B	F6		NOT AL
021C	D0		
021D	EE		OUT DX,AL
021E	CD		INT 20
021F	20		

Problem B-1

Change Program B-2 to make the status signal active-high. How would you make the program wait for the status signal to go low and then back high?

Problem B-2

Revise Program B-2 to use bit 2 of port C as the status signal. Be sure to modify Program B-1 to make the lower half of port C input. Also remember to restore the original initialization before doing the next problem or example.

Problem B-3

Extend Program B-2 to read data into an array of four elements starting at 340. It should read a data item each time the status signal (bit 4 of port C) goes low. Because the status switches are debounced, no delay is necessary.

During output, the status signal may show whether the peripheral is ready for more data (for example, whether a printer has finished with the last character). We often call this kind of signal an *acknowledgment*. The next program waits for the status switch to close before sending data from 340. Program B-3 is the DEBUG version.

```
          MOV   DX,0FF02H        ;ACCESS STATUS/CONTROL PORT
WAITR:    IN    AL,DX            ;IS PERIPHERAL READY?
          TEST  AL,00010000B
          JNZ   WAITR            ;NO, WAIT
          MOV   AL,[340H]        ;YES, GET DATA FROM MEMORY
          MOV   DX,0FF01H        ;ACCESS OUTPUT PORT
          NOT   AL               ;REVERSE POLARITY OF DATA
          OUT   DX,AL            ;SEND DATA TO LEDS
          INT   20H
```

PROGRAM B-3				
Memory Address (Hex)	Memory Contents (Hex)		Instruction (DEBUG Form)	
020C	BA		MOV	DX,FF02
020D	02			
020E	FF			
020F	EC	WAITR:	IN	AL,DX
0210	A8		TEST	AL,10
0211	10			
0212	75		JNZ	20F
0213	FB			
0214	A0		MOV	AL,[340]
0215	40			
0216	03			
0217	BA		MOV	DX,FF01
0218	01			
0219	FF			
021A	F6		NOT	AL
021B	D0			
021C	EE		OUT	DX,AL
021D	CD		INT	20
021E	20			

Run Program B-3 with [0340] = AA (10101010 binary). What happens before you close the status switch? Does it matter what 340 contains? What happens when you close the status switch? The old data stays until the peripheral specifically requests new data or informs the computer that it is ready.

Note how different input and output are. An input peripheral tells the CPU when it has new data, thus starting a transfer. An output peripheral tells the CPU when it is ready for more data, thus completing a transfer. Input peripherals are normally not ready (that is, they usually have no data), whereas output peripherals are normally ready (that is, they usually can accept data). Later we will see these differences reflected in the 8255 PPI's operating modes.

Problem B-4

Make Program B-3 send data from an array of eight elements starting at 340. It should send a new item each time the status signal goes low.

Example array (single light moves right, starting in bit 7):

$$[0340] = 80$$
$$[0341] = 40$$
$$[0342] = 20$$
$$[0343] = 10$$
$$[0344] = 08$$
$$[0345] = 04$$
$$[0346] = 02$$
$$[0347] = 01$$

An alternative sequence (01, 03, 07, 0F, 1F, 3F, 7F, FF) lights one more LED (to the left) in each iteration.

Problem B-5

Make your answer to Problem B-4 exit after sending a zero value. How would you make it stop after sending a value of 0D (an ASCII carriage return)?

Using Data Outputs for Control

We can also use data lines for control signals. A control signal for an input device may show that the computer has read the latest data. The next program stores the data from port A in 340 and then lights the control LED by clearing bit 3 of port C. Program B-4 is the DEBUG version.

```
MOV   DX,0FF00H      ;ACCESS INPUT PORT
IN    AL,DX          ;GET DATA FROM INPUT PORT
MOV   [340H],AL      ;SAVE DATA IN MEMORY
MOV   DX,0FF02H      ;ACCESS STATUS/CONTROL PORT
MOV   AL,11110111B   ;TURN CONTROL LIGHT ON
OUT   DX,AL
INT   20H
```

PROGRAM B-4		
Memory Address (Hex)	Memory Contents (Hex)	Instruction (DEBUG Form)
020C	BA	MOV DX,FF00
020D	00	
020E	FF	
020F	EC	IN AL,DX
0210	A2	MOV [340],AL
0211	40	
0212	03	
0213	BA	MOV DX,FF02
0214	02	
0215	FF	
0216	B0	MOV AL,F7
0217	F7	
0218	EE	OUT DX,AL
0219	CD	INT 20
021A	20	

Enter and run Program B-4. The light shows that the computer has accepted the latest data and is ready for more. Such a signal may be called READY FOR DATA, DATA ACCEPTED, or DATA BUFFER EMPTY.

Problem B-6

Extend Program B-4 to leave the control light on for 1 s. Use the delay routine in Problem 8-8.

In the output case, the control signal tells the peripheral that new data is available. Program B-5 sends the data from 340 to port B and then lights the control LED.

```
MOV   DX,0FF01H          ;ACCESS OUTPUT PORT
MOV   AL,[340H]          ;GET DATA FROM MEMORY
NOT   AL                 ;REVERSE POLARITY OF DATA
OUT   DX,AL              ;SEND DATA TO LEDS
MOV   DX,0FF02H          ;ACCESS STATUS/CONTROL PORT
MOV   AL,11110111B       ;TURN CONTROL LIGHT ON
OUT   DX,AL
INT   20H
```

PROGRAM B-5		
Memory Address (Hex)	Memory Contents (Hex)	Instruction (DEBUG Form)
020C	BA	MOV DX,FF01
020D	01	
020E	FF	
020F	A0	MOV AL,[340]
0210	40	
0211	03	
0212	F6	NOT AL
0213	D0	
0214	EE	OUT DX,AL
0215	BA	MOV DX,FF02
0216	02	
0217	FF	
0218	B0	MOV AL,F7
0219	F7	
021A	EE	OUT DX,AL
021B	CD	INT 20
021C	20	

Problem B-7

Extend Program B-5 to send a data array of eight elements, starting at location 340, to the LEDs. Leave each value on the displays for 1 s and wait 1 s between values. Use the sample data from Problem B-4 and the 1-s delay from Problem 8-8.

Programs B-4 and B-5 assume that we can freely change all of port C when turning on the control light. But in practical applications, this is generally not the case, as the other bits are in use. One way to avoid affecting them is by using the logical functions. For example, procedures to change only bit 3 of port C are

1. Set bit 3 (turn off control light):

```
MOV   DX,0FF02H      ;ACCESS STATUS/CONTROL PORT
IN    AL,DX          ;GET CURRENT DATA
OR    AL,00001000B   ;TURN CONTROL LIGHT OFF
OUT   DX,AL
```

2. Clear bit 3 (turn on control light):

```
MOV   DX,0FF02H      ;ACCESS STATUS/CONTROL PORT
IN    AL,DX          ;GET CURRENT DATA
AND   AL,11110111B   ;TURN CONTROL LIGHT ON
OUT   DX,AL
```

Problem B-8

Revise the answer to Problem B-6 to use logical functions to turn the control light on and off. How would you change your answer if port C were not readable (that is, if IN AL,DX did not read the output latch)?

Although the logical functions work, they are awkward to use. Furthermore, the effects of reading an output port are hardware dependent. Fortunately, the 8255 device has a special way to set or clear (reset) individual bits of port C. It involves sending the device a control byte organized as follows (see Figure B-3):

- Bit 7 = 0 to indicate a bit set/reset operation.
- Bits 6, 5, and 4 are not used.
- Bits 3, 2, and 1 are the bit number (0 through 7).
- Bit 0 is the new value.

Here are some typical examples, assuming that the control register's address is PPICR. Note that we must send the byte to the control register, not to port C.

1. Set bit 0 of port C (that is, make it 1).

```
MOV   DX,PPICR  [FF03]
MOV   AL,00000001B
OUT   DX,AL
```

Here the bit number is 000 (bits 1 through 3) and bit 0 is 1 to set the target bit.

2. Clear bit 5 of port C (that is, make it 0).

```
MOV   DX,PPICR
MOV   AL,00001010B
OUT   DX,AL
```

Here the bit number is 101 (bits 1 through 3) and bit 0 is 0 to clear the target bit.

Figure B-3

Bit set/reset format for 8255 PPI. (Reprinted by permission of Intel Corporation, Santa Clara, CA).

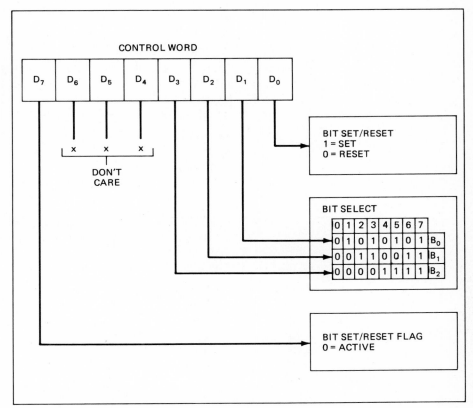

Problem B-9

Revise the answer to Problem B-6 to use the 8255's bit set/reset capability to turn the control light on and off. This approach is shorter and faster than using logical functions, but it is difficult to follow without a thorough understanding of the 8255 device.

Handshaking with Data Lines

Combining Programs B-2 and B-4 (see Program B-6) makes the computer wait for the status signal to become active before accepting the data. It then turns on the control light to indicate the acceptance. Here we have a complete handshake (see Figure B-4). The peripheral indicates that new data is available and the computer, in response, reads the data and acknowledges it.

```
        MOV   DX,0FF02H      ;ACCESS STATUS/CONTROL PORT
WAITR:  IN    AL,DX          ;IS DATA READY?
        TEST  AL,00010000B
        JNZ   WAITR          ;NO, WAIT
        MOV   DX,0FF00H      ;YES, READ DATA
        IN    AL,DX
        MOV   DX,0FF01H      ;SHOW INVERTED DATA ON LEDS
        NOT   AL
        OUT   DX,AL
        MOV   DX,0FF02H      ;TURN ON CONTROL LIGHT
        MOV   AL,11110111B
        OUT   DX,AL
        INT   20H
```

		PROGRAM B-6		
Memory Address (Hex)	Memory Contents (Hex)		Instruction (DEBUG Form)	
020C	BA		MOV	DX,FF02
020D	02			
020E	FF			
020F	EC	WAITR:	IN	AL,DX
0210	A8		TEST	AL,10
0211	10			
0212	75		JNZ	20F
0213	FB			
0214	BA		MOV	DX,FF00
0215	00			
0216	FF			
0217	EC		IN	AL,DX
0218	BA		MOV	DX,FF01
0219	01			
021A	FF			
021B	F6		NOT	AL
021C	D0			

Memory Address (Hex)	Memory Contents (Hex)	Instruction (DEBUG Form)	
021D	EE	OUT	DX,AL
021E	BA	MOV	DX,FF02
021F	02		
0220	FF		
0221	B0	MOV	AL,F7
0222	F7		
0223	EE	OUT	DX,AL
0224	CD	INT	20
0225	20		

PROGRAM B-6 (continued)

Enter and run Program B-6. An obvious problem is that the control light stays on. Clearly, it should go off eventually to allow the next transfer. The control signal may, for example:

1. Stay active only briefly, thus forming a pulse that can be counted (for example, to multiplex displays or communications channels) or latched.
2. Go off when the status signal becomes active again to begin the next transfer. The control signal then indicates that the processor has accepted the latest data (that is, it is a BUFFER EMPTY signal). As we will see later, the 8255 PPI provides this option automatically.
3. Remain active until the program turns it off. This option can meet the timing needs of a variety of peripherals.

Problem B-10

Modify Program B-6 to make the acknowledgment last until the status signal from the peripheral goes high again.

Problem B-11

Modify Program B-6 to use bit 2 of port C as the status input and bit 5 of port C as the control output. Be sure to assign the lower half of port C as input and the upper half as output.

Combining Programs B-3 and B-5 (see Program B-7) makes the computer wait for the status signal to become active before sending the data. It then turns

Figure B-4
Procedure for a
complete input
handshake.

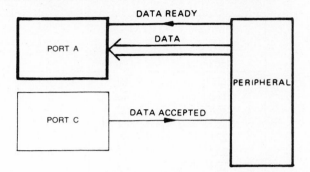

STEP 1
PERIPHERAL PROVIDES DATA AND ACTIVATES DATA READY

The peripheral provides both the data and an active DATA READY signal.

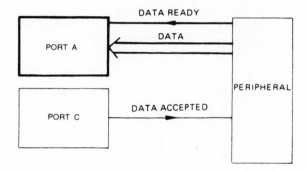

STEP 2
CPU RECOGNIZES THAT DATA READY IS ACTIVE AND READS THE DATA,
THUS PERFORMING THE ACTUAL DATA TRANSFER.

STEP 3
CPU ACTIVATES DATA ACCEPTED, INDICATING THE SUCCESSFUL
COMPLETION OF THE TRANSFER.

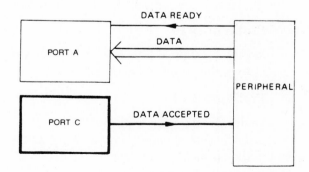

on the control light to mark the transmission. Here again we have a complete
handshake (see Figure B-5), although the order and meaning of the signals

differ from the input case. The peripheral indicates that it can accept data; in response, the computer sends the data and indicates its availability. Run Program B-7 with [0340] = 55.

```
          MOV   DX,0FF02H    ;ACCESS STATUS/CONTROL PORT
WAITR:    IN    AL,DX        ;IS PERIPHERAL READY?
          TEST  AL,00010000B
          JNZ   WAITR        ;NO, WAIT
          MOV   DX,0FF01H    ;YES, ACCESS OUTPUT PORT
          MOV   AL,[340H]    ;GET OUTPUT DATA
          NOT   AL           ;REVERSE DATA POLARITY
          OUT   DX,AL        ;SEND DATA TO LEDS
          MOV   DX,0FF02H    ;INDICATE DATA AVAILABLE
          MOV   AL,11110111B
          OUT   DX,AL
          INT   20H
```

PROGRAM B-7

Memory Address (Hex)	Memory Contents (Hex)		Instruction (DEBUG Form)	
020C	BA		MOV	DX,FF02
020D	02			
020E	FF			
020F	EC	WAITR:	IN	AL,DX
0210	A8		TEST	AL,10
0211	10			
0212	75		JNZ	20F
0213	FB			
0214	BA		MOV	DX,FF01
0215	01			
0216	FF			
0217	A0		MOV	AL,[340]
0218	40			
0219	03			
021A	F6		NOT	AL
021B	D0			
021C	EE		OUT	DX,AL
021D	BA		MOV	DX,FF02
021E	02			
021F	FF			
0220	B0		MOV	AL,F7

	PROGRAM B-7 (continued)	
Memory Address (Hex)	Memory Contents (Hex)	Instruction (DEBUG Form)
0221	F7	
0222	EE	OUT DX,AL
0223	CD	INT 20
0224	20	

Problem B-12

Modify Program B-7 to send data from an array of eight elements, starting at
address 340. Make the data available signal last 1 s after each output operation.

8255 Programmable Peripheral Interface

LSI I/O devices can greatly simplify interfacing and I/O programming. Furthermore, they are smaller, cheaper, more flexible, and more reliable and use
less power than do circuits made from TTL parts.

As an example, consider the 8255 Programmable Peripheral Interface (PPI).
This generalized I/O device can operate in many useful ways. The programmer
selects the operating mode for each port by storing a value in the control register. The value activates circuits in the PPI, much as an instruction does in the
CPU. The circuits in the PPI, however, are much simpler than those in the CPU
and are intended for common I/O functions, such as handshaking.

As mentioned earlier, each PPI contains three 8-bit ports (A, B, and C) and a
control register. Sending a byte to the control register with bit 7 set (1) estab-
lishes the operating mode, as shown in Figure B-6. Note the following:

1. Ports A and B can operate in either mode 0 (ordinary I/O) or mode 1
   (strobed I/O). In mode 1, bits of port C act automatically as status and
   control signals (see Table B-3). Port A can also operate in the bidirectional
   mode 2, in which most of port C acts as its status and control signals. We will
   not discuss mode 2; for a description of it, see Intel's *Microcystem Components Handbook*.

Figure B-5

Procedure for a
complete output
handshake.

STEP 1
PERIPHERAL ACTIVATES PERIPHERAL READY, INDICATING THAT IT
IS ABLE TO ACCEPT DATA.

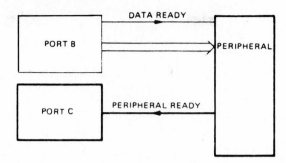

The output peripheral must provide the
input status signal PERIPHERAL READY

STEP 2
CPU RECOGNIZES THAT PERIPHERAL READY IS ACTIVE AND SENDS
THE DATA, THUS PERFORMING THE ACTUAL DATA TRANSFER.

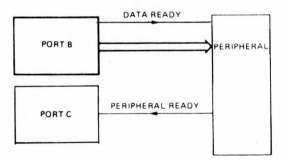

STEP 3
CPU ACTIVATES DATA READY, THUS INFORMING THE PERIPHERAL
THAT NEW DATA IS AVAILABLE.

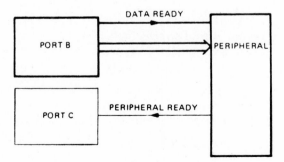

2. RESET makes all ports operate as inputs in mode 0 and clears the output latches.
3. The positions (and meanings) of the bits in the control register are arbitrary and can be determined only from the device specifications.

Figure B-6

Mode definition format for 8255 Programmable Peripheral Interface (PPI). (Reprinted by permission of Intel Corporation, Santa Clara, CA).

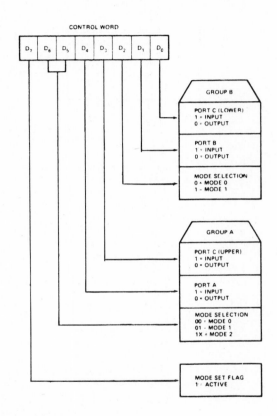

PPI Automatic Status and Control Signals

The PPI's status and control signals work as follows in mode 1, assuming that port A is input and port B is output:

1. A INPUT BUFFER FULL (bit PC5) goes high (1) after A STROBE goes low. It remains high until after port A is read. INPUT BUFFER FULL thus indicates that the port contains data the CPU has not yet read.
2. A STROBE (bit PC4) is a status signal from the input peripheral. A low value (0) allows data to enter the input latch.
3. B ACKNOWLEDGE (bit PC2) is a status signal from the output peripheral. A low value (0) indicates that the peripheral has accepted the latest data and is ready for more.

Table B-3

Mode Definition Summary

Summary of 8255
PPI operating
modes.

	MODE 0		MODE 1		MODE 2
	IN	OUT	IN	OUT	GROUP A ONLY
PA_0	IN	OUT	IN	OUT	←——→
PA_1	IN	OUT	IN	OUT	←——→
PA_2	IN	OUT	IN	OUT	←——→
PA_3	IN	OUT	IN	OUT	←——→
PA_4	IN	OUT	IN	OUT	←——→
PA_5	IN	OUT	IN	OUT	←——→
PA_6	IN	OUT	IN	OUT	←——→
PA_7	IN	OUT	IN	OUT	←——→
PB_0	IN	OUT	IN	OUT	——
PB_1	IN	OUT	IN	OUT	——
PB_2	IN	OUT	IN	OUT	——
PB_3	IN	OUT	IN	OUT	——
PB_4	IN	OUT	IN	OUT	——
PB_5	IN	OUT	IN	OUT	——
PB_6	IN	OUT	IN	OUT	——
PB_7	IN	OUT	IN	OUT	——
PC_0	IN	OUT	$INTR_B$	$INTR_B$	I/O
PC_1	IN	OUT	IBF_B	$\overline{OBF}_B$	I/O
PC_2	IN	OUT	$\overline{STB}_B$	$\overline{ACK}_B$	I/O
PC_3	IN	OUT	$INTR_A$	$INTR_A$	$INTR_A$
PC_4	IN	OUT	$\overline{STB}_A$	I/O	$\overline{STB}_A$
PC_5	IN	OUT	IBF_A	I/O	IBF_A
PC_6	IN	OUT	I/O	$\overline{ACK}_A$	$\overline{ACK}_A$
PC_7	IN	OUT	I/O	$\overline{OBF}_A$	$\overline{OBF}_A$

(MODE 0 OR MODE 1 ONLY — applies to the PB rows in Group A Only column)

Reprinted by permission of Intel Corporation, Santa Clara, CA.

4. B OUTPUT BUFFER FULL (bit PC1) goes low (0) after data has been written into the port and remains low until after B ACKNOWLEDGE goes low. A low value thus indicates that port B contains data that the peripheral has not yet accepted. Note that OUTPUT BUFFER FULL is active-low, whereas INPUT BUFFER FULL is active-high.

8255 PPI Handshake Input

Input through port A proceeds as follows (see Figure B-7):

1. The peripheral sends the data and brings STROBE (VALID DATA) low. INPUT BUFFER FULL goes high.
2. The peripheral brings STROBE high, latching the data into the input port. The data may now change without affecting the port's contents.
3. In response to INPUT BUFFER FULL going high, the CPU reads the data from the port. This returns INPUT BUFFER FULL to its usual (low) state.

Figure B-7

Handshake input
using port A of an
8255 PPI in
mode 1.

Step 1

Peripheral provides data and brings STROBE low.

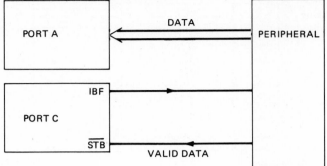

The peripheral provides both the data and an active-low valid data signal.
Data enters the port, and INPUT BUFFER FULL goes high, informing
the peripheral that the port contains data that the CPU has not yet read.

Step 2

Peripheral brings STROBE high, latching data into the port.

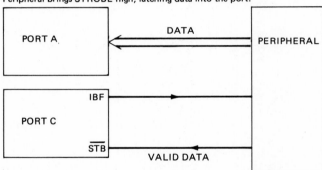

The data is now latched, and the peripheral need not hold it any longer.

Step 3

CPU reads data, bringing INPUT BUFFER FULL LOW.

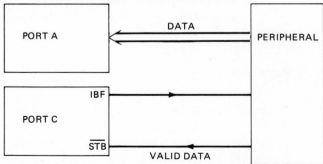

All signals are now inactive and ready for the next transfer.

Here the connection between ports A and C is in hardware rather than in software. Note that the STROBE pulse may be very brief, whereas a VALID DATA signal would have to last much longer for the CPU to handle it in software. Note also that INPUT BUFFER FULL is set and cleared automatically.

The following program (Program B-8 is the DEBUG version) waits until the A INPUT BUFFER FULL signal (bit 5 of port C) goes high. It then reads the data from port A and displays it on the LEDs. The control byte puts both ports in mode 1 (strobed I/O). Closing the A STROBE switch makes the A INPUT BUFFER FULL signal go high. Opening that switch then latches the data into the port.

```
        MOV   DX,0FF03H      ;GET CONTROL REGISTER
                             ;  ADDRESS
        MOV   AL,10110100B   ;MAKE PORT A INPUT, PORT B
                             ;  OUTPUT
        OUT   DX,AL          ;BOTH PORTS IN STROBED MODE
                             ;  (1)
        MOV   DX,0FF01H      ;GET PORT B ADDRESS
        MOV   AL,0FFH        ;TURN OFF THE LEDS
        OUT   DX,AL
        MOV   DX,0FF02H      ;ACCESS STATUS/CONTROL PORT
WAITR:  IN    AL,DX          ;IS DATA AVAILABLE?
        TEST  AL,00100000B
        JZ    WAITR          ;NO, WAIT
        MOV   DX,0FF00H      ;YES, ACCESS INPUT PORT
        IN    AL,DX          ;GET INPUT DATA
        NOT   AL             ;REVERSE DATA POLARITY
        MOV   DX,0FF01H      ;ACCESS OUTPUT PORT
        OUT   DX,AL          ;DISPLAY DATA
        INT   20H
```

Note that a mode 1 initialization supersedes the assignments of halves of port C to input or output. However, the assignments still apply to bits not used for status and control. The positions of the unused bits vary (see Table B-3); they are bits 6 and 7 if A is an input port, but bits 4 and 5 if it is an output port.

	PROGRAM B-8		
Memory Address (Hex)	Memory Contents (Hex)		Instruction (DEBUG Form)
0200	BA		MOV DX,FF03
0201	03		
0202	FF		
0203	B0		MOV AL,B4
0204	B4		
0205	EE		OUT DX,AL
0206	BA		MOV DX,FF01
0207	01		
0208	FF		
0209	B0		MOV AL,FF
020A	FF		
020B	EE		OUT DX,AL
020C	BA		MOV DX,FF02
020D	02		
020E	FF		
020F	EC	WAITR:	IN AL,DX
0210	A8		TEST AL,20
0211	20		
0212	74		JZ 20F
0213	FB		
0214	BA		MOV DX,FF00
0215	00		
0216	FF		
0217	EC		IN AL,DX
0218	F6		NOT AL
0219	D0		
021A	BA		MOV DX,FF01
021B	01		
021C	FF		
021D	EE		OUT DX,AL
021E	CD		INT 20
021F	20		

Enter Program B-8 into memory and single-step it with T commands. Be sure the status switch (bit 4 of port C) is open initially. Watch the buffer full signals (bits 1 and 5). Remember that OUTPUT BUFFER FULL is active-low and the LEDs are connected to the port by their cathodes, so zeros light them. As soon as the program loads the PPI's control register, INPUT BUFFER FULL should go low (LED on) and OUTPUT BUFFER FULL high (LED off). That is, both are initially inactive. Turning off the LEDs at port B should then send OUTPUT

BUFFER FULL low, as this fills the output port. Single-step the program until it enters the polling loop (locations 20F through 213). Here it should simply wait for the input port to be filled.

Now close and open the status switch. INPUT BUFFER FULL should go high as soon as you close it. The program should exit from the polling loop and read the input port, sending INPUT BUFFER FULL low again. Be sure to reopen the status switch before the program reads the input port. If you leave it closed, the port will remain open for new data, and INPUT BUFFER FULL will stay high.

Problem B-13

Revise Program B-8 to load data from port A into four memory locations starting at 340. The new version should load one location each time you close the switch attached to bit 4 of port C. Be sure to reopen the switch and wait for INPUT BUFFER FULL to go low before starting the next iteration. Note that you cannot read the status switch directly in mode 1.

8255 PPI Handshake Output

Output through port B proceeds as follows (see Figure B-8, and remember that OUTPUT BUFFER FULL is active-low):

1. The CPU tests OUTPUT BUFFER FULL. If it is high, the CPU latches the data into the output port, sending OUTPUT BUFFER FULL low. Remember that OUTPUT BUFFER FULL is low when the port is full, unlike INPUT BUFFER FULL, which is high.
2. The peripheral brings the ACKNOWLEDGE (or PERIPHERAL READY) line low, sending OUTPUT BUFFER FULL back high.
3. The peripheral brings the ACKNOWLEDGE line high, ending the acknowledgment and letting the next output send OUTPUT BUFFER FULL low again.

The following program (Program B-9 is the DEBUG version) sends data from location 340 to port B after the switch attached to bit 2 of port C is closed and then reopened. Trace Program B-9 with [0340] = AA. Note that OUTPUT BUFFER FULL goes low when the program turns off the LEDs, high when you close the status switch, and low again when the program actually sends the data (assuming that you have reopened the status switch).

Figure B-8

Handshake output
using port B of an
8255 PPI in
mode 1.

Step 1
CPU checks OUTPUT BUFFER FULL. If it is high, the CPU will perform
an output operation, sending OUTPUT BUFFER FULL low.

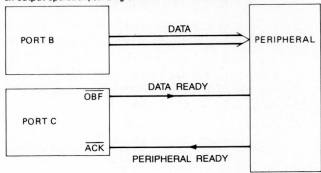

Step 2
Peripheral brings ACKNOWLEDGE low, sending OUTPUT BUFFER FULL high.

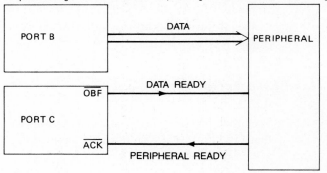

Step 3
Peripheral brings ACKNOWLEDGE high in preparation for the next operation.

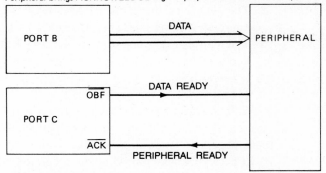

The signals are now ready for the next data transfer.

```
            MOV    DX,0FF03H        ;GET CONTROL REGISTER
                                    ;   ADDRESS
            MOV    AL,10110100B     ;MAKE PORT A INPUT, PORT B
                                    ;   OUTPUT
            OUT    DX,AL            ;BOTH PORTS IN STROBED
                                    ;   MODE(1)
            MOV    DX,0FF01H        ;GET PORT B ADDRESS
            MOV    AL,0FFH          ;TURN OFF THE LEDS
            OUT    DX,AL
            MOV    DX,0FF02H        ;ACCESS STATUS/CONTROL PORT
WAITR:      IN     AL,DX            ;IS PERIPHERAL READY?
            TEST   AL,00000010B
            JNZ    WAITR            ;NO, WAIT
            MOV    DX,0FF01H        ;YES, ACCESS OUTPUT PORT
            MOV    AL,[340H]        ;GET OUTPUT DATA
            NOT    AL               ;REVERSE DATA POLARITY
            OUT    DX,AL            ;DISPLAY DATA
            INT    20H
```

PROGRAM B-9

Memory Address (Hex)	Memory Contents (Hex)		Instruction (DEBUG Form)	
0200	BA		MOV	DX,FF03
0201	03			
0202	FF			
0203	B0		MOV	AL,B4
0204	B4			
0205	EE		OUT	DX,AL
0206	BA		MOV	DX,FF01
0207	01			
0208	FF			
0209	B0		MOV	AL,FF
020A	FF			
020B	EE		OUT	DX,AL
020C	BA		MOV	DX,FF02
020D	02			
020E	FF			
020F	EC	WAITR:	IN	AL,DX
0210	A8		TEST	AL,2
0211	02			

	PROGRAM B-9 (continued)			
Memory Address (Hex)	Memory Contents (Hex)		Instruction (DEBUG Form)	
0212	74	JZ	20F	
0213	FB			
0214	BA	MOV	DX,FF01	
0215	01			
0216	FF			
0217	A0	MOV	AL,[340]	
0218	40			
0219	03			
021A	F6	NOT	AL	
021B	D0			
021C	EE	OUT	DX,AL	
021D	CD	INT	20	
021E	20			

Problem B-14

Make Program B-9 send data from an array of four elements, starting at 340. The program should send an item each time the switch attached to bit 2 of port C is closed. Be sure to reopen the switch and wait for OUTPUT BUFFER FULL to go high before starting the next iteration. Note that you cannot read the status switch directly in mode 1.

Problem B-15

Revise Program B-9 to respond to the switch attached to bit 4 of port C instead of the one attached to bit 2. Be careful—you must send the data to port B, but you must also clear the status by reading port A. You can use control lines from other ports as long as you manage the status and control signals properly. Trace the program to see the signals change, but remember to reopen the status switch before trying to clear the status.

Programmable I/O Devices

The 8255 PPI has many operating modes (see Figures B-3 and B-6 and Table B-3) The program selects one of them by storing a value in the control register. Such devices allow designers to build flexible hardware suited to many applications. Furthermore, you can make changes or corrections in software. The disadvantages are the extra programming and the lack of standards. The device's manufacturer determines arbitrarily what modes are available and how to select them. For example, the functions and positions of the bits in the PPI's control register are arbitrary; similar devices from other manufacturers could have completely different registers.

The following features are, nonetheless, typical of programmable I/O devices:

1. Control or command registers that determine how the device operates.
2. Status registers that describe the current state of the device and the data transfer. The 8255 PPI does not have a separately addressed status register, but you can read its status from port C in the strobed I/O mode.
3. Separate data and status or control inputs and outputs.

Most or all bits in the control registers are set during initialization to implement a particular interface. The main program does not change them. When using the PPI, for example, most applications programs do not change the arrangement of input and output ports or the operating mode.

Programmable I/O devices require careful documentation. The instructions that set their operating modes and use them are arbitrary and are seldom described clearly in manuals.

Key Point Summary

1. Input and output can proceed properly only if there is a way to determine when the receiver is ready, when new data is available, and when the receiver has accepted the data.
2. Synchronous transfers use a clock, whereas asynchronous transfers require a handshake in which sender and receiver exchange status and control signals.
3. Status and control signals can use ordinary data ports. Such implementations are simple in theory, but require a lot of software and hardware in practice.
4. If status and control signals are treated as data, determining the status of a peripheral (polling) is much like determining the state of a switch. Managing a control output is much like turning an LED on and off. A handshake requires a series of input and output operations.
5. The 8255 Programmable Peripheral Interface (PPI) is an LSI device that simplifies polling and handshaking. Besides two 8-bit I/O ports, a PPI contains two 4-bit ports that can provide automatic status and control signals. The PPI also allows direct setting and resetting (clearing) of individual control lines.

6. During input, the 8255's status and control port provides a STROBE input and an INPUT BUFFER FULL output. The STROBE from the peripheral shows that new data is available and latches it into the input port. INPUT BUFFER FULL indicates whether the port contains data that the processor has not yet read.

7. During output, the 8255's status and control port provides an ACKNOWLEDGE input and an OUTPUT BUFFER FULL output. The ACKNOWLEDGE from the peripheral shows that it has finished with the latest data and is ready for more. OUTPUT BUFFER FULL indicates that the port contains data that the peripheral has not yet accepted.

8. Programmable I/O devices simplify hardware design. However, the lack of standards for them makes careful program documentation essential. Each programmable device has its own set of operating modes, ways to select those modes, and special features.

Interrupts

Purpose To learn when and how to use interrupts.

What You Should Learn
1. The features of the 8088 interrupt system.
2. How the IBM PC handles interrupts.
3. How the keyboard interrupt works.
4. How to write a simple interrupt service routine.
5. How to use the 8255 PPI with interrupts.
6. How to use interrupts for handshake I/O.
7. How to pass information between the main program and the interrupt service routines.
8. How to buffer interrupt-driven I/O.
9. How to manage interrupt systems with many sources.
10. Guidelines for programming with interrupts.

Parts Required A connection between pins PC0 (INTERRUPT REQUEST B) and PC3 (INTERRUPT REQUEST A) of 8255 device P1 and the IRQ7 signal on the IBM PC's external bus (pin B21; see Figure A4-1), as shown in Figure C-1.

Reference Materials Comer, D. J. *Microprocessor-Based System Design.* New York: Holt, Rinehart and Winston, 1986, secs. 3.8 (8086 interrupts), 5.4B and 5.5B (programmed I/O with interrupts), 5.4C and 5.5C (interrupt-driven I/O), 5.5D (choosing a data exchange method), 5.6E (programmable interrupt controllers).

Gorsline, G. W. *16-Bit Modern Microcomputers.* Englewood Cliffs, NJ: Prentice-Hall, 1985, pp. 156–166 (noticing events).

Figure C-1

Connections for
interrupting I/O
ports from 8255
device P1.

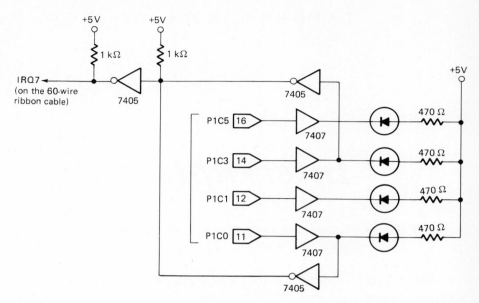

Liu, Y. C., and G. A. Gibson. *Microcomputer Systems: The 8086/8088 Family*, (2nd ed.). Englewood Cliffs, NJ: Prentice-Hall, 1986, pp. 169–173 (interrupts), 240–251 (interrupt I/O), 329–339 (interrupt priority management).

Microsystem Components Handbook: Microprocessors and Peripherals, Volume I. Santa Clara, CA: Intel Corporation, 1985, pp. 2-89 to 2-106 (8259A Programmable Interrupt Controller), 2-118 to 2-155 (using the 8259A Programmable Interrupt Controller).

Norton, P. *Programmer's Guide to the IBM PC.* Redmond, WA: Microsoft Press, 1985, chap. 6 (keyboard basics), pp. 270-71 (universal DOS functions), 284 (set interrupt vector), 303 (get interrupt vector).

Terms **Coprocessor:** a secondary processor that executes instructions in parallel with the main CPU. Coprocessors usually perform specific functions, such as numerical data processing, I/O, signal processing, or communications tasks.

Disable: keep an activity from proceeding.

Enable: allow an activity to proceed.

Interrupt: a signal that temporarily suspends the computer's normal operations and transfers control to a special routine.

Interrupt-driven: dependent on interrupts for its operation.

Interrupt enable (or **interrupt mask**): a bit that determines whether interrupts will be recognized. A mask or disable bit must be cleared to allow interrupts, whereas an enable bit must be set.

Interrupt request: a signal that is active when a peripheral is requesting service, often used to interrupt the CPU.

Interrupt service routine: a program that responds to an interrupt.

Interrupt vector: a pointer that directs the CPU to an interrupt service routine.

Maskable interrupt: an interrupt that the CPU can disable.

Nonmaskable interrupt: an interrupt that the CPU cannot disable.

Polling interrupt system: an interrupt system that identifies sources by having a program examine their status one at a time.

Power fail interrupt: an interrupt that is activated when the system power supply drops below a specified voltage.

Priority interrupt system: an interrupt system in which some interrupts take precedence over others, that is, are serviced first or can interrupt the others' service routines.

Reentrant: can be executed correctly while the same routine is being interrupted.

Transparent routine: a routine that runs without interfering with other routines.

Vectored interrupt: an interrupt that produces an identification code (or *vector*) used to transfer control to the service routine.

8088 Instructions

CLI: clear interrupt enable flag (IF), thus disabling maskable interrupts (INTR input).

INT: software interrupt; save the flags, code segment register, and instruction pointer in the stack (as shown in Figure C-2), clear the interrupt enable flag, and jump to the address in memory locations $4 \times N$ through $4 \times N + 3$, where N is the interrupt type (less than 256). Locations $4 \times N$ and $4 \times N + 1$ contain the new instruction pointer value, locations $4 \times N + 2$ and $4 \times N + 3$ the new code segment register value.

IRET: return from interrupt; load the instruction pointer, code segment register, and flags from the stack, assuming that they were saved as shown in Figure C-2.

STI: set interrupt enable flag (IF), thus enabling maskable interrupts (INTR input).

Figure C-2

Saving the status of
the 8088
microprocessor in
the stack.

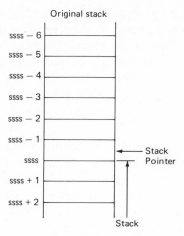

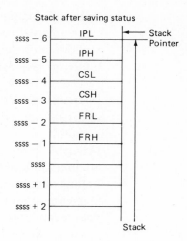

ss = original stack pointer

FRH = MSB of flag register after executing current instruction.
FRL = LSB of flag register after executing current instruction.
CSH = MSB of code segment register after executing current instruction.
CSL = LSB of code segment register after executing current instruction.
IPH = MSB of instruction pointer after executing current instruction.
IPL = LSB of instruction pointer after executing current instruction.

Overview of Interrupts

Interrupts go directly into the CPU. They inform it that something has happened, much as the ringing of a telephone tells you that someone is on the line. The program then need not test status inputs. Instead, interrupts force the CPU to suspend normal operations and respond immediately.

Although interrupts provide rapid response to inputs, they also introduce new problems. They make testing and debugging difficult, as they can occur at any time. Extra hardware (much like a telephone switchboard or PBX) is often necessary to control them and simplify their identification. Furthermore, the designer must decide when to allow them and how to pass information between the main program and the service routines.

8088 Interrupt System

The 8088 has two interrupt inputs:

1. NMI (nonmaskable interrupt) is edge sensitive, so that it will not interrupt its own service routine. Nonmaskable means that it cannot be shut out.
   Many applications use NMI as a *power fail interrupt*. That is, a drop in

the supply voltage below a specified level causes a nonmaskable interrupt. In response, the processor saves essential data in a low-power memory attached to a battery. Obviously, loss of power should have top priority, as it will quickly shut down everything anyway. We will not deal with NMI here, since the IBM PC does not provide access to it.

2. INTR (interrupt request) is a maskable interrupt generally used for I/O and other common operating functions. The input is level sensitive. The IF (interrupt enable flag) controls whether the processor recognizes INTR interrupts. Setting IF (with STI) enables them, whereas clearing it (with CLI) disables them.

The 8088 responds to an interrupt as follows after finishing its current instruction:

1. It saves the instruction pointer, code segment register, and flag register in the stack, as shown in Figure C-2. (To review the function and use of the code segment register, see the last section of Laboratory 0.)
2. It clears the interrupt enable flag, thus disabling maskable interrupts.
3. It reads an 8-bit vector (called the *interrupt type*) generated by external circuitry.
4. It uses the vector to get new values for the instruction pointer and code segment register. These values are located in the lowest part of memory (segment 0), starting at an address four times the vector. For example, a type 5 interrupt is serviced at the address in memory locations 14 through 17 hex ($4 \times 5 = 14$ in hexadecimal). An IRET instruction at the end of the service routine restores the registers saved during the interrupt response.

The 8088's way of handling interrupts forces us to reserve the bottom 1K bytes of memory (addresses 0000 through 03FF in segment 0, that is, addresses 00000 through 003FF in the 20-bit form) for interrupt service addresses. As Figure C-3 shows, some of these locations (pointer types 0 through 4, addresses 0000 through 0013) are dedicated to specific commands, signals, and software (that is, program-generated) interrupts. Intel Corporation has reserved others (types 5 through 31, addresses 0014 through 007F) for its own purposes. Note, however, that IBM has ignored Intel's claims; the PC uses interrupt types 5, 8, 9, E, and 10 through 3F for BIOS and DOS functions (see Tables A5-1, A5-3, and A5-4).

RESET clears IF, disabling maskable interrupts and letting the program set up the system before it accepts any interrupts. Accepting an interrupt also clears IF, so that a maskable interrupt cannot disturb its own service routine. IRET usually reenables maskable interrupts automatically, as it restores the old IF (as part of the flag register) from the stack. IF must have been 1 or the interrupt would not have been recognized in the first place.

Figure C-3

Memory map for 8088 interrupt vectors. (Reprinted by permission of Intel Corporation, Santa Clara, CA).

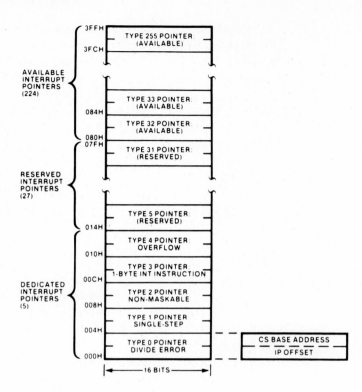

IBM PC Interrupts

Table C-1 lists the interrupt vectors governed by the PC's 8259 Programmable Interrupt Controller (PIC). The PIC manages eight interrupt inputs; it latches and prioritizes them, and generates vectors. The PC's PIC services interrupt types 8 through F. As Figure C-1 shows, we have tied the PPI's interrupt outputs to the PIC's INT7 input so they produce interrupts of type F. F is available since we are not using the printer cluster alternate function (whatever it may be).

Table C-1

Interrupt Service Addresses for the IBM PC's 8259 PIC

Type	Purpose	Vector Address (Hex)
8	On-board timer	0040 – 0043
9	Keyboard	0044 – 0047
A	Reserved	0048 – 004B
B	Asynchronous communications alternate	004C – 004F
C	Asynchronous communications primary	0050 – 0053
D	Fixed (hard) disk	0054 – 0057
E	Floppy disk	0058 – 005B
F	Printer cluster alternate	005C – 005F

1111
× 4   =0011 1100   => 3C   003c

DEBUG and DOS together handle most interrupt overhead. DEBUG initial-izes the stack pointer, and DOS provides vectors for standard devices (timer, keyboard, disk, and so on). DOS also has the following functions (part of INT 21H) to read and set interrupt vectors:

25 hex: set interrupt vector (type in AL) to the value in registers DS (seg-ment number) and DX (offset).

35 hex: get interrupt vector (type in AL) and return it in registers ES (seg-ment number) and BX (offset).

The function number, as usual, goes in register AH.

Keyboard Interrupts

In fact, we have already used interrupts in Laboratory 4. After all, the PC's keyboard is interrupt driven. To show this, let us move the keyboard interrupt vector (type 9; see Table C-1) into user memory. The following program (Pro-gram C-1 is the DEBUG version) makes the vector 280.

```
        MOV   AL,9        ;GET INTERRUPT TYPE
        MOV   DX,280H     ;GET VECTOR IN USER
                          ;   MEMORY
        MOV   AH,25H      ;SET INTERRUPT VECTOR
        INT   21H
        STI               ;ENABLE CPU INTERRUPTS
HERE:   JMP   HERE        ;WAIT FOR INTERRUPT

        ORG   280H        ;INTERRUPT SERVICE ROUTINE
        INT   3           ;EXIT AND DISPLAY REGISTERS
```

PROGRAM C-1		
Memory Address (Hex)	Memory Contents (Hex)	Instruction (DEBUG Form)
0200	B0	*MOV* *AL,9*
0201	09	
0202	BA	*MOV* *DX,280*
0203	80	
0204	02	
0205	B4	*MOV* *AH,25*
0206	25	

	PROGRAM C-1 (continued)			
Memory Address (Hex)	Memory Contents (Hex)		Instruction (DEBUG Form)	
0207	CD		INT	21
0208	21			
0209	FB		STI	
020A	EB	HERE:	JMP	20A
020B	FE			
0280	CC		INT	3

Program C-1 exits immediately, instead of waiting for you to press a key. The reason is that keyboard interrupts occur both when a key is pressed and when one is released. DEBUG starts commands (such as G) when you press the Enter key. Releasing Enter then causes an interrupt and forces Program C-1 to exit. To verify this, read the keyboard (port 60H in the IBM PC) in the interrupt service routine. The result is the scan code (see Table A2-3) for a key closure, and the scan code plus 80 hex for a key release. The code for the release of the Enter key is thus 9C hex.

One obvious drawback to Program C-1 is that it locks out the keyboard. This is not surprising, since the keyboard interrupt no longer does anything. The only way to regain control is to turn the computer off and then back on again. A more sensible, but more complex approach is to use function 35 hex to save the old interrupt vector and then transfer control to it. Be sure to save and restore both the segment number and the offset.

Problem C-1

What happens if you simply hold the Enter key down after issuing the G command for Program C-1? Remember that the IBM PC lets you repeat a key by holding it down for a while. What scan code is in AL after an IN from the keyboard (port 60 hex)?

8255 PPI Interrupts

In practice, interrupts are used most often as service requests from peripheral chips such as the 8255 PPI. In mode 1, the PPI produces interrupt request signals automatically. Bit 3 of port C (INTERRUPT REQUEST A) indicates whether port A needs service, and bit 0 (INTERRUPT REQUEST B) does the same for port B.

Note how INTERRUPT REQUEST differs from BUFFER FULL. For an input port, INTERRUPT REQUEST goes active (high) only after the peripheral's STROBE pulse ends. BUFFER FULL, on the other hand, becomes active as soon as the STROBE pulse begins. Both are deactivated when the port is read. For an output port, INTERRUPT REQUEST is deactivated when the port is written and remains inactive until the ACKNOWLEDGE pulse ends. BUFFER FULL, on the other hand, remains inactive only until the ACKNOWLEDGE pulse begins. In practice, BUFFER FULL usually serves as an acknowledgment to the peripheral, whereas INTERRUPT REQUEST is the computer's ready signal.

As with handshakes, input and output are quite different. An input interrupt is normally inactive; the STROBE pulse from the peripheral activates it. An output interrupt, on the other hand, is normally active; an ACKNOWLEDGE pulse from the peripheral clears it. As noted earlier, input peripherals are usually not ready, and the computer must wait for them to provide data; output peripherals are usually ready and must wait for the computer to send them data.

Before we can generate interrupts from a PPI, we must enable its interrupt outputs. This means setting the following bits in mode 1:

> PC2 for port B
> PC4 for port A if it is input, PC6 if it is output

We can change these bits with the bit set/reset capability described in Laboratory B (see Figure B-3). For example, to enable interrupts from input port A, we use

```
MOV    DX,PPICR
MOV    AL,00001001B
OUT    DX,AL
```

Here the bit number is 100 (bits 1 through 3), and bit 0 is 1 to set the target bit. Similarly, to disable interrupts from output port B (that is, to clear the enable bit), we use

```
MOV    DX,PPICR
MOV    AL,00000100B
OUT    DX,AL
```

Here the bit number is 010 (bits 1 through 3), and bit 0 is 0 to clear the target bit. Note that the output goes to the control register, not to port C.

Problem C-2

Write a program that puts port A of 8255 device P1 in mode 1 and enables its
  interrupt. Does it matter whether port A is input or output? Leave port B in
  mode 0 and make port C all outputs.

Let us now use interrupts from 8255 device P1. Its interrupt outputs cause
interrupts of type F via the 8259 PIC (Figure C-1 shows the connections). The
main program must enable the PIC's interrupts (by clearing bit 7 of its interrupt
mask register); enable the PPI interrupts (by setting bits 2 and 4 of PPI port C);
load the interrupt vector for type F; and enable the CPU interrupt with STI.
The service routine must clear the interrupt in the 8259 (port 20 hex) by
sending it an End-of-Interrupt (EOI) command byte (20 hex). Be careful—the
port address, the EOI command byte, and our program-ending instruction are
unrelated, despite the ubiquitous 20 hex value. For details about initializing and
using the 8259 device, see the Intel manual listed in the references.

The following program (Program C-2 is the DEBUG version) responds to the
closing and reopening of the switch attached to bit 4 of port C. Note that the
switches and interrupt enables occupy the same bit positions. Internal 8255 circuitry resolves this apparent conflict. Be sure to note, however, that reading port
C returns the enable bits, not the switch positions.

```
MOV   DX,21H           ;ENABLE 8259 INTERRUPT BY
IN    AL,DX            ;  CLEARING BIT 7 OF THE
AND   AL,01111111B     ;  INTERRUPT MASK REGISTER
OUT   DX,AL
MOV   AL,0FH           ;GET INTERRUPT TYPE
MOV   DX,280H          ;GET VECTOR IN USER MEMORY
MOV   AH,25H           ;SET INTERRUPT VECTOR
INT   21H
MOV   DX,0FF03H        ;GET CONTROL REGISTER
                       ;  ADDRESS
MOV   AL,10110100B     ;MAKE PORT A INPUT, PORT B
                       ;  OUTPUT
OUT   DX,AL            ;BOTH PORTS IN STROBED
                       ;  MODE (1)
MOV   AL,00001001B     ;ENABLE INPUT INTERRUPT
OUT   DX,AL
MOV   AL,00000101B     ;ENABLE OUTPUT INTERRUPT
OUT   DX,AL
MOV   DX,0FF01H        ;TURN OFF THE LEDS
```

```
          MOV    AL,0FFH
          OUT    DX,AL
          STI                    ;ENABLE CPU INTERRUPT
HERE:     JMP    HERE            ;WAIT FOR INTERRUPT

          ORG    280H            ;INTERRUPT SERVICE ROUTINE
          MOV    DX,20H          ;CLEAR 8259 INTERRUPT
          MOV    AL,20H
          OUT    DX,AL
          INT    20H
```

PROGRAM C-2

Memory Address (Hex)	Memory Contents (Hex)	Instruction (DEBUG Form)	
0200	BA	MOV	DX,21
0201	21		
0202	00		
0203	EC	IN	AL,DX
0204	24	AND	AL,7F
0205	7F		
0206	EE	OUT	DX,AL
0207	B0	MOV	AL,F
0208	0F		
0209	BA	MOV	DX,280
020A	80		
020B	02		
020C	B4	MOV	AH,25
020D	25		
020E	CD	INT	21
020F	21		
0210	BA	MOV	DX,FF03
0211	03		
0212	FF		
0213	B0	MOV	AL,B4
0214	B4		
0215	EE	OUT	DX,AL
0216	B0	MOV	AL,9
0217	09		
0218	EE	OUT	DX,AL
0219	B0	MOV	AL,5
021A	05		
021B	EE	OUT	DX,AL
021C	BA	MOV	DX,FF01

			PROGRAM C-2 (continued)	

Memory Address (Hex)	Memory Contents (Hex)		Instruction (DEBUG Form)	
021D	01			
021E	FF			
021F	B0		MOV	AL,FF
0220	FF			
0221	EE		OUT	DX,AL
0222	FB		STI	
0223	EB	HERE:	JMP	223
0224	FE			
0280	BA		MOV	DX,20
0281	20			
0282	00			
0283	B0		MOV	AL,20
0284	20			
0285	EE		OUT	DX,AL
0286	CD		INT	20
0287	20			

Enter and run Program C-2. Closing and reopening the STROBE switch causes an interrupt. Note that INPUT BUFFER FULL (bit 5) goes high as soon as you close the STROBE switch. INTERRUPT REQUEST (bit 3) goes high only when you reopen the switch. Afterward, clear the interrupt by examining port FF00 from the keyboard with the I command. This makes both INTER-RUPT REQUEST and INPUT BUFFER FULL go low.

Program C-2 will also respond to the opening and closing of the port B ACKNOWLEDGE switch. Try this interrupt. How do you clear it?

Handshaking with Interrupts

Interrupts are often used in handshake I/O (see Figures B-4 and B-5). To experiment with this, we need the startup routine in addresses 200 through 221 of Program C-2. It loads the PPI's control register and the IBM PC's interrupt vector, enables PIC and PPI interrupts, and turns off all the LEDs. We leave the enabling of the CPU interrupts for later, as some examples require more initialization.

The following program (Program C-3 is the DEBUG version) is the interrupt-driven equivalent of Program B-2. It loads data from port A when you close and reopen the STROBE switch. The main program clears the DATA

READY flag (400) and waits for it to be set. In response to the interrupt, the service routine reads the data from the input port and sets the DATA READY flag.

Note the following features of Program C-3:

1. We enable the CPU interrupts last, after initializing all system parameters. Otherwise, an early interrupt could cause problems if it found the PPI in the wrong mode.
2. We must set the PPI's interrupt enables and the CPU's I flag to allow interrupt-driven I/O. However, we must clear the mask in the PIC's interrupt mask register. The schoolboy rule is "Set an enable, clear a mask."
3. The final CLI (CLEAR INTERRUPT ENABLE FLAG) disables the CPU interrupt before returning control to DEBUG. This precaution avoids conflict with DEBUG's functions or later user programs.
4. The IN AL,DX instruction in the service routine clears the interrupt and reads the data from port A.

You need not change the I flag to EI before running programs that enable interrupts anyway.

```
           SUB    AL,AL                  ;CLEAR READY FLAG
           MOV    [400H],AL
           STI
WTRDY:     MOV    AL,[400H]              ;IS DATA READY?
           TEST   AL,AL
           JZ     WTRDY                  ;NO, WAIT
           CLI                           ;YES, DISABLE CPU INTERRUPT
           INT    20H

           ORG    280H                   ;INTERRUPT SERVICE
                                         ;   ROUTINE
           PUSH   AX                     ;SAVE ACCUMULATOR
           PUSH   DX                     ;SAVE REGISTER DX
           MOV    DX,0FF00H              ;GET DATA, CLEAR
                                         ;   INTERRUPT
           IN     AL,DX
           MOV    [401H],AL              ;SAVE DATA IN MEMORY
           INC    BYTE PTR [400H]        ;SET READY FLAG
           MOV    DX,20H                 ;CLEAR 8259 INTERRUPT
           MOV    AL,20H
           OUT    DX,AL
           POP    DX                     ;RESTORE REGISTER DX
           POP    AX                     ;RESTORE ACCUMULATOR
           IRET
```

The service routine only has to save and restore registers AX and DX, because the interrupt response saves the flags automatically. Try running Program C-3 for various inputs at port A. What do you find in 400 and 401?

PROGRAM C-3				
Memory Address (Hex)	Memory Contents (Hex)		Instruction (DEBUG Form)	
0222	28		SUB	AL,AL
0223	C0			
0224	A2		MOV	[400],AL
0225	00			
0226	04			
0227	FB		STI	
0228	A0	WTRDY:	MOV	AL,[400]
0229	00			
022A	04			
022B	84		TEST	AL,AL
022C	C0			
022D	74		JZ	228
022E	F9			
022F	FA		CLI	
0230	CD		INT	20
0231	20			
0280	50		PUSH	AX
0281	52		PUSH	DX
0282	BA		MOV	DX,FF00
0283	00			
0284	FF			
0285	EC		IN	AL,DX
0286	A2		MOV	[401],AL
0287	01			
0288	04			
0289	FE		INC	BY[400]
028A	06			
028B	00			
028C	04			
028D	BA		MOV	DX,20
028E	20			
028F	00			
0290	B0		MOV	AL,20
0291	20			
0292	EE		OUT	DX,AL
0293	5A		POP	DX
0294	58		POP	AX
0295	CF		IRET	

Note that you cannot trace an interruptable routine, as the computer does not recognize interrupts while executing a T command. However, you can put a breakpoint in the service routine to check its operation. As you will surely discover, debugging interrupt service routines is difficult because of limited tools and endless timing problems.

Problem C-3

Make the service routine in Program C-3 show the data on the LEDs at port B.

Problem C-4

Make Program C-3 save up to four input data values, starting at 340. That is, each time you close and reopen the STROBE switch, the program should read the data from port A and store it in the next available location. Use locations 402 and 403 for the buffer pointer, and make the service routine save and restore any registers it uses. Set the data switches to give the following values:

$$[\,0340\,] = C3$$
$$[\,0341\,] = 03$$
$$[\,0342\,] = C0$$
$$[\,0343\,] = FC$$

Problem C-5

Make the main part of Program C-3 wait for a 7F input, the synchronization character from Laboratory 2. If the input is not 7F, the main program should simply clear the DATA READY flag and wait.

Problem C-6

Write an interrupt-driven version of Program B-3. The main program should clear 400 to show that data is available for output. When the B ACKNOWLEDGE switch is closed and reopened, the service routine should send the data from 401 and set 400 to 1, indicating that the data has been sent. Set [0401] = AA to make the response easy to spot.

Problem C-7

Change the answer to Problem C-6 so that the service routine sends the data only if it is a synchronization character (7F hex). Otherwise, the routine simply sets 400 to 1 and clears the interrupt by sending FF to port B. All the LEDs should remain off unless [0401] = 7F.

Communicating with Interrupt Service Routines

We cannot use registers to move data to or from an interrupt service routine, because the main program generally needs them for its own work. Rather, we need a method that makes service routines transparent to the main program, so that we can change either independently of the other.

One approach is to use memory locations (called a *mailbox*) for data transfers. They serve the same purpose as the drops in popular spy books. The agent puts orders, requests, and payments in the drop; the informant picks them up and supplies the information in return. The two never talk or meet. Either can be replaced without disrupting the flow of information (as long as the newcomers know where the drop is).

For example, in Program C-3, the main program clears 400 and waits for the service routine to change it. When that happens, the main program exits. Here the interrupt acts like a RUN command, causing the main program to proceed.

Problem C-8

Make Program C-3 use bit 7 of 400 as the READY flag and put the data in bits 0 through 6. This is sensible if the data consists of 7-bit ASCII characters (see Table A2-1, Appendix 2).

Problem C-9

Make Program C-3 wait until 400 contains 5. How would you make the main program wait until 400 contains the same value as 340? This approach is useful when the computer must count external events, such as clock pulses or activations of a sensor.

Obviously, the receiver must check the mailbox often enough to avoid missing messages. One problem is that other programs may use the mailbox accidentally. Imagine an informant hiding valuable papers in a trash container. Unfortunately, before the agent can retrieve them, the garbage collector picks up the trash.

Buffering Interrupts

Program C-3 handles the input data one character at a time. This creates timing and interpretation problems if the data rate is high or if only sequences of data are meaningful (as is typical when the inputs are from a terminal or communications line). The obvious solution is to buffer the data in memory. Then the service routine can fill a buffer, and the main program need not handle individual characters. The buffer serves the same purpose as a buffer memory in a printer or terminal. The computer can send the peripheral a block of data at one time, and the peripheral can then handle the data at its own speed. In our case, the service routine plays the role of the peripheral.

In the following program (Program C-4 is the DEBUG version), the main part waits until the count in 400 reaches 4. The service routine stores the inputs in successive locations starting at 340. Note that common practice is to keep service routines short to reduce response time; this is particularly important if the system may send or receive rapid bursts of data.

```
        SUB    AL,AL              ;CLEAR COUNT TO START
        MOV    [400H],AL
        MOV    AX,340H            ;INITIALIZE BUFFER POINTER
        MOV    [402H],AX
        STI
        MOV    AL,4               ;GET TARGET COUNT
WTCNT:  CMP    AL,[400H]          ;ENOUGH INPUTS RECEIVED?
        JNE    WTCNT              ;NO, WAIT
        CLI                       ;YES, DISABLE CPU INTERRUPT
        INT    20H


        ORG    280H               ;INTERRUPT SERVICE ROUTINE
        PUSH   AX                 ;SAVE REGISTERS
        PUSH   DI
        PUSH   DX
        MOV    DX,0FF00H          ;GET DATA, CLEAR INTERRUPT
        IN     AL,DX
        MOV    DI,[402H]          ;GET BUFFER POINTER
        CLD                       ;SELECT AUTOINCREMENTING
        STOSB                     ;SAVE DATA IN BUFFER
        MOV    [402H],DI          ;SAVE UPDATED BUFFER
                                  ;   POINTER
        INC    BYTE PTR[400H]     ;SET READY FLAG
        MOV    DX,20H             ;CLEAR 8259 INTERRUPT
        MOV    AL,20H
        OUT    DX,AL
        POP    DX                 ;RESTORE REGISTERS
        POP    DI
        POP    AX
        IRET
```

PROGRAM C-4			
Memory Address (Hex)	Memory Contents (Hex)	Instruction (DEBUG Form)	
0222	28	SUB	AL,AL
0223	C0		
0224	A2	MOV	[400],AL
0225	00		
0226	04		
0227	B8	MOV	AX,340
0228	40		
0229	03		
022A	A3	MOV	[402],AX
022B	02		
022C	04		
022D	FB	STI	
022E	B0	MOV	AL,4
022F	04		
0230	3A	WTCNT: CMP	AL,[400]
0231	06		
0232	00		
0233	04		
0234	75	JNE	230
0235	FA		
0236	FA	CLI	
0237	CD	INT	20
0238	20		
0280	50	PUSH	AX
0281	57	PUSH	DI
0282	52	PUSH	DX
0283	BA	MOV	DX,FF00
0284	00		
0285	FF		
0286	EC	IN	AL,DX
0287	8B	MOV	DI,[402]
0288	3E		
0289	02		
028A	04		
028B	FC	CLD	
028C	AA	STOSB	
028D	89	MOV	[402],DI
028E	3E		
028F	02		
0290	04		
0291	FE	INC	BY [400]
0292	06		

		PROGRAM C-4 (continued)	
Memory Address (Hex)	Memory Contents (Hex)	Instruction (DEBUG Form)	
0293	00		
0294	04		
0295	BA	MOV	DX,20
0296	20		
0297	00		
0298	B0	MOV	AL,20
0299	20		
029A	5A	POP	DX
029B	5F	POP	DI
029C	58	POP	AX
029D	CF	IRET	

This service routine must save and restore DI as well as AX and DX. Remember that the processor automatically saves only the instruction pointer, code segment register, and flags.

Enter and run Program C-4. Set the switches to form the following array:

$$[0340] = F0 \qquad (11110000 \text{ binary})$$
$$[0341] = 0F \qquad (00001111 \text{ binary})$$
$$[0342] = AA \qquad (10101010 \text{ binary})$$
$$[0343] = 55 \qquad (01010101 \text{ binary})$$

Problem C-10

Revise Program C-4 to fill the buffer until it receives an input of 0D, an ASCII carriage return character. Use 403 as an END OF LINE flag. The main program should clear the flag initially and then wait for it to be set. The service routine should set the flag when it receives a 0D input. A program like this handles input from a terminal one line at a time.

Problem C-11

Make Program C-4 fill the buffer with a message that starts with an ASCII STX (Start of Text) character (02) and ends with an ASCII ETX (End of Text) character (03). All inputs before the STX are ignored, and the STX and ETX characters themselves do not appear in the buffer. Such control characters are often used for synchronization.

EXAMPLE:

If the inputs are (in order of receipt)

67	
B2	
02	ASCII STX
47	ASCII G
5F	ASCII O (letter)
0D	ASCII Carriage Return
03	ASCII ETX

the final buffer contents will be

[0340] = 47	ASCII G
[0341] = 5F	ASCII O (letter)
[0342] = 0D	ASCII Carriage Return

The two inputs preceding the STX are ignored. The STX and ETX characters do not appear in the buffer. (*Hint*: Use 403 as a TRANSMISSION IN PROGRESS flag. The main program should clear the flag initially, and the service routine should set it when it receives an STX input.)

Problem C-12

A common practice, called *double buffering*, has the service routine fill one buffer while the main program processes another. Extend Program C-4 to first fill the buffer starting at 340 with four inputs and then fill the buffer starting at 360. Use location 400 for the count in the current buffer and 402 and 403 for the buffer pointer. Be sure to disable CPU interrupts while switching buffers. (Why?)

EXAMPLE:

If the inputs are

FE	(all switches open except 0)
FD	(all switches open except 1)
FB	(all switches open except 2)
F7	(all switches open except 3)

EF	(all switches open except 4)
DF	(all switches open except 5)
BF	(all switches open except 6)
7F	(all switches open except 7)

the first four values end up in the first buffer and the second four in the second buffer. That is, we have

[0340] = FE
[0341] = FD
[0342] = FB
[0343] = F7

[0360] = EF
[0361] = DF
[0362] = BF
[0363] = 7F

Problem C-13

Write an interrupt-driven output routine that transmits data from a buffer starting at 340 until it finds a 0D value, an ASCII carriage return.

EXAMPLE:

[0340] = 80
[0341] = 40
[0342] = 20
[0343] = 10
[0344] = 0D

The output should be a single light that moves right one position after each interrupt. The program should exit with the displays showing 0D (00001101B).

Multiple Sources of Interrupts

So far, we have assumed a single source of interrupts. Real applications normally have several sources, such as input devices, output devices, alarms, timers, coprocessors, control panels, and remote stations. The problem is identifying the source of an interrupt, so the processor can decide which service routine to execute.

The simplest approach is to examine the status of one source at a time. This is like answering a multiline telephone by trying each line successively until you find the caller. The first active source is serviced, and the others are handled in the order of examination. This approach (called *polling*) is similar to the approach used to handle non-interrupt-driven I/O; in fact, the only difference is the initiation by an interrupt rather than under program control.

The next program (Program C-5 is the DEBUG version) waits for an interrupt from either port A or port B of 8255 device P1. The polling routine examines the BUFFER FULL signals and services the first interrupt it finds active. If the input buffer is full, the routine sets 400 to 1 and loads the input data into 402. But if the output buffer is empty, the routine sets 401 to 1 and sends the output data from 403.

The polling routine disables the PPI interrupts so you can see the effects of priority. Otherwise, the second interrrupt would be serviced as soon as the first service routine ended. The disabling causes the lower-priority interrupt to go unserviced.

```
            SUB    AX,AX              ;CLEAR READY FLAGS
            MOV    [400H],AX
            STI
WTINT:      CMP    AL,[400H]          ;INPUT DATA AVAILABLE?
            JNE    DONE               ;YES, DONE
            CMP    AL,[401H]          ;OUTPUT DATA SENT?
            JE     WTINT              ;NO, WAIT
DONE:       CLI                       ;YES, DISABLE CPU INTERRUPT
            INT    20H

            ORG    280H               ;INTERRUPT POLLING ROUTINE
            PUSH   AX                 ;SAVE REGISTERS
            PUSH   DX
            MOV    DX,0FF03H
            MOV    AL,00001000B       ;DISABLE INPUT INTERRUPTS
            OUT    DX,AL
            MOV    AL,00000100B       ;DISABLE OUTPUT INTERRUPTS
            OUT    DX,AL
            MOV    DX,0FF02H          ;GET STATUS BITS
            IN     AL,DX
            TEST   AL,00100000B       ;INPUT BUFFER FULL?
            JNZ    SRVIN              ;YES, SERVICE INPUT
```

```
        TEST  AL,00000010B        ;OUTPUT BUFFER EMPTY?
        JNZ   SRVOUT              ;YES, SERVICE OUTPUT
                                  ;OTHERWISE, JUST EXIT
SREXIT: MOV   DX,20H              ;CLEAR 8259 INTERRUPT
        MOV   AL,20H
        OUT   DX,AL
        POP   DX                  ;RESTORE REGISTERS
        POP   AX
        IRET

        ORG   2C0H                ;INPUT INTERRUPT SERVICE
SRVIN:  MOV   DX,0FF00H           ;GET INPUT DATA
        IN    AL,DX
        MOV   [402H],AL           ;SAVE DATA IN MEMORY
        INC   BYTE PTR [400H]     ;SET INPUT READY FLAG
        JMP   SREXIT

        ORG   2E0H                ;OUTPUT INTERRUPT
                                  ;  SERVICE
SRVOUT: MOV   DX,0FF01H           ;SEND DATA TO LEDS
        MOV   AL,[403H]
        NOT   AL
        OUT   DX,AL
        INC   BYTE PTR [401H]     ;SET OUTPUT ACKNOWLEDGE
                                  ;  FLAG
        JMP   SREXIT
```

To test the priority scheme, you must set both interrupts simultaneously. The easiest way to do this is to connect them to the same switch temporarily with a jumper wire. The program will service only the input interrupt, as it is first in the polling order.

PROGRAM C-5				
Memory Address (Hex)	Memory Contents (Hex)		Instruction (DEBUG Form)	
0222	29		*SUB*	*AX,AX*
0223	*C0*			
0224	A3		*MOV*	*[400],AX*
0225	00			
0226	04			
0227	FB		*STI*	

	PROGRAM C-5 (continued)			
Memory Address (Hex)	Memory Contents (Hex)		Instruction (DEBUG Form)	
0228	3A	WTINT:	CMP	AL,[400]
0229	06			
022A	00			
022B	04			
022C	75		JNE	234
022D	06			
022E	3A		CMP	AL,[401]
022F	06			
0230	01			
0231	04			
0232	74		JE	228
0233	F4			
0234	FA	DONE:	CLI	
0235	CD		INT	20
0236	20			
0280	50		PUSH	AX
0281	52		PUSH	DX
0282	BA		MOV	DX,FF03
0283	03			
0284	FF			
0285	B0		MOV	AL,8
0286	08			
0287	EE		OUT	DX,AL
0288	B0		MOV	AL,4
0289	04			
028A	EE		OUT	DX,AL
028B	BA		MOV	DX,FF02
028C	02			
028D	FF			
028E	EC		IN	AL,DX
028F	A8		TEST	AL,20
0290	20			
0291	75		JNZ	2C0
0292	2D			
0293	A8		TEST	AL,2
0294	02			
0295	75		JNZ	2E0
0296	49			
0297	BA	SREXIT:	MOV	DX,20
0298	20			
0299	00			
029A	B0		MOV	AL,20

PROGRAM C-5 (continued)

Memory Address (Hex)	Memory Contents (Hex)		Instruction (DEBUG Form)	
029B	20			
029C	EE		OUT	DX,AL
029D	5A		POP	DX
029E	58		POP	AX
029F	CF		IRET	
02C0	BA	SRVIN:	MOV	DX,FF00
02C1	00			
02C2	FF			
02C3	EC		IN	AL,DX
02C4	A2		MOV	[402],AL
02C5	02			
02C6	04			
02C7	FE		INC	BY [400]
02C8	06			
02C9	00			
02CA	04			
02CB	EB		JMP	297
02CC	CA			
02E0	BA	SRVOUT:	MOV	DX,FF01
02E1	01			
02E2	FF			
02E3	A0		MOV	AL,[403]
02E4	03			
02E5	04			
02E6	F6		NOT	AL
02E7	D0			
02E8	EE		OUT	DX,AL
02E9	FE		INC	BY [401]
02EA	06			
02EB	01			
02EC	04			
02ED	EB		JMP	297
02EE	A8			

Problem C-14

How could you invert the priority in Program C-5? That is, make the output interrupt take precedence over the input interrupt.

Problem C-15

Some interrupt systems may ignore low-priority interrupts indefinitely if there are many high-priority interrupts. The situation is like that of a caller who is left on hold forever. One way to ensure that all interrupts get serviced is to rotate the priorities. Make the polling routine invert the order in which it examines interrupts as part of each execution. Use 405 as a flag indicating the order of examination (00 means "input interrupt first" and FF means "output interrupt first"). Set this flag from the keyboard initially so that you can control the priority.

Problem C-16

Write a program for a complete interrupt-driven I/O system. The program should start by enabling only the input interrupt and waiting for data to appear. When it receives data, it should disable the input interrupt, enable the output interrupt, and wait for the output device to become ready. When the output device is ready, the program should send it the data, disable the output interrupt, and complete the cycle by enabling the input interrupt.

Note that the 8255 PPI latches interrupts that occur while its outputs are disabled. Be careful, however, not to service a disabled interrupt. Remember that the port's BUFFER FULL signal can still be activated; no interrupt will occur, but a polling routine will find BUFFER FULL active. Thus, if you disable some PPI interrupts, check only the enabled ports. You can determine whether an interrupt is enabled by testing its enable bit in port C.

What happens to your solution if you start by setting an output interrupt? What happens if you then set the input interrupt? What if you change the switch positions and set another input interrupt after the program has just serviced one? Note that the processor services a pending PPI interrupt as soon as both it and the CPU interrupt are enabled simultaneously.

Polling makes sense when there are only a few sources. As the number increases, however, polling becomes slow and cumbersome. The alternative is a vectored system in which each interrupt directs the CPU to its own service routine. For example, we could connect the two PPI interrupts to different inputs on the 8259 programmable Interrupt Controller. Note, however, that we would have to unmask both interrupts by clearing both corresponding bits in the PIC's interrupt mask register.

Guidelines for Programming with Interrupts

In designing interrupt-based systems, the programmer should use the following guidelines:

1. Initialize all parameters before enabling interrupts.
2. Make all service routines transparent to the programs they can interrupt.
3. Provide a well-defined method for transferring data between the main program and the service routines. This method should be flexible and program independent.

There are many aspects of programming with interrupts that we have not discussed. Among them are reentrant programs that can be interrupted and resumed even if an interrupt service routine executes them. Such programs must use the registers and the stack for temporary storage, not specific memory addresses, as values stored there would be overwritten.

Still another issue is the need to disable interrupts during activities that cannot be resumed properly or are indivisible. Delay loops are typical examples of routines that cannot be resumed, whereas the updating of multiword data that a service routine uses is a typical example of an indivisible activity. Obviously, a service routine can cause havoc if it finds the current time or a segmented address (that is, a segment number and an offset) only partially changed.

Key Point Summary

1. Interrupts allow a computer to respond rapidly and directly to external events, such as changes in the status of peripherals. The program need not test the status, since the changes affect hardware inputs.
2. The 8088 microprocessor has two interrupts: maskable (INTR) and nonmaskable (NMI). In response to them, the processor saves the instruction pointer, code segment register, and flags in the stack; disables the maskable interrupt; and fetches new code segment and instruction pointer values from specified pairs of memory locations. The locations are addresses $4 \times N$ through $4 \times N + 3$, where N is the interrupt's type. An IRET instruction at the end of the service routine restores the old instruction pointer, code segment register, and flags from the stack. The service routine must save and restore any other registers it uses.
3. Before enabling interrupts, the main program must load the stack pointer and initialize any parameters that the service routines use.

It must also determine the operating modes for PPIs and other I/O devices. RESET disables the CPU interrupt and the PPI interrupts.

4. To get interrupts from an 8255 PPI, the program must enable its interrupt outputs using the bit set/reset capability. Transitions on the status lines then both cause interrupts and change the BUFFER FULL bits.

5. The main program and the service routines cannot communicate through the registers, because each needs them for its own purposes. A simple way to communicate is through memory locations, which act like a mailbox. One program can put information in the mailbox for the other to read.

6. Buffering allows the main program and the service routine to communicate less often. The main program need only concern itself with an entire buffer's worth of data. Either a large buffer or multiple buffers (double buffering) gives the main program extra time to do its work without missing data or ignoring requests for service.

7. If there are many sources of interrupts, the program must have a way of identifying them. Polling means that the processor examines the status of successive sources until it finds one that is active. Vectoring means that each source provides its own identification.

8. In polling interrupt systems, the sources' priority depends on the order of examination. This order can be changed or varied, but not conveniently. Because the average time required to identify a source depends directly on how many sources there are, polling is reasonable only when the number is small.

Timing Methods

Purpose To learn how to time I/O operations.

What You Should Learn
1. How to synchronize with an external clock.
2. How to measure the period of an external clock.
3. Why programmable timers are useful.
4. How to use an elapsed time interrupt.
5. How to use a real-time clock.
6. What a real-time operating system does.

Parts Required A low-frequency clock input (5–200 Hz), such as one generated from a 555 timer (see Figure D-1). Tie the clock to pin PC6 of 8255 device P1 (pin 17 of the I/O connector), as shown in Figure D-2. A potentiometer in the circuit will let you vary the frequency.

Figure D-1

Simple circuit for generating a clock from a 555 timer chip. The frequency is approximately 100 Hz.

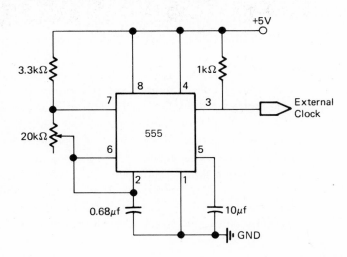

Figure D-2

Connection of the external clock to bit 6 of port C of 8255 device P1.

External
Clock

Reference Materials

Comer, D. J. *Microprocessor-Based System Design*. New York: Holt, Rinehart and Winston, 1986, secs. 5.6D (timers), 6.3C (design example).

Eccles, W. J. *Microprocessor Systems: A 16-Bit Approach*. Reading, MA: Addison-Wesley, 1985, pp. 142 (program-controlled I/O), 169–172 (time-of-day clock).

Gorsline, G. W. *16-Bit Modern Microcomputers*. Englewood Cliffs, NJ: Prentice-Hall, 1985, pp. 334–339 (iRMX 86 operating system).

Liu, Y. C., and G. A. Gibson. *Microcomputer Systems: The 8086/8088 Family* (2nd ed.). Englewood Cliffs, NJ: Prentice-Hall, 1986, pp. 272–274 (multiprogramming), 274–282 (iRMX 86 operating system), 282–287 (semaphores), 287–291 (procedure sharing), 378–383 (programmable timers and event counters), 520–523 (80130 operating system processor).

Microsystem Components Handbook. Microprocessors and Peripherals, Volume II. Santa Clara, CA: Intel Corporation, 1985, pp. 5-229 to 5-272 (8253 and 8254 programmable interval timers).

Norton, P. *Programmer's Guide to the IBM PC*. Redmond, WA: Microsoft Press, 1985, pp. 56 (clock count in memory), 148–150 (timer-chip sound control), 222–224 (time-of-day services), 287–288 (date and time functions in DOS).

Software Handbook. Santa Clara, CA: Intel Corporation, 1985, pp. 2-5 to 2-23 (iRMX 86 Operating System), 2-193 to 2-233 (task management in iRMX 86), 2-241 to 2-247 (real-time operating systems).

Terms

Multitasking: doing many tasks in one time period, usually by working on the highest priority task that is currently active and suspending tasks that must wait for I/O, the completion of other tasks, or external events.

One-shot: a device that produces a single pulse of known length in response to a pulse input.

Programmable timer: a device that can do many timing functions, such as generating delays, pulses, and waveforms, under program control.

Real-time: in synchronization with the occurrence of events.

Real-time clock: a device that interrupts a CPU at regular time intervals.

Real-time operating system: an operating system that can manage programs with real-time requirements.

Scheduler: a program that decides when to start and stop other programs.

Supervisor: a program that loads, runs, and stops other programs.

Suspend (a task): halt a task and preserve its status.

Task: a self-contained program that forms part of a system under a supervisor's control.

Task status: the parameters that specify a task's current state.

Utility: a program that does a common overhead function such as sorting, converting data from one format to another, or copying a file.

Timing Requirements and Methods

Timing is always a problem in microprocessor applications. Systems must handle inputs and outputs at the proper rates and do their work on schedule. Delay programs, such as the ones shown in Laboratory 3, can meet simple timing needs. However, because they occupy the processor completely, they are inadequate for applications with complex, varying timing requirements.

Many applications, particularly in process and industrial control, have real-time constraints; that is, the microcomputer must take measurements and do operations at specific times. Some applications, such as energy and utility management systems, navigation systems, and security systems, must actually maintain a time-of-day clock and a calendar. A clock and calendar may also be necessary to stamp the date and time on reports, files, and messages.

We will explore the following ways to handle timing.

1. Adapting to the frequencies of external clocks.
2. Using programmable timers.
3. Using an elapsed time interrupt.
4. Using a real-time clock.

These methods are more flexible than fixed delay routines; external timers also reduce the burden on the processor.

Waiting for a Clock Transition

Many systems use either hardware (such as synchronizing circuits) or fixed parameter values to determine when time intervals begin and end. This approach is simple and compatible with systems that are not computer based, but it is inflexible. The user cannot readily modify the systems to handle new or improved peripherals. This is a major concern because of recent rapid advances in peripheral (for example, printer, terminal, tape, and disk) technology. A system that cannot be upgraded easily soon becomes obsolete.

An alternative approach is for the program to determine the time constants for its I/O devices. For example, the system could synchronize itself with a clock input. Attach a low-frequency (5–200 Hz) clock to bit 6 of port C of 8255 device P1, as shown in Figure D-2. The following program (see Program D-1 and Figure D-3) waits for a rising edge on the clock:

```
            MOV   DX,0FF03H      ;GET CONTROL REGISTER
                                 ;  ADDRESS
            MOV   AL,10011001B   ;MAKE PORTS A,C INPUT,
            OUT   DX,AL          ;  PORT B OUTPUT
            MOV   DX,0FF02H      ;GET CLOCK PORT ADDRESS
            ;
            ;WAIT UNTIL CLOCK LINE GOES LOW
            ;
WAITL:      IN    AL,DX          ;IS CLOCK LINE LOW?
            TEST  AL,01000000B
            JNZ   WAITL          ;NO, WAIT
            ;
            ;WAIT UNTIL CLOCK LINE GOES HIGH
            ;
WAITH:      IN    AL,DX          ;IS CLOCK LINE HIGH?
            TEST  AL,01000000B
            JZ    WAITH          ;NO, WAIT
            INT   20H
```

PROGRAM D-1		
Memory Address (Hex)	Memory Contents (Hex)	Instruction (DEBUG Form)
0200	BA	MOV DX,FF03
0201	03	
0202	FF	
0203	B0	MOV AL,99
0204	99	
0205	EE	OUT DX,AL
0206	BA	MOV DX,FF02

		PROGRAM D-1 (continued)		

Memory Address (Hex)	Memory Contents (Hex)		Instruction (DEBUG Form)	
0207	02			
0208	FF			
0209	EC	WAITL:	IN	AL,DX
020A	A8		TEST	AL,40
020B	40			
020C	75		JNZ	209
020D	FB			
020E	EC	WAITH:	IN	AL,DX
020F	A8		TEST	AL,40
0210	40			
0211	74		JZ	20E
0212	FB			
0213	CD		INT	20
0214	20			

Enter and run Program D-1. Vary the clock's frequency. How would you make the program wait for a falling edge?

One way to test Program D-1 is to use a debounced switch as the clock input. For example, you could use either the one attached to bit 2 of port C of 8255 device P1 or the one attached to bit 4 (see Figure B-1). If you do this, remember to change the masks in the TEST instructions to 04 (bit 2) or 10 (bit 4).

Another approach is to single-step the program with the T command. You will then be able to watch the two loops run. Remember, however, that the traced program is only checking the clock at very long intervals compared to its period.

Problem D-1

Make Program D-1 wait for a full clock pulse (that is, a rising edge followed by a falling edge).

Problem D-2

Make Program D-1 wait for 500 (01F4 hex) rising edges. This should take about 5 s.

Figure D-3
Flowchart of clock
synchronization
program.

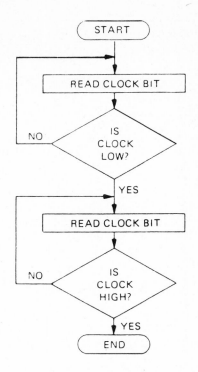

Problem D-3

Extend Program D-1 to control the LEDs attached to port B of 8255 device P1.
Make the LEDs go on initially and remain on for 100 (64 hex) rising edges
(about 1 s).

Measuring the Clock Period

We can make Program D-1 actually measure the clock's period. This involves:

1. Waiting for an edge.
2. Counting time intervals until the next similar edge.

Obviously, the period must last many CPU clock cycles for this method to work.
  The following program (see Figure D-4 for a flowchart) waits for a rising
edge and then counts milliseconds until the next one occurs. The length of the
period ends up in register BX. Program D-2 is the DEBUG version; check its
accuracy on some low-frequency clocks.

Figure D-4
Flowchart of the
program that
measures a clock
period.

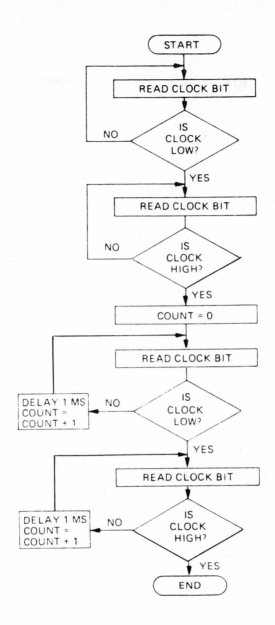

```
MOV   DX,0FF03H    ;GET CONTROL REGISTER
                   ;   ADDRESS
MOV   AL,10011001B ;MAKE PORTS A,C INPUT,
OUT   DX,AL        ;   B OUTPUT
MOV   DX,0FF02H    ;GET CLOCK PORT ADDRESS
SUB   BX,BX        ;MILLISECOND COUNT = ZERO
```

```
WTL1:       IN      AL,DX           ;IS CLOCK LINE LOW?
            TEST    AL,01000000B
            JNZ     WTL1            ;NO, WAIT
WTH1:       IN      AL,DX           ;IS CLOCK LINE HIGH?
            TEST    AL,01000000B
            JZ      WTH1            ;NO, WAIT
WTL2:       INC     BX              ;ADD 1 TO MILLISECOND COUNT
            MOV     CX,0CBH         ;WAIT 1 MS
DLYL:       DEC     CX
            JNZ     DLYL
            IN      AL,DX           ;IS CLOCK LINE LOW?
            TEST    AL,01000000B
            JNZ     WTL2            ;NO, WAIT
WTH2:       INC     BX              ;ADD 1 TO MILLISECOND COUNT
            MOV     CX,0CBH         ;WAIT 1 MS
DLYH:       DEC     CX
            JNZ     DLYH
            IN      AL,DX           ;IS CLOCK LINE HIGH?
            TEST    AL,01000000B
            JZ      WTH2            ;NO, WAIT
            INT     3               ;DISPLAY REGISTERS — PERIOD
                                    ;   IN REGISTER BX
```

PROGRAM D-2			
Memory Address (Hex)	**Memory Contents (Hex)**		**Instruction (DEBUG Form)**
0200	BA		MOV DX,FF03
0201	03		
0202	FF		
0203	B0		MOV AL,99
0204	99		
0205	EE		OUT DX,AL
0206	BA		MOV DX,FF02
0207	02		
0208	FF		
0209	29		SUB BX,BX
020A	DB		
020B	EC	WTL1:	IN AL,DX
020C	A8		TEST AL,40
020D	40		

Memory Address (Hex)	Memory Contents (Hex)		Instruction (DEBUG Form)	
		PROGRAM D-2 (continued)		
020E	75		JNZ	20B
020F	FB			
0210	EC	WTH1:	IN	AL,DX
0211	A8		TEST	AL,40
0212	40			
0213	74		JZ	210
0214	FB			
0215	43	WTL2:	INC	BX
0216	B9		MOV	CX,CB
0217	CB			
0218	00			
0219	49	DLYL:	DEC	CX
021A	75		JNZ	219
021B	FD			
021C	EC		IN	AL,DX
021D	A8		TEST	AL,40
021E	40			
021F	75		JNZ	215
0220	F4			
0221	43	WTH2:	INC	BX
0222	B9		MOV	CX,CB
0223	CB			
0224	00			
0225	49	DLYH:	DEC	CX
0226	75		JNZ	225
0227	FD			
0228	EC		IN	AL,DX
0229	A8		TEST	AL,40
022A	40			
022B	74		JZ	221
022C	F4			
022D	CC		INT	3

Problem D-4

Make Program D-2 measure the width of the clock's high phase.

Problem D-5

Make Program D-2's resolution 100 μs instead of 1 ms. Measure the periods of some clocks using both resolutions.

Problem D-6

Program D-2 assumes that the delay loops take all the execution time. How much should you reduce the delay constants to account for the instructions that add 1 to the clock count and test the clock line? See how the changes affect the period measurements at resolutions of 1 ms and 100 μs.

By using the measured clock period to time input and output, a program can operate at different rates. For example, it could handle serial I/O with a terminal at any common data rate (10 or 30 characters per second for low-speed units, 1200 to 19,200 bits per second for high-speed units).

Programmable Timers

The methods we have described so far all depend on the processor generating intervals with delay routines. An alternative is to use an external timer. The processor then only has to determine how the timer will operate, start it, and wait for it to indicate the end of the interval. Note that intervals generated in this way do not depend on the CPU's clock frequency and will not change if a faster CPU is introduced.

The simplest hardware timer is a one-shot that produces a single pulse of fixed length in response to a pulse input. More complex timers contain counters and latches; input controls may determine how many stages are used.

Like the programmable I/O devices described in Laboratory B, programmable timers have many operating modes; the program selects one by loading control registers. The timer's current state may be determined by examining its status registers. Typical options are binary or decimal (BCD) counts; the shape of output pulses (for example, square wave or brief pulse on terminal count); whether an interrupt is produced; whether the clock is divided; and whether the timer does a single task or runs continuously (that is, reloads its counters with their initial values after counting them down to zero).

Like programmable I/O devices, programmable timers simplify hardware design, save parts, and allow the use of standard boards in many applications. On the other hand, they are difficult to use and document because of their arbitrary features and unique programming requirements.

The 8253 and 8254 timers are often used in 8088-based microcomputers. Both have three 16-bit counter/timers that can be loaded under program control. Both have many operating modes; a control word register selects among them. The alternatives include:

1. Single interrupt on terminal count.
2. Programmable one-shot (that is, a single wide pulse).
3. Rate generator (that is, a periodic series of narrow pulses).
4. Square wave generator.
5. Hardware- or software-triggered strobe (that is, a single narrow pulse at the end of an interval).

For more details about the 8253 and 8254 timers, see the Intel handbook listed in this laboratory's references.

Elapsed Time Interrupts

The IBM PC has a timer interrupt (interrupt 8) based on its 8253 device. This interrupt occurs approximately 18.2 times per second. DOS provides the following functions that use the timer interrupt:

Service 0 of interrupt 1A hex returns the number of system-clock ticks since midnight. The high-order part of the number is in CX, the low-order part in DX. We will ignore the midnight-crossing problem (insomniacs beware!).

Function 2C of interrupt 21 hex returns the time of day. CH contains the hour (0 through 23), CL the minutes (0 through 59), DH the seconds (0 through 59), and DL hundredths of seconds (0 through 99).

The timer interrupt is easy to use, as DOS provides the vector and the interrupt service routine. The following program (Program D-3 is the DEBUG version) reads the clock count and then waits for it to change. This routine allows you to synchronize with the clock.

```
;
;WAIT FOR NEXT CLOCK TICK
;
        STI                     ;ENABLE CPU INTERRUPT
        SUB     AH,AH           ;GET CURRENT CLOCK
                                ;  COUNT
        INT     1AH
        MOV     [400H],DX       ;SAVE LOW-ORDER PART OF
                                ;  CLOCK COUNT
```

```
WTTICK:  SUB    AH,AH         ;GET CURRENT CLOCK
                              ;  COUNT

         INT    1AH
         CMP    DX,[400H]     ;HAS CLOCK COUNT
                              ;  CHANGED?

         JE     WTTICK        ;NO, WAIT
         CLI                  ;YES, DISABLE CPU INTER-
                              ;  RUPT

         INT    20H
```

PROGRAM D-3

Memory Address (Hex)	Memory Contents (Hex)		Instruction (DEBUG Form)	
0200	FB		STI	
0201	28		SUB	AH,AH
0202	E4			
0203	CD		INT	1A
0204	1A			
0205	89		MOV	[400],DX
0206	16			
0207	00			
0208	04			
0209	28	WTTICK:	SUB	AH,AH
020A	E4			
020B	CD		INT	1A
020C	1A			
020D	3B		CMP	DX,[400]
020E	16			
020F	00			
0210	04			
0211	74		JE	209
0212	F6			
0213	FA		CLI	
0214	CD		INT	20
0215	20			

Obviously, Program D-3 runs much too fast for you to see anything. One way to show that something has happened is to turn the LEDs attached to port B off initially, then on when the clock count changes. The next program (Program D-4 is the DEBUG version) extends Program D-3 to do this. You must look closely to see the LEDs flash, as they are only off for a few milliseconds.

```
        MOV    DX,0FF03H    ;GET CONTROL REGISTER ADDRESS
        MOV    AL,10010000B ;PORT A INPUT, PORT B OUTPUT
        OUT    DX,AL
        MOV    DX,0FF01H    ;TURN LEDS OFF INITIALLY
        MOV    AL,0FFH
        OUT    DX,AL
        STI                 ;ENABLE CPU INTERRUPT
        SUB    AH,AH        ;GET CURRENT CLOCK COUNT
        INT    1AH
        MOV    [400H],DX    ;SAVE LOW-ORDER PART OF
                            ;   CLOCK COUNT
WTTICK: SUB    AH,AH        ;GET CURRENT CLOCK COUNT
        INT    1AH
        CMP    DX,[400H]    ;HAS CLOCK COUNT CHANGED?
        JE     WTTICK       ;NO, WAIT
        MOV    DX,0FF01H    ;YES, TURN LEDS ON
        SUB    AL,AL
        OUT    DX,AL
        CLI                 ;DISABLE CPU INTERRUPT
        INT    20H
```

PROGRAM D-4

Memory Address (Hex)	Memory Contents (Hex)	Instruction (DEBUG Form)
0200	BA	MOV DX,FF03
0201	03	
0202	FF	
0203	B0	MOV AL,90
0204	90	
0205	EE	OUT DX,AL
0206	BA	MOV DX,FF01
0207	01	
0208	FF	
0209	B0	MOV AL,FF
020A	FF	
020B	EE	OUT DX,AL
020C	FB	STI
020D	28	SUB AH,AH
020E	E4	
020F	CD	INT 1A
0210	1A	
0211	89	MOV [400],DX

		PROGRAM D-4 (continued)		
Memory Address (Hex)	Memory Contents (Hex)		Instruction (DEBUG Form)	
0212	16			
0213	00			
0214	04			
0215	28	WTTICK:	SUB	AH,AH
0216	E4			
0217	CD		INT	1A
0218	1A			
0219	39		CMP	DX,[400]
021A	16			
021B	00			
021C	04			
021D	74		JE	215
021E	F6			
021F	BA		MOV	DX,FF01
0220	01			
0221	FF			
0222	28		SUB	AL,AL
0223	C0			
0224	EE		OUT	DX,AL
0225	FA		CLI	
0226	CD		INT	20
0227	20			

Problem D-7

Extend Program D-3 to first synchronize with the clock (by waiting for the next tick), then wait for a complete period before exiting.

Problem D-8

Write a program that waits for 18 (12 hex) timer interrupts and then lights the LEDs at port B of 8255 device P1 for 9 timer interrupts. The LEDs should be off for about 1 s and then on for about 0.5 s.

Real-Time Clock

A real-time clock simply produces interrupts continuously. The computer can keep time by counting them. On the IBM PC, the count is in units of 1/18.2 s.

Other programs can use the clock count to measure time, much as you would use your watch. If your watch now reads 2:33, for example, you can produce a 15-min delay by adding 15 to 2:33 and waiting for your watch to read 2:48. Similarly, a program can produce a delay by reading the clock count, adding the required number of clock periods, and waiting until the sum and the count are equal. The following program makes the computer wait 1 s (about 18 clock periods). Program D-5 is the DEBUG version.

```
                STI                     ;ENABLE CPU INTERRUPT
                SUB     AH,AH           ;GET INITIAL CLOCK COUNT
                INT     1AH
                ADD     DX,18           ;CALCULATE TARGET CLOCK COUNT
                MOV     [400H],DX
WTCNT:          SUB     AH,AH           ;GET CURRENT CLOCK COUNT
                INT     1AH
                CMP     DX,[400H]       ;HAS CLOCK COUNT REACHED
                                        ;  TARGET?
                JNE     WTCNT           ;NO, WAIT
                CLI                     ;YES, DISABLE CPU INTERRUPT
                INT     20H
```

PROGRAM D-5

Memory Address (Hex)	Memory Contents (Hex)		Instruction (DEBUG Form)	
0200	FB		STI	
0201	28		SUB	AH,AH
0202	E4			
0203	CD		INT	1A
0204	1A			
0205	83		ADD	DX,12
0206	C2			
0207	12			
0208	89		MOV	[400],DX
0209	16			
020A	00			
020B	04			
020C	28	WTCNT:	SUB	AH,AH
020D	E4			
020E	CD		INT	1A
020F	1A			
0210	3B		CMP	DX,[400]
0211	16			

	PROGRAM D-5 (continued)	
Memory Address (Hex)	Memory Contents (Hex)	Instruction (DEBUG Form)
0212	00	
0213	04	
0214	74	JNE 20C
0215	F6	
0216	FA	CLI
0217	CD	INT 20
0218	20	

Enter and run Program D-5. Make it wait for 5 s.

Problem D-9

Make Program D-5 run for ten iterations, turning the LEDs at port B on and off according to the duty cycle in 340 and 341. To determine when a time interval ends, add its length to the current clock count. Does it matter if the addition generates a carry?

Run the program for the following test cases and describe what happens.

  a. OFF − [0340] = 1
       ON − [0341] = 1
  b. OFF − [0340] = 1
       ON − [0341] = 7
  c. OFF − [0340] = 4
       ON − [0341] = 4
  d. OFF − [0340] = 7
       ON − [0341] = 1

(*Hint:* Use the instruction ADD [mem],reg which adds a register to a memory location. The sum ends up in memory.)

Problem D-10

Make the answer to Problem D-9 turn the LEDs on and off according to the following duty cycle for each iteration:

$$OFF - 12 \text{ hex } (1 \text{ s})$$
$$ON - 24 \text{ hex } (2 \text{ s})$$

$$\text{OFF} - 48 \text{ hex } (4 \text{ s})$$
$$\text{ON} \ \ - 90 \text{ hex } (8 \text{ s})$$

Industrial and process controllers often have complex duty cycles with many variations in length and amplitude.

To make the program shorter and more general, put the ON-OFF values in a table. For example, you could use 340 through 344, as follows:

$$[0340] = 12 \ (\text{first OFF period})$$
$$[0341] = 24 \ (\text{first ON period})$$
$$[0342] = 48 \ (\text{second OFF period})$$
$$[0343] = 90 \ (\text{second ON period})$$
$$[0344] = 00 \ (\text{terminator})$$

Longer Intervals

We can handle longer intervals with the time-of-day function (function 2C of interrupt 21 hex). The following program (Program D-6 is the DEBUG version) uses the count in register DH to wait for 10 s, ignoring any fractions. Note that we must do mod 60 arithmetic when handling seconds.

```
        STI                      ;ENABLE CPU INTERRUPT
        MOV    AH,2CH            ;GET INITIAL TIME OF DAY
        INT    21H
        ADD    DH,10             ;CALCULATE TARGET
                                 ;   SECONDS
        CMP    DH,60             ;MOD 60
        JB     SVSEC
        SUB    DH,60
SVSEC:  MOV    [400H],DH         ;SAVE TARGET MOD 60
WTSEC:  MOV    AH,2CH            ;GET CURRENT TIME OF DAY
        INT    21H
        CMP    DH,[400H]         ;HAVE SECONDS REACHED
                                 ;   TARGET?
        JNE    WTSEC             ;NO, WAIT
        CLI                      ;YES, DISABLE CPU INTERRUPT
        INT    20H
```

	PROGRAM D-6		
Memory Address (Hex)	Memory Contents (Hex)		Instruction (DEBUG Form)
0200	FB		STI
0201	B4		MOV AH,2C
0202	2C		
0203	CD		INT 21
0204	21		
0205	80		ADD DH,A
0206	C6		
0207	0A		
0208	80		CMP DH,3C
0209	FE		
020A	3C		
020B	72		JB 210
020C	03		
020D	80		SUB DH,3C
020E	EE		
020F	3C		
0210	88	SVSEC:	MOV [400],DH
0211	36		
0212	00		
0213	04		
0214	B4	WTSEC:	MOV AH,2C
0215	2C		
0216	CD		INT 21
0217	21		
0218	3A		CMP DH,[400]
0219	36		
021A	00		
021B	04		
021C	75		JNE 214
021D	F6		
021E	FA		CLI
021F	CD		INT 20
0220	20		

Note that 60 decimal = 3C hex.

Problem D-11

Extend Program D-6 to turn all the LEDs at port B off for 10 s and then on for

15 s. Change your program to get the following ON-OFF periods

a. OFF − 15 s
   ON − 10 s
b. OFF − 10 s
   ON − 10 s

Problem D-12

Make the answer to Problem D-11 operate for four iterations, turning the LEDs on and off according to 340 (OFF period) and 341 (ON period). Try the following cases:

a. [0340] = 14 (20 s)
   [0341] = 0F (15 s)
b. [0340] = 0A (10 s)
   [0341] = 0A (10 s)

We can easily extend Program D-6 to handle minutes as well as seconds. The following program (Program D-7 is the DEBUG version) waits for 1 min by first waiting for the minute count to change, then waiting for the second count to get back to its initial value.

```
        STI                    ;ENABLE CPU INTERRUPT
        MOV    AH,2CH          ;GET INITIAL TIME OF DAY
        INT    21H
        MOV    [400H],CL       ;SAVE INITIAL MINUTE COUNT
        MOV    [401H],DH       ;SAVE INITIAL SECOND COUNT
WTMIN:  MOV    AH,2CH          ;GET CURRENT TIME OF DAY
        INT    21H
        CMP    CL,[400H]       ;WAIT UNTIL MINUTE CHANGES
        JE     WTMIN
WTSEC:  MOV    AH,2CH          ;GET CURRENT TIME OF DAY
        INT    21H
        CMP    DH,[401H]       ;WAIT UNTIL SECOND COUNT IS
        JNE    WTSEC           ;   SAME AS INITIAL VALUE
        CLI
        INT    20H
```

	PROGRAM D-7			
Memory Address (Hex)	Memory Contents (Hex)		Instruction (DEBUG Form)	
0200	FB		STI	
0201	B4		MOV	AH,2C
0202	2C			
0203	CD		INT	21
0204	21			
0205	88		MOV	[400],CL
0206	0E			
0207	00			
0208	04			
0209	88		MOV	[401],DH
020A	36			
020B	01			
020C	04			
020D	B4	WTMIN:	MOV	AH,2C
020E	2C			
020F	CD		INT	21
0210	21			
0211	3A		CMP	CL,[400]
0212	0E			
0213	00			
0214	04			
0215	74		JE	20D
0216	F6			
0217	B4	WTSEC:	MOV	AH,2C
0218	2C			
0219	CD		INT	21
021A	21			
021B	3A		CMP	DH,[401]
021C	36			
021D	01			
021E	04			
021F	75		JNZ	217
0220	F6			
0221	FA		CLI	
0222	CD		INT	20
0223	20			

Problem D-13

Extend Program D-7 to turn all the LEDs off for 1 min and 30 s and then on for 1 min and 15 s.

Problem D-14

We can use tables to produce complex timing sequences. Write a program that
turns the LEDs at port B on and off according to the following table. Each
entry is the length of a period in seconds and the final zero is a terminator.

[0340] = 0A (first OFF period is 10 s)
[0341] = 0F (first ON period is 15 s)
[0342] = 14 (second OFF period is 20 s)
[0343] = 0F (second ON period is 15 s)
[0344] = 0A (third OFF period is 10 s)
[0345] = 14 (third ON period is 20 s)
[0346] = 00 (terminator)

The LEDs should be off for 10 s (0A hex), on for 15 s, off for 20 s, on for 15 s, off
for 10 s, and on for 20 s.

Problem D-15

Extend the answer to Problem D-14 to show arbitrary values on the LEDs.
Write a program that operates the LEDs from a table with entries consisting
of a length in seconds followed by an output data value. The final zero is a
terminator. Turn all the LEDs off before ending.

[0340] = 14 (first period is 20 s long)
[0341] = 00 (all LEDs on)
[0342] = 1E (second period is 30 s long)
[0343] = 01 (all LEDs on except 0)
[0344] = 0F (third period is 15 s long)
[0345] = 03 (all LEDs on except 0 and 1)
[0346] = 00 (terminator)

Real-Time Operating Systems

A real-time clock can satisfy many timing needs. Tasks can be scheduled or
suspended, delays can be produced, and real-time inputs and outputs can be
handled. The programmer must, however, determine the tasks' order and priority and specify how they use the clock.

A typical example application is a real-time monitoring system for process or industrial control. The system must collect data periodically (for example, readings from sensors located in a pipeline, tank, or reactor), respond immediately to alarms, and report status to a central computer. The times when alarms occur must be printed for permanent records. This system has many tasks to do: data logging, alarm recognition, alarm recording, printing, and communications with the central computer. The priority of the tasks is critical. For example, if an alarm occurs while a record is being printed, the system must suspend the printing, mark when the alarm occurred, prepare a new record for later printing, and then resume the suspended task. A similar procedure is necessary if the central computer requests a report while the system is busy. The programmer must manage the computer's resources so that it does its work without missing any data, alarms, or requests for reports.

A real-time operating system removes much of the burden of task management from the programmer. This packaged software schedules tasks, handles communications between them (for example, its routines would let the alarm-recording task send information about the alarm to the printer task), generates time intervals, and provides real-time interrupt control for I/O devices. The programmer must learn only how to use the operating system. The obvious advantages of such systems are that they can be bought rather than written and that they provide standard procedures and formats.

To use a real-time operating system in the monitoring application, you would have to write programs in the proper form to handle data logging, alarm monitoring, printing, and status reporting. Each program (or *task*) would call operating system subroutines (sometimes called *utilities*). Thus the user tasks and the operating system would together control the monitoring system. Note that you could change one task (for example, attach a new printer, allow more alarms, or add a local data buffer) without changing the other tasks. We would like to thank Bill Renwick of Kadak Products Ltd. (Vancouver, B.C., Canada) for suggesting this example and describing how it would run under Kadak's AMX Operating System. Intel offers a widely used real-time operating system called iRMX 86 (see this laboratory's references for more details about it).

Key Point Summary

1. Programs can be made more flexible by allowing them to determine timing parameters from system inputs. The same program can then handle peripherals operating at different data rates.
2. A program can easily examine a clock line, synchronize with it, and measure its period as long as its frequency is much lower than the CPU's clock frequency.

3. A programmable timer can replace a delay routine. It simply indicates when a starting value loaded into it has been counted down to zero. Programmable timers make systems more flexible because they can operate in different modes under program control. However, these timers require careful use and documentation because there are no standards for their options or programming.

4. Interrupts are a convenient way to handle timing. A real-time clock is a regular source of interrupts that can be counted for timing and scheduling. Time is specified in counts.

5. A real-time operating system does scheduling, coordination, and communications on a real-time basis. It provides a standard supervisor for applications with real-time needs.

Serial Input/Output

To learn how to send and receive serial data.

What You
Should Learn

1. How to convert data between serial and parallel forms.
2. How to provide timing for serial communications.
3. How to generate and recognize start and stop bits.
4. How to detect false start bits using majority logic.
5. How to generate and check parity.

Reference
Materials

Comer, D. J. *Microprocessor-Based System Design*. New York: Holt, Rinehart and Winston, 1986, sec. 5.6F (UART).

Eccles, W. J. *Microprocessor Systems: A 16-Bit Approach*. Reading, MA: Addison-Wesley, chap. 9 (serial interfaces).

Gorsline, G. W. *16-Bit Modern Microcomputers*. Englewood Cliffs, NJ: Prentice-Hall, 1985, pp. 142–156 (I/O protocols), 437–469 (computer-to-computer communication).

Liu, Y. C., and G. A. Gibson. *Microcomputer Systems: The 8086/8088 Family* (2nd ed.). Englewood Cliffs, NJ: Prentice-Hall, 1986, pp. 349–369 (serial communication interfaces).

McNamara, J. E. *Technical Aspects of Data Communications* (2nd ed.). Maynard, MA: Educational Services Department, Digital Equipment Corp., 1982, chaps. 1–3, 5, 15.

Microsystem Components Handbook: Microprocessors and Peripherals, Volume II. Santa Clara, CA: Intel Corporation, 1985, pp. 6-1 to 6-2 (overview of Intel communications devices), 6-3 to 6-19 (8251A programmable communication interface), 6-20 to 6-84 (8273 and 8274 serial communications controllers), 6-113 to 6-143 (using the 8251 serial interface chip), 6-144 to 6-267 (using the 8273 and 8274 serial communications controllers).

Norton, P. *Programmer's Guide to the IBM PC*. Redmond, WA: Microsoft Press, 1985, pp. 210–213 (RS-232 serial communications services), 273 (serial I/O).

Terms **Baud:** rate of serial data transmission, bits per second but including both data bits and bits used for synchronization, error checking, and other purposes. Common baud rates are 110, 300, 1200, 2400, 4800, and 9600.

Baud rate generator: a device that generates time intervals between bits for serial data transmission.

Error-correcting code: a code that the receiver can use to correct errors in messages.

Error-detecting code: a code that the receiver can use to detect errors in messages.

False start bit: a start bit that does not last the minimum required amount of time.

Majority logic: a logic function that is true when more than half its inputs are true.

Parallel: more than one bit at a time.

Parity: a 1-bit code that makes the total number of 1 bits in the word, including the parity bit, odd (odd parity) or even (even parity).

Protocol: a set of conventions governing the format and timing of data transfers.

Serial: one bit at a time.

Start bit: a bit indicating the start of data transmission by an asynchronous device.

Stop bit: a bit indicating the end of data transmission by an asynchronous device.

Universal asynchronous receiver/transmitter (UART): an LSI device that interfaces parallel systems to asynchronous serial peripherals.

8088 **CMC: complement (invert) the Carry flag.**
Instructions

JPE (or JP): jump if parity even (Parity flag = 1).

JPO (or JNP): jump if parity odd (Parity flag = 0).

RCL: rotate left through Carry; shift a register or memory location left as if its most significant and least significant bits were connected through the Carry flag (see Figure E-1).

Figure E-1
8088 shift
instructions RCL
and RCR in their
1-bit forms.

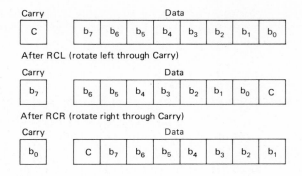

RCR: rotate right through Carry; shift a register or memory location
right as if its most significant and least significant bits were connected through the Carry flag (see Figure E-1).

Serial Interfacing

Most communications equipment (for example, modems and computer-to-
computer connections) and many other peripherals transfer data one bit at a
time (*serially*) rather than in larger units (in *parallel*). The serial approach is
cheaper to implement because it requires only one data line. However, special
interfaces are needed to connect serial peripherals to a computer that handles
data in parallel.

This laboratory describes the interfacing of serial peripherals using software.
We will show how to convert data between serial and parallel forms, provide
timing, add and detect start and stop bits, and check and generate parity.

Serial interfaces allow many tradeoffs between hardware and software. A
common hardware interface is the universal asynchronous receiver/transmitter
(UART). UARTs do all the interfacing tasks mentioned above without processor
intervention. This laboratory's references describe the Intel 8251, a common
UART in 8088-based systems. IBM PCs, compatibles, and add-on boards generally use National Semiconductor's 8250, a UART with its own built-in timer or
baud rate generator.

Serial/Parallel Conversion

Shift instructions can convert data between parallel and serial forms. Because
serial data transmission generally starts with bit 0, the next program puts bit 0 of

register BL on the LED connected to bit 7 of port B of 8255 device P1 (LED 7, for short). Program E-1 is the DEBUG version. SHR BL,1 moves the data's rightmost bit to the Carry; RCR AL,1 then moves it on to bit 7 of register AL for output. *We have complemented the data, so it appears on the LEDs in positive logic.* Program E-1 initially turns off all the LEDs and starts the output data at all ones. It also makes port C input, thus keeping its LEDs off to avoid distraction.

```
MOV    DX,0FF03H        ;GET CONTROL REGISTER ADDRESS
MOV    AL,10011001B     ;PORT A INPUT, PORT B OUTPUT,
OUT    DX,AL            ;   PORT C INPUT
MOV    DX,0FF01H        ;TURN OFF THE LEDS AND START
MOV    AL,0FFH          ;   DATA AT ALL 1'S
OUT    DX,AL
MOV    BL,[340H]        ;GET DATA
NOT    BL               ;INVERT DATA TO SHOW ON LEDS
SHR    BL,1             ;SERIALIZE NEXT BIT
RCR    AL,1
OUT    DX,AL
INT    3                ;EXIT, DISPLAY AND PRESERVE
                        ;   REGISTERS
```

	PROGRAM E-1	
Memory Address (Hex)	Memory Contents (Hex)	Instruction (DEBUG Form)
0200	BA	MOV DX,FF03
0201	03	
0202	FF	
0203	B0	MOV AL,99
0204	99	
0205	EE	OUT DX,AL
0206	BA	MOV DX,FF01
0207	01	
0208	FF	
0209	B0	MOV AL,FF
020A	FF	
020B	EE	OUT DX,AL
020C	8A	MOV BL,[340]
020D	1E	
020E	40	

		PROGRAM E-1 (continued)	
Memory Address (Hex)	Memory Contents (Hex)	Instruction (DEBUG Form)	
020F	03		
0210	F6	NOT	BL
0211	D3		
0212	D0	SHR	BL,1
0213	EB		
0214	D0	RCR	AL,1
0215	D8		
0216	EE	OUT	DX,AL
0217	CC	INT	3

Program E-1 transmits 1 bit. Run it eight times starting with [0340] = AA (10101010 binary). *After the first time, start at 212 to skip the initialization instructions.* Be sure to end the program with INT 3, not INT 20H, to preserve the registers between iterations. LED 7 should alternate between off and on, since the data consists of alternating 0 and 1 bits, starting with a 0 in bit 0. RCR AL,1 shifts the previous serial outputs right, so you can see all the transmitted bits. What does register BL contain when you finish? Note how Program E-1 simulates the effects of a shift register on the LEDs.

Problem E-1

Revise Program E-1 to use bit 0 of port B of 8255 device P1 as the serial output. The data now appears on the LEDs in inverted order, starting with bit 0 at the far left.

Converting inputs from serial to parallel is also simple. The following program (Program E-2 is the DEBUG version) fetches a serial input from bit 7 of port A and combines it with the data in register BL. We assume that bit 0 of the data is received first. Repeating Program E-2 makes the data bits move right on the LEDs and end up in their normal order.

Run Program E-2 eight times to assemble a data byte in register BL. *After the first time, start at 20E to skip the initialization.* Vary the switch position to make BL's final contents AA hex; remember that the bits are received in right-to-left order.

```
MOV   DX,0FF03H      ;GET CONTROL REGISTER ADDRESS
MOV   AL,10011001B   ;PORT A INPUT, PORT B OUTPUT,
OUT   DX,AL          ;   PORT C INPUT
MOV   DX,0FF01H      ;TURN OFF THE LEDS
MOV   AL,0FFH
OUT   DX,AL
SUB   BL,BL          ;CLEAR DATA INITIALLY
MOV   DX,0FF00H      ;GET SERIAL DATA
IN    AL,DX
SHL   AL,1           ;MOVE SERIAL DATA TO CARRY
RCR   BL,1           ;COMBINE IT WITH PREVIOUS DATA
MOV   DX,0FF01H      ;SHOW DATA ON LEDS
MOV   AL,BL
NOT   AL
OUT   DX,AL
INT   3              ;EXIT AND DISPLAY REGISTERS
```

PROGRAM E-2		
Memory Address (Hex)	Memory Contents (Hex)	Instruction (DEBUG Form)
0200	BA	MOV DX,FF03
0201	03	
0202	FF	
0203	B0	MOV AL,99
0204	99	
0205	EE	OUT DX,AL
0206	BA	MOV DX,FF01
0207	01	
0208	FF	
0209	B0	MOV AL,FF
020A	FF	
020B	EE	OUT DX,AL
020C	28	SUB BL,BL
020D	DB	
020E	BA	MOV DX,FF00
020F	00	
0210	FF	
0211	EC	IN AL,DX
0212	D0	SHL AL,1
0213	E0	
0214	D0	RCR BL,1
0215	DB	
0216	BA	MOV DX,FF01

Memory Address (Hex)	Memory Contents (Hex)	Instruction (DEBUG Form)
\multicolumn{3}{c}{**PROGRAM E-2 (continued)**}		
0217	01	
0218	FF	
0219	88	MOV AL,BL
021A	D8	
021B	F6	NOT AL
021C	D0	
021D	EE	OUT DX,AL
021E	CC	INT 3

Problem E-2

Make Program E-2 start with data bit 7, and use switch 0 as the serial input.

Generating Bit Rates

In actual applications, the computer must wait between bits. One way to do this is with a software delay. The next program (Program E-3 is the DEBUG version) uses a subroutine DELAY that waits for 1/8 s times the contents of register AH. DELAY affects only the flags. Run Program E-3 with [0340] = AA and with [0340] = 55; the 2-s wait between bits makes the serialization easy to see.

```
MOV    SP,180H        ;INITIALIZE USER STACK
                      ;   POINTER
MOV    DX,0FF03H      ;GET CONTROL
                      ;   REGISTER ADDRESS
MOV    AL,10011001B   ;PORT A INPUT, PORT B
                      ;   OUTPUT, PORT C
OUT    DX,AL          ;   INPUT
MOV    DX,0FF01H      ;TURN OFF THE LEDS
MOV    AL,0FFH
OUT    DX,AL
```

```
              MOV     BL,[340H]      ;GET DATA
              NOT     BL             ;INVERT DATA TO SHOW ON
                                     ;  LEDS
              MOV     CX,8           ;NUMBER OF BITS = 8
OUTBIT:       SHR     BL,1           ;SERIALIZE NEXT BIT
              RCR     AL,1
              OUT     DX,AL
              MOV     AH,16          ;BIT TIME = 2 SECONDS
              CALL    DELAY
              LOOP    OUTBIT         ;COUNT BITS
              INT     20H


              ORG     300H           ;WAIT 1/8 S TIMES [AH]
DELAY:        PUSH    AX             ;SAVE REGISTERS
              PUSH    CX
DLY8:         MOV     CX,62A5H       ;WAIT 1/8 S
DLY:          DEC     CX
              JNZ     DLY
              DEC     AH             ;COUNT 1/8 S UNITS
              JNZ     DLY8
              POP     CX             ;RESTORE REGISTERS
              POP     AX
              RET
```

PROGRAM E-3

Memory Address (Hex)	Memory Contents (Hex)	Instruction (DEBUG Form)	
0200	BC	MOV	SP,180
0201	80		
0202	01		
0203	BA	MOV	DX,FF03
0204	03		
0205	FF		
0206	B0	MOV	AL,99
0207	99		
0208	EE	OUT	DX,AL
0209	BA	MOV	DX,FF01
020A	01		
020B	FF		
020C	B0	MOV	AL,FF
020D	FF		

	PROGRAM E-3 (continued)			
Memory Address (Hex)	Memory Contents (Hex)		Instruction (DEBUG Form)	
020E	EE		OUT	DX,AL
020F	8A		MOV	BL,[340]
0210	1E			
0211	40			
0212	03			
0213	F6		NOT	BL
0214	D3			
0215	B9		MOV	CX,8
0216	08			
0217	00			
0218	D0	OUTBIT:	SHR	BL,1
0219	EB			
021A	D0		RCR	AL,1
021B	D8			
021C	EE		OUT	DX,AL
021D	B4		MOV	AH,10
021E	10			
021F	E8		CALL	300
0220	DE			
0221	00			
0222	E2		LOOP	218
0223	F4			
0224	CD		INT	20
0225	20			
0300	50	DELAY:	PUSH	AX
0301	51		PUSH	CX
0302	B9	DLY8:	MOV	CX,62A5
0303	A5			
0304	62			
0305	49	DLY:	DEC	CX
0306	75		JNZ	305
0307	FD			
0308	FE		DEC	AH
0309	CC			
030A	75		JNZ	302
030B	F6			
030C	59		POP	CX
030D	58		POP	AX
030E	C3		RET	

Problem E-3

Write a serial reception program that waits 2 seconds between bits. Assume that the data starts with bit 0 and comes from switch 7. Run the program, setting the switch to give a final result of 55 hex in location 341. Start with the switch in the 1 (open) position, and move it each time the display changes.

Using the Real-Time Clock

We can also use a real-time clock to wait between bits. The following program synchronizes with the clock and sends a bit each time the second count changes (that is, at 1-s intervals). Program E-4 is the DEBUG version. Note that we use memory locations for the data, second count, and bit count to avoid dependence on which registers INT 21H affects. Enter and run Program E-4 with [0340] = AA and with [0340] = 0F.

		PROGRAM E-4	
Memory Address (Hex)	Memory Contents (Hex)	Instruction (DEBUG Form)	
0200	BA	MOV	DX,FF03
0201	03		
0202	FF		
0203	B0	MOV	AL,99
0204	99		
0205	EE	OUT	DX,AL
0206	BA	MOV	DX,FF01
0207	01		
0208	FF		
0209	B0	MOV	AL,FF
020A	FF		
020B	EE	OUT	DX,AL
020C	A2	MOV	[401],AL
020D	01		
020E	04		
020F	FB	STI	
0210	B4	MOV	AH,2C

PROGRAM E-4 (continued)		
Memory Address (Hex)	Memory Contents (Hex)	Instruction (DEBUG Form)
0211	2C	
0212	CD	INT 21
0213	21	
0214	88	MOV [400],DH
0215	36	
0216	00	
0217	04	
0218	B4	WTSYN: MOV AH,2C
0219	2C	
021A	CD	INT 21
021B	21	
021C	3A	CMP DH,[400]
021D	36	
021E	00	
021F	04	
0220	74	JZ 218
0221	F6	
0222	88	MOV [400],DH
0223	36	
0224	00	
0225	04	
0226	A0	MOV AL,[340]
0227	40	
0228	03	
0229	F6	NOT AL
022A	D0	
022B	A2	MOV [402],AL
022C	08	
022D	00	
022E	C6	MOV BY [403],8
022F	06	
0230	03	
0231	04	
0232	08	
0233	D0	OUTBIT: SHR BY [402],1
0234	2E	
0235	02	
0236	04	
0237	D0	RCR BY [401],1
0238	1E	
0239	01	
023A	04	

PROGRAM E-4 (continued)		
Memory Address (Hex)	Memory Contents (Hex)	Instruction (DEBUG Form)
023B	BA	MOV DX,FF01
023C	01	
023D	FF	
023E	A0	MOV AL,[401]
023F	01	
0240	04	
0241	EE	OUT DX,AL
0242	B4	WTSEC: MOV AH,2C
0243	2C	
0244	CD	INT 21
0245	21	
0246	3A	CMP DH,[400]
0247	36	
0248	00	
0249	04	
024A	74	JE 242
024B	F6	
024C	88	MOV [400],DH
024D	36	
024E	00	
024F	04	
0250	FE	DEC BY [403]
0251	0E	
0252	03	
0253	04	
0254	75	JNZ 233
0255	DD	
0256	FA	CLI
0257	CD	INT 20
0258	20	

```
MOV   DX,0FF03H      ;GET CONTROL REGISTER ADDRESS
MOV   AL,10011001B   ;PORT A INPUT, PORT B OUTPUT,
OUT   DX,AL          ;   PORT C INPUT
MOV   DX,0FF01H      ;TURN OFF LEDS INITIALLY
MOV   AL,0FFH
OUT   DX,AL
MOV   [401H],AL      ;SAVE INITIAL STATE OF LEDS
STI                  :ENABLE CPU INTERRUPT
MOV   AH,2CH         ;GET INITIAL SECOND COUNT
```

```
                INT    21H
                MOV    [400H],DH            ;SAVE INITIAL SECOND COUNT
WTSYN:          MOV    AH,2CH               ;SYNCHRONIZE TRANSMISSION
                                            ;WITH CLOCK BY WAITING FOR
                INT    21H                  ;NEXT SECOND TO START
                CMP    DH,[400H]
                JE     WTSYN
                MOV    [400H],DH            ;SAVE SECOND COUNT
                MOV    AL,[340H]            ;GET DATA
                NOT    AL                   ;INVERT DATA TO SHOW ON LEDS
                MOV    [402H],AL            ;SAVE INVERTED DATA
                MOV    BYTE PTR [403H],8    ;NUMBER OF BITS = 8
OUTBIT:         SHR    BYTE PTR [402H],1    ;SERIALIZE NEXT BIT
                RCR    BYTE PTR [401H],1
                MOV    DX,0FF01H            ;SHOW DATA ON LEDS
                MOV    AL,[401H]
                OUT    DX,AL
WTSEC:          MOV    AH,2CH               ;WAIT FOR NEXT SECOND
                                            ;   TO START
                INT    21H
                CMP    DH,[400H]
                JE     WTSEC
                MOV    [400H],DH            ;SAVE SECOND COUNT
                DEC    BYTE PTR [403H]      ;COUNT BITS
                JNZ    OUTBIT
                CLI                         ;DISABLE CPU INTERRUPT
                INT    20H
```

Problem E-4

Make the serial reception program wait for 1 s (18 ticks) between bits. Use the clock count (that is, INT 1AH) to create the delay.

SAMPLE CASES

a. All inputs 1's (leave the switch open).
   Result: [0341] = FF
b. All inputs 0's (leave the switch closed).
   Results: [0341] = 00

Start and Stop Bits

So far, we have assumed that reception can occur at any time. Of course, in practice, the receiver (computer or peripheral) must determine when the data starts and ends.

One way to allow for this is to put markers around the data. Figure E-2 shows a popular format with a start bit (0) before each character and two stop bits (1s) afterward. Note that the data line is normally 1.

Although this approach is simple and easy to implement, it has drawbacks. Noise can product false start bits; later we will discuss methods for detecting them. Adding start and stop bits reduces the actual data rate (because of the extra bits that contain no information) and creates extra overhead for each character. An alternative is to group the characters into blocks and synchronize only on a block-by-block basis. Most protocols (see the book by McNamara listed in the references) use this approach to increase speed and reliability.

We can easily modify Program E-3 to produce a start bit. We must clear the Carry initially and shift register BL at the end of the loop instead of at the beginning. Now the program transmits a 0 first and data bit 0 second. Of course, the bit count must be 9 instead of 8. Program E-5 is the DEBUG version.

Figure E-2
Serial data format
with a start bit and
two stop bits.

Each character requires 11 bits.

PROGRAM E-5		
Memory Address (Hex)	Memory Contents (Hex)	Instruction (DEBUG Form)
0200	BC	*MOV* *SP,180*
0201	80	
0202	01	
0203	BA	*MOV* *DX,FF03*
0204	03	
0205	FF	
0206	B0	*MOV* *AL,99*
0207	99	
0208	EE	*OUT* *DX,AL*
0209	BA	*MOV* *DX,FF01*
020A	01	
020B	FF	
020C	B0	*MOV* *AL,FF*
020D	FF	
020E	EE	*OUT* *DX,AL*
020F	8A	*MOV* *BL,[340]*
0210	1E	
0211	40	

	PROGRAM E-5 (continued)		

Memory Address (Hex)	Memory Contents (Hex)		Instruction (DEBUG Form)
0212	03		
0213	F6		NOT BL
0214	D3		
0215	B9		MÓV CX,9
0216	09		
0217	00		
0218	F8		CLC
0219	D0	OUTBIT:	RCR AL,1
021A	D8		
021B	EE		OUT DX,AL
021C	B4		MOV AH,10
021D	10		
021E	E8		CALL 300
021F	DF		
0220	00		
0221	D0		SHR BL,1
0222	EB		
0223	E2		LOOP 219
0224	F4		
0225	CD		INT 20
0226	20		

```
         MOV   SP,180H          ;INITIALIZE USER STACK
                                ;   POINTER
         MOV   DX,0FF03H        ;GET CONTROL REGISTER
                                ;   ADDRESS
         MOV   AL,10011001B     ;PORT A INPUT, PORT B OUTPUT,
         OUT   DX,AL            ;   PORT C INPUT
         MOV   DX,0FF01H        ;TURN OFF THE LEDS
         MOV   AL,0FFH
         OUT   DX,AL
         MOV   BL,[340H]        ;GET DATA
         NOT   BL               ;INVERT DATA TO SHOW ON
                                ;   LEDS
         MOV   CX,9             ;NUMBER OF BITS = 9
         CLC                    ;FORM START BIT
OUTBIT:  RCR   AL,1             ;SERIALIZE NEXT BIT
         OUT   DX,AL
```

```
MOV    AH,16              ;BIT TIME = 2 SECONDS
CALL   DELAY
SHR    BL,1               ;GET NEXT DATA BIT
LOOP   OUTBIT             ;COUNT BITS
INT    20H
```

Enter Program E-5 into memory and run it with [0340] = 00 and with [0340] = AA. The DELAY routine is the same as in Program E-3. The start bit appears as a light in front of the actual data, as 0 lights an LED. When the last data bit (bit 7) is sent, the start bit vanishes at the far right.

Problem E-5

a. Write and run a transmission program that generates a start bit and 2 stop bits. Remember to change the bit count.

Hint: The easiest way to generate a stop bit is to replace SHR BL,1 with STC (SET CARRY); RCR BL,1. This sequence shifts in 1's automatically at the left as it shifts the data right. Note that the stop bits appear as two unlit LEDs to the left of the remaining data bits (bits 2 through 7).

b. How could you make your program produce 1 stop bit instead of 2? Many terminals use a 10-bit format with 1 stop bit.

Receiving data with start and stop bits is more difficult than transmitting it. The next program (Program E-6 is the DEBUG version) first detects the falling edge that marks the beginning of a start bit. It then waits 1.5 bit times to center the reception. This delay makes the computer read the data bits near the centers of the pulses rather than at the edges, thus avoiding the transition areas. Centering also makes precise bit times unnecessary, because a slight drift will still leave the input instructions well within their target data bits.

```
MOV    SP,180H            ;INITIALIZE USER STACK
                          ;   POINTER
MOV    DX,0FF03H          ;GET CONTROL REGISTER
                          ;   ADDRESS
MOV    AL,10011001B       ;PORT A INPUT, PORT B OUTPUT,
OUT    DX,AL              ;   PORT C INPUT
MOV    DX,0FF01H          ;TURN OFF THE LEDS
MOV    AL,0FFH
OUT    DX,AL
MOV    DX,0FF00H          ;WAIT FOR A START BIT
```

```
WTSTB:  IN      AL,DX
        SHL     AL,1
        JC      WTSTB
        MOV     AH,24           ;WAIT 1 1/2 BIT TIMES TO
        CALL    DELAY           ;   CENTER FIRST DATA BIT
        MOV     CX,8            ;NUMBER OF BITS = 8
INBIT:  IN      AL,DX           ;GET NEXT BIT
        SHL     AL,1            ;COMBINE IT WITH PREVIOUS
                                ;   DATA
        RCR     BL,1
        MOV     AH,16           ;BIT TIME = 2 SECONDS
        CALL    DELAY
        LOOP    INBIT           ;COUNT BITS
        MOV     [340H],BL       ;SAVE DATA BYTE
        INT     20H
```

	PROGRAM E-6	
Memory Address (Hex)	Memory Contents (Hex)	Instruction (DEBUG Form)
0200	BC	MOV SP,180
0201	80	
0202	01	
0203	BA	MOV DX,FF03
0204	03	
0205	FF	
0206	B0	MOV AL,99
0207	99	
0208	EE	OUT DX,AL
0209	BA	MOV DX,FF01
020A	01	
020B	FF	
020C	B0	MOV AL,FF
020D	FF	
020E	EE	OUT DX,AL
020F	BA	MOV DX,FF00
0210	00	
0211	FF	
0212	EC	WTSTB: IN AL,DX
0213	D0	SHL AL,1
0214	E0	
0215	72	JC 212
0216	FB	

PROGRAM E-6 (continued)

Memory Address (Hex)	Memory Contents (Hex)		Instruction (DEBUG Form)	
0217	B4		MOV	AH,18
0218	18			
0219	E8		CALL	300
021A	E4			
021B	00			
021C	B9		MOV	CX,8
021D	08			
021E	00			
021F	EC	INBIT:	IN	AL,DX
0220	D0		SHL	AL,1
0221	E0			
0222	D0		RCR	BL,1
0223	DB			
0224	B4		MOV	AH,10
0225	10			
0226	E8		CALL	300
0227	D7			
0228	00			
0229	E2		LOOP	21F
022A	F4			
022B	88		MOV	[340],BL
022C	1E			
022D	40			
022E	03			
022F	CD		INT	20
0230	20			

Enter and run Program E-6. Single-stepping it with the T command will give you a long time to set the switch for each data value. The program will not leave the initial loop until you form a start bit by closing the switch. Be sure to replace the delay routine with an RET instruction in 300, as single-stepping through 370,000 decrements can be dangerous to your fingers! Try the following sample cases:

1. Close the switch initially and move it each time the computer enters DELAY.
   Result: [0340] = 55 hex

2. Close the switch to form the start bit and then immediately open it and leave it open.
Result: [0340] = FF

A breakpoint is a convenient alternative to the tedious tracing procedure. An easy way to implement one is to put RETs in both 300 and 301. Now you can make the program stop after it first enters DELAY with

G=200 300

To resume the program after each data input, use

G=301 300

Problem E-6

Make Program E-6 check whether 2 stop bits follow the data. The revised program should set 342 to 00 if the 2 stop bits are present and to FF otherwise. Lack of the proper number of stop bits is called a *framing error*.

Detecting False Start Bits

Many errors may occur in communications, particularly over noisy connections (such as telephone lines) or long distances. One problem is that noise may make the input briefly 0, thus producing a *false start bit*. The receiver can tell a short noise pulse from a start bit by sampling the line several times and requiring that most samples be zeros. This approach is called *majority logic*; it works like voting: The value that occurs most often "wins."

The following program samples the data at one-quarter, one-half, and three-quarters of a bit time after the initial detection of a zero. At least two samples must be zeros for the start bit to be accepted. Program E-7 is the DEBUG version. If the computer accepts the start bit, it must wait three-quarters of a bit time to reach the center of data bit 0 (see Figure E-2).

Run Program E-7 with a breakpoint in 300 as described earlier. You can then control the switch and check the sampling. Remember to replace DELAY with

RET instructions in locations 300 and 301. Try the following cases (starting with the switch closed to form the start bit):

1. Move the switch each time the computer reaches the breakpoint. The sample values will be 1, 0, and 1. Because only one is 0, the computer should reject the start bit and repeat the program.
2. Leave the switch closed until the computer reaches the breakpoint for the second time. Then move it after each entry. The sample values will be 0, 1, and 0. Because two are 0, the computer should accept the start bit and return to DEBUG.

```
            MOV    SP,180H        ;INITIALIZE USER STACK
                                  ;   POINTER
            MOV    DX,0FF03H      ;GET CONTROL REGISTER
                                  ;   ADDRESS
            MOV    AL,10011001B   ;PORT A INPUT, PORT B OUTPUT,
            OUT    DX,AL          ;   PORT C INPUT
            MOV    DX,0FF01H      ;TURN OFF THE LEDS
            MOV    AL,0FFH
            OUT    DX,AL
            MOV    DX,0FF00H      ;WAIT FOR A START BIT
WTSTB:      IN     AL,DX
            SHL    AL,1
            JC     WTSTB
            MOV    CX,3           ;NUMBER OF SAMPLES = 3
            SUB    BL,BL          ;NUMBER OF ONES = 0
CHBIT:      MOV    AH,4           ;WAIT 1/4 BIT TIME
            CALL   DELAY
            IN     AL,DX          ;CHECK NEXT SAMPLE
            SHL    AL,1
            ADC    BL,0           ;ADD 1 TO COUNT FOR EACH
                                  ;   1 BIT
            LOOP   CHBIT          ;COUNT SAMPLES
            CMP    BL,2           ;WAS MAJORITY OF SAMPLES
                                  ;   ZERO?
            JAE    WTSTB          ;NO, LOOK FOR ANOTHER
                                  ;   START BIT
            MOV    AX,12          ;YES, WAIT 3/4 BIT TIME TO
            CALL   DELAY          ;   CENTER FIRST DATA BIT
            INT    20H
```

ADC BL,0 adds the Carry to register BL, thus adding 1 to the count for each sample that is 1.

	PROGRAM E-7		

Memory Address (Hex)	Memory Contents (Hex)		Instruction (DEBUG Form)
0200	BC		MOV SP,180
0201	80		
0202	01		
0203	BA		MOV DX,FF03
0204	03		
0205	FF		
0206	B0		MOV AL,99
0207	99		
0208	EE		OUT DX,AL
0209	BA		MOV DX,FF01
020A	01		
020B	FF		
020C	B0		MOV AL,FF
020D	FF		
020E	EE		OUT DX,AL
020F	BA		MOV DX,FF00
0210	00		
0211	FF		
0212	EC	WTSTB:	IN AL,DX
0213	D0		SHL AL,1
0214	E0		
0215	72		JC 212
0216	FB		
0217	B9		MOV CX,3
0218	03		
0219	00		
021A	28		SUB BL,BL
021B	DB		
021C	B4	CHBIT:	MOV AH,4
021D	04		
021E	E8		CALL 300
021F	DF		
0220	00		
0221	EC		IN AL,DX
0222	D0		SHL AL,1
0223	E0		
0224	80		ADC BL,0
0225	D3		
0226	00		
0227	E2		LOOP 21C
0228	F3		
0229	80		CMP BL,2
022A	FB		

Memory Address (Hex)	Memory Contents (Hex)	Instruction (DEBUG Form)	
022B	02		
022C	73	JAE	212
022D	E4		
022E	B4	MOV	AH,C
022F	0C		
0230	E8	CALL	300
0231	CD		
0232	00		
0233	CD	INT	20
0234	20		

PROGRAM E-7 (continued)

Problem E-7

Revise Program E-7 to check the input at intervals of one-eighth of a bit time. At least four samples must be zero to accept the start bit.

Problem E-8

Write a reception program that checks each bit at one-fourth, one-half, and three-fourths of a bit time and determines the actual value by majority logic. That is, the bit value is the value of at least two samples.

Generating and Checking Parity

Still another way to avoid errors is to add error-detecting or correcting codes to the data. These codes show whether the data was received correctly and, if not, where the errors were; they contain no additional information and thus reduce the rate at which actual data can be sent.

Parity is a simple error-detecting code. It is a single bit added to each character, which makes the total number of 1 bits even (if even parity) or odd (if odd parity). For example:

1. Data = 01101101: Even parity = 1, as the data contains an odd number of 1 bits (5).

2. Data = 00010001: Even parity = 0, as the data contains an even number of 1 bits (2).

Parity has the following features:

1. It allows the receiver to detect single but not double errors. Two wrong bits give the same parity as the correct data.
2. It does not allow for error correction. If the parity is wrong, the receiver knows that an error occurred but has no way of determining which bit is wrong. All the receiver can do is request retransmission.

Parity is particularly convenient with 7-bit ASCII characters, because it can occupy bit 7. Most UARTs and other communications chips, as we have mentioned, will automatically generate parity for transmission and check it on reception. There are usually ways to control whether a UART implements parity, whether the parity is even or odd, and how many bits it includes in each character.

Parity is easy to handle with the 8088 microprocessor, because it has a (even) Parity flag. This flag is 1 if the last arithmetic or logical operation produced a result with even parity, and 0 if it produced a result with odd parity. The following program (Program E-8 is the DEBUG version) fetches 7-bit data from location 340, puts odd parity in bit 7 (assumed to be 0 originally), and saves the result in location 341.

```
       MOV    AL,[340H]          ;GET DATA
       TEST   AL,AL              ;IS PARITY ALREADY ODD?
       JPO    DONE               ;YES, DONE
       OR     AL,10000000B       ;NO, SET MSB OF DATA
DONE:  MOV    [341H],AL          ;SAVE DATA WITH ODD PARITY
       INT    20H
```

PROGRAM E-8		
Memory Address (Hex)	Memory Contents (Hex)	Instruction (DEBUG Form)
0200	*A0*	*MOV AL,[340]*
0201	*40*	
0202	*03*	
0203	*84*	*TEST AL,AL*

Memory Address (Hex)	Memory Contents (Hex)		Instruction (DEBUG Form)
		PROGRAM E-8 (continued)	
0204	C0		
0205	7B		JPO 209
0206	02		
0207	0C		OR AL,80
0208	80		
0209	A2	DONE:	MOV [341],AL
020A	41		
020B	03		
020C	CD		INT 20
020D	20		

Enter and run Program E-8 for the following examples:

1. [0340] = 41 (ASCII A)
   Result: [0341] = C1
2. [0340] = 43 (ASCII C)
   Result: [0341] = 43

Problem E-9

Many computers and peripherals use 7-bit ASCII characters and reserve bit 7 for parity. Make Program E-7 transmit 7-bit characters followed by even parity. Keep everything (including the parity) in negative logic, so it will appear correctly on the LEDs. This has no net effect on the parity, as it is inverted once because of the inversion of the data and again because of the LED connections.

EXAMPLES:

a. [0340] = 41 (ASCII A)
   Result: Transmitted data is 41, as its parity is even.
b. [0340] = 43 (ASCII C)
   Result: Transmitted data is C3, as 43 has odd parity.

Problem E-10

Write a serial reception program that checks the parity of 8-bit characters. The program should save the parallel data in 340 and set 341 to 0 if the parity is even and to 1 if it is odd.

EXAMPLES:

a. Received data is 41 hex = 01000001 binary.
Result: [0340] = 41 (parallel data)
[0341] = 00, as 41 hex has an even number of 1 bits.
b. Received data is C1 hex = 11000001 binary.
Result: [0340] = C1 (parallel data)
[0341] = 01, as C1 hex has an odd number of 1 bits.

Key Point Summary

1. Serial interfaces require parallel/serial conversion, the addition and detection of start and stop bits, clocking, and parity generation and checking. Either software or hardware such as UARTs can perform these functions.
2. Shift instructions can easily convert data between serial and parallel forms. Different initial and final conditions are all that is needed to generate or detect start and stop bits.
3. Serial data can be clocked using either software delay loops or an external timer or clock.
4. You can reduce the number of errors in serial communications by centering the reception, by sampling bits several times and using majority logic, and by including an error-detecting or correcting code such as parity. Parity is easy to implement on the 8088 microprocessor because of its (even) Parity flag.

Microcomputer Timing and Control

Purpose   To learn how the 8088 microprocessor executes instructions and how the addresses in the memory and I/O sections of 8088-based microcomputers are decoded.

What You Should Learn
1. Why a logic analyzer is necessary to troubleshoot microprocessor-based systems.
2. What kind of clock the 8088 microprocessor uses.
3. How the 8088 transfers data to and from memory and I/O ports.
4. How the 8088 fetches and executes instructions.
5. How the 8088 transfers 8-bit and 16-bit data.
6. How to decode address lines to select memories.
7. What tradeoffs the designer can make between a computer's memory capacity and the number of parts required to decode addresses.
8. How to decode I/O addresses efficiently by using linear select.

Parts Required   A dual-trace oscilloscope with a bandwidth of at least 10 MHz.

Reference Materials   Alexy, G. *8086 System Design*. Santa Clara, CA: Intel Application Note AP-67, Intel Corporation, 1979. Also in *Microsystem Components Handbook: Microprocessors and Peripherals* (Vol. I). Santa Clara, CA: Intel Corporation, 1985, pp. 3-285 to 3-348.

Comer, D. J. *Microprocessor-Based System Design*. New York: Holt, Rinehart and Winston, 1986, sec. 3.4A (8086 CPU), 3.4B (8086 pin connections), 3.5 (8086 storage organization and addressing), 5.1 (interfacing to a microprocessor bus), 5.2 (microprocessor interface).

Gorsline, G. W. *16-Bit Modern Microcomputers*. Englewood Cliffs, NJ: Prentice-Hall, 1985, pp. 129–138 (bus organization).

Liu, Y. C., and G. A. Gibson. *Microcomputer Systems: The 8086/8088 Family*, (2nd ed.). Englewood Cliffs, NJ: Prentice-Hall, 1986, chaps. 8 (system bus structure), 10 (semiconductor memory).

Norton, P. *Programmer's Guide to the IBM PC*. Redmond, WA: Microsoft Press, 1985, pp. 14–17 (memory chips), 36–40 (how the 8088 uses ports).

Peatman, J. B. *Digital Hardware Design*. New York: McGraw-Hill, 1980.

Terms   **Address bus:** the bus the CPU uses to select a memory location or I/O port.

Address space: the total range of addresses to which a computer may refer.

Bus: parallel lines that connect devices.

Bus contention: more than one device trying to control a bus at the same time.

Bus cycle (in 8088-based systems): the time it takes the processor to transfer data to or from memory or an I/O port.

Decoder: a device that produces unencoded outputs from coded inputs.

Demultiplex: direct a time-shared input to one of several outputs.

Dynamic memory: a memory that loses its contents gradually without any external causes. The contents must be rewritten periodically to be retained; the rewriting process is called **refresh**.

Instruction: a group of bits that defines a computer operation.

Linear select: using coded bus lines individually for selection, rather than decoding them. Linear select requires no decoders but can address only n devices rather than 2^n with n lines.

Logic analyzer: a piece of test equipment that detects, stores, and displays parallel digital signals.

Memory capacity: the total number of memory locations that may be attached to a computer.

Multiplex: use a unit for several purposes on a shared basis, interleave different signals on the same channel.

Pipelining: dividing a complex function into a series of simpler operations that can be done in assembly-line fashion. The idea is that inputs to later operations should always be available when needed.

Prefetch: obtain an input before the system needs it.

Queue: a structure that is accessed in a first-in, first-out manner. That is, the first item entered into it is also the first one removed.

Refresh: the process of rewriting the contents of a dynamic memory before they are lost.

Tristate: logic outputs with three states: high, low, and inactive (high-impedance or open-circuit). Inactive (disabled) outputs can be combined without gates.

T state (in 8088-based systems): one clock cycle.

Special Problems in Microcomputer Hardware Design

Describing the flow of signals in a microcomputer is not simple. Not only does data move in parallel (typically 8, 16, or 32 bits at a time), but also the clock rate is high, and there are few periodic sequences. The result is that microprocessor-based products are difficult to debug, maintain, and repair. In practice, engineers often buy board computers rather than design their own, and companies often have service people replace entire circuit boards rather than try to pinpoint a malfunction.

The designer must nevertheless understand how a microcomputer operates and how its parts are connected. This laboratory gives only a brief overview of hardware design. We assume that you have a dual-trace oscilloscope with a bandwidth of at least 10 MHz. Unfortunately, even a good oscilloscope is inadequate for design or troubleshooting. To diagnose hardware faults, you must be able simultaneously to examine the clock, data bus, address bus, and control signals. This requires a test instrument called a *logic analyzer* that can display many lines in a comprehensible form. Because logic analyzers are expensive, we will content ourselves with examining signals one at a time on an oscilloscope.

Timing and Control Functions

To design or understand a microcomputer, we must answer the following questions:

1. How does the processor transfer data to or from memory and I/O ports? Clearly, timing is a critical factor.
2. How does the processor decode and execute instructions? Although this is an internal function, understanding it is important, as it governs the computer's operations.
3. How does the processor distinguish different types of cycles? The designer must use the processor's signals to control external hardware and monitor system operation.
4. How are memory addresses and I/O ports selected? Address lines and control signals must be decoded properly.
5. How can memories, I/O ports, and other devices share system buses? Most

microprocessors have a tristate data bus. Only one memory or input port is enabled at a time; the disabled ones do not affect the bus, as they are in the high-impedance state.

The microcomputer designer also must consider economic and physical factors such as cost, speed, board size, and power consumption. Other important factors are consistency with other applications and standards, as well as how easy the computer is to test, expand, update, and maintain.

System Clock

Let us now look at processor signals on the oscilloscope. Figure F-1 contains the pin assignments for the 8088 microprocessor. Figure F-2 and Table F-1 describe the IBM PC's system board I/O channel (often called the *IBM PC bus*). Attach the oscilloscope ground to a ground connection. Put your oscilloscope in the CHOP mode so that it maintains timing relationships and does not retrigger when you switch channels; do not use the ALTERNATE mode.

Because of the inaccessibility of the IBM PC bus, we have brought its signals out through the B side of the 60-pin connector used to attach the experiment board. Figure F-3 shows the pin assignments for the connector.

Figure F-1

Pin assignments for the 8088 microprocessor. (Reprinted by permission of Intel Corporation, Santa Clara, CA).

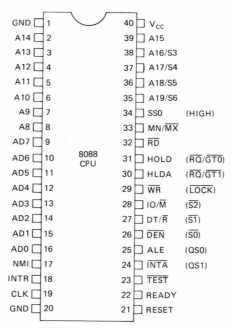

MAXIMUM MODE PIN FUNCTIONS (e.g., $\overline{\text{LOCK}}$) ARE SHOWN IN PARENTHESES

Figure F-2

Diagram of the
IBM PC's System
Board I/O Channel
(the IBM PC bus).
(Reprinted by
permission of IBM
Corporation, Boca
Raton, FL).

I/O Channel Diagram

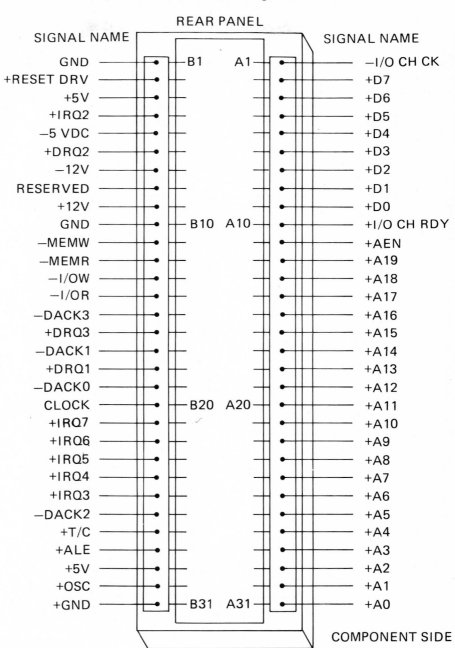

SIGNAL NAME			SIGNAL NAME
GND	B1	A1	−I/O CH CK
+RESET DRV			+D7
+5V			+D6
+IRQ2			+D5
−5 VDC			+D4
+DRQ2			+D3
−12V			+D2
RESERVED			+D1
+12V			+D0
GND	B10	A10	+I/O CH RDY
−MEMW			+AEN
−MEMR			+A19
−I/OW			+A18
−I/OR			+A17
−DACK3			+A16
+DRQ3			+A15
−DACK1			+A14
+DRQ1			+A13
−DACK0			+A12
CLOCK	B20	A20	+A11
+IRQ7			+A10
+IRQ6			+A9
+IRQ5			+A8
+IRQ4			+A7
+IRQ3			+A6
−DACK2			+A5
+T/C			+A4
+ALE			+A3
+5V			+A2
+OSC			+A1
+GND	B31	A31	+A0

REAR PANEL

COMPONENT SIDE

Figure F-3

Pin assignments for
the 60-pin
connector used to
attach the
experiment board.

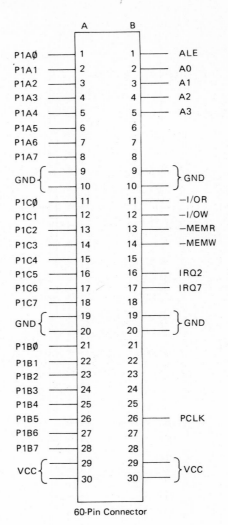

60-Pin Connector

Attach one probe to connection B20 of the I/O channel (60-pin connector pin B26; see Figure F-3). This is the system clock (see Figure F-4) that governs processor operations. Intel calls the clock period a *T state*.

Figure F-4
8088 system clock.

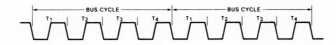

I/O Channel Description

The following is a description of the IBM Personal Computer I/O Channel. All lines are TTL-compatible.

Signal	I/O	Description
A0–A19	O	Address bits 0 to 19: These lines are used to address memory and I/O devices within the system. The 20 address lines allow access of up to 1M-byte of memory. A0 is the least significant bit (LSB) and A19 is the most significant bit (MSB). These lines are generated by either the microprocessor or DMA controller. They are active high.
AEN	O	Address Enable: This line is used to de-gate the microprocessor and other devices from the I/O channel to allow DMA transfers to take place. When this line is active (high), the DMA controller has control of the address bus, data bus, Read command lines (memory and I/O), and the Write command lines (memory and I/O).
ALE	O	Address Latch Enable: This line is provided by the 8288 Bus Controller and is used on the system board to latch valid addresses from the microprocessor. It is available to the I/O channel as an indicator of a valid microprocessor address (when used with AEN). Microprocessor addresses are latched with the falling edge of ALE.
CLK	O	System clock: It is a divide-by-three of the oscillator and has a period of 210-ns (4.77-MHz) The clock has a 33% duty cycle.

D0–D7 I/O Data Bits 0 to 7. These lines provide data bus bits 0 to 7 for the microprocessor, memory, and I/O devices. D0 is the least significant bit (LSB) and D7 is the most significant bit (MSB). These lines are active high.

-DACK0 to O -DMA Acknowledge 0 to 3: These lines
-DACK3 are used to acknowledge DMA requests (DRQ1–DRQ3) and refresh system dynamic memory (-DACK0). They are active low.

DRQ1–DRQ3 I DMA Request 1 to 3: These lines are asynchronous channel requests used by peripheral devices to gain DMA service. They are prioritized with DRQ3 being the lowest and DRQ1 being the highest. A request is generated by bringing a DRQ line to an active level (high). A DRQ line must be held high until the corresponding DACK line goes active.

-I/O CH CK I -I/O Channel Check: This line provides the microprocessor with parity (error) information on memory or devices in the I/O channel. When this signal is active low, a parity error is indicated.

I/O CH RDY I I/O Channel Ready: This line, normally high (ready), is pulled low (not ready) by a memory or I/O device to lengthen I/O or memory cycles. It allows slower devices to attach to the I/O channel with a minimum of difficulty. Any slow device using this line should drive it low immediately upon detecting a valid address and a Read or Write command. This line should never be held low longer than 10

		clock cycles. Machine cycles (I/O or memory) are extended by an integral number of clock cycles (210-ns).
-IOR	O	-I/O Read Command: This command line instructs an I/O device to drive its data onto the data bus. It may be driven by the microprocessor or the DMA controller. This signal is active low.
-IOW	O	-I/O Write Command: This command line instructs an I/O device to read the data on the data bus. It may be driven by the microprocessor or the DMA controller. This signal is active low.
IRQ2–IRQ7	I	Interrupt Request 2 to 7: These lines are used to signal the microprocessor that an I/O device requires attention. They are prioritized with IRQ2 as the highest priority and IRQ7 as the lowest . An Interrupt Request is generated by raising an IRQ line (low to high) and holding it high until it is acknowledged by the microprocessor (interrupt service routine).
-MEMR	O	-Memory Read Command: This command line instructs the memory to drive its data onto the data bus. It may be driven by the microprocessor or the DMA controller. This signal is active low.
-MEMW	O	-Memory Write Command: This command line instructs the memory to store the data present on the data bus. It may be driven by the microprocessor or the DMA controller. This signal is active low.

OSC   O   Oscillator: High-speed clock with a
70-ns period (14.31818-MHz). It has a
50% duty cycle.

RESET DRV   O   Reset Drive: This line is used to reset
or initialize system logic upon power-up
or during a low line-voltage outage.
This signal is synchronized to the falling
edge of CLK and is active high.

T/C   O   Terminal Count: This line provides a
pulse when the terminal count for any
DMA channel is reached. This signal is
active high.

Section 1

Problem F-1

Determine the system clock's frequency and pulse width.

Memory Accesses

Put the following instruction in locations 200 and 201:

HERE: JMP   HERE

The jump transfers control to itself, producing an endless repetitive pattern of signals. Program F-1 is the DEBUG version. Be sure to start it with the I flag set to EI. You can then press Ctrl-Alt-Del to stop the program and restart DEBUG; of course, you must reenter the program (and set the I flag) each time. You can use a command file (see Laboratory 8) to speed the process.

PROGRAM F-1			
Memory Address (Hex)	Memory Contents (Hex)		Instruction (DEBUG Form)
0200	EB	HERE:	JMP 200
0201	FE		

To conserve pins (and allow a 40-pin package), the 8088 processor multiplexes (that is, time-shares) the eight least significant lines of its address bus (AD0 through AD7). For part of the time, these lines carry address bits from the CPU to the memory and I/O ports. For the rest of the time (with the exception of a brief idle period to avoid contention), they carry data. Note that only the CPU produces addresses, whereas data may move in either direction.

Intel calls the time needed to transfer data to or from memory a *bus cycle*. As Figure F-4 shows, a bus cycle lasts at least four clock cycles or T states. During the first T state, the processor puts an address on its multiplexed bus and the more significant address lines. During the second through fourth states, it transfers data on the multiplexed bus. The data transfer time can be extended by an integral number of states to allow for slow memory.

Note that the processor cannot fetch and execute instructions at a rate higher than one-quarter of its clock rate, since fetching an instruction byte (which might contain an entire instruction) always takes at least four clock cycles. Clearly, the actual rate will be much lower, as most instructions occupy at least two bytes and many require more memory cycles to transfer data. Thus the 8088's clock rate is much higher than its instruction execution rate.

Note also that the memory's access time (from stable address) must be less than three clock cycles for the transfer to occur at full speed. This requirement is further tightened by the need for input data to be available at the processor well before the end of the bus cycle. Delays caused by buffering and other control signals must also be considered.

The multiplexed address/data bus causes design problems. Among the obvious questions are:

1. How do external devices such as memories and I/O ports distinguish between addresses and data?
2. How does the system remember the active address after part of it is no longer on the multiplexed bus?

The signal that indicates when an address is on the multiplexed bus is called Address Latch Enable (ALE). Attach one oscilloscope probe to the system clock and the other to ALE (connection B28 on the I/O channel or B1 on the 60-pin connector). You should see groups of three ALE pulses followed by a gap. Within a group, pulses should occur four clock cycles apart. ALE thus marks the start of an active bus cycle; the gap is an idle period when the processor is not using the bus.

As its name implies, ALE is generally used to latch the address into a register, thus making it available for the rest of the bus cycle. This demultiplexes the address/data bus. In the IBM PC, the falling edge of ALE stores the low byte of the address in a 74373 octal latch.

Problem F-2

Determine the width of the ALE pulses.

Data transfers on the multiplexed bus require more control signals. Many devices, including the microprocessor, memories, input ports, and output ports, must share the bus. Control signals must prevent *bus contention*, that is, two or more devices trying to control the bus simultaneously.

Bus contention would occur if a memory put data on the bus at the same time as the processor was putting an address on it. The way to avoid this is to gate or enable the outputs from each memory with the $\overline{\text{MEMR}}$ signal, as shown in Figure F-5. $\overline{\text{MEMR}}$ is active only when the latched address is stable, memory (rather than I/O) is being accessed, and the multiplexed bus is available for data transfers.

Figure F-5

Gating data from memory with the $\overline{\text{MEMR}}$ signal.

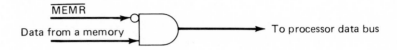

Note: The output of the gate is always 0 except when $\overline{\text{MEMR}}$ is 0.

Attach one probe to the clock and the other to $\overline{\text{MEMR}}$ (connection B12 on the I/O channel or B13 on the 60-pin connector). Note that $\overline{\text{MEMR}}$ is active (low) during about half of each active bus cycle. This means that the data bus is available for transfers only half of the time. Attaching one probe to ALE and the other to $\overline{\text{MEMR}}$ will show that they do not overlap. $\overline{\text{MEMR}}$ is active only after the address has been latched. When observing the two signals, remember that ALE is active-high, whereas $\overline{\text{MEMR}}$ is active-low.

Tracing Instruction Execution

Tracing the 8088's operations is difficult because it overlaps instruction fetch and execution. In fact, the 8088 consists of two largely independent units. One, the bus interface unit (BIU), transfers data to or from memory, and the other, the execution unit (EU), actually executes instructions. The BIU can fetch new instructions (called *instruction prefetch*) while the EU is busy executing previous ones.

As Figure F-6 shows, the BIU saves up to four instruction bytes in a queue until the EU needs them. As a result, the EU seldom has to wait for the next byte to be fetched. Instead, it is almost always waiting in the queue when needed. This overlapping of operations, called *pipelining*, is like having a helper fetch new materials while a worker does the current job.

Note that the BIU contains the segment registers and adds shifted segment numbers and offset values (see the last section of Laboratory 0). The EU handles only 16-bit addresses. It contains the other registers, flags, and arithmetic facilities.

Figure F-6
Block diagram of
the 8088
microprocessor.
(Reprinted by
permission of Intel
Corporation, Santa
Clara, CA).

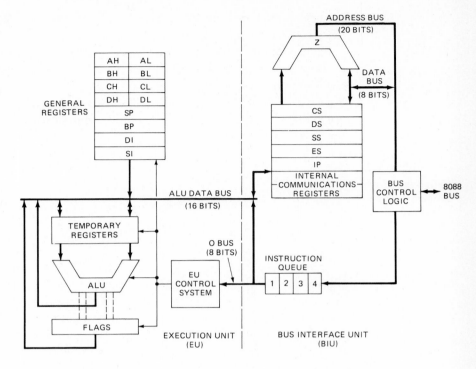

Pipelining complicates the tracing of instructions (and hardware debugging in general) because the processor may be working on more than one instruction at a time. That is, it may interleave instruction fetches with data transfers from previous instructions. Furthermore, the processor will stop fetching instructions if its queue is full. This is the reason for the gap in the ALE signals you saw on your oscilloscope.

Furthermore, instruction fetches may be wasted. Every jump makes the queue's contents worthless, thus forcing the processor to clear it out and start over from scratch.

Instructions involving only registers, flags, and program memory generally execute so quickly that the processor has no time to fill its instruction queue. The key to maximum pipeline efficiency is for some instructions to spend time computing effective addresses or doing internal calculations. Then the queue will fill, minimizing instruction fetch overhead.

For the jump-to-self instruction (Program F-1), the processor actually needs only two bus cycles (eight clock cycles) to fetch the operation code and relative offset. It spends the rest of the execution time adding the relative offset to the instruction pointer, thus computing the pointer's new value. It then repeats the entire process.

While the execution unit is busy calculating the effective address, however, the bus interface unit is not idle. Because it has free time, it goes ahead and fetches the next instruction byte. This is why the ALE pulses occur in groups of three rather than in pairs as you might expect. Of course, the next byte is never executed because of the jump.

Each instruction fetch involves:

1. Putting the sum of the instruction pointer and the shifted code segment register (see Laboratory 0) on the address bus (including the multiplexed part). The processor adds 1 to the instruction pointer (or, at least, to the bus interface unit's copy of it) after each bus cycle in which it is used.
2. Reading the data from memory and placing it at the end of the instruction queue (see Figure F-6).

To see the addresses change while Program F-1 runs, connect one probe to the clock (or to ALE) and the other to address line A0 (connection A31 on the I/O channel or B2 on the 60-pin connector). Triggering on the leading edge of ALE generally gives the clearest results. Repeat the process with A1 (connection A30 on the I/O channel or B3 on the 60-pin connector). Because of the shifting of the code segment register's contents, address lines A0 through A3 do not depend on the segment number.

Can you find an instruction cycle on the oscilloscope? It begins just before a new group of three ALE pulses. A major problem in identifying cycles is the irregularity caused by the PC's memory refresh; it uses a five-clock cycle every 72 clocks. The result is a large disturbance of Program F-1's pattern, making it difficult to stabilize events on the oscilloscope.

Another way to identify the start of an instruction cycle is by noting when A1 goes low. A1 is low during the first two bus cycles while the processor is fetching instructions from locations 200 and 201. It is then high while the processor is fetching the instruction from 202 (the one it never executes). A1 remains high during the idle period, since the value derived from offset 202 is latched and no new ALE pulse is produced.

Problem F-3

Measure how long A0 remains high during each instruction cycle. Explain your result.

Because of pipelining, adding a byte of code to the loop has little external effect unless the new instruction requires additional memory cycles. To see this, add a NOP to the loop as shown in Program F-2. Examine the address lines, ALE, and $\overline{\text{MEMR}}$. You should now see groups of four ALE pulses instead of three, as the NOP executes quickly and the bus interface unit therefore has time to fetch another byte.

PROGRAM F-2

Memory Address (Hex)	Memory Contents (Hex)		Instruction (DEBUG Form)	
0200	90	*HERE:*	*NOP*	
0201	EB		*JMP*	*200*
0202	FD			

We can also add other instructions that do not require extra memory cycles. For example, replace NOP with INC AX. Does this affect the address or control signals? Try other one-byte instructions such as CLC. Note that externally it is difficult to tell what the processor is doing. Minor variations in instruction length and execution time have little or no external effect.

Accessing Data Memory

Instructions that transfer data to or from memory take more bus cycles. For example, consider MOV AL,[DI]. To see how it executes, put 408 hex in DI and run Program F-3.

PROGRAM F-3

Memory Address (Hex)	Memory Contents (Hex)		Instruction (DEBUG Form)	
0200	8A	*HERE:*	*MOV*	*AL, [DI]*
0201	05			
0202	EB		*JMP*	*200*
0203	FC			

Examining ALE should show groups of seven pulses instead of four. The processor now has time to fetch two extra instruction bytes (that it never executes), as well as get the data from the address in DI. To determine when it reads the data, examine address line A3 (connection A28 on the I/O channel or B5 on the 60-pin connector). This line is the key because it is 0 in the memory addresses for the instruction fetches, but 1 in the address for the data fetch. Thus A3 should be high only during the bus cycle in which the processor is moving data from address 408 to register AL. Remember that segmentation does not affect address line A3, as the segment register's contents are shifted left four bits before being added to the offset.

Problem F-4

When does the new data read cycle occur during an iteration? Explain your
answer.

Instructions that store data in memory must produce a signal indicating when data is available. The $\overline{\text{MEMW}}$ signal (connection B11 on the I/O channel or B14 on the 60-pin connector) serves this purpose. In Programs F-1 through F-3, this line should always be inactive (1). Verify this by examining $\overline{\text{MEMW}}$ while Program F-3 is running.

Problem F-5

What happens to $\overline{\text{MEMW}}$ and $\overline{\text{MEMR}}$ if you replace MOV AL,[DI] with MOV
[DI],AL? Does the change affect ALE or address lines A0 through A3?

Byte- and Word-Length Transfers

Byte-length transfers are straightforward on the 8088 since it always transfers data a byte at a time. Word-length transfers simply consist of two consecutive byte-length transfers. The processor adds 1 to the address between operations.

Problem F-6

What happens to ALE, A0, and A3 if you replace MOV AL,[DI] with MOV
AX,[DI] in Program F-3? Explain the result.

Decoding Address Lines

The IBM PC decodes memory as shown in Table F-2. Note that the lowest addresses (through 9FFFF) are user RAM, the highest ones are ROM (because the 8088 resets to address FFFF0), and the middle ones are video display memory. The dedication of part of the address space to ROM and video display memory is the reason why standard IBM PCs are limited to 640K of memory despite the 8088's 1M address space.

Table F-2

IBM PC Memory Assignments

Addresses	Purpose
00000 – 9FFFF	Working RAM
A0000 – BFFFF	Display memory
C0000 – CFFFF	ROM (BIOS extensions)
D0000 – EFFFF	Cartridge ROM area
F0000 – FFFFF	ROM (BIOS, BASIC, diagnostics)

We can easily design decoding hardware to divide memory into the 64K sections used in the IBM PC. All we need is a single 4-line to 16-line decoder such as the 74154 (see Table F-3 and Figure F-7). Its inputs would be address lines A16 through A19, and each output would control 64K of memory. The outputs would, of course, have to be made available externally if some memory were not on the main system board.

Figure F-7

Pin assignments for the 74154 4-line to 16-line decoder.

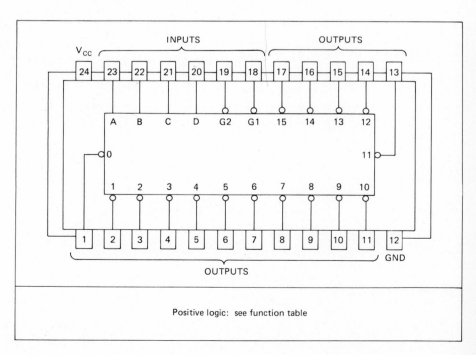

Positive logic: see function table

Table F-3

Function Table for the 74154 4-Line to 16-Line Decoder

G1	G2	D	C	B	A	0	1	2	3	4	5	6	7	8	9	10	11	12	13	14	15
			Inputs											Ouputs							
L	L	L	L	L	L	L	H	H	H	H	H	H	H	H	H	H	H	H	H	H	H
L	L	L	L	L	H	H	L	H	H	H	H	H	H	H	H	H	H	H	H	H	H
L	L	L	L	H	L	H	H	L	H	H	H	H	H	H	H	H	H	H	H	H	H
L	L	L	L	H	H	H	H	H	L	H	H	H	H	H	H	H	H	H	H	H	H
L	L	L	H	L	L	H	H	H	H	L	H	H	H	H	H	H	H	H	H	H	H
L	L	L	H	L	H	H	H	H	H	H	L	H	H	H	H	H	H	H	H	H	H
L	L	L	H	H	L	H	H	H	H	H	H	L	H	H	H	H	H	H	H	H	H
L	L	L	H	H	H	H	H	H	H	H	H	H	L	H	H	H	H	H	H	H	H
L	L	H	L	L	L	H	H	H	H	H	H	H	H	L	H	H	H	H	H	H	H
L	L	H	L	L	H	H	H	H	H	H	H	H	H	H	L	H	H	H	H	H	H
L	L	H	L	H	L	H	H	H	H	H	H	H	H	H	H	L	H	H	H	H	H
L	L	H	L	H	H	H	H	H	H	H	H	H	H	H	H	H	L	H	H	H	H
L	L	H	H	L	L	H	H	H	H	H	H	H	H	H	H	H	H	L	H	H	H
L	L	H	H	L	H	H	H	H	H	H	H	H	H	H	H	H	H	H	L	H	H
L	L	H	H	H	L	H	H	H	H	H	H	H	H	H	H	H	H	H	H	L	H
L	L	H	H	H	H	H	H	H	H	H	H	H	H	H	H	H	H	H	H	H	L
L	H	X	X	X	X	H	H	H	H	H	H	H	H	H	H	H	H	H	H	H	H
H	L	X	X	X	X	H	H	H	H	H	H	H	H	H	H	H	H	H	H	H	H
H	H	X	X	X	X	H	H	H	H	H	H	H	H	H	H	H	H	H	H	H	H

H = high level, L = low level, X = irrelevant

An alternative is to use switches to select the four most significant bits of the addresses on a board as shown in Figure F-8. Here moving the four switches to specified positions is equivalent to choosing a decoder output. This approach (or an alternative based on a comparator) works with external boards, as it uses only signals from the PC's bus.

Figure F-8

Creating a memory enable (ME) signal from switches. The switch connections control the four most significant bits of the memory addresses.

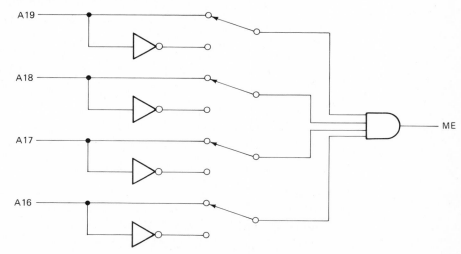

Multiple Addresses and Memory Expansion

What happens if the external memory contains less than 64K? A simple approach is to just let it occupy 64K of address space. Although memory decoding must ensure that two locations never respond to the same address (as reading that address would cause bus contention), it need not ensure a unique address for each location. After all, no contention occurs if many addresses select the same location. This sounds odd, but it does not affect computer operation, any more than assigning a large building several street addresses (for different entrances) affects mail delivery.

For example, suppose we want to add 16K of memory to an IBM PC. Perhaps we were able to get old, small memories at a discount (maybe free!), or they are some special technology that is not affected by radiation, extreme temperatures, electromagnetic interference, or cigarette smoke. Rather than decode the address space further, we could simply enable the memory with a decoder output or with an output derived from switches as shown in Figure F-8. Address lines A15 and A14 would not be connected to the memory or to the decoding circuit, so their values would not affect selection.

The advantage of multiple addresses is obvious. To decode the 16K completely would require a 2-line to 4-line decoder (for example, 74139). Adding it would mean another part, more connections, and more board space. Furthermore, dedicating the full section in this way makes upgrading simple when either our finances or the technology improves.

The disadvantage of multiple addresses is that they reduce the computer's memory capacity. In the example, 16K bytes of memory would occupy an address space that could hold 64K bytes, thus reducing the capacity by 48K bytes. The reduction does not matter, of course, if we have no further expansion plans.

The tradeoff here is clear. Decoding all address lines allows us to attach the maximum amount of memory. On the other hand, it requires more circuitry. In simple applications, the extra parts are an unnecessary expense. Thus designers usually decode all address lines in large systems, such as personal computers, graphics terminals, or robot controllers. They often leave address lines undecoded in small systems, such as printers, electronic games, or simple instruments.

Problem F-7

If we add 16K of memory as proposed (enabling it when A19 = A17 = 1 and A18 = A16 = 0), which addresses does it occupy? Which addresses refer to the same memory location as A1000 hex?

Addressing I/O Devices

The IO/$\overline{\text{MEMORY}}$ pin is the only external difference between 8088 instructions that reference memory and those that reference I/O. The IN and OUT instructions bring this line high; all other external transfer instructions bring it low, as they all reference memory. As far as the processor is concerned, a memory is anything activated by this signal being low; an I/O device is anything activated by it being high. All other distinctions are beyond the 8088's comprehension.

The IBM PC combines the IO/$\overline{\text{M}}$ signal with other signals to form the enabling signals $\overline{\text{MEMR}}$, $\overline{\text{MEMW}}$, $\overline{\text{I/OR}}$, and $\overline{\text{I/OW}}$. Examine $\overline{\text{I/OR}}$ (connection B14 on the I/O channel or B11 on the 60-pin connector) while Program F-3 is running. It should be high always, as the program does no I/O. Now put **FF00** in DX and run the next program (Program F-4 is the DEBUG version). $\overline{\text{I/OR}}$ should go low during the cycle in which the input port is read. Note that an I/O bus cycle takes five clocks rather than the usual four.

```
HERE:  IN   AL,DX    ;READ INPUT PORT
       JMP  HERE     ;CONTINUE FOREVER
```

PROGRAM F-4

Memory Address (Hex)	Memory Contents (Hex)		Instruction (DEBUG Form)	
0200	EC	HERE:	IN	AL,DX
0201	EB		JMP	200
0202	FD			

Problem F-8

What happens if you run Program F-4 with OUT DX,AL instead of IN AL,DX? Is the $\overline{\text{I/OR}}$ signal affected? How about $\overline{\text{I/OW}}$ (connection B13 on the I/O channel or B12 on the 60-pin connector)?

We could fully decode I/O addresses just like memory addresses, except using only lines A0 through A15 (all that the processor allows in I/O transfers). Remember that I/O addresses are not segmented, so the segment registers are not involved. As I/O devices generally come in small units (1 to 16 ports in a package), this would require many decoders. Imagine decoding 16 address lines with standard 4-line to 16-line or 3-line to 8-line decoders down to the level required to select individual ports!

A cheaper alternative is to simply use address lines directly without decoding. For example, if the I/O section consists of 8255 PPIs (each containing four ports), we need A0 and A1 for internal decoding. Since the I/O ports on the system board all have addresses below 8000 hex (see Figure 2-9 of P. Norton, *Programmer's Guide to the IBM PC*, given in Laboratory references), we can use A15 to distinguish between system board and external I/O. Lines A2 through A14 are then available to generate PPI selection signals from a single AND gate, as shown in Figure F-9. This approach allows us to add 13 PPIs to an IBM PC, thus providing 39 I/O ports, surely more than enough for most applications.

Figure F-9
Creating a PPI selection signal from a single AND gate.

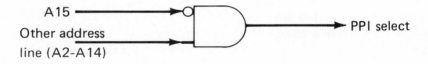

The advantages of this approach are obvious: We have attached PPIs without any expensive parts. Decoding requires only a few small TTL packages. The disadvantage is that the approach uses a large amount of I/O address space (32K, to be precise) for just 39 ports. If, for example, we use A14 as the other address line in Figure F-9, the attached PPI responds to all addresses with A15 = 1 and A14 = 1, regardless of the values of A2 through A13. Thus the PPI's port A (port 0 internally) responds not only to I/O address C000 hex, but also to addresses C004, C008, C00C, and so on, through FFFC. We call this approach *linear select*, because it uses address lines directly (on a linear basis) rather than decoding them.

Problem F-9

Linear select produces discontinuous addresses. Each 1 bit in the selection lines activates a PPI, so only addresses with one 1 bit in those lines are occupied. Which addresses do PPIs occupy if we attach 13 of them using linear select, as shown in Figure F-8?

Problem F-10

One result of the discontinuous addresses in Problem F-9 is that we can actually send data to several PPIs at once. This is done by storing the data in a port address with 1 bits in several selection lines. The result is called a *broadcast*, since it is like a general broadcast on a communications network. Assuming that we have 13 PPIs addressed according to the answer to Problem F-9, write a program that makes all ports operate in mode 0, assigns all A ports as input and all B and C ports as output, and stores 55 hex in all B ports. Note that port A, port B, port C, and the control register are port addresses 0, 1, 2, and 3, respectively, inside the PPI.

Key Point Summary

1. A logic analyzer is needed to understand fully or debug the hardware in microprocessor-based systems. An analyzer can display many signals simultaneously in a comprehensible format.

2. The 8088 transfers data to or from memory in a bus cycle consisting of at least four clock periods. During the first period, the processor puts an address on the multiplexed address/data bus and the more significant address lines. This address must be latched externally using the Address Latch Enable (ALE) signal. The processor uses the rest of the bus cycle to transfer data on the multiplexed bus. All memories must have their outputs gated or enabled with the $\overline{\text{MEMR}}$ signal so they do not contend with the processor for bus control.

3. The 8088 consists of two largely independent units. The bus interface unit fetches instructions and saves them in a queue. It also transfers data to or from memory. The execution unit does internal operations. This division allows the processor to fetch later instructions while it is executing earlier ones. It therefore seldom has to wait for an instruction fetch.

4. Although the pipelining of instruction fetch and execution speeds up operations, it also results in wasted effort. Every jump forces the processor to clear the instruction queue and refill the pipeline.

5. The more significant address lines are usually decoded to form enabling signals. These signals select a particular memory or I/O device. In general, only one memory or I/O device can be selected at a time. The IO/$\overline{\text{MEMORY}}$ signal distinguishes between memories and I/O devices.

6. The designer can make tradeoffs between a computer's memory capacity and the complexity of its decoding system. Full decoding of addresses maximizes memory capacity but increases

parts count. Partial decoding is often sufficient in small systems.

7. I/O addresses are seldom decoded fully because few applications require more than a small fraction of the available capacity. Linear select (using an address line directly to select an I/O device) is a convenient way to provide a reasonable I/O capacity without complex decoding circuits.

Appendixes

*8088 Microprocessor Instruction Set**

*Reprinted by permission of Intel Corporation, Santa Clara, CA.

Table A1-1

8088
Microprocessor
Operation Codes
and Execution
Times

Table 2-18. Key to Flag Effects

IDENTIFIER	EXPLANATION
(blank)	not altered
0	cleared to 0
1	set to 1
X	set or cleared according to result
U	undefined—contains no reliable value
R	restored from previously-saved value

Table 2-19. Key to Operand Types

IDENTIFIER	EXPLANATION
(no operands)	No operands are written
register	An 8- or 16-bit general register
reg 16	A 16-bit general register
seg-reg	A segment register
accumulator	Register AX or AL
immediate	A constant in the range 0-FFFFH
immed8	A constant in the range 0-FFH
memory	An 8- or 16-bit memory location[1]
mem8	An 8-bit memory location[1]
mem16	A 16-bit memory location[1]
source-table	Name of 256-byte translate table
source-string	Name of string addressed by register SI
dest-string	Name of string addressed by register DI
DX	Register DX
short-label	A label within −128 to +127 bytes of the end of the instruction
near-label	A label in current code segment
far-label	A label in another code segment
near-proc	A procedure in current code segment
far-proc	A procedure in another code segment
memptr16	A word containing the offset of the location in the current code segment to which control is to be transferred[1]
memptr32	A doubleword containing the offset and the segment base address of the location in another code segment to which control is to be transferred[1]
regptr16	A 16-bit general register containing the offset of the location in the current code segment to which control is to be transferred
repeat	A string instruction repeat prefix

For control transfer instructions, the timings given include any additional clocks required to reinitialize the instruction queue as well as the time required to fetch the target instruction. For instructions executing on an 8086, four clocks should be added for each instruction reference to a word operand located at an odd memory address to reflect any additional operand bus cycles required. Similarly for instructions executing on an 8088, four clocks should be added to each instruction reference to a 16-bit memory operand; this includes all stack operations. The required number of data references is listed in table 2-21 for each instruction to aid in this calculation.

Several additional factors can increase actual execution time over the figures shown in table 2-21. The time provided assumes that the instruction has already been prefetched and that it is waiting in the instruction queue, an assumption that is valid under most, but not all, operating conditions. A series of fast executing (fewer than two clocks per opcode byte) instructions can drain the queue and increase execution time. Execution time also is slightly impacted by the interaction of the EU and BIU when memory operands must be read or written. If the EU needs access to memory, it may have to wait for up to one clock if the BIU has already started an instruction fetch bus cycle. (The EU can detect the need for a memory operand and post a bus request far enough in advance of its need for this operand to avoid waiting a full 4-clock bus cycle). Of course the EU does not have to wait if the queue is full, because the BIU is idle. (This discussion assumes

[1]Any addressing mode—direct, register indirect, based, indexed, or based indexed—may be used (see section 2.8).

Mnemonics Intel, 1978

Table 2-17. Key to Instruction Coding Formats

IDENTIFIER	USED IN	EXPLANATION
destination	data transfer, bit manipulation	A register or memory location that may contain data operated on by the instruction, and which receives (is replaced by) the result of the operation.
source	data transfer, arithmetic, bit manipulation	A register, memory location or immediate value that is used in the operation, but is not altered by the instruction.
source-table	XLAT	Name of memory translation table addressed by register BX.
target	JMP, CALL	A label to which control is to be transferred directly, or a register or memory location whose *content* is the address of the location to which control is to be transferred indirectly.
short-label	cond. transfer, iteration control	A label to which control is to be conditionally transferred; must lie within −128 to +127 bytes of the first byte of the next instruction.
accumulator	IN, OUT	Register AX for word transfers, AL for bytes.
port	IN, OUT	An I/O port number; specified as an immediate value of 0-255, or register DX (which contains port number in range 0-64k).
source-string	string ops.	Name of a string in memory that is addressed by register SI; used only to identify string as byte or word and specify segment override, if any. This string is used in the operation, but is not altered.
dest-string	string ops.	Name of string in memory that is addressed by register DI; used only to identify string as byte or word. This string receives (is replaced by) the result of the operation.
count	shifts, rotates	Specifies number of bits to shift or rotate; written as immediate value 1 or register CL (which contains the count in the range 0-255).
interrupt-type	INT	Immediate value of 0-255 identifying interrupt pointer number.
optional-pop-value	RET	Number of bytes (0-64k, ordinarily an even number) to discard from stack.
external-opcode	ESC	Immediate value (0-63) that is encoded in the instruction for use by an external processor.

Mnemonics © Intel, 1978

Table 2-20. Effective Address Calculation Time

EA COMPONENTS		CLOCKS*
Displacement Only		6
Base or Index Only	(BX,BP,SI,DI)	5
Displacement + Base or Index	(BX,BP,SI,DI)	9
Base + Index	BP + DI, BX + SI	7
	BP + SI, BX + DI	8
Displacement + Base + Index	BP + DI + DISP BX + SI + DISP	11
	BP + SI + DISP BX + DI + DISP	12

*Add 2 clocks for segment override

that the BIU can obtain the bus on demand, i.e., that no other processors are competing for the bus.)

With typical instruction mixes, the time actually required to execute a sequence of instructions will typically be within 5-10% of the sum of the individual timings given in table 2-21. Cases can be constructed, however, in which execution time may be much higher than the sum of the figures provided in the table. The execution time for a given sequence of instructions, however, is always repeatable, assuming comparable external conditions (interrupts, coprocessor activity, etc.). If the execution time for a given series of instructions must be determined exactly, the instructions should be run on an execution vehicle such as the SDK-86 or the iSBC 86/12™ board.

Table 2-21. Instruction Set Reference Data

AAA	AAA (no operands) ASCII adjust for addition			Flags	O D I T S Z A P C U U U X U X
Operands	Clocks	Transfers*	Bytes	**Coding Example**	
(no operands)	4	—	1	AAA	

AAD	AAD (no operands) ASCII adjust for division			Flags	O D I T S Z A P C U X X U X U
Operands	Clocks	Transfers*	Bytes	**Coding Example**	
(no operands)	60	—	2	AAD	

AAM	AAM (no operands) ASCII adjust for multiply			Flags	O D I T S Z A P C U X X U X U
Operands	Clocks	Transfers*	Bytes	**Coding Example**	
(no operands)	83	—	1	AAM	

AAS	AAS (no operands) ASCII adjust for subtraction			Flags	O D I T S Z A P C U U U X U X
Operands	Clocks	Transfers*	Bytes	**Coding Example**	
(no operands)	4	—	1	AAS	

*For the 8086, add four clocks for each 16-bit word transfer with an odd address. For the 8088, add four clocks for each 16-bit word transfer.

Table 2-21. Instruction Set Reference Data (Cont'd.)

ADC	ADC destination,source Add with carry			Flags	O D I T S Z A P C X X X X X X
Operands	**Clocks**	**Transfers***	**Bytes**	**Coding Example**	
register, register	3	—	2	ADC AX, SI	
register, memory	9 + EA	1	2-4	ADC DX, BETA [SI]	
memory, register	16 + EA	2	2-4	ADC ALPHA [BX] [SI], DI	
register, immediate	4	—	3-4	ADC BX, 256	
memory, immediate	17 + EA	2	3-6	ADC GAMMA, 30H	
accumulator, immediate	4	—	2-3	ADC AL, 5	

ADD	ADD destination,source Addition			Flags	O D I T S Z A P C X X X X X X
Operands	**Clocks**	**Transfers***	**Bytes**	**Coding Example**	
register, register	3	—	2	ADD CX, DX	
register, memory	9 + EA	1	2-4	ADD DI, [BX].ALPHA	
memory, register	16 + EA	2	2-4	ADD TEMP, CL	
register, immediate	4	—	3-4	ADD CL, 2	
memory, immediate	17 + EA	2	3-6	ADD ALPHA, 2	
accumulator, immediate	4	—	2-3	ADD AX, 200	

AND	AND destination,source Logical and			Flags	O D I T S Z A P C 0 X X U X 0
Operands	**Clocks**	**Transfers***	**Bytes**	**Coding Example**	
register, register	3	—	2	AND AL,BL	
register, memory	9 + EA	1	2-4	AND CX,FLAG__WORD	
memory, register	16 + EA	2	2-4	AND ASCII [DI],AL	
register, immediate	4	—	3-4	AND CX,0F0H	
memory, immediate	17 + EA	2	3-6	AND BETA, 01H	
accumulator, immediate	4	—	2-3	AND AX, 01010000B	

CALL	CALL target Call a procedure			Flags	O D I T S Z A P C
Operands	**Clocks**	**Transfers***	**Bytes**	**Coding Examples**	
near-proc	19	1	3	CALL NEAR__PROC	
far-proc	28	2	5	CALL FAR__PROC	
memptr 16	21 + EA	2	2-4	CALL PROC__TABLE [SI]	
regptr 16	16	1	2	CALL AX	
memptr 32	37 + EA	4	2-4	CALL [BX].TASK [SI]	

CBW	CBW (no operands) Convert byte to word			Flags	O D I T S Z A P C
Operands	**Clocks**	**Transfers***	**Bytes**	**Coding Example**	
(no operands)	2	—	1	CBW	

*For the 8086, add four clocks for each 16-bit word transfer with an odd address. For the 8088, add four clocks for each 16-bit word transfer.

Mnemonics © Intel, 1978

Table 2-21. Instruction Set Reference Data (Cont'd.)

CLC	CLC (no operands) Clear carry flag				Flags	O D I T S Z A P C 0
Operands		**Clocks**	**Transfers***	**Bytes**	**Coding Example**	
(no operands)		2	—	1	CLC	

CLD	CLD (no operands) Clear direction flag				Flags	O D I T S Z A P C 0
Operands		**Clocks**	**Transfers***	**Bytes**	**Coding Example**	
(no operands)		2	—	1	CLD	

CLI	CLI (no operands) Clear interrupt flag				Flags	O D I T S Z A P C 0
Operands		**Clocks**	**Transfers***	**Bytes**	**Coding Example**	
(no operands)		2	—	1	CLI	

CMC	CMC (no operands) Complement carry flag				Flags	O D I T S Z A P C X
Operands		**Clocks**	**Transfers***	**Bytes**	**Coding Example**	
(no operands)		2	—	1	CMC	

CMP	CMP destination,source Compare destination to source				Flags	O D I T S Z A P C X X X X X
Operands		**Clocks**	**Transfers***	**Bytes**	**Coding Example**	
register, register		3	—	2	CMP BX, CX	
register, memory		9 + EA	1	2-4	CMP DH, ALPHA	
memory, register		9 + EA	1	2-4	CMP [BP + 2], SI	
register, immediate		4	—	3-4	CMP BL, 02H	
memory, immediate		10 + EA	1	3-6	CMP [BX].RADAR [DI], 3420H	
accumulator, immediate		4	—	2-3	CMP AL, 00010000B	

CMPS	CMPS dest-string,source-string Compare string				Flags	O D I T S Z A P C X X X X X
Operands		**Clocks**	**Transfers***	**Bytes**	**Coding Example**	
dest-string, source-string		22	2	1	CMPS BUFF1, BUFF2	
(repeat) dest-string, source-string		9 + 22/rep	2/rep	1	REPE CMPS ID, KEY	

*For the 8086, add four clocks for each 16-bit word transfer with an odd address. For the 8088, add four clocks for each 16-bit word transfer.

Mnemonics © Intel, 1978

Table 2-21. Instruction Set Reference Data (Cont'd.)

CWD	CWD (no operands) Convert word to doubleword			Flags	O D I T S Z A P C
Operands	Clocks	Transfers*	Bytes	Coding Example	
(no operands)	5	—	1	CWD	

DAA	DAA (no operands) Decimal adjust for addition			Flags	O D I T S Z A P C X X X X X X
Operands	Clocks	Transfers*	Bytes	Coding Example	
(no operands)	4	—	1	DAA	

DAS	DAS (no operands) Decimal adjust for subtraction			Flags	O D I T S Z A P C U X X X X X
Operands	Clocks	Transfers*	Bytes	Coding Example	
(no operands)	4	—	1	DAS	

DEC	DEC destination Decrement by 1			Flags	O D I T S Z A P C X X X X X
Operands	Clocks	Transfers*	Bytes	Coding Example	
reg16	2	—	1	DEC AX	
reg8	3	—	2	DEC AL	
memory	15 + EA	2	2-4	DEC ARRAY [SI]	

DIV	DIV source Division, unsigned			Flags	O D I T S Z A P C U U U U U U
Operands	Clocks	Transfers*	Bytes	Coding Example	
reg8	80-90	—	2	DIV CL	
reg16	144-162	—	2	DIV BX	
mem8	(86-96) + EA	1	2-4	DIV ALPHA	
mem16	(150-168) + EA	1	2-4	DIV TABLE [SI]	

ESC	ESC external-opcode,source Escape			Flags	O D I T S Z A P C
Operands	Clocks	Transfers*	Bytes	Coding Example	
immediate, memory	8 + EA	1	2-4	ESC 6,ARRAY [SI]	
immediate, register	2	—	2	ESC 20,AL	

*For the 8086, add four clocks for each 16-bit word transfer with an odd address. For the 8088, add four clocks for each 16-bit word transfer.

Mnemonics : Intel, 1978

Table 2-21. Instruction Set Reference Data (Cont'd.)

HLT	HLT (no operands) Halt			Flags O D I T S Z A P C
Operands	**Clocks**	**Transfers***	**Bytes**	**Coding Example**
(no operands)	2	—	1	HLT

IDIV	IDIV source Integer division			Flags O D I T S Z A P C U U U U U
Operands	**Clocks**	**Transfers***	**Bytes**	**Coding Example**
reg8	101-112	—	2	IDIV BL
reg16	165-184	—	2	IDIV CX
mem8	(107-118) +EA	1	2-4	IDIV DIVISOR__BYTE [SI]
mem16	(171-190) +EA	1	2-4	IDIV [BX].DIVISOR__WORD

IMUL	IMUL source Integer multiplication			Flags O D I T S Z A P C X U U U U X
Operands	**Clocks**	**Transfers***	**Bytes**	**Coding Example**
reg8	80-98	—	2	IMUL CL
reg16	128-154	—	2	IMUL BX
mem8	(86-104) +EA	1	2-4	IMUL RATE__BYTE
mem16	(134-160) +EA	1	2-4	IMUL RATE__WORD [BP] [DI]

IN	IN accumulator,port Input byte or word			Flags O D I T S Z A P C
Operands	**Clocks**	**Transfers***	**Bytes**	**Coding Example**
accumulator, immed8	10	1	2	IN AL, 0FFEAH
accumulator, DX	8	1	1	IN AX, DX

INC	INC destination Increment by 1			Flags O D I T S Z A P C X X X X X
Operands	**Clocks**	**Transfers***	**Bytes**	**Coding Example**
reg16	2	—	1	INC CX
reg8	3	—	2	INC BL
memory	15+EA	2	2-4	INC ALPHA [DI] [BX]

*For the 8086, add four clocks for each 16-bit word transfer with an odd address. For the 8088, add four clocks for each 16-bit word transfer.

Table 2-21. Instruction Set Reference Data (Cont'd.)

INT				Flags	O D I T S Z A P C 0 0
	INT interrupt-type Interrupt				
Operands	**Clocks**	**Transfers***	**Bytes**	**Coding Example**	
immed8 (type = 3) immed8 (type ≠ 3)	52 51	5 5	1 2	INT 3 INT 67	

INTR †				Flags	O D I T S Z A P C 0 0
	INTR (external maskable interrupt) Interrupt if INTR and IF=1				
Operands	**Clocks**	**Transfers***	**Bytes**	**Coding Example**	
(no operands)	61	7	N/A	N/A	

INTO				Flags	O D I T S Z A P C 0 0
	INTO (no operands) Interrupt if overflow				
Operands	**Clocks**	**Transfers***	**Bytes**	**Coding Example**	
(no operands)	53 or 4	5	1	INTO	

IRET				Flags	O D I T S Z A P C R R R R R R R R
	IRET (no operands) Interrupt Return				
Operands	**Clocks**	**Transfers***	**Bytes**	**Coding Example**	
(no operands)	24	3	1	IRET	

JA/JNBE				Flags	O D I T S Z A P C
	JA/JNBE short-label Jump if above/Jump if not below nor equal				
Operands	**Clocks**	**Transfers***	**Bytes**	**Coding Example**	
short-label	16 or 4	—	2	JA ABOVE	

JAE/JNB				Flags	O D I T S Z A P C
	JAE/JNB short-label Jump if above or equal/Jump if not below				
Operands	**Clocks**	**Transfers***	**Bytes**	**Coding Example**	
short-label	16 or 4	—	2	JAE ABOVE__EQUAL	

JB/JNAE				Flags	O D I T S Z A P C
	JB/JNAE short-label Jump if below/Jump if not above nor equal				
Operands	**Clocks**	**Transfers***	**Bytes**	**Coding Example**	
short-label	16 or 4	—	2	JB BELOW	

*For the 8086, add four clocks for each 16-bit word transfer with an odd address. For the 8088, add four clocks for each 16-bit word transfer.

†INTR is not an instruction; it is included in table 2-21 only for timing information.

Mnemonics © Intel, 1978

Table 2-21. Instruction Set Reference Data (Cont'd.)

JBE/JNA	JBE/JNA short-label Jump if below or equal/Jump if not above			Flags	O D I T S Z A P C
Operands		**Clocks**	**Transfers***	**Bytes**	**Coding Example**
short-label		16 or 4	—	2	JNA NOT__ABOVE

JC	JC short-label Jump if carry			Flags	O D I T S Z A P C
Operands		**Clocks**	**Transfers***	**Bytes**	**Coding Example**
short-label		16 or 4	—	2	JC CARRY__SET

JCXZ	JCXZ short-label Jump if CX is zero			Flags	O D I T S Z A P C
Operands		**Clocks**	**Transfers***	**Bytes**	**Coding Example**
short-label		18 or 6	—	2	JCXZ COUNT__DONE

JE/JZ	JE/JZ short-label Jump if equal/Jump if zero			Flags	O D I T S Z A P C
Operands		**Clocks**	**Transfers***	**Bytes**	**Coding Example**
short-label		16 or 4	—	2	JZ ZERO

JG/JNLE	JG/JNLE short-label Jump if greater/Jump if not less nor equal			Flags	O D I T S Z A P C
Operands		**Clocks**	**Transfers***	**Bytes**	**Coding Example**
short-label		16 or 4	—	2	JG GREATER

JGE/JNL	JGE/JNL short-label Jump if greater or equal/Jump if not less			Flags	O D I T S Z A P C
Operands		**Clocks**	**Transfers***	**Bytes**	**Coding Example**
short-label		16 or 4	—	2	JGE GREATER__EQUAL

JL/JNGE	JL/JNGE short-label Jump if less/Jump if not greater nor equal			Flags	O D I T S Z A P C
Operands		**Clocks**	**Transfers***	**Bytes**	**Coding Example**
short-label		16 or 4	—	2	JL LESS

*For the 8086, add four clocks for each 16-bit word transfer with an odd address. For the 8088, add four clocks for each 16-bit word transfer.

Mnemonics © Intel, 1978

Table 2-21. Instruction Set Reference Data (Cont'd.)

JLE/JNG	JLE/JNG short-label Jump if less or equal/Jump if not greater			Flags	O D I T S Z A P C
Operands		**Clocks**	**Transfers***	**Bytes**	**Coding Example**
short-label		16 or 4	—	2	JNG NOT__GREATER

JMP	JMP target Jump			Flags	O D I T S Z A P C
Operands		**Clocks**	**Transfers***	**Bytes**	**Coding Example**
short-label		15	—	2	JMP SHORT
near-label		15	—	3	JMP WITHIN__SEGMENT
far-label		15	—	5	JMP FAR__LABEL
memptr16		18 + EA	1	2-4	JMP [BX].TARGET
regptr16		11	—	2	JMP CX
memptr32		24 + EA	2	2-4	JMP OTHER.SEG [SI]

JNC	JNC short-label Jump if not carry			Flags	O D I T S Z A P C
Operands		**Clocks**	**Transfers***	**Bytes**	**Coding Example**
short-label		16 or 4	—	2	JNC NOT__CARRY

JNE/JNZ	JNE/JNZ short-label Jump if not equal/Jump if not zero			Flags	O D I T S Z A P C
Operands		**Clocks**	**Transfers***	**Bytes**	**Coding Example**
short-label		16 or 4	—	2	JNE NOT__EQUAL

JNO	JNO short-label Jump if not overflow			Flags	O D I T S Z A P C
Operands		**Clocks**	**Transfers***	**Bytes**	**Coding Example**
short-label		16 or 4	—	2	JNO NO__OVERFLOW

JNP/JPO	JNP/JPO short-label Jump if not parity/Jump if parity odd			Flags	O D I T S Z A P C
Operands		**Clocks**	**Transfers***	**Bytes**	**Coding Example**
short-label		16 or 4	—	2	JPO ODD__PARITY

JNS	JNS short-label Jump if not sign			Flags	O D I T S Z A P C
Operands		**Clocks**	**Transfers***	**Bytes**	**Coding Example**
short-label		16 or 4	—	2	JNS POSITIVE

*For the 8086, add four clocks for each 16-bit word transfer with an odd address. For the 8088, add four clocks for each 16-bit word transfer.

Mnemonics © Intel, 1978

Table 2-21. Instruction Set Reference Data (Cont'd.)

JO	JO short-label Jump if overflow			Flags	O D I T S Z A P C
Operands	**Clocks**	**Transfers***	**Bytes**	**Coding Example**	
short-label	16 or 4	—	2	JO SIGNED__OVRFLW	

JP/JPE	JP/JPE short-label Jump if parity / Jump if parity even			Flags	O D I T S Z A P C
Operands	**Clocks**	**Transfers***	**Bytes**	**Coding Example**	
short-label	16 or 4	—	2	JPE EVEN__PARITY	

JS	JS short-label Jump if sign			Flags	O D I T S Z A P C
Operands	**Clocks**	**Transfers***	**Bytes**	**Coding Example**	
short-label	16 or 4	—	2	JS NEGATIVE	

LAHF	LAHF (no operands) Load AH from flags			Flags	O D I T S Z A P C
Operands	**Clocks**	**Transfers***	**Bytes**	**Coding Example**	
(no operands)	4	—	1	LAHF	

LDS	LDS destination,source Load pointer using DS			Flags	O D I T S Z A P C
Operands	**Clocks**	**Transfers**	**Bytes**	**Coding Example**	
reg16, mem32	16 + EA	2	2-4	LDS SI,DATA.SEG [DI]	

LEA	LEA destination,source Load effective address			Flags	O D I T S Z A P C
Operands	**Clocks**	**Transfers***	**Bytes**	**Coding Example**	
reg16, mem16	2 + EA	—	2-4	LEA BX, [BP] [DI]	

LES	LES destination,source Load pointer using ES			Flags	O D I T S Z A P C
Operands	**Clocks**	**Transfers***	**Bytes**	**Coding Example**	
reg16, mem32	16 + EA	2	2-4	LES DI, [BX].TEXT_ BUFF	

*For the 8086, add four clocks for each 16-bit word transfer with an odd address. For the 8088, add four clocks for each 16-bit word transfer

Table 2-21. Instruction Set Reference Data (Cont'd.)

LOCK	LOCK (no operands) Lock bus			Flags	O D I T S Z A P C
Operands	**Clocks**	**Transfers***	**Bytes**	**Coding Example**	
(no operands)	2	—	1	LOCK XCHG FLAG,AL	

LODS	LODS source-string Load string			Flags	O D I T S Z A P C
Operands	**Clocks**	**Transfers***	**Bytes**	**Coding Example**	
source-string	12	1	1	LODS CUSTOMER_NAME	
(repeat) source-string	9 + 13/rep	1/rep	1	REP LODS NAME	

LOOP	LOOP short-label Loop			Flags	O D I T S Z A P C
Operands	**Clocks**	**Transfers***	**Bytes**	**Coding Example**	
short-label	17/5	—	2	LOOP AGAIN	

LOOPE/LOOPZ	LOOPE/LOOPZ short-label Loop if equal/Loop if zero			Flags	O D I T S Z A P C
Operands	**Clocks**	**Transfers***	**Bytes**	**Coding Example**	
short-label	18 or 6	—	2	LOOPE AGAIN	

LOOPNE/LOOPNZ	LOOPNE/LOOPNZ short-label Loop if not equal/Loop if not zero			Flags	O D I T S Z A P C
Operands	**Clocks**	**Transfers***	**Bytes**	**Coding Example**	
short-label	19 or 5	—	2	LOOPNE AGAIN	

NMI†	NMI (external nonmaskable interrupt) Interrupt if NMI = 1			Flags	O S I T S Z A P C 0 0
Operands	**Clocks**	**Transfers***	**Bytes**	**Coding Example**	
(no operands)	50	5	N/A	N/A	

*For the 8086, add four clocks for each 16-bit word transfer with an odd address. For the 8088, add four clocks for each 16-bit word transfer.

†NMI is not an instruction; it is included in table 2-21 only for timing information.

Mnemonics © Intel, 1978

Table 2-21. Instruction Set Reference Data (Cont'd.)

MOV	MOV destination,source Move			Flags	O D I T S Z A P C
Operands	**Clocks**	**Transfers***	**Bytes**	**Coding Example**	
memory, accumulator	10	1	3	MOV ARRAY [SI], AL	
accumulator, memory	10	1	3	MOV AX, TEMP__RESULT	
register, register	2	—	2	MOV AX,CX	
register, memory	8 + EA	1	2-4	MOV BP, STACK__TOP	
memory, register	9 + EA	1	2-4	MOV COUNT [DI], CX	
register, immediate	4	—	2-3	MOV CL, 2	
memory, immediate	10 + EA	1	3-6	MOV MASK [BX] [SI], 2CH	
seg-reg, reg16	2	—	2	MOV ES, CX	
seg-reg, mem16	8 + EA	1	2-4	MOV DS, SEGMENT__BASE	
reg16, seg-reg	2	—	2	MOV BP, SS	
memory, seg-reg	9 + EA	1	2-4	MOV [BX].SEG__SAVE, CS	

MOVS	MOVS dest-string,source-string Move string			Flags	O D I T S Z A P C
Operands	**Clocks**	**Transfers***	**Bytes**	**Coding Example**	
dest-string, source-string	18	2	1	MOVS LINE EDIT__DATA	
(repeat) dest-string, source-string	9 + 17/rep	2/rep	1	REP MOVS SCREEN, BUFFER	

MOVSB/MOVSW	MOVSB/MOVSW (no operands) Move string (byte/word)			Flags	O D I T S Z A P C
Operands	**Clocks**	**Transfers***	**Bytes**	**Coding Example**	
(no operands)	18	2	1	MOVSB	
(repeat) (no operands)	9 + 17/rep	2/rep	1	REP MOVSW	

MUL	MUL source Multiplication, unsigned			Flags	O D I T S Z A P C X U U U U X
Operands	**Clocks**	**Transfers***	**Bytes**	**Coding Example**	
reg8	70-77	—	2	MUL BL	
reg16	118-133	—	2	MUL CX	
mem8	(76-83) + EA	1	2-4	MUL MONTH [SI]	
mem16	(124-139) + EA	1	2-4	MUL BAUD__RATE	

*For the 8086, add four clocks for each 16-bit word transfer with an odd address. For the 8088, add four clocks for each 16-bit word transfer.

Mnemonics © Intel, 1978

Table 2-21. Instruction Set Reference Data (Cont'd.)

NEG	NEG destination Negate				Flags	O D I T S Z A P C X X X X X 1*
Operands	**Clocks**	**Transfers***	**Bytes**	**Coding Example**		
register memory	3 16 + EA	— 2	2 2-4	NEG AL NEG MULTIPLIER		

*0 if destination = 0

NOP	NOP (no operands) No Operation				Flags	O D I T S Z A P C
Operands	**Clocks**	**Transfers***	**Bytes**	**Coding Example**		
(no operands)	3	—	1	NOP		

NOT	NOT destination Logical not				Flags	O D I T S Z A P C
Operands	**Clocks**	**Transfers***	**Bytes**	**Coding Example**		
register memory	3 16 + EA	— 2	2 2-4	NOT AX NOT CHARACTER		

OR	OR destination,source Logical inclusive or				Flags	O D I T S Z A P C 0 X X U X 0
Operands	**Clocks**	**Transfers***	**Bytes**	**Coding Example**		
register, register	3	—	2	OR AL, BL		
register, memory	9 + EA	1	2-4	OR DX, PORT_ID [DI]		
memory, register	16 + EA	2	2-4	OR FLAG_BYTE, CL		
accumulator, immediate	4	—	2-3	OR AL, 01101100B		
register, immediate	4	—	3-4	OR CX,01H		
memory, immediate	17 + EA	2	3-6	OR [BX].CMD_WORD,0CFH		

OUT	OUT port,accumulator Output byte or word				Flags	O D I T S Z A P C
Operands	**Clocks**	**Transfers***	**Bytes**	**Coding Example**		
immed8, accumulator	10	1	2	OUT 44, AX		
DX, accumulator	8	1	1	OUT DX, AL		

POP	POP destination Pop word off stack				Flags	O D I T S Z A P C
Operands	**Clocks**	**Transfers***	**Bytes**	**Coding Example**		
register	8	1	1	POP DX		
seg-reg (CS illegal)	8	1	1	POP DS		
memory	17 + EA	2	2-4	POP PARAMETER		

*For the 8086, add four clocks for each 16-bit word transfer with an odd address. For the 8088, add four clocks for each 16-bit word transfer.

Mnemonics © Intel, 1978

Table 2-21. Instruction Set Reference Data (Cont'd.)

POPF	POPF (no operands) Pop flags off stack			Flags	O D I T S Z A P C R R R R R R R R
Operands	**Clocks**	**Transfers***	**Bytes**	**Coding Example**	
(no operands)	8	1	1	POPF	

PUSH	PUSH source Push word onto stack			Flags	O D I T S Z A P C
Operands	**Clocks**	**Transfers***	**Bytes**	**Coding Example**	
register seg-reg (CS legal) memory	11 10 16 + EA	1 1 2	1 1 2-4	PUSH SI PUSH ES PUSH RETURN__CODE [SI]	

PUSHF	PUSHF (no operands) Push flags onto stack			Flags	O D I T S Z A P C
Operands	**Clocks**	**Transfers***	**Bytes**	**Coding Example**	
(no operands)	10	1	1	PUSHF	

RCL	RCL destination,count Rotate left through carry			Flags	O D I T S Z A P C X X
Operands	**Clocks**	**Transfers***	**Bytes**	**Coding Example**	
register, 1 register, CL memory, 1 memory, CL	2 8 + 4/bit 15 + EA 20 + EA + 4/bit	— — 2 2	2 2 2-4 2-4	RCL CX, 1 RCL AL, CL RCL ALPHA, 1 RCL [BP].PARM, CL	

RCR	RCR designation,count Rotate right through carry			Flags	O D I T S Z A P C X X
Operands	**Clocks**	**Transfers***	**Bytes**	**Coding Example**	
register, 1 register, CL memory, 1 memory, CL	2 8 + 4/bit 15 + EA 20 + EA + 4/bit	— — 2 2	2 2 2-4 2-4	RCR BX, 1 RCR BL, CL RCR [BX].STATUS, 1 RCR ARRAY [DI], CL	

REP	REP (no operands) Repeat string operation			Flags	O D I T S Z A P C
Operands	**Clocks**	**Transfers***	**Bytes**	**Coding Example**	
(no operands)	2	—	1	REP MOVS DEST, SRCE	

*For the 8086, add four clocks for each 16-bit word transfer with an odd address. For the 8088, add four clocks for each 16-bit word transfer.

Mnemonics   Intel, 1978

Table 2-21. Instruction Set Reference Data (Cont'd.)

REPE/REPZ	REPE/REPZ (no operands) Repeat string operation while equal/while zero			Flags O D I T S Z A P C
Operands	**Clocks**	**Transfers***	**Bytes**	**Coding Example**
(no operands)	2	—	1	REPE CMPS DATA, KEY

REPNE/REPNZ	REPNE/REPNZ (no operands) Repeat string operation while not equal/not zero			Flags O D I T S Z A P C
Operands	**Clocks**	**Transfers***	**Bytes**	**Coding Example**
(no operands)	2	—	1	REPNE SCAS INPUT__LINE

RET	RET optional-pop-value Return from procedure			Flags O D I T S Z A P C
Operands	**Clocks**	**Transfers***	**Bytes**	**Coding Example**
(intra-segment, no pop)	8	1	1	RET
(intra-segment, pop)	12	1	3	RET 4
(inter-segment, no pop)	18	2	1	RET
(inter-segment, pop)	17	2	3	RET 2

ROL	ROL destination,count Rotate left			Flags O D I T S Z A P C X X
Operands	**Clocks**	**Transfers**	**Bytes**	**Coding Examples**
register, 1	2	—	2	ROL BX, 1
register, CL	8 + 4/bit	—	2	ROL DI, CL
memory, 1	15 + EA	2	2-4	ROL FLAG__BYTE [DI],1
memory, CL	20 + EA + 4/bit	2	2-4	ROL ALPHA , CL

ROR	ROR destination,count Rotate right			Flags O D I T S Z A P C X X
Operand	**Clocks**	**Transfers***	**Bytes**	**Coding Example**
register, 1	2	—	2	ROR AL, 1
register, CL	8 + 4/bit	—	2	ROR BX, CL
memory, 1	15 + EA	2	2-4	ROR PORT__STATUS, 1
memory, CL	20 + EA + 4/bit	2	2-4	ROR CMD__WORD, CL

SAHF	SAHF (no operands) Store AH into flags			Flags O D I T S Z A P C R R R R R
Operands	**Clocks**	**Transfers***	**Bytes**	**Coding Example**
(no operands)	4	—	1	SAHF

*For the 8086, add four clocks for each 16-bit word transfer with an odd address. For the 8088, add four clocks for each 16-bit word transfer.

Mnemonics © Intel, 1978

Table 2-21. Instruction Set Reference Data (Cont'd.)

SAL/SHL	SAL/SHL destination,count Shift arithmetic left/Shift logical left				Flags	O D I T S Z A P C X X
Operands		**Clocks**	**Transfers***	**Bytes**	**Coding Examples**	
register,1		2	—	2	SAL AL,1	
register, CL		8 + 4/bit	—	2	SHL DI, CL	
memory,1		15 + EA	2	2-4	SHL [BX].OVERDRAW, 1	
memory, CL		20 + EA + 4/bit	2	2-4	SAL STORE__COUNT, CL	

SAR	SAR destination,source Shift arithmetic right				Flags	O D I T S Z A P C X X X U X X
Operands		**Clocks**	**Transfers***	**Bytes**	**Coding Example**	
register, 1		2	—	2	SAR DX, 1	
register, CL		8 + 4/bit	—	2	SAR DI, CL	
memory, 1		15 + EA	2	2-4	SAR N__BLOCKS, 1	
memory, CL		20 + EA + 4/bit	2	2-4	SAR N__BLOCKS, CL	

SBB	SBB destination,source Subtract with borrow				Flags	O D I T S Z A P C X X X X X X
Operands		**Clocks**	**Transfers***	**Bytes**	**Coding Example**	
register, register		3	—	2	SBB BX, CX	
register, memory		9 + EA	1	2-4	SBB DI, [BX].PAYMENT	
memory, register		16 + EA	2	2-4	SBB BALANCE, AX	
accumulator, immediate		4	—	2-3	SBB AX, 2	
register, immediate		4	—	3-4	SBB CL, 1	
memory, immediate		17 + EA	2	3-6	SBB COUNT [SI], 10	

SCAS	SCAS dest-string Scan string				Flags	O D I T S Z A P C X X X X X
Operands		**Clocks**	**Transfers***	**Bytes**	**Coding Example**	
dest-string		15	1	1	SCAS INPUT__LINE	
(repeat) dest-string		9 + 15/rep	1/rep	1	REPNE SCAS BUFFER	

SEGMENT†	SEGMENT override prefix Override to specified segment				Flags	O D I T S Z A P C
Operands		**Clocks**	**Transfers***	**Bytes**	**Coding Example**	
(no operands)		2	—	1	MOV SS:PARAMETER, AX	

*For the 8086, add four clocks for each 16-bit word transfer with an odd address. For the 8088, add four clocks for each 16-bit word transfer.

†ASM-86 incorporates the segment override prefix into the operand specification and not as a separate instruction. SEGMENT is included in table 2-21 only for timing information.

Mnemonics © Intel, 1978

SHR AX, CL MEANTS shift ℰ of AX how many time of content CL
ex: SHR AX, CL WHEN CL = 02 AX = 0150H
AFTER SHR AX = 0000 0000 0101 0100

Table 2-21. Instruction Set Reference Data (Cont'd.)

SHR	SHR destination,count Shift logical right			Flags	O D I T S Z A P C X X
Operands	**Clocks**	**Transfers***	**Bytes**	**Coding Example**	
register, 1	2	—	2	SHR SI, 1	
register, CL	8 + 4/bit	—	2	SHR SI, CL	
memory, 1	15 + EA	2	2-4	SHR ID__BYTE [SI] [BX], 1	
memory, CL	20 + EA + 4/bit	2	2-4	SHR INPUT__WORD, CL	

SINGLE STEP†	SINGLE STEP (Trap flag interrupt) Interrupt if TF = 1			Flags	O D I T S Z A P C 0 0
Operands	**Clocks**	**Transfers***	**Bytes**	**Coding Example**	
(no operands)	50	5	N/A	N/A	

STC	STC (no operands) Set carry flag			Flags	O D I T S Z A P C 1
Operands	**Clocks**	**Transfers***	**Bytes**	**Coding Example**	
(no operands)	2	—	1	STC	

STD	STD (no operands) Set direction flag			Flags	O D I T S Z A P C 1
Operands	**Clocks**	**Transfers***	**Bytes**	**Coding Example**	
(no operands)	2	—	1	STD	

STI	STI (no operands) Set interrupt enable flag			Flags	O D I T S Z A P C 1
Operands	**Clocks**	**Transfers***	**Bytes**	**Coding Example**	
(no operands)	2	—	1	STI	

STOS	STOS dest-string Store byte or word string			Flags	O D I T S Z A P C
Operands	**Clocks**	**Transfers***	**Bytes**	**Coding Example**	
dest-string	11	1	1	STOS PRINT__LINE	
(repeat) dest-string	9 + 10/rep	1/rep	1	REP STOS DISPLAY	

*For the 8086, add four clocks for each 16-bit word transfer with an odd address. For the 8088, add four clocks for each 16-bit word transfer.

†SINGLE STEP is not an instruction; it is included in table 2-21 only for timing information.

Mnemonics   Intel, 1978

Table 2-21. Instruction Set Reference Data (Cont'd.)

SUB	SUB destination,source Subtraction				Flags	O D I T S Z A P C X X X X X X
Operands	**Clocks**	**Transfers***	**Bytes**	**Coding Example**		
register, register	3	—	2	SUB CX, BX		
register, memory	9 + EA	1	2-4	SUB DX, MATH__TOTAL [SI]		
memory, register	16 + EA	2	2-4	SUB [BP + 2], CL		
accumulator, immediate	4	—	2-3	SUB AL, 10		
register, immediate	4	—	3-4	SUB SI, 5280		
memory, immediate	17 + EA	2	3-6	SUB [BP].BALANCE, 1000		

TEST	TEST destination,source Test or non-destructive logical and				Flags	O D I T S Z A P C 0 X X U X 0
Operands	**Clocks**	**Transfers***	**Bytes**	**Coding Example**		
register, register	3	—	2	TEST SI, DI		
register, memory	9 + EA	1	2-4	TEST SI, END__COUNT		
accumulator, immediate	4	—	2-3	TEST AL, 00100000B		
register, immediate	5	—	3-4	TEST BX, 0CC4H		
memory, immediate	11 + EA	—	3-6	TEST RETURN__CODE, 01H		

WAIT	WAIT (no operands) Wait while $\overline{\text{TEST}}$ pin not asserted				Flags	O D I T S Z A P C
Operands	**Clocks**	**Transfers***	**Bytes**	**Coding Example**		
(no operands)	3 + 5n	—	1	WAIT		

XCHG	XCHG destination,source Exchange				Flags	O D I T S Z A P C
Operands	**Clocks**	**Transfers***	**Bytes**	**Coding Example**		
accumulator, reg16	3	—	1	XCHG AX, BX		
memory, register	17 + EA	2	2-4	XCHG SEMAPHORE, AX		
register, register	4	—	2	XCHG AL, BL		

XLAT	XLAT source-table Translate				Flags	O D I T S Z A P C
Operands	**Clocks**	**Transfers***	**Bytes**	**Coding Example**		
source-table	11	1	1	XLAT ASCII__TAB		

*For the 8086, add four clocks for each 16-bit word transfer with an odd address. For the 8088, add four clocks for each 16-bit word transfer.

Mnemonics © Intel, 1978

Table 2-21. Instruction Set Reference Data (Cont'd.)

XOR		XOR destination,source Logical exclusive or			Flags	O D I T S Z A P C 0 X X U X 0
Operands		**Clocks**	**Transfers***	**Bytes**	**Coding Example**	
register, register		3	—	2	XOR CX, BX	
register, memory		9 + EA	1	2-4	XOR CL, MASK__BYTE	
memory, register		16 + EA	2	2-4	XOR ALPHA [SI], DX	
accumulator, immediate		4	—	2-3	XOR AL, 01000010B	
register, immediate		4	—	3-4	XOR SI, 00C2H	
memory, immediate		17 + EA	2	3-6	XOR RETURN__CODE, 0D2H	

*For the 8086, add four clocks for each 16-bit word transfer with an odd address. For the 8088, add four clocks for each 16-bit word transfer.

2.8 Addressing Modes

The 8086 and 8088 provide many different ways to access instruction operands. Operands may be contained in registers, within the instruction itself, in memory or in I/O ports. In addition, the addresses of memory and I/O port operands can be calculated in several different ways. These addressing modes greatly extend the flexibility and convenience of the instruction set. This section briefly describes register and immediate operands and then covers the 8086/8088 memory and I/O addressing modes in detail.

Register and Immediate Operands

Instructions that specify only register operands are generally the most compact and fastest executing of all instruction forms. This is because the register "addresses" are encoded in instructions in just a few bits, and because these operations are performed entirely within the CPU (no bus cycles are run). Registers may serve as source operands, destination operands, or both.

Immediate operands are constant data contained in an instruction. The data may be either 8 or 16 bits in length. Immediate operands can be accessed quickly because they are available directly from the instruction queue; like a register operand, no bus cycles need to be run to obtain an immediate operand. The limitations of immediate operands are that they may only serve as source operands and that they are constant values.

Mnemonics · Intel, 1978

Memory Addressing Modes

Whereas the EU has direct access to register and immediate operands, memory operands must be transferred to or from the CPU over the bus. When the EU needs to read or write a memory operand, it must pass an offset value to the BIU. The BIU adds the offset to the (shifted) content of a segment register producing a 20-bit physical address and then executes the bus cycle(s) needed to access the operand.

The Effective Address

The offset that the EU calculates for a memory operand is called the operand's effective address or EA. It is an unsigned 16-bit number that expresses the operand's distance in bytes from the beginning of the segment in which it resides. The EU can calculate the effective address in several different ways. Information encoded in the second byte of the instruction tells the EU how to calculate the effective address of each memory operand. A compiler or assembler derives this information from the statement or instruction written by the programmer. Assembly language programmers have access to all addressing modes.

Figure 2-34 shows that the execution unit calculates the EA by summing a displacement, the content of a base register and the content of an index register. The fact that any combination of these three components may be present in a given instruction gives rise to the variety of 8086/8088 memory addressing modes.

Table A1-2

8088 Microprocessor Operation Code Matrix

Hi \ Lo	0	1	2	3	4	5	6	7	8	9	A	B	C	D	E	F
0	ADD b,f,r/m	ADD w,f,r/m	ADD b,t,r/m	ADD w,t,r/m	ADD b,ia	ADD w,ia	PUSH ES	POP ES	OR b,f,r/m	OR w,f,r/m	OR b,t,r/m	OR w,t,r/m	OR b,i	OR w,i	PUSH CS	
1	ADC b,f,r/m	ADC w,f,r/m	ADC b,t,r/m	ADC w,t,r/m	ADC b,i	ADC w,i	PUSH SS	POP SS	SBB b,f,r/m	SBB w,f,r/m	SBB b,t,r/m	SBB w,t,r/m	SBB b,i	SBB w,i	PUSH DS	POP DS
2	AND b,f,r/m	AND w,f,r/m	AND b,t,r/m	AND w,t,r/m	AND b,i	AND w,i	SEG ES	DAA	SUB b,f,r/m	SUB w,f,r/m	SUB b,t,r/m	SUB w,t,r/m	SUB b,i	SUB w,i	SEG CS	DAS
3	XOR b,f,r/m	XOR w,f,r/m	XOR b,t,r/m	XOR w,t,r/m	XOR b,i	XOR w,i	SEG SS	AAA	CMP b,f,r/m	CMP w,f,r/m	CMP b,t,r/m	CMP w,t,r/m	CMP b,i	CMP w,i	SEG DS	AAS
4	INC AX	INC CX	INC DX	INC BX	INC SP	INC BP	INC SI	INC DI	DEC AX	DEC CX	DEC DX	DEC BX	DEC SP	DEC BP	DEC SI	DEC DI
5	PUSH AX	PUSH CX	PUSH DX	PUSH BX	PUSH SP	PUSH BP	PUSH SI	PUSH DI	POP AX	POP CX	POP DX	POP BX	POP SP	POP BP	POP SI	POP DI
6																
7	JO	JNO	JB/JNAE	JNB/JAE	JE/JZ	JNE/JNZ	JBE/JNA	JNBE/JA	JS	JNS	JP/JPE	JNP/JPO	JL/JNGE	JNL/JGE	JLE/JNG	JNLE/JG
8	Immed b,r/m	Immed w,r/m	Immed b,r/m	Immed is,r/m	TEST b,r/m	TEST w,r/m	XCHG b,r/m	XCHG w,r/m	MOV b,f,r/m	MOV w,f,r/m	MOV b,t,r/m	MOV w,t,r/m	MOV sr,f,r/m	LEA	MOV sr,t,r/m	POP r/m
9	XCHG AX	XCHG CX	XCHG DX	XCHG BX	XCHG SP	XCHG BP	XCHG SI	XCHG DI	CBW	CWD	CALL l,d	WAIT	PUSHF	POPF	SAHF	LAHF
A	MOV m→AL	MOV m→AX	MOV AL→m	MOV AX→m	MOVS	MOVS	CMPS	CMPS	TEST b,i,a	TEST w,i,a	STOS	STOS	LODS	LODS	SCAS	SCAS
B	MOV i→AL	MOV i→CL	MOV i→DL	MOV i→BL	MOV i→AH	MOV i→CH	MOV i→DH	MOV i→BH	MOV i→AX	MOV i→CX	MOV i→DX	MOV i→BX	MOV i→SP	MOV i→BP	MOV i→SI	MOV i→DI
C			RET (i+SP)	RET	LES	LDS	MOV b,i,r/m	MOV w,i,r/m			RET l,(i+SP)	RET l	INT Type 3	INT (Any)	INTO	IRET
D	Shift b	Shift w	Shift b,v	Shift w,v	AAM	AAD		XLAT	ESC 0	ESC 1	ESC 2	ESC 3	ESC 4	ESC 5	ESC 6	ESC 7
E	LOOPNZ/LOOPNE	LOOPZ/LOOPE	LOOP	JCXZ	IN b	IN w	OUT b	OUT w	CALL d	JMP d	JMP l,d	JMP si,d	IN v,b	IN v,w	OUT v,b	OUT v,w
F	LOCK		REP	REP z	HLT	CMC	Grp 1 b,r/m	Grp 1 w,r/m	CLC	STC	CLI	STI	CLD	STD	Grp 2 b,r/m	Grp 2 w,r/m

where

mod☐r/m	000	001	010	011	100	101	110	111
Immed	ADD	OR	ADC	SBB	AND	SUB	XOR	CMP
Shift	ROL	ROR	RCL	RCR	SHL/SAL	SHR	—	SAR
Grp 1	TEST	—	NOT	NEG	MUL	IMUL	DIV	IDIV
Grp 2	INC	DEC	CALL id	CALL l,id	JMP id	JMP l,id	PUSH	—

b = byte operation
d = direct
f = from CPU reg
i = immediate
ia = immed. to accum.
id = indirect
is = immed. byte, sign ext.
l = long ie. intersegment

m = memory
r/m = EA is second byte
si = short intrasegment
sr = segment register
t = to CPU reg
v = variable
w = word operation
z = zero

Table A1-3

Object Codes and
Timings for 8086
Instructions Used
in This Book

Instruction	Object Code	Bytes	Clock Cycles
ADC AH,DATA8	80 D4 DATA8	3	4
ADC AL,BH	10 F8	2	3
ADC AL,DATA8	14 DATA8	2	4
ADC AL,[DI]	12 05	2	14
ADC BL,DATA8	80 D3 DATA8	3	4
ADD [ADDR],AX	01 06 ADDR	4	22
ADD AH,DATA8	80 C4 DATA8	3	4
ADD AL,[ADDR]	02 06 ADDR	4	15
ADD AL,AL	00 C0	2	3
ADD AL,BH	00 F8	2	3
ADD AL,BL	00 D8	2	3
ADD AL,CL	00 C8	2	3
ADD AL,DATA8	04 DATA8	2	4
ADD AL,[SI]	02 04	2	14
ADD AX,AX	01 C0	2	3
ADD AX,DATA16	05 DATA16	3	4
ADD AX,[SI]	03 04	2	14
ADD BL,[ADDR]	02 1E ADDR	4	15
ADD BL,AL	00 C3	2	3
ADD BL,[SI]	02 1C	2	14
ADD BX,[ADDR]	03 1E ADDR	4	15
ADD BX,AX	01 C3	2	3
ADD BX,BX	01 DB	2	3
ADD BX,DATA16	81 C3 DATA16	4	4
ADD CL,DATA8	80 C1 DATA8	3	4
ADD DH,DATA8	80 C6 DATA8	3	4
ADD DX,DATA8	83 C2 DATA8	3	4
AND AL,[ADDR]	22 06 ADDR	4	15
AND AL,AL	20 C0	2	3
AND AL,BL	20 D8	2	3
AND AL,DATA8	24 DATA8	2	4
AND CH,DATA8	80 E5 DATA8	3	4
CALL ADDR	E8 DISP16	3	19
CALL [BX+ADDR]	FF 97 ADDR	4	30
CLC	F8	1	2
CLD	FC	1	2
CLI	FA	1	2
CMC	F5	1	2
CMP AH,[ADDR]	3A 26 ADDR	4	15
CMP AL,[ADDR]	3A 06 ADDR	4	15
CMP AL,AH	38 E0	2	3
CMP AL,[BX+ADDR]	3A 87 ADDR	4	18
CMP AL,DATA8	3C DATA8	2	4
CMP AL,[DI]	3A 05	2	14
CMP AX,[ADDR]	3B 06 ADDR	4	15
CMP AX,DATA16	3D DATA16	3	4

Instruction	Object Code	Bytes	Clock Cycles
CMP BH,[ADDR]	3A 3E ADDR	4	15
CMP BH,DATA8	80 FF DATA8	3	4
CMP BL,[ADDR]	3A 1E ADDR	4	15
CMP BL,DATA8	80 FB DATA8	3	4
CMP BX,[ADDR]	3B 1E ADDR	4	15
CMP BX,DATA16	81 FB DATA16	4	4
CMP CL,[ADDR]	3A 0E ADDR	4	15
CMP CL,DATA8	80 F9 DATA8	3	4
CMP DH,[ADDR]	3A 36 ADDR	4	15
CMP DH,DATA8	80 FE DATA8	3	4
CMP DX,[ADDR]	3B 16 ADDR	4	15
CMP SI,DATA8	83 FE DATA8	3	4
DAA	27	1	4
DAS	2F	1	4
DEC BYTE PTR [ADDR]	FE 0E ADDR	4	21
DEC WORD PTR [ADDR]	FF 0E ADDR	4	21
DEC AH	FE CC	2	3
DEC AL	FE C8	2	3
DEC AX	48	1	2
DEC BL	FE CB	2	3
DEC BP	4D	1	2
DEC BX	4B	1	2
DEC CH	FE CD	2	3
DEC CX	49	1	2
DEC DI	4F	1	2
DEC SI	4E	1	2
IN AL,DX	EC	1	8
INC BYTE PTR [ADDR]	FE 06 ADDR	4	21
INC WORD PTR [ADDR]	FF 06 ADDR	4	21
INC AL	FE C0	2	3
INC AX	40	1	2
INC BH	FE C7	2	3
INC BL	FE C3	2	3
INC BX	43	1	2
INC BYTE PTR [BX+ADDR]	FE 87 ADDR	4	24
INC CL	FE C1	2	3
INC CX	41	1	2
INC DI	47	1	2
INC SI	46	1	2
INT 3	CC	1	52
INT TYPE (Type Not 3)	CD TYPE	2	51
INTR	External Interrupt		61
IRET	CF	1	24
JA ADDR	77 DISP	2	4/16*

Instruction	Object Code	Bytes	Clock Cycles
JAE ADDR	73 DISP	2	4/16*
JB ADDR	72 DISP	2	4/16*
JBE ADDR	76 DISP	2	4/16*
JC ADDR	72 DISP	2	4/16*
JE ADDR	74 DISP	2	4/16*
JMP ADDR	EB DISP	2	15
JMP [BX+ADDR]	FF A7 ADDR	4	27
JNB ADDR	73 DISP	2	4/16*
JNBE ADDR	77 DISP	2	4/16*
JNC ADDR	73 DISP	2	4/16*
JNE ADDR	75 DISP	2	4/16*
JNS ADDR	79 DISP	2	4/16*
JNZ ADDR	75 DISP	2	4/16*
JPE ADDR	7A DISP	2	4/16*
JPO ADDR	7B DISP	2	4/16*
JS ADDR	78 DISP	2	4/16*
JZ ADDR	74 DISP	2	4/16*
LODSB(W)	AC(AD)	1	12
(after REP)			9+13/repetition
LOOP ADDR	E2 DISP	2	5/17*
MOV BYTE PTR [ADDR],DATA8	C6 06 ADDR DATA8	5	16
MOV WORD PTR [ADDR],DATA16	C7 06 ADDR DATA16	6	16
MOV AH,[ADDR]	8A 26 ADDR	4	14
MOV AH,AL	88 C4	2	2
MOV AH,DATA8	B4 DATA8	2	4
MOV AL,[ADDR]	A0 ADDR	3	10
MOV [ADDR],AL	A2 ADDR	3	10
MOV AL,AH	88 E0	2	2
MOV AL,BH	88 F8	2	2
MOV AL,BL	88 D8	2	2
MOV AL,[BX+ADDR]	8A 87 ADDR	4	17
MOV [BX+ADDR],AL	88 87 ADDR	4	18
MOV AL,CL	88 C8	2	2
MOV AL,DATA8	B0 DATA8	2	4
MOV AL,[DI]	8A 05	2	13
MOV [DI],AL	88 05	2	14
MOV AL,DL	88 D0	2	2
MOV AL,[SI]	8A 04	2	13
MOV AL,[SI+ADDR]	8A 84 ADDR	4	17
MOV AX,[ADDR]	A1 ADDR	3	10

Instruction	Object Code	Bytes	Clock Cycles
MOV [ADDR],AX	A3 ADDR	3	10
MOV AX,BX	89 D8	2	2
MOV AX,[BX+ADDR]	8B 87 ADDR	4	17
MOV [BX+ADDR],AX	89 87 ADDR	4	18
MOV AX,DATA16	B8 DATA16	3	4
MOV AX,[DI]	8B 05	2	13
MOV [DI],AX	89 05	2	14
MOV [ADDR],BH	88 1F ADDR	4	15
MOV BH,AL	88 C7	2	2
MOV BL,[ADDR]	8A 1E ADDR	4	14
MOV [ADDR],BL	88 1E ADDR	4	15
MOV BL,AL	88 C3	2	2
MOV BL,DATA8	B3 DATA8	2	4
MOV BL,[SI]	8A 1C	2	13
MOV BP,DATA16	BD DATA16	3	4
MOV [ADDR],BX	89 1E ADDR	4	15
MOV BX,AX	89 C3	2	2
MOV BX,DATA16	BB DATA16	3	4
MOV BYTE PTR [BX+ADDR],DATA8	C6 87 ADDR DATA8	5	19
MOV WORD PTR [BX+ADDR],DATA16	C7 87 ADDR DATA16	6	19
MOV CH,CL	88 CD	2	2
MOV CL,[ADDR]	8A 0E ADDR	4	14
MOV [ADDR],CL	88 0E ADDR	4	15
MOV CL,AL	88 C1	2	2
MOV DX, [ADDR]	8B 16 ADDR	4	14
MOV [ADDR],DX	89 16 ADDR	4	15
MOV CL,[BX+ADDR]	8A 8F ADDR	4	17
MOV CL,DATA8	B1 DATA8	2	4
MOV CX,[ADDR]	8B 0E ADDR	4	14
MOV [ADDR],CX	89 0E ADDR	4	15
MOV CX,DATA16	B9 DATA16	3	4
MOV DH,[ADDR]	8A 36 ADDR	4	14
MOV [ADDR],DH	88 36 ADDR	4	15
MOV DH,DATA8	B6 DATA8	2	4
MOV DI,[ADDR]	8B 3E ADDR	4	14
MOV [ADDR],DI	89 3E ADDR	4	15
MOV DI,DATA16	BF DATA16	3	4
MOV DL,[ADDR]	8A 16 ADDR	4	14
MOV [ADDR],DL	88 16 ADDR	4	15
MOV DL,AL	88 C2	2	2

Instruction	Object Code	Bytes	Clock Cycles
MOV DL,BL	88 DA	2	2
MOV DL,DATA8	B2 DATA8	2	4
MOV DX,ADDR	BA ADDR	3	4
MOV DX,[ADDR]	8B 16 ADDR	4	14
MOV [ADDR],DX	89 16 ADDR	4	15
MOV DX,[BX+ADDR]	8B 97 ADDR	4	17
MOV SI,ADDR	BE ADDR	3	4
MOV SI,[ADDR]	8B 36 ADDR	4	14
MOV [ADDR],SI	89 36 ADDR	4	15
MOV [SI+OFFSET8],AL	88 44 OFFSET8	3	18
MOV SI,DI	89 FE	2	2
MOV SP,ADDR	BC ADDR	3	4
MOV [ADDR],SP	89 26 ADDR	4	15
MOVSB(W) (after REP)	A4(A5)	1	18 9+17/repetition
NOP	90	1	3
NOT BYTE PTR [ADDR]	F6 16 ADDR	4	22
NOT AL	F6 D0	2	3
NOT BL	F6 D3	2	3
NOT CL	F6 D1	2	3
OR AL,[ADDR]	0A 06 ADDR	4	15
OR AL,DATA8	0C DATA8	2	4
OR CH,DATA8	80 CD DATA8	3	4
OUT DX,AL	EE	1	8
OUT DX,AX	EF	1	8
POP AX	58	1	8
POP BX	5B	1	8
POP CX	59	1	8
POP DI	5F	1	8
POP DX	5A	1	8
POPF	9D	1	8
POP SI	5E	1	8
PUSH AX	50	1	11
PUSH BX	53	1	11
PUSH CX	51	1	11
PUSH DI	57	1	11
PUSH DX	52	1	11
PUSHF	9C	1	10
PUSH SI	56	1	11
RCL AL,1	D0 D0	2	2

Instruction	Object Code	Bytes	Clock Cycles
RCL BL,1	D0 D3	2	2
RCR AL,1	D0 D8	2	2
RCR BH,1	D0 DF	2	2
RCR BL,1	D0 DB	2	2
REP	F3	1	2
REPNE	F2	1	2
RET	C3	1	8
SAR AL,1	D0 F8	2	2
SBB AL,[DI]	1A 05	2	14
SBB AL,[SI]	1A 04	2	14
SCASB(W)	AE(AF)	1	15
(after REP)			9+15/repetition
SHL AL,CL	D2 E0	2	8+4/bit
SHL AL,1	D0 E0	2	2
SHL AX,1	D1 E0	2	2
SHL BL,1	D0 E3	2	2
SHL BX,1	D1 E3	2	2
SHR AL,1	D0 E8	2	2
SHR BL,1	D0 EB	2	2
STC	F9	1	2
STD	FD	1	2
STI	FB	1	2
STOSB(W)	AA(AB)	1	11
(after REP)			9+10/repetition
SUB AH,AH	28 E4	2	3
SUB AL,[ADDR]	2A 06 ADDR	4	15
SUB AL,AL	28 C0	2	3
SUB AL,DATA8	2C DATA8	2	4
SUB AX,AX	29 C0	2	3
SUB AX,BX	29 D8	2	3
SUB BH,BH	28 FF	2	3
SUB BL,BL	28 DB	2	3
SUB BL,DATA8	80 EB DATA8	3	4
SUB BX,BX	29 DB	2	3
SUB CH,CH	28 ED	2	3
SUB CL,DATA8	80 E9 DATA8	3	4
SUB DH,DATA8	80 EE DATA8	3	4
SUB DX,DX	29 D2	2	3
SUB SI,SI	29 F6	2	3
TEST AL,AL	84 C0	2	3
TEST AL,BL	84 D8	2	3

Instruction	Object Code	Bytes	Clock Cycles
TEST AL,DATA8	A8 DATA8	2	4
TEST BL,BL	84 DB	2	3
TEST CL,CL	84 C9	2	3
TEST DL,DL	84 D2	2	3
XLAT	D7	1	11
XOR AL,[ADDR]	32 06 ADDR	4	15
XOR AL,DATA8	34 DATA8	2	4
XOR AL,[SI]	32 04	2	14

*The larger number of cycles applies if a jump actually occurs.

Character Code Tables

Table A2-1

ASCII Characters

LSD \ MSD		0 000	1 001	2 010	3 011	4 100	5 101	6 110	7 111
0	0000	NUL	DLE	SP	0	@	P	`	p
1	0001	SOH	DC1	!	1	A	Q	a	q
2	0010	STX	DC2	"	2	B	R	b	r
3	0011	ETX	DC3	#	3	C	S	c	s
4	0100	EOT	DC4	$	4	D	T	d	t
5	0101	ENQ	NAK	%	5	E	U	e	u
6	0110	ACK	SYN	&	6	F	V	f	v
7	0111	BEL	ETB	'	7	G	W	g	w
8	1000	BS	CAN	(	8	H	X	h	x
9	1001	HT	EM	)	9	I	Y	i	y
A	1010	LF	SUB	•	:	J	Z	j	z
B	1011	VT	ESC	+	;	K	[	k	}
C	1100	FF	FS	,	<	L	\	l	:
D	1101	CR	GS	—	=	M	]	m	{
E	1110	SO	RS	•	>	N	·	n	~
F	1111	SI	US	/	?	O	_	o	DEL

Table A2-2

Auxiliary Byte Values for the Special Keys and Combinations on the Standard IBM PC Keyboard

Value (Hex)	Key	Value (Hex)	Key
0F	Shift-Tab	16	Alt-U
10	Alt-Q	17	Alt-I
11	Alt-W	18	Alt-O
12	Alt-E	19	Alt-P
13	Alt-R	1E	Alt-A
14	Alt-T	1F	Alt-S
15	Alt-Y	20	Alt-D

Value (Hex)	Key	Value (Hex)	Key
21	Alt-F	5C	Shift-F9
22	Alt-G	5D	Shift-F10
23	Alt-H	5E	Ctrl-F1
24	Alt-J	5F	Ctrl-F2
25	Alt-K	60	Ctrl-F3
26	Alt-L	61	Ctrl-F4
2C	Alt-Z	62	Ctrl-F5
2D	Alt-X	63	Ctrl-F6
2E	Alt-C	64	Ctrl-F7
2F	Alt-V	65	Ctrl-F8
30	Alt-B	66	Ctrl-F9
31	Alt-N	67	Ctrl-F10
32	Alt-M	68	Alt-F1
3B	F1	69	Alt-F2
3C	F2	6A	Alt-F3
3D	F3	6B	Alt-F4
3E	F4	6C	Alt-F5
3F	F5	6D	Alt-F6
40	F6	6E	Alt-F7
41	F7	6F	Alt-F8
42	F8	70	Alt-F9
43	F9	71	Alt-F10
44	F10	72	Ctrl-PrtSc
47	Home	73	Ctrl-Left arrow
48	Up arrow	74	Ctrl-Right arrow
49	PgUp	75	Ctrl-End
4B	Left arrow	76	Ctrl-PgDn
4D	Right arrow	77	Ctrl-Home
4F	End	78	Alt-1
50	Down arrow	79	Alt-2
51	PgDn	7A	Alt-3
52	Insert	7B	Alt-4
53	Delete	7C	Alt-5
54	Shift-F1	7D	Alt-6
55	Shift-F2	7E	Alt-7
56	Shift-F3	7F	Alt-8
57	Shift-F4	80	Alt-9
58	Shift-F5	81	Alt-0
59	Shift-F6	82	Alt-Hyphen
5A	Shift-F7	83	Alt-=
5B	Shift-F8	84	Ctrl-PgUp

Table A2-3
Keyboard Scan
Codes for the
Standard IBM PC
Keyboard

Value (Hex)	Key	Value (Hex)	Key
1	Esc	2B	/
2	1	2C	Z
3	2	2D	X
4	3	2E	C
5	4	2F	V
6	5	30	B
7	6	31	N
8	7	32	M
9	8	33	,
A	9	34	.
B	0	35	/
C	-	36	Right Shift
D	=	37	° (PrtSc)
E	Backspace	38	Alt
F	Tab	39	Space Bar
10	Q	3A	Caps Lock
11	W	3B	F1
12	E	3C	F2
13	R	3D	F3
14	T	3E	F4
15	Y	3F	F5
16	U	40	F6
17	I	41	F7
18	O	42	F8
19	P	43	F9
1A	[	44	F10
1B	]	45	Num Lock
1C	Enter	46	Scroll Lock
1D	Ctrl	47	Home
1E	A	48	Up Arrow
1F	S	49	PgUp
20	D	4A	- (on numeric pad)
21	F	4B	Left Arrow
22	G	4C	Blank key (on pad)
23	H	4D	Right Arrow
24	J	4E	+ (on numeric pad)
25	K	4F	End
26	L	50	Down Arrow
27	;	51	PgDn
28	'	52	Ins
29	`	53	Del
2A	Left Shift		

Table A2-4

Character Codes
for the IBM PC
Video Display

Value (Hex)	Character	Value (Hex)	Character
00	(null)	27	'
01	☺	28	(
02	●	29	)
03	♥	2A	*
04	♦	2B	+
05	♣	2C	,
06	♠	2D	-
07	(beep)	2E	.
08	(backspace)	2F	/
09	(tab)	30	0
0A	(line feed)	31	1
0B	(home)	32	2
0C	(form feed)	33	3
0D	(carriage return)	34	4
0E	♫	35	5
0F	☼	36	6
10	►	37	7
11	◄	38	8
12	↕	39	9
13	!!	3A	:
14	¶	3B	;
15	§	3C	<
16	▬	3D	=
17	↨	3E	>
18	↑	3F	?
19	↓	40	@
1A	→	41	A
1B	←	42	B
1C	(cursor right)	43	C
1D	(cursor left)	44	D
1E	(cursor up)	45	E
1F	(cursor down)	46	F
20	(space)	47	G
21	!	48	H
22	"	49	I
23	#	4A	J
24	$	4B	K
25	%	4C	L
26	&	4D	M

Value (Hex)	Character	Value (Hex)	Character
4E	N	75	u
4F	O	76	v
50	P	77	w
51	Q	78	x
52	R	79	y
53	S	7A	z
54	T	7B	{
55	U	7C	|
56	V	7D	}
57	W	7E	~
58	X	7F	⌂
59	Y	80	Ç
5A	Z	81	ü
5B	[	82	é
5C	\	83	â
5D	]	84	ä
5E	∧	85	à
5F	—	86	å
60	'	87	ç
61	a	88	ê
62	b	89	ë
63	c	8A	è
64	d	8B	ï
65	e	8C	î
66	f	8D	ì
67	g	8E	Ä
68	h	8F	Å
69	i	90	É
6A	j	91	œ
6B	k	92	Æ
6C	l	93	ô
6D	m	94	ö
6E	n	95	ò
6F	o	96	û
70	p	97	ù
71	q	98	ÿ
72	r	99	Ö
73	s	9A	Ü
74	t	9B	¢

Value (Hex)	Character	Value (Hex)	Character
9C	£	C3	⊦
9D	¥	C4	—
9E	Pt	C5	+
9F	ƒ	C6	⊨
A0	á	C7	⊩
A1	í	C8	⊾
A2	ó	C9	⌐
A3	ú	CA	⊥
A4	ñ	CB	⊤
A5	Ñ	CC	⊩
A6	ª	CD	=
A7	º	CE	╬
A8	¿	CF	⊥
A9	⌐	D0	⊥
AA	¬	D1	⊤
AB	½	D2	⊤
AC	¼	D3	⊔
AD	¡	D4	⊢
AE	«	D5	⌐
AF	»	D6	⊤
B0	░	D7	╫
B1	▒	D8	╪
B2	▓	D9	⌟
B3	│	DA	⌜
B4	┤	DB	■
B5	╡	DC	▬
B6	╢	DD	▌
B7	╖	DE	▮
B8	╕	DF	▬
B9	╣	E0	α
BA	║	E1	β
BB	╗	E2	Γ
BC	╝	E3	π
BD	╜	E4	Σ
BE	╛	E5	σ
BF	┐	E6	μ
C0	└	E7	τ
C1	┴	E8	Φ
C2	┬	E9	Θ

Value (Hex)	Character
EA	Ω
EB	δ
EC	∞
ED	Ø
EE	ε
EF	∩
F0	≡
F1	±
F2	≥
F3	≤
F4	⌠
F5	⌡
F6	÷
F7	≈
F8	°
F9	•
FA	·
FB	√
FC	ⁿ
FD	²
FE	■
FF	(blank 'FF')

*Brief Descriptions of 8088 Family Devices**

*The following specification sheets are reprinted here with the permission of Intel Corporation, Santa Clara, CA.

iAPX 88/10
8-BIT HMOS MICROPROCESSOR
8088/8088-2

- **8-Bit Data Bus Interface**

- **16-Bit Internal Architecture**

- **Direct Addressing Capability to 1 Mbyte of Memory**

- **Direct Software Compatibility with iAPX 86/10 (8086 CPU)**

- **14-Word by 16-Bit Register Set with Symmetrical Operations**

- **24 Operand Addressing Modes**

- **Byte, Word, and Block Operations**

- **8-Bit and 16-Bit Signed and Unsigned Arithmetic in Binary or Decimal, Including Multiply and Divide**

- **Compatible with 8155-2, 8755A-2 and 8185-2 Multiplexed Peripherals**

- **Two Clock Rates:**
  5 MHz for 8088
  8 MHz for 8088-2

- **Available in EXPRESS**
  – Standard Temperature Range
  – Extended Temperature Range

The Intel® iAPX 88/10 is a new generation, high performance microprocessor implemented in N-channel, depletion load, silicon gate technology (HMOS), and packaged in a 40-pin CerDIP package. The processor has attributes of both 8- and 16-bit microprocessors. It is directly compatible with iAPX 86/10 software and 8080/8085 hardware and peripherals.

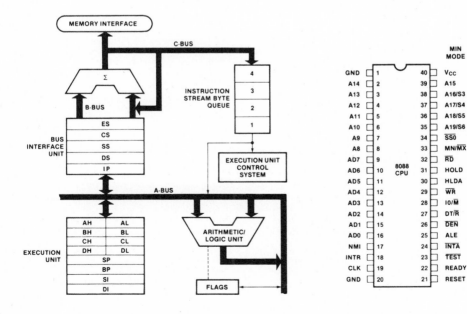

Figure 1. iAPX 88/10 CPU Functional Block Diagram   **Figure 2. iAPX 88/10 Pin Configuration**

iAPX 88/10   PRELIMINARY

Table 1. Pin Description

The following pin function descriptions are for 8088 systems in either minimum or maximum mode. The "local bus" in these descriptions is the direct multiplexed bus interface connection to the 8088 (without regard to additional bus buffers).

Symbol	Pin No.	Type	Name and Function
AD7–AD0	9-16	I/O	**Address Data Bus:** These lines constitute the time multiplexed memory/IO address (T1) and data (T2, T3, Tw, and T4) bus. These lines are active HIGH and float to 3-state OFF during interrupt acknowledge and local bus "hold acknowledge".
A15–A8	2-8, 39	O	**Address Bus:** These lines provide address bits 8 through 15 for the entire bus cycle (T1–T4). These lines do not have to be latched by ALE to remain valid. A15–A8 are active HIGH and float to 3-state OFF during interrupt acknowledge and local bus "hold acknowledge".
A19/S6, A18/S5, A17/S4, A16/S3	35-38	O	**Address/Status:** During T1, these are the four most significant address lines for memory operations. During I/O operations, these lines are LOW. During memory and I/O operations, status information is available on these lines during T2, T3, Tw, and T4. S6 is always low. The status of the interrupt enable flag bit (S5) is updated at the beginning of each clock cycle. S4 and S3 are encoded as shown. This information indicates which segment register is presently being used for data accessing. These lines float to 3-state OFF during local bus "hold acknowledge".
RD	32	O	**Read:** Read strobe indicates that the processor is performing a memory or I/O read cycle, depending on the state of the IO/M̄ pin or S2. This signal is used to read devices which reside on the 8088 local bus. RD is active LOW during T2, T3 and Tw of any read cycle, and is guaranteed to remain HIGH in T2 until the 8088 local bus has floated. This signal floats to 3-state OFF in "hold acknowledge".
READY	22	I	**READY:** is the acknowledgement from the addressed memory or I/O device that it will complete the data transfer. The RDY signal from memory or I/O is synchronized by the 8284 clock generator to form READY. This signal is active HIGH. The 8088 READY input is not synchronized. Correct operation is not guaranteed if the set up and hold times are not met.
INTR	18	I	**Interrupt Request:** is a level triggered input which is sampled during the last clock cycle of each instruction to determine if the processor should enter into an interrupt acknowledge operation. A subroutine is vectored to via an interrupt vector lookup table located in system memory. It can be internally masked by software resetting the interrupt enable bit. INTR is internally synchronized. This signal is active HIGH.
TEST	23	I	**TEST:** input is examined by the "wait for test" instruction. If the TEST input is LOW, execution continues, otherwise the processor waits in an "idle" state. This input is synchronized internally during each clock cycle on the leading edge of CLK.
NMI	17	I	**Non-Maskable Interrupt:** is an edge triggered input which causes a type 2 interrupt. A subroutine is vectored to via an interrupt vector lookup table located in system memory. NMI is not maskable internally by software. A transition from a LOW to HIGH initiates the interrupt at the end of the current instruction. This input is internally synchronized.

The following small table appears in the Address/Status row:

S4	S3	CHARACTERISTICS
0 (LOW)	0	Alternate Data
0	1	Stack
1 (HIGH)	0	Code or None
1	1	Data
S6 is 0 (LOW)		

intel IAPX 88/10 PRELIMINARY

Table 1. Pin Description (Continued)

Symbol	Pin No.	Type	Name and Function
RESET	21	I	**RESET:** causes the processor to immediately terminate its present activity. The signal must be active HIGH for at least four clock cycles. It restarts execution, as described in the instruction set description, when RESET returns LOW. RESET is internally synchronized.
CLK	19	I	**Clock:** provides the basic timing for the processor and bus controller. It is asymmetric with a 33% duty cycle to provide optimized internal timing.
V$_{CC}$	40		**V$_{CC}$:** is the +5V ±10% power supply pin.
GND	1, 20		**GND:** are the ground pins.
MN/$\overline{\text{MX}}$	33	I	**Minimum/Maximum:** indicates what mode the processor is to operate in. The two modes are discussed in the following sections.

The following pin function descriptions are for the 8088 minimum mode (i.e., MN/MX = V$_{CC}$). Only the pin functions which are unique to minimum mode are described; all other pin functions are as described above.

Symbol	Pin No.	Type	Name and Function
IO/$\overline{\text{M}}$	28	O	**Status Line:** is an inverted maximum mode $\overline{\text{S2}}$. It is used to distinguish a memory access from an I/O access. IO/$\overline{\text{M}}$ becomes valid in the T4 preceding a bus cycle and remains valid until the final T4 of the cycle (I/O=HIGH, M=LOW). IO/$\overline{\text{M}}$ floats to 3-state OFF in local bus "hold acknowledge".
$\overline{\text{WR}}$	29	O	**Write:** strobe indicates that the processor is performing a write memory or write I/O cycle, depending on the state of the IO/$\overline{\text{M}}$ signal. WR is active for T2, T3, and Tw of any write cycle. It is active LOW, and floats to 3-state OFF in local bus "hold acknowledge".
$\overline{\text{INTA}}$	24	O	**INTA:** is used as a read strobe for interrupt acknowledge cycles. It is active LOW during T2, T3, and Tw of each interrupt acknowledge cycle.
ALE	25	O	**Address Latch Enable:** is provided by the processor to latch the address into the 8282/8283 address latch. It is a HIGH pulse active during clock low of T1 of any bus cycle. Note that ALE is never floated.
DT/$\overline{\text{R}}$	27	O	**Data Transmit/Receive:** is needed in a minimum system that desires to use an 8286/8287 data bus transceiver. It is used to control the direction of data flow through the transceiver. Logically, DT/$\overline{\text{R}}$ is equivalent to $\overline{\text{S1}}$ in the maximum mode, and its timing is the same as for IO/$\overline{\text{M}}$ (T=HIGH, R=LOW). This signal floats to 3-state OFF in local "hold acknowledge".
$\overline{\text{DEN}}$	26	O	**Data Enable:** is provided as an output enable for the 8286/8287 in a minimum system which uses the transceiver. $\overline{\text{DEN}}$ is active LOW during each memory and I/O access, and for $\overline{\text{INTA}}$ cycles. For a read or $\overline{\text{INTA}}$ cycle, it is active from the middle of T2 until the middle of T4, while for a write cycle, it is active from the beginning of T2 until the middle of T4. $\overline{\text{DEN}}$ floats to 3-state OFF during local bus "hold acknowledge".
HOLD, HLDA	30,31	I, O	**HOLD:** indicates that another master is requesting a local bus "hold". To be acknowledged, HOLD must be active HIGH. The processor receiving the "hold" request will issue HLDA (HIGH) as an acknowledgement, in the middle of a T4 or TI clock cycle. Simultaneous with the issuance of HLDA the processor will float the local bus and control lines. After HOLD is detected as being LOW, the processor lowers HLDA, and when the processor needs to run another cycle, it will again drive the local bus and control lines. Hold is not an asynchronous input. External synchronization should be provided if the system cannot otherwise guarantee the set up time.
$\overline{\text{SSO}}$	34	O	**Status line:** is logically equivalent to $\overline{\text{SO}}$ in the maximum mode. The combination of $\overline{\text{SSO}}$, IO/$\overline{\text{M}}$ and DT/$\overline{\text{R}}$ allows the system to completely decode the current bus cycle status.

IO/$\overline{\text{M}}$	DT/$\overline{\text{R}}$	$\overline{\text{SSO}}$	CHARACTERISTICS
1 (HIGH)	0	0	Interrupt Acknowledge
1	0	1	Read I/O port
1	1	0	Write I/O port
1	1	1	Halt
0 (LOW)	0	0	Code access
0	0	1	Read memory
0	1	0	Write memory
0	1	1	Passive

Table 1. Pin Description (Continued)

The following pin function descriptions are for the 8088, 8228 system in maximum mode (i.e., MN/MX=GND.) Only the pin functions which are unique to maximum mode are described; all other pin functions are as described above.

<table>
<tr><th>Symbol</th><th>Pin No.</th><th>Type</th><th>Name and Function</th></tr>
<tr><td>$\overline{S2}$, $\overline{S1}$, $\overline{S0}$</td><td>26-28</td><td>O</td><td>**Status:** is active during clock high of T4, T1, and T2, and is returned to the passive state (1,1,1) during T3 or during Tw when READY is HIGH. This status is used by the 8288 bus controller to generate all memory and I/O access control signals. Any change by $\overline{S2}$, $\overline{S1}$, or $\overline{S0}$ during T4 is used to indicate the beginning of a bus cycle, and the return to the passive state in T3 or Tw is used to indicate the end of a bus cycle.

| $\overline{S2}$ | $\overline{S1}$ | $\overline{S0}$ | CHARACTERISTICS |
| 0 (LOW) | 0 | 0 | Interrupt Acknowledge |
| 0 | 0 | 1 | Read I/O port |
| 0 | 1 | 0 | Write I/O port |
| 0 | 1 | 1 | Halt |
| 1 (HIGH) | 0 | 0 | Code access |
| 1 | 0 | 1 | Read memory |
| 1 | 1 | 0 | Write memory |
| 1 | 1 | 1 | Passive |

These signals float to 3-state OFF during "hold acknowledge". During the first clock cycle after RESET becomes active, these signals are active HIGH. After this first clock, they float to 3-state OFF.</td></tr>
<tr><td>$\overline{RQ}/\overline{GT0}$,
$\overline{RQ}/\overline{GT1}$</td><td>30, 31</td><td>I/O</td><td>**Request/Grant:** pins are used by other local bus masters to force the processor to release the local bus at the end of the processor's current bus cycle. Each pin is bidirectional with $\overline{RQ}/\overline{GT0}$ having higher priority than $\overline{RQ}/\overline{GT1}$. $\overline{RQ}/\overline{GT}$ has an internal pull-up resistor, so may be left unconnected. The request/grant sequence is as follows (See Figure 8):

1. A pulse of one CLK wide from another local bus master indicates a local bus request ("hold") to the 8088 (pulse 1).
2. During a T4 or TI clock cycle, a pulse one clock wide from the 8088 to the requesting master (pulse 2), indicates that the 8088 has allowed the local bus to float and that it will enter the "hold acknowledge" state at the next CLK. The CPU's bus interface unit is disconnected logically from the local bus during "hold acknowledge". The same rules as for HOLD/HOLDA apply as for when the bus is released.
3. A pulse one CLK wide from the requesting master indicates to the 8088 (pulse 3) that the "hold" request is about to end and that the 8088 can reclaim the local bus at the next CLK. The CPU then enters T4.

Each master-master exchange of the local bus is a sequence of three pulses. There must be one idle CLK cycle after each bus exchange. Pulses are active LOW.

If the request is made while the CPU is performing a memory cycle, it will release the local bus during T4 of the cycle when all the following conditions are met:

1. Request occurs on or before T2.
2. Current cycle is not the low bit of a word.
3. Current cycle is not the first acknowledge of an interrupt acknowledge sequence.
4. A locked instruction is not currently executing.

If the local bus is idle when the request is made the two possible events will follow:

1. Local bus will be released during the next clock.
2. A memory cycle will start within 3 clocks. Now the four rules for a currently active memory cycle apply with condition number 1 already satisfied.</td></tr>
</table>

iAPX 88/10 PRELIMINARY

FUNCTIONAL DESCRIPTION

Memory Organization

The processor provides a 20-bit address to memory which locates the byte being referenced. The memory is organized as a linear array of up to 1 million bytes, addressed as 00000(H) to FFFFF(H). The memory is logically divided into code, data, extra data, and stack segments of up to 64K bytes each, with each segment falling on 16-byte boundaries. (See Figure 3.)

All memory references are made relative to base addresses contained in high speed segment registers. The segment types were chosen based on the addressing needs of programs. The segment register to be selected is automatically chosen according to the rules of the following table. All information in one segment type share the same logical attributes (e.g. code or data). By structuring memory into relocatable areas of similar characteristics and by automatically selecting segment registers, programs are shorter, faster, and more structured.

Word (16-bit) operands can be located on even or odd address boundaries. For address and data operands, the least significant byte of the word is stored in the lower valued address location and the most significant byte in the next higher address location. The BIU will automatically execute two fetch or write cycles for 16-bit operands.

Certain locations in memory are reserved for specific CPU operations. (See Figure 4.) Locations from addresses FFFF0H through FFFFFH are reserved for operations including a jump to the initial system initialization routine. Following RESET, the CPU will always begin execution at location FFFF0H where the jump must be located. Locations 00000H through 003FFH are reserved for interrupt operations. Four-byte pointers consisting of a 16-bit segment address and a 16-bit offset address direct program flow to one of the 256 possible interrupt service routines. The pointer elements are assumed to have been stored at their respective places in reserved memory prior to the occurrence of interrupts.

Minimum and Maximum Modes

The requirements for supporting minimum and maximum 8088 systems are sufficiently different that they cannot be done efficiently with 40 uniquely defined pins. Consequently, the 8088 is equipped with a strap pin (MN/$\overline{\text{MX}}$) which defines the system configuration. The definition of a certain subset of the pins changes, dependent on the condition of the strap pin. When the MN/$\overline{\text{MX}}$ pin is strapped to GND, the 8088 defines pins 24 through 31 and 34 in maximum mode. When the MN/$\overline{\text{MX}}$ pin is strapped to V$_{CC}$, the 8088 generates bus control signals itself on pins 24 through 31 and 34.

Figure 3. Memory Organization

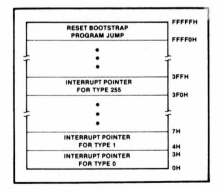

Figure 4. Reserved Memory Locations

Memory Reference Need	Segment Register Used	Segment Selection Rule
Instructions	CODE (CS)	Automatic with all instruction prefetch.
Stack	STACK (SS)	All stack pushes and pops. Memory references relative to BP base register except data references.
Local Data	DATA (DS)	Data references when: relative to stack, destination of string operation, or explicitly overridden.
External (Global) Data	EXTRA (ES)	Destination of string operations: Explicitly selected using a segment override.

The minimum mode 8088 can be used with either a multiplexed or demultiplexed bus. The multiplexed bus configuration is compatible with the MCS-85™ multiplexed bus peripherals (8155, 8156, 8355, 8755A, and 8185). This configuration (See Figure 5) provides the user with a minimum chip count system. This architecture provides the 8088 processing power in a highly integrated form.

The demultiplexed mode requires one latch (for 64K addressability) or two latches (for a full megabyte of addressing). A third latch can be used for buffering if the address bus loading requires it. An 8286 or 8287 transceiver can also be used if data bus buffering is required. (See Figure 6.) The 8088 provides $\overline{\text{DEN}}$ and DT/$\overline{\text{R}}$ to con-trol the transceiver, and ALE to latch the addresses. This configuration of the minimum mode provides the standard demultiplexed bus structure with heavy bus buffering and relaxed bus timing requirements.

The maximum mode employs the 8288 bus controller. (See Figure 7.) The 8288 decodes status lines $\overline{\text{S0}}$, $\overline{\text{S1}}$, and $\overline{\text{S2}}$, and provides the system with all bus control signals. Moving the bus control to the 8288 provides better source and sink current capability to the control lines, and frees the 8088 pins for extended large system features. Hardware lock, queue status, and two request/grant interfaces are provided by the 8088 in maximum mode. These features allow co-processors in local bus and remote bus configurations.

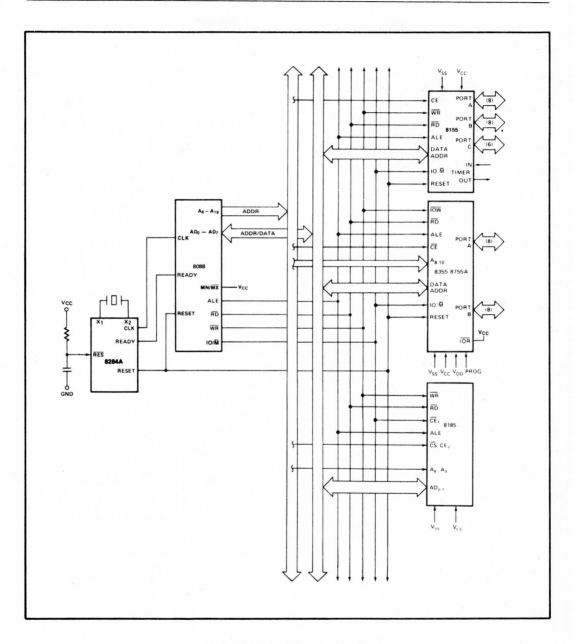

Figure 5. Multiplexed Bus Configuration

IAPX 88/10 PRELIMINARY

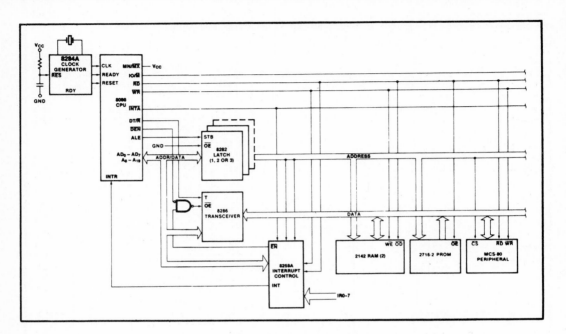

Figure 6. Demultiplexed Bus Configuration

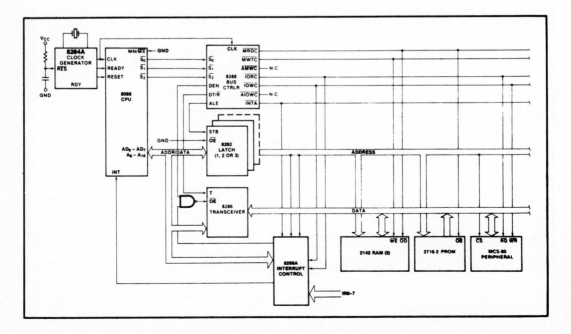

Figure 7. Fully Buffered System Using Bus Controller

Bus Operation

The 8088 address/data bus is broken into three parts — the lower eight address/data bits (AD0–AD7), the middle eight address bits (A8–A15), and the upper four address bits (A16–A19). The address/data bits and the highest four address bits are time multiplexed. This technique provides the most efficient use of pins on the processor, permitting the use of a standard 40 lead package. The middle eight address bits are not multiplexed, i.e. they remain valid throughout each bus cycle. In addi-

tion, the bus can be demultiplexed at the processor with a single address latch if a standard, non-multiplexed bus is desired for the system.

Each processor bus cycle consists of at least four CLK cycles. These are referred to as T1, T2, T3, and T4. (See Figure 8). **The address is emitted from the processor** during T1 and data transfer occurs on the bus during T3 and T4. T2 is used primarily for changing the direction of the bus during read operations. In the event that a "NOT READY" indication is given by the addressed device,

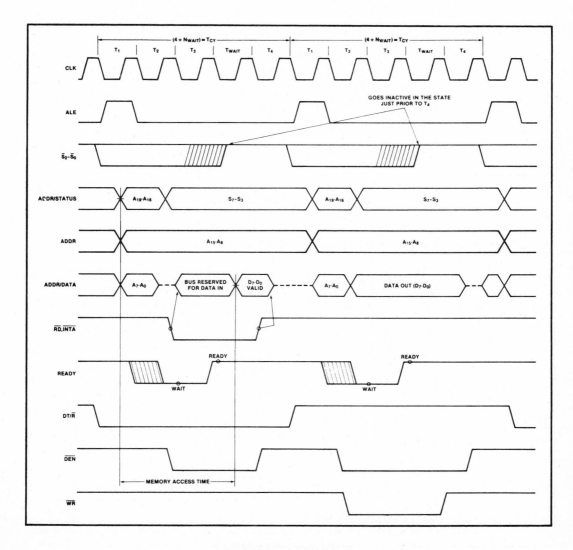

Figure 8. Basic System Timing

IAPX 88/10   PRELIMINARY

"wait" states (Tw) are inserted between T3 and T4. Each inserted "wait" state is of the same duration as a CLK cycle. Periods can occu between 8088 driven bus cycles. These are referred to as "idle" states (Ti), or inactive CLK cycles. The processor uses these cycles for internal housekeeping.

During T1 of any bus cycle, the ALE (address latch enable) signal is emitted (by either the processor or the 8288 bus controller, depending on the MN/$\overline{\text{MX}}$ strap). At the trailing edge of this pulse, a valid address and certain status information for the cycle may be latched.

Status bits $\overline{\text{S0}}$, $\overline{\text{S1}}$, and $\overline{\text{S2}}$ are used by the bus controller, in maximum mode, to identify the type of bus transaction according to the following table:

$\overline{\text{S}}_2$	$\overline{\text{S}}_1$	$\overline{\text{S}}_0$	CHARACTERISTICS
0 (LOW)	0	0	Interrupt Acknowledge
0	0	1	Read I/O
0	1	0	Write I/O
0	1	1	Halt
1 (HIGH)	0	0	Instruction Fetch
1	0	1	Read Data from Memory
1	1	0	Write Data to Memory
1	1	1	Passive (no bus cycle)

Status bits S3 through S6 are multiplexed with high order address bits and are therefore valid during T2 through T4. S3 and S4 indicate which segment register was used for this bus cycle in forming the address according to the following table:

S_4	S_3	CHARACTERISTICS
0 (LOW)	0	Alternate Data (extra segment)
0	1	Stack
1 (HIGH)	0	Code or None
1	1	Data

S5 is a reflection of the PSW interrupt enable bit. S6 is always equal to 0.

I/O Addressing

In the 8088, I/O operations can address up to a maximum of 64K I/O registers. The I/O address appears in the same format as the memory address on bus lines A15-A0. The address lines A19-A16 are zero in I/O operations. The variable I/O instructions, which use register DX as a pointer, have full address capability, while the direct I/O instructions directly address one or two of the 256 I/O byte locations in page 0 of the I/O address space. I/O ports are addressed in the same manner as memory locations.

Designers familiar with the 8085 or upgrading an 8085 design should note that the 8085 addresses I/O with an 8-bit address on both halves of the 16-bit address bus. The 8088 uses a full 16-bit address on its lower 16 address lines.

EXTERNAL INTERFACE

Processor Reset and Initialization

Processor initialization or start up is accomplished with activation (HIGH) of the RESET pin. The 8088 RESET is required to be HIGH for greater than four clock cycles. The 8088 will terminate operations on the high-going edge of RESET and will remain dormant as long as RESET is HIGH. The low-going transition of RESET triggers an internal reset sequence for approximately 7 clock cycles. After this interval the 8088 operates normally, beginning with the instruction in absolute location FFFF0H. (See Figure 4.) The RESET input is internally synchronized to the processor clock. At initialization, the HIGH to LOW transition of RESET must occur no sooner than 50 μs after power up, to allow complete initialization of the 8088.

If INTR is asserted sooner than nine clock cycles after the end of RESET, the processor may execute one instruction before responding to the interrupt.

All 3-state outputs float to 3-state OFF during RESET. Status is active in the idle state for the first clock after RESET becomes active and then floats to 3-state OFF.

Interrupt Operations

Interrupt operations fall into two classes: software or hardware initiated. The software initiated interrupts and software aspects of hardware interrupts are specified in the instruction set description in the iAPX 88 book or the iAPX 86,88 User's Manual. Hardware interrupts can be classified as nonmaskable or maskable.

Interrupts result in a transfer of control to a new program location. A 256 element table containing address pointers to the interrupt service program locations resides in absolute locations 0 through 3FFH (see Figure 4), which are reserved for this purpose. Each element in the table is 4 bytes in size and corresponds to an interrupt "type." An interrupting device supplies an 8-bit type number, during the interrupt acknowledge sequence, which is used to vector through the appropriate element to the new interrupt service program location.

Non-Maskable Interrupt (NMI)

The processor provides a single non-maskable interrupt (NMI) pin which has higher priority than the maskable interrupt request (INTR) pin. A typical use would be to activate a power failure routine. The NMI is edge-triggered on a LOW to HIGH transition. The activation of this pin causes a type 2 interrupt.

NMI is required to have a duration in the HIGH state of greater than two clock cycles, but is not required to be synchronized to the clock. Any higher going transition of NMI is latched on-chip and will be serviced at the end of the current instruction or between whole moves (2 bytes in the case of word moves) of a block type instruction. Worst case response to NMI would be for multiply, divide, and variable shift instructions. There is no specification on the occurrence of the low-going edge; it may occur before, during, or after the servicing of NMI. Another high-going edge triggers another response if it occurs after the start of the NMI procedure. The signal must be free of logical spikes in general and be free of bounces on the low-going edge to avoid triggering extraneous responses.

Maskable Interrupt (INTR)

The 8088 provides a single interrupt request input (INTR) which can be masked internally by software with the resetting of the interrupt enable (IF) flag bit. The interrupt request signal is level triggered. It is internally synchronized during each clock cycle on the high-going edge of CLK. To be responded to, INTR must be present (HIGH) during the clock period preceding the end of the current instruction or the end of a whole move for a block type instruction. During interrupt response sequence, further interrupts are disabled. The enable bit is reset as part of the response to any interrupt (INTR, NMI, software interrupt, or single step), although the FLAGS register which is automatically pushed onto the stack reflects the state of the processor prior to the interrupt. Until the old FLAGS register is restored, the enable bit will be zero unless specifically set by an instruction.

During the response sequence (See Figure 9), the processor executes two successive (back to back) interrupt acknowledge cycles. The 8088 emits the LOCK signal (maximum mode only) from T2 of the first bus cycle until T2 of the second. A local bus "hold" request will not be honored until the end of the second bus cycle. In the second bus cycle, a byte is fetched from the external interrupt system (e.g., 8259A PIC) which identifies the source (type) of the interrupt. This byte is multiplied by four and used as a pointer into the interrupt vector lookup table. An INTR signal left HIGH will be continually responded to within the limitations of the enable bit

and sample period. The interrupt return instruction includes a flags pop which returns the status of the original interrupt enable bit when it restores the flags.

HALT

When a software HALT instruction is executed, the processor indicates that it is entering the HALT state in one of two ways, depending upon which mode is strapped. In minimum mode, the processor issues ALE, delayed by one clock cycle, to allow the system to latch the halt status. Halt status is available on $IO/\overline{M}$, $DT/\overline{R}$, and $\overline{SSO}$. In maximum mode, the processor issues appropriate HALT status on $\overline{S2}$, $\overline{S1}$, and $\overline{S0}$, and the 8288 bus controller issues one ALE. The 8088 will not leave the HALT state when a local bus hold is entered while in HALT. In this case, the processor reissues the HALT indicator at the end of the local bus hold. An interrupt request or RESET will force the 8088 out of the HALT state.

Read/Modify/Write (Semaphore) Operations via LOCK

The LOCK status information is provided by the processor when consecutive bus cycles are required during the execution of an instruction. This allows the processor to perform read/modify/write operations on memory (via the "exchange register with memory" instruction), without another system bus master receiving intervening memory cycles. This is useful in multiprocessor system configurations to accomplish "test and set lock" operations. The $\overline{LOCK}$ signal is activated (LOW) in the clock cycle following decoding of the LOCK prefix instruction. It is deactivated at the end of the last bus cycle of the instruction following the LOCK prefix. While $\overline{LOCK}$ is active, a request on a $\overline{RQ/GT}$ pin will be recorded, and then honored at the end of the LOCK.

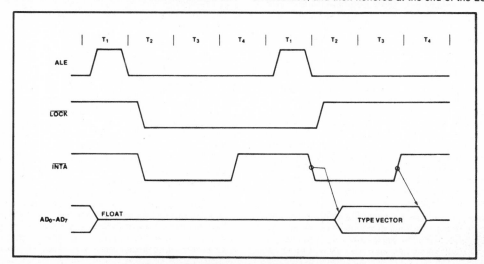

Figure 9. Interrupt Acknowledge Sequence

intel   **iAPX 88/10**   PRELIMINARY

External Synchronization via TEST

As an alternative to interrupts, the 8088 provides a single software-testable input pin (TEST). This input is utilized by executing a WAIT instruction. The single WAIT instruction is repeatedly executed until the TEST input goes active (LOW). The execution of WAIT does not consume bus cycles once the queue is full.

If a local bus request occurs during WAIT execution, the 8088 3-states all output drivers. If interrupts are enabled, the 8088 will recognize interrupts and process them. The WAIT instruction is then refetched, and reexecuted.

Basic System Timing

In minimum mode, the MN/MX pin is strapped to V_{CC} and the processor emits bus control signals compatible with the 8085 bus structure. In maximum mode, the MN/MX pin is strapped to GND and the processor emits coded status information which the 8288 bus controller uses to generate MULTIBUS compatible bus control signals.

System Timing — Minimum System

(See Figure 8.)

The read cycle begins in T1 with the assertion of the address latch enable (ALE) signal. The trailing (low going) edge of this signal is used to latch the address information, which is valid on the address/data bus (AD0–AD7) at this time, into the 8282/8283 latch. Address lines A8 through A15 do not need to be latched because they remain valid throughout the bus cycle. From T1 to T4 the IO/M signal indicates a memory or I/O operation. At T2 the address is removed from the address/data bus and the bus goes to a high impedance state. The read control signal is also asserted at T2. The read (RD) signal causes the addressed device to enable its data bus drivers to the local bus. Some time later, valid data will be available on the bus and the addressed device will drive the READY line HIGH. When the processor returns the read signal to a HIGH level, the addressed device will again 3-state its bus drivers. If a transceiver (8286/8287) is required to buffer the 8088 local bus, signals DT/R and DEN are provided by the 8088.

A write cycle also begins with the assertion of ALE and the emission of the address. The IO/M signal is again asserted to indicate a memory or I/O write operation. In T2, immediately following the address emission, the processor emits the data to be written into the addressed location. This data remains valid until at least the middle of T4. During T2, T3, and T_W, the processor asserts the write control signal. The write (WR) signal becomes active at the beginning of T2, as opposed to the read, which is delayed somewhat into T2 to provide time for the bus to float.

The basic difference between the interrupt acknowledge cycle and a read cycle is that the interrupt acknowledge (INTA) signal is asserted in place of the read (RD) signal and the address bus is floated. (See Figure 9.). In the second of two successive INTA cycles,

a byte of information is read from the data bus, as supplied by the interrupt system logic (i.e. 8259A priority interrupt controller). This byte identifies the source (type) of the interrupt. It is multiplied by four and used as a pointer into the interrupt vector lookup table, as described earlier.

Bus Timing — Medium Complexity Systems

(See Figure 10.)

For medium complexity systems, the MN/MX pin is connected to GND and the 8288 bus controller is added to the system, as well as an 8282/8283 latch for latching the system address, and an 8286/8287 transceiver to allow for bus loading greater than the 8088 is capable of handling. Signals ALE, DEN, and DT/R are generated by the 8288 instead of the processor in this configuration, although their timing remains relatively the same. The 8088 status outputs (S2, S1, and S0) provide type of cycle information and become 8288 inputs. This bus cycle information specifies read (code, data, or I/O), write (data or I/O), interrupt acknowledge, or software halt. The 8288 thus issues control signals specifying memory read or write, I/O read or write, or interrupt acknowledge. The 8288 provides two types of write strobes, normal and advanced, to be applied as required. The normal write strobes have data valid at the leading edge of write. The advanced write strobes have the same timing as read strobes, and hence, data is not valid at the leading edge of write. The 8286/8287 transceiver receives the usual T and OE inputs from the 8288's DT/R and DEN outputs.

The pointer into the interrupt vector table, which is passed during the second INTA cycle, can derive from an 8259A located on either the local bus or the system bus. If the master 8289A priority interrupt controller is positioned on the local bus, a TTL gate is required to disable the 8286/8287 transceiver when reading from the master 8259A during the interrupt acknowledge sequence and software "poll"

The 8088 Compared to the 8086

The 8088 CPU is an 8-bit processor designed around the 8086 internal structure. Most internal functions of the 8088 are identical to the equivalent 8086 functions. The 8088 handles the external bus the same way the 8086 does with the distinction of handling only 8 bits at a time. Sixteen-bit operands are fetched or written in two consecutive bus cycles. Both processors will appear identical to the software engineer, with the exception of execution time. The internal register structure is identical and all instructions have the same end result. The differences between the 8088 and 8086 are outlined below. The engineer who is unfamiliar with the 8086 is referred to the iAPX 86, 88 User's Manual, Chapters 2 and 4, for function description and instruction set information. Internally, there are three differences between the 8088 and the 8086. All changes are related to the 8-bit bus interface.

intel   **iAPX 88/10**   PRELIMINARY

- The queue length is 4 bytes in the 8088, whereas the 8086 queue contains 6 bytes, or three words. The queue was shortened to prevent overuse of the bus by the BIU when prefetching instructions. This was required because of the additional time necessary to fetch instructions 8 bits at a time.

- To further optimize the queue, the prefetching algorithm was changed. The 8088 BIU will fetch a new instruction to load into the queue each time there is a 1 byte hole (space available) in the queue. The 8086 waits until a 2-byte space is available.

- The internal execution time of the instruction set is affected by the 8-bit interface. All 16-bit fetches and writes from/to memory take an additional four clock cycles. The CPU is also limited by the speed of instruction fetches. This latter problem only occurs when a series of simple operations occur. When the more sophisticated instructions of the 8088 are being used, the queue has time to fill and the execution proceeds as fast as the execution unit will allow.

The 8088 and 8086 are completely software compatible by virture of their identical execution units. Software that is system dependent may not be completely transferable, but software that is not system dependent will operate equally as well on an 8088 or an 8086.

The hardware interface of the 8088 contains the major differences between the two CPUs. The pin assignments are nearly identical, however, with the following functional changes:

- A8–A15 — These pins are only address outputs on the 8088. These address lines are latched internally and remain valid throughout a bus cycle in a manner similar to the 8085 upper address lines.

- $\overline{BHE}$ has no meaning on the 8088 and has been eliminated.

- $\overline{SSO}$ provides the $\overline{SO}$ status information in the minimum mode. This output occurs on pin 34 in minimum mode only. DT/$\overline{R}$, IO/$\overline{M}$, and $\overline{SSO}$ provide the complete bus status in minimum mode.

- IO/$\overline{M}$ has been inverted to be compatible with the MCS-85 bus structure.

- ALE is delayed by one clock cycle in the minimum mode when entering HALT, to allow the status to be latched with ALE.

8255A/8255A-5
PROGRAMMABLE PERIPHERAL INTERFACE

- MCS-85™ Compatible 8255A-5
- 24 Programmable I/O Pins
- Completely TTL Compatible
- Fully Compatible with Intel® Microprocessor Families
- Improved Timing Characteristics

- Direct Bit Set/Reset Capability Easing Control Application Interface
- Reduces System Package Count
- Improved DC Driving Capability
- Available in EXPRESS
  —Standard Temperature Range
  —Extended Temperature Range

The Intel® 8255A is a general purpose programmable I/O device designed for use with Intel® microprocessors. It has 24 I/O pins which may be individually programmed in 2 groups of 12 and used in 3 major modes of operation. In the first mode (MODE 0), each group of 12 I/O pins may be programmed in sets of 4 to be input or output. In MODE 1, the second mode, each group may be programmed to have 8 lines of input or output. Of the remaining 4 pins, 3 are used for hand-shaking and interrupt control signals. The third mode of operation (MODE 2) is a bidirectional bus mode which uses 8 lines for a bidirectional bus, and 5 lines, borrowing one from the other group, for handshaking.

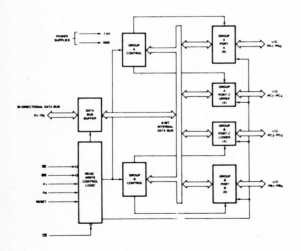

Figure 1. 8255A Block Diagram

Figure 2. Pin Configuration

Order Number: 231308-001

8255A FUNCTIONAL DESCRIPTION

General

The 8255A is a programmable peripheral interface (PPI) device designed for use in Intel® microcomputer systems. Its function is that of a general purpose I/O component to interface peripheral equipment to the microcomputer system bus. The functional configuration of the 8255A is programmed by the system software so that normally no external logic is necessary to interface peripheral devices or structures.

Data Bus Buffer

This 3-state bidirectional 8-bit buffer is used to interface the 8255A to the system data bus. Data is transmitted or received by the buffer upon execution of input or output instructions by the CPU. Control words and status information are also transferred through the data bus buffer.

Read/Write and Control Logic

The function of this block is to manage all of the internal and external transfers of both Data and Control or Status words. It accepts inputs from the CPU Address and Control busses and in turn, issues commands to both of the Control Groups.

(CS̄)

Chip Select. A "low" on this input pin enables the communiction between the 8255A and the CPU.

(RD̄)

Read. A "low" on this input pin enables the 8255A to send the data or status information to the CPU on the data bus. In essence, it allows the CPU to "read from" the 8255A.

(WR̄)

Write. A "low" on this input pin enables the CPU to write data or control words into the 8255A.

(A₀ and A₁)

Port Select 0 and Port Select 1. These input signals, in conjunction with the RD and WR inputs, control the selection of one of the three ports or the control word registers. They are normally connected to the least significant bits of the address bus (A_0 and A_1).

8255A BASIC OPERATION

A_1	A_0	$\overline{RD}$	$\overline{WR}$	$\overline{CS}$	INPUT OPERATION (READ)
0	0	0	1	0	PORT A ⇒ DATA BUS
0	1	0	1	0	PORT B ⇒ DATA BUS
1	0	0	1	0	PORT C ⇒ DATA BUS
					OUTPUT OPERATION (WRITE)
0	0	1	0	0	DATA BUS ⇒ PORT A
0	1	1	0	0	DATA BUS ⇒ PORT B
1	0	1	0	0	DATA BUS ⇒ PORT C
1	1	1	0	0	DATA BUS ⇒ CONTROL
					DISABLE FUNCTION
X	X	X	X	1	DATA BUS ⇒ 3-STATE
1	1	0	1	0	ILLEGAL CONDITION
X	X	1	1	0	DATA BUS ⇒ 3-STATE

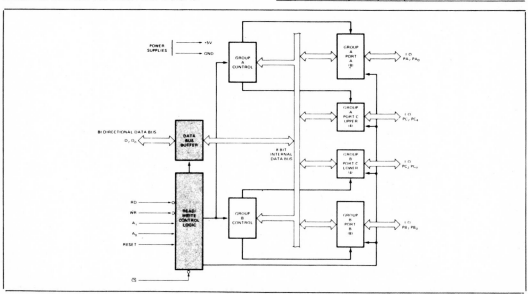

Figure 3. 8255A Block Diagram Showing Data Bus Buffer and Read/Write Control Logic Functions

(RESET)

Reset. A "high" on this input clears the control register and all ports (A. B. C) are set to the input mode.

Group A and Group B Controls

The functional configuration of each port is programmed by the systems software. In essence, the CPU "outputs" a control word to the 8255A. The control word contains information such as "mode", "bit set", "bit reset", etc., that initializes the functional configuration of the 8255A.

Each of the Control blocks (Group A and Group B) accepts "commands" from the Read/Write Control Logic, receives "control words" from the internal data bus and issues the proper commands to its associated ports.

  Control Group A – Port A and Port C upper (C7-C4)
  Control Group B – Port B and Port C lower (C3-C0)

The Control Word Register can **Only** be written into. No Read operation of the Control Word Register is allowed.

Ports A, B, and C

The 8255A contains three 8-bit ports (A, B, and C). All can be configured in a wide variety of functional characteristics by the system software but each has its own special features or "personality" to further enhance the power and flexibility of the 8255A.

Port A. One 8-bit data output latch/buffer and one 8-bit data input latch.

Port B. One 8-bit data input/output latch/buffer and one 8-bit data input buffer.

Port C. One 8-bit data output latch/buffer and one 8-bit data input buffer (no latch for input). This port can be divided into two 4-bit ports under the mode control. Each 4-bit port contains a 4-bit latch and it can be used for the control signal outputs and status signal inputs in conjunction with ports A and B.

PIN CONFIGURATION

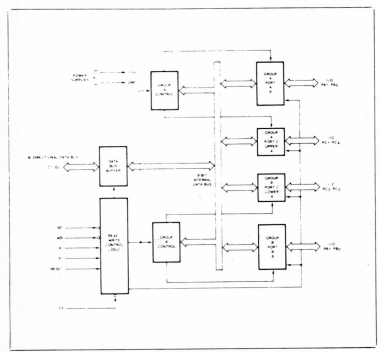

PIN NAMES

D_7 D_0	DATA BUS (BI DIRECTIONAL)
RESET	RESET INPUT
$\overline{CS}$	CHIP SELECT
$\overline{RD}$	READ INPUT
$\overline{WR}$	WRITE INPUT
A0 A1	PORT ADDRESS
PA7 PA0	PORT A (BIT)
PB7 PB0	PORT B (BIT)
PC7 PC0	PORT C (BIT)
V_{CC}	+5 VOLTS
GND	0 VOLTS

Figure 4. 8225A Block Diagram Showing Group A and Group B Control Functions

8255A OPERATIONAL DESCRIPTION

Mode Selection

There are three basic modes of operation that can be selected by the system software:

    Mode 0 – Basic Input/Output
    Mode 1 – Strobed Input/Output
    Mode 2 – Bi-Directional Bus

When the reset input goes "high" all ports will be set to the input mode (i.e., all 24 lines will be in the high impedance state). After the reset is removed the 8255A can remain in the input mode with no additional initialization required. During the execution of the system program any of the other modes may be selected using a single output instruction. This allows a single 8255A to service a variety of peripheral devices with a simple software maintenance routine.

The modes for Port A and Port B can be separately defined, while Port C is divided into two portions as required by the Port A and Port B definitions. All of the output registers, including the status flip-flops, will be reset whenever the mode is changed. Modes may be combined so that their functional definition can be "tailored" to almost any I/O structure. For instance; Group B can be programmed in Mode 0 to monitor simple switch closings or display computational results, Group A could be programmed in Mode 1 to monitor a keyboard or tape reader on an interrupt-driven basis.

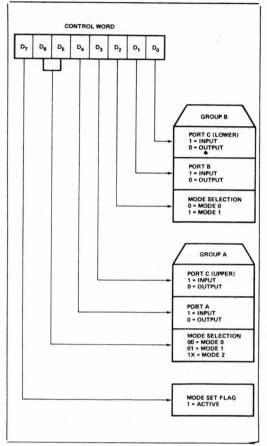

Figure 6. Mode Definition Format

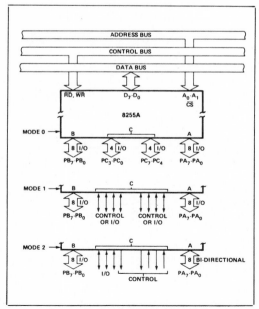

Figure 5. Basic Mode Definitions and Bus Interface

The mode definitions and possible mode combinations may seem confusing at first but after a cursory review of the complete device operation a simple, logical I/O approach will surface. The design of the 8255A has taken into account things such as efficient PC board layout, control signal definition vs PC layout and complete functional flexibility to support almost any peripheral device with no external logic. Such design represents the maximum use of the available pins.

Single Bit Set/Reset Feature

Any of the eight bits of Port C can be Set or Reset using a single OUTput instruction. This feature reduces software requirements in Control-based applications.

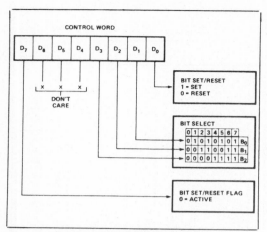

Figure 7. Bit Set/Reset Format

When Port C is being used as status/control for Port A or B, these bits can be set or reset by using the Bit Set/Reset operation just as if they were data output ports.

Interrupt Control Functions

When the 8255A is programmed to operate in mode 1 or mode 2, control signals are provided that can be used as interrupt request inputs to the CPU. The interrupt request signals, generated from port C, can be inhibited or enabled by setting or resetting the associated INTE flip-flop, using the bit set/reset function of port C.

This function allows the Programmer to disallow or allow a specific I/O device to interrupt the CPU without affecting any other device in the interrupt structure.

INTE flip-flop definition:

(BIT-SET) — INTE is SET — Interrupt enable
(BIT-RESET) — INTE is RESET — Interrupt disable

Note: All Mask flip-flops are automatically reset during mode selection and device Reset.

Operating Modes

MODE 0 (Basic Input/Output). This functional configuration provides simple input and output operations for each of the three ports. No "handshaking" is required, data is simply written to or read from a specified port.

Mode 0 Basic Functional Definitions:

• Two 8-bit ports and two 4-bit ports.
• Any port can be input or output.
• Outputs are latched.
• Inputs are not latched.
• 16 different Input/Output configurations are possible in this Mode.

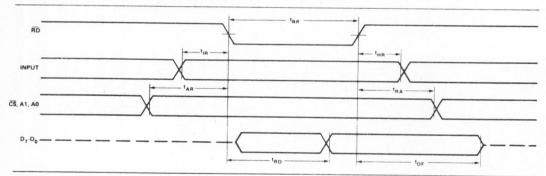

MODE 0 (Basic Input)

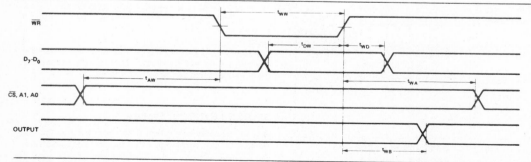

MODE 0 (Basic Output)

MODE 0 Port Definition

A		B		GROUP A			GROUP B	
D_4	D_3	D_1	D_0	PORT A	PORT C (UPPER)	#	PORT B	PORT C (LOWER)
0	0	0	0	OUTPUT	OUTPUT	0	OUTPUT	OUTPUT
0	0	0	1	OUTPUT	OUTPUT	1	OUTPUT	INPUT
0	0	1	0	OUTPUT	OUTPUT	2	INPUT	OUTPUT
0	0	1	1	OUTPUT	OUTPUT	3	INPUT	INPUT
0	1	0	0	OUTPUT	INPUT	4	OUTPUT	OUTPUT
0	1	0	1	OUTPUT	INPUT	5	OUTPUT	INPUT
0	1	1	0	OUTPUT	INPUT	6	INPUT	OUTPUT
0	1	1	1	OUTPUT	INPUT	7	INPUT	INPUT
1	0	0	0	INPUT	OUTPUT	8	OUTPUT	OUTPUT
1	0	0	1	INPUT	OUTPUT	9	OUTPUT	INPUT
1	0	1	0	INPUT	OUTPUT	10	INPUT	OUTPUT
1	0	1	1	INPUT	OUTPUT	11	INPUT	INPUT
1	1	0	0	INPUT	INPUT	12	OUTPUT	OUTPUT
1	1	0	1	INPUT	INPUT	13	OUTPUT	INPUT
1	1	1	0	INPUT	INPUT	14	INPUT	OUTPUT
1	1	1	1	INPUT	INPUT	15	INPUT	INPUT

MODE 0 Configurations

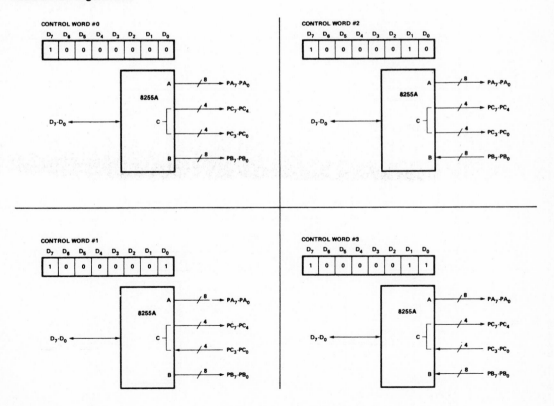

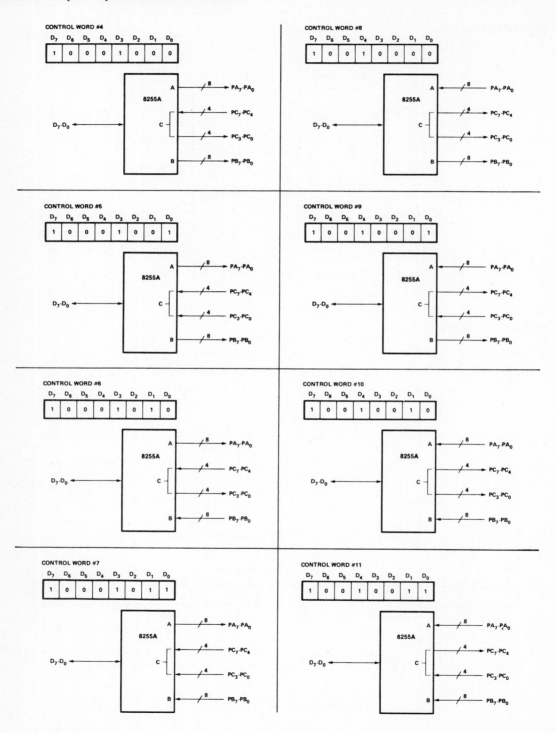

CONTROL WORD #4

D₇	D₆	D₅	D₄	D₃	D₂	D₁	D₀
1	0	0	0	1	0	0	0

CONTROL WORD #8

D₇	D₆	D₅	D₄	D₃	D₂	D₁	D₀
1	0	0	1	0	0	0	0

CONTROL WORD #5

D₇	D₆	D₅	D₄	D₃	D₂	D₁	D₀
1	0	0	0	1	0	0	1

CONTROL WORD #9

D₇	D₆	D₅	D₄	D₃	D₂	D₁	D₀
1	0	0	1	0	0	0	1

CONTROL WORD #6

D₇	D₆	D₅	D₄	D₃	D₂	D₁	D₀
1	0	0	0	1	0	1	0

CONTROL WORD #10

D₇	D₆	D₅	D₄	D₃	D₂	D₁	D₀
1	0	0	1	0	0	1	0

CONTROL WORD #7

D₇	D₆	D₅	D₄	D₃	D₂	D₁	D₀
1	0	0	0	1	0	1	1

CONTROL WORD #11

D₇	D₆	D₅	D₄	D₃	D₂	D₁	D₀
1	0	0	1	0	0	1	1

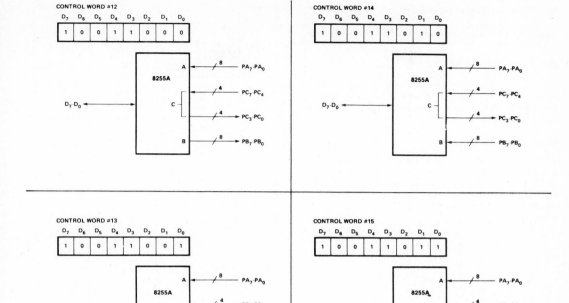

CONTROL WORD #12

D_7	D_6	D_5	D_4	D_3	D_2	D_1	D_0
1	0	0	1	1	0	0	0

CONTROL WORD #14

D_7	D_6	D_5	D_4	D_3	D_2	D_1	D_0
1	0	0	1	1	0	1	0

CONTROL WORD #13

D_7	D_6	D_5	D_4	D_3	D_2	D_1	D_0
1	0	0	1	1	0	0	1

CONTROL WORD #15

D_7	D_6	D_5	D_4	D_3	D_2	D_1	D_0
1	0	0	1	1	0	1	1

Operating Modes

MODE 1 (Strobed Input/Output). This functional configuration provides a means for transferring I/O data to or from a specified port in conjunction with strobes or "handshaking" signals. In mode 1, port A and Port B use the lines on port C to generate or accept these "handshaking" signals.

Mode 1 Basic Functional Definitions:

- Two Groups (Group A and Group B)
- Each group contains one 8-bit data port and one 4-bit control/data port.
- The 8-bit data port can be either input or output. Both inputs and outputs are latched.
- The 4-bit port is used for control and status of the 8-bit data port.

Input Control Signal Definition

$\overline{\text{STB}}$ **(Strobe Input).** A "low" on this input loads data into the input latch.

IBF (Input Buffer Full F/F)

A "high" on this output indicates that the data has been loaded into the input latch; in essence, an acknowledgement. IBF is set by STB input being low and is reset by the rising edge of the RD input.

INTR (Interrupt Request)

A "high" on this output can be used to interrupt the CPU when an input device is requesting service. INTR is set by the $\overline{\text{STB}}$ is a "one", IBF is a "one" and INTE is a "one". It is reset by the falling edge of $\overline{\text{RD}}$. This procedure allows an input device to request service from the CPU by simply strobing its data into the port.

INTE A
Controlled by bit set/reset of PC_4.
INTE B
Controlled by bit set/reset of PC_2.

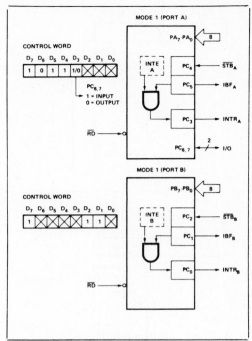

Figure 8. MODE 1 Input

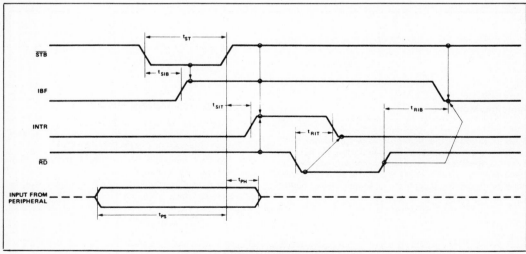

Figure 9. MODE 1 (Strobed Input)

Output Control Signal Definition

OBF (Output Buffer Full F/F). The $\overline{OBF}$ output will go "low" to indicate that the CPU has written data out to the specified port. The $\overline{OBF}$ F/F will be set by the rising edge of the $\overline{WR}$ input and reset by $\overline{ACK}$ input being low.

$\overline{ACK}$ (Acknowledge Input). A "low" on this input informs the 8255A that the data from port A or port B has been accepted. In essence, a response from the peripheral device indicating that it has recieved the data output by the CPU.

INTR (Interrupt Request). A "high" on this output can be used to interrupt the CPU when an output device has accepted data transmitted by the CPU. INTR is set when $\overline{ACK}$ is a "one", $\overline{OBF}$ is a "one", and INTE is a "one". It is reset by the falling edge of $\overline{WR}$.

INTR (Interrupt Request). A "high" on this output can be used to interrupt the CPU when an output device has accepted data transmitted by the CPU. INTR is set when $\overline{ACK}$ is a "one", $\overline{OBF}$ is a "one", and INTE is a "one". It is reset by the falling edge of WR.

INTE A

Controlled by bit set/reset of PC_6.

INTE B

Controlled by bit set/reset of PC_2.

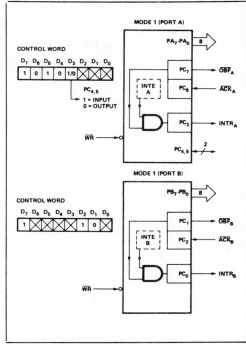

Figure 10. MODE 1 Output

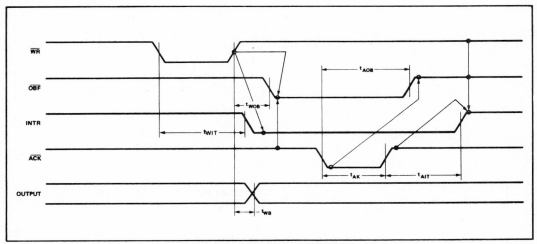

Figure 11. Mode 1 (Strobed Output)

Combinations of MODE 1

Port A and Port B can be individually defined as input or output in Mode 1 to support a wide variety of strobed I/O applications.

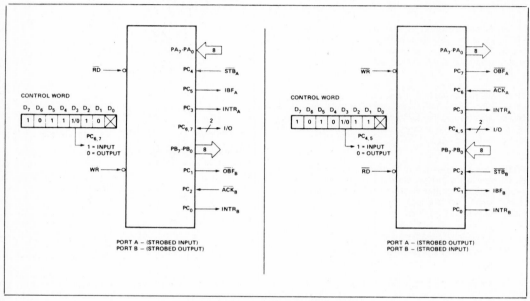

Figure 12. Combinations of MODE 1

Operating Modes

MODE 2 (Strobed Bidirectional Bus I/O). This functional configuration provides a means for communicating with a peripheral device or structure on a single 8-bit bus for both transmitting and receiving data (bidirectional bus I/O). "Handshaking" signals are provided to maintain proper bus flow discipline in a similar manner to MODE 1. Interrupt generation and enable/disable functions are also available.

MODE 2 Basic Functional Definitions:
- Used in Group A only.
- One 8-bit, bi-directional bus Port (Port A) and a 5-bit control Port (Port C).
- Both inputs and outputs are latched.
- The 5-bit control port (Port C) is used for control and status for the 8-bit, bi-directional bus port (Port A).

Bidirectional Bus I/O Control Signal Definition

INTR (Interrupt Request). A high on this output can be used to interrupt the CPU for both input or output operations.

Output Operations

OBF (Output Buffer Full). The OBF output will go "low" to indicate that the CPU has written data out to port A.

ACK (Acknowledge). A "low" on this input enables the tri-state output buffer of port A to send out the data. Otherwise, the output buffer will be in the high impedance state.

INTE 1 (The INTE Flip-Flop Associated with OBF). Controlled by bit set/reset of PC_6.

Input Operations

STB (Strobe Input). A "low" on this input loads data into the input latch.

IBF (Input Buffer Full F/F). A "high" on this output indicates that data has been loaded into the input latch.

INTE 2 (The INTE Flip-Flop Associated with IBF). Controlled by bit set/reset of PC_4.

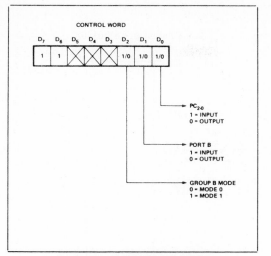

Figure 13. MODE Control Word

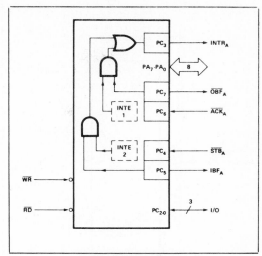

Figure 14. MODE 2

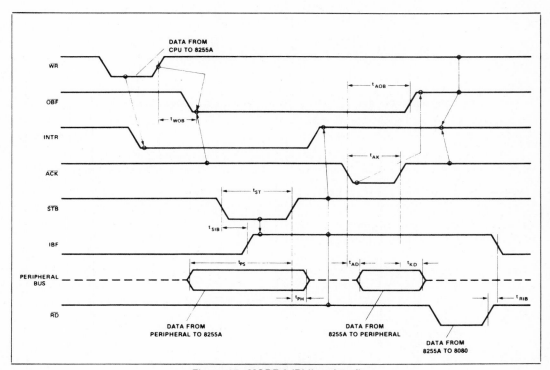

Figure 15. MODE 2 (Bidirectional)

NOTE   Any sequence where $\overline{WR}$ occurs before $\overline{ACK}$ and $\overline{STB}$ occurs before $\overline{RD}$ is permissible.
        (INTR = IBF · $\overline{MASK}$ · $\overline{STB}$ · $\overline{RD}$ + $\overline{OBF}$ · $\overline{MASK}$ · $\overline{ACK}$ · $\overline{WR}$)

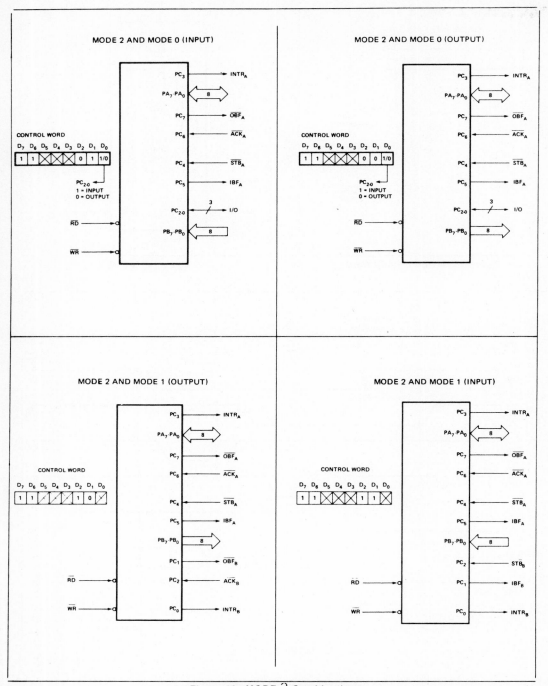

Figure 16. MODE 2 Combinations

Mode Definition Summary

	MODE 0		MODE 1		MODE 2
	IN	OUT	IN	OUT	GROUP A ONLY
PA_0	IN	OUT	IN	OUT	←→
PA_1	IN	OUT	IN	OUT	←→
PA_2	IN	OUT	IN	OUT	←→
PA_3	IN	OUT	IN	OUT	←→
PA_4	IN	OUT	IN	OUT	←→
PA_5	IN	OUT	IN	OUT	←→
PA_6	IN	OUT	IN	OUT	←→
PA_7	IN	OUT	IN	OUT	←→
PB_0	IN	OUT	IN	OUT	——
PB_1	IN	OUT	IN	OUT	——
PB_2	IN	OUT	IN	OUT	——
PB_3	IN	OUT	IN	OUT	——
PB_4	IN	OUT	IN	OUT	——
PB_5	IN	OUT	IN	OUT	——
PB_6	IN	OUT	IN	OUT	——
PB_7	IN	OUT	IN	OUT	——
PC_0	IN	OUT	$INTR_B$	$INTR_B$	I/O
PC_1	IN	OUT	IBF_B	$\overline{OBF}_B$	I/O
PC_2	IN	OUT	$\overline{STB}_B$	$\overline{ACK}_B$	I/O
PC_3	IN	OUT	$INTR_A$	$INTR_A$	$INTR_A$
PC_4	IN	OUT	$\overline{STB}_A$	I/O	$\overline{STB}_A$
PC_5	IN	OUT	IBF_A	I/O	IBF_A
PC_6	IN	OUT	I/O	$\overline{ACK}_A$	$\overline{ACK}_A$
PC_7	IN	OUT	I/O	$\overline{OBF}_A$	$\overline{OBF}_A$

(MODE 0 OR MODE 1 ONLY — applies to PB block)

Special Mode Combination Considerations

There are several combinations of modes when not all of the bits in Port C are used for control or status. The remaining bits can be used as follows:

If Programmed as Inputs —
All input lines can be accessed during a normal Port C read.

If Programmed as Outputs —
Bits in C upper (PC_7-PC_4) must be individually accessed using the bit set/reset function.

Bits in C lower (PC_3-PC_0) can be accessed using the bit set/reset function or accessed as a threesome by writing into Port C.

Source Current Capability on Port B and Port C

Any set of **eight** output buffers, selected randomly from Ports B and C can source 1mA at 1.5 volts. This feature allows the 8255 to directly drive Darlington type drivers and high-voltage displays that require such source current.

Reading Port C Status

In Mode 0, Port C transfers data to or from the peripheral device. When the 8255 is programmed to function in Modes 1 or 2, Port C generates or accepts "hand-shaking" signals with the peripheral device. Reading the contents of Port C

allows the programmer to test or verify the "status" of each peripheral device and change the program flow accordingly.

There is no special instruction to read the status information from Port C. A normal read operation of Port C is executed to perform this function.

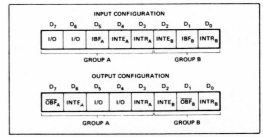

Figure 17. MODE 1 Status Word Format

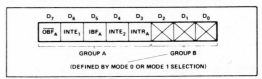

Figure 18. MODE 2 Status Word Format

APPENDIX 4

Laboratory Interfaces and Parts Lists

These are the interfaces required to do the experiments. The main text contains explanations of the interfaces' functions and operations. The next page contains a diagram of the IBM PC's System Board I/O Channel (the IBM PC bus). It is reprinted here by permission of IBM Corporation, Boca Raton, FL.

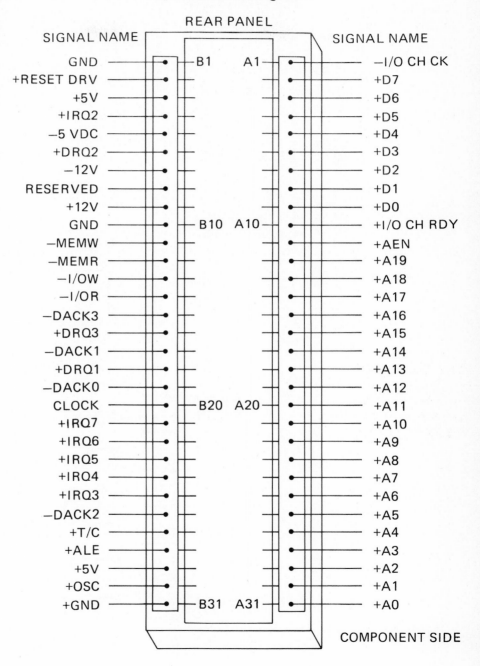

Figure A4-1

Diagram of the IBM PC's System **Board** I/O Channel (the IBM PC Bus). Reprinted by permission of IBM Corporation, Boca Raton, FL).

I/O Channel Diagram

REAR PANEL

SIGNAL NAME			SIGNAL NAME
GND	B1	A1	−I/O CH CK
+RESET DRV			+D7
+5V			+D6
+IRQ2			+D5
−5 VDC			+D4
+DRQ2			+D3
−12V			+D2
RESERVED			+D1
+12V			+D0
GND	B10	A10	+I/O CH RDY
−MEMW			+AEN
−MEMR			+A19
−I/OW			+A18
−I/OR			+A17
−DACK3			+A16
+DRQ3			+A15
−DACK1			+A14
+DRQ1			+A13
−DACK0			+A12
CLOCK	B20	A20	+A11
+IRQ7			+A10
+IRQ6			+A9
+IRQ5			+A8
+IRQ4			+A7
+IRQ3			+A6
−DACK2			+A5
+T/C			+A4
+ALE			+A3
+5V			+A2
+OSC			+A1
+GND	B31	A31	+A0

COMPONENT SIDE

Figure A4-2

Schematic for the add-on I/O board.

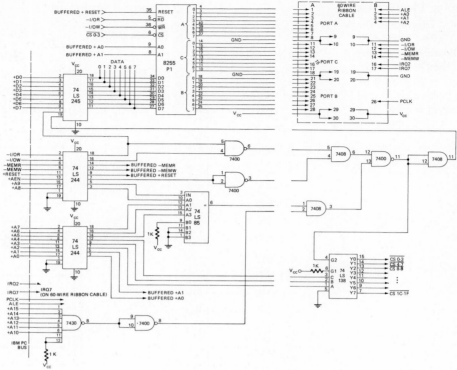

Figure A4-3

Attachment of switches to port A of 8255 device P1 (on the add-on I/O board).

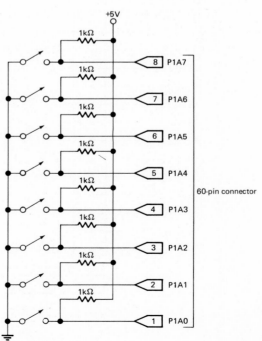

Figure A4-4

Attachment of LEDs to port B of 8255 device P1 (on the add-on I/O board).

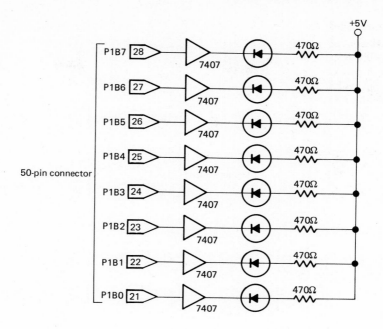

Figure A4-5

Attachment of switches to bits 2 and 4 of port C of 8255 device P1 (on the add-on I/O board).

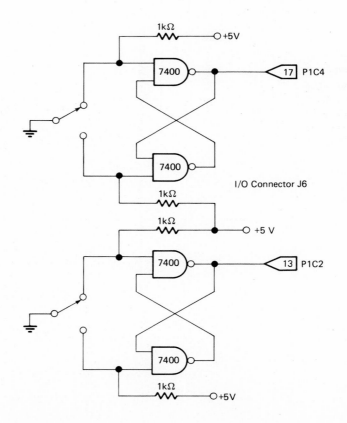

Figure A4-6

Attachment of LEDs to bits 0, 1, 3, and 5 of port C of 8255 device P1 (on the add-on I/O board).

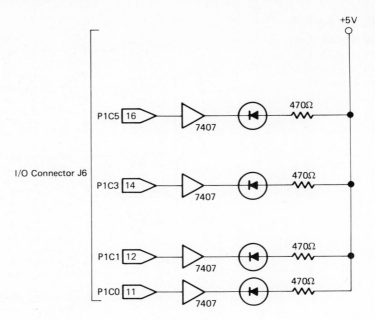

Figure A4-7

Connections for interrupting I/O ports from 8255 device P1 (on the add-on I/O board).

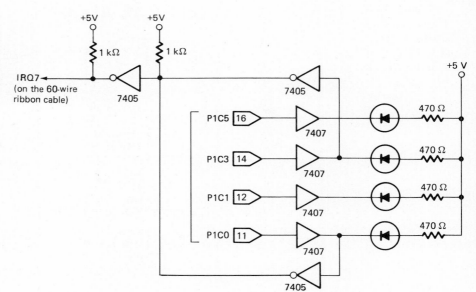

Figure A4-8

Simple circuit for generating a low-frequency clock from a 555 timer chip. The frequency is approximately 100 Hz.

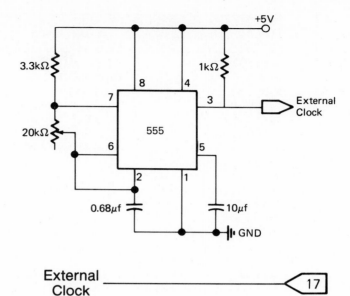

Figure A4-9

Connection of the external clock to bit 6 of port C of 8255 device P1 (on the add-on I/O board).

External Clock ————————————⟨ 17 ⟩

Table A4-1

Parts List for Laboratory Exercises

Item	Description	Quantity	Laboratories
SPDT switch	Alco TT 11DG-WW-2T	8	2,7,B,C,E
1-kΩ resistor pack	Bourns 4114R-002-102	1	2,7,B,C,E
or 1-kΩ resistors		8	2,7,B,C,E
LED display	Red	8	3,B,C,E
470Ω resistor pack	Bourns 4114R-002-471	1	3,B,C,E
or 470Ω resistors		8	
7407 IC	Hex Buffer/Driver	2	3,B,C,E
SPDT switch	Alco TT 11DG-WW-2T	2	B,C
1-kΩ resistor pack	Bourns 4114R-002-102	1	B,C
or 1-kΩ resistors		4	
7400 IC	Quad NAND	1	B,C
LED display	Red	4	B,C
470Ω resistor pack	Bourns 4114R-002-471	1	B,C
or 470Ω resistors			
7407 IC	Hex Buffer/Driver	1	B,C
7405 IC	Hex Inverters	1	B,C
8255 IC	I/O Port	1	2,3,4,7,B,C,D,E
74LS244 IC	Octal Buffer	2	2,3,4,7,B,C,D,E
74LS245 IC	Octal Bus Transceiver	1	2,3,4,7,B,C,D,E

Item	Description	Quantity	Laboratories
7430 IC	8-Input NAND	1	2,3,4,7,B,C,D,E
7400 IC	Quad NAND	1	2,3,4,7,B,C,D,E
7408 IC	Quad AND	1	2,3,4,7,B,C,D,E
74LS85 IC	Magnitude Comparator	1	2,3,4,7,B,C,D,E
74LS138 IC	Decoder	1	2,3,4,7,B,C,D,E
3.3-kΩ resistor		1	D
20K trimmer resistor	Bourns 3099P-1-203	1	D
.68-μF capacitor		1	D
1-kΩ resistor		1	D
10-μF capacitor		1	D
555 timer IC		1	D
Miscellaneous:			
IBM prototype card		1	
8-pin wire-wrap sockets		1	
14-pin wire-wrap sockets		14	
16-pin wire-wrap sockets		6	
20-pin wire-wrap sockets		3	
40-pin wire-wrap sockets		1	

Note: You may find it convenient to use 8-position DIP switches (such as the Archer 275-1301 from Radio Shack) instead of individual SPDT switches and 10-position LED displays (such as the Archer 276-081 from Radio Shack) instead of individual LEDs.

Example Laboratory Setup

The example laboratory setup consists of two boards:

- An add-on I/O board that occupies a slot inside the IBM PC. It contains an 8255 PPI, address decoding and device enabling logic, and data bus transceivers. Such boards are available at low cost in assembled form from several sources, including MetraByte Corporation, Taunton, MA. MetraByte's version is the 24-bit parallel digital I/O interface model PIO-12.
- An experiment board outside the PC itself. It contains switches, LEDs, a timer, and a few other connections required for the laboratory experiments.

The two boards are connected using a 60-conductor ribbon cable as shown in Figure A4-10. We constructed our setup from the following equipment:

- An IBM (PC) prototype card inside the PC. Such cards are available from many sources; we used the IBM-PR2 board from JDR Microdevices of San

Jose, CA. JDR Microdevices provides the decoding circuitry shown in Figure A4-2 as a parts kit.

- A Vector 3677-2 prototyping board externally.

Figure A4-11 shows the pinouts for the 60-pin connector used to attach the experiment board.

Figure A4-10

Connection between the add-on I/O board (inside the IBM PC) and the experiment board (external to the PC).

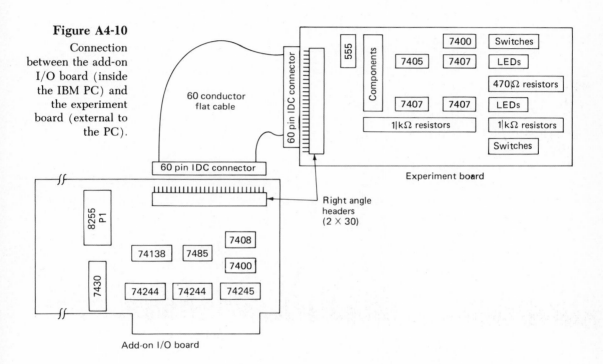

Figure A4-11

Pin assignments for the 60-pin connector used to attach the experiment board.

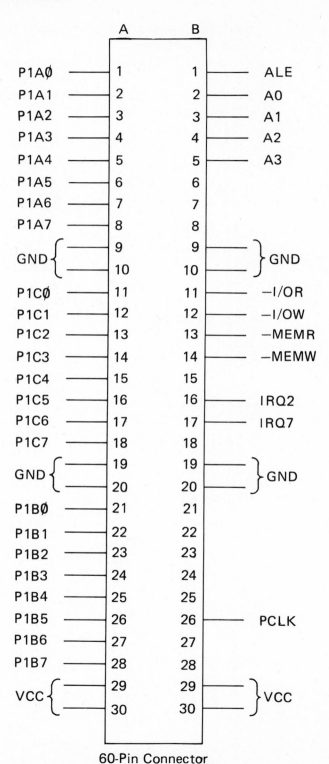

60-Pin Connector

APPENDIX 5

Summary of the DEBUG Monitor

The following descriptions are taken from the *IBM PC Technical Reference Manual* and from the *Disk Operating System Reference Manual* and are reprinted here by permission of IBM Corporation, Boca Raton, FL.

How to Start the DEBUG Program

To start DEBUG, enter:

DEBUG [d:][*path*][*filename*[*.ext*]][*parm1*][*parm2*]

If you enter *filename*, the DEBUG program loads the specified file into memory. You may now enter commands to alter, display, or execute the contents of the specified file.

If you do *not* enter a filename, you must either work with the present memory contents, or load the required file into memory by using the Name and Load commands. Then you can enter commands to alter, display, or execute the memory contents.

The optional parameters, *parm1* and *parm2*, represent the optional parameters for the named *filespec*. For example,

DEBUG DISKCOMP.COM A: B:

In this command, the A: and B: are the parameters that DEBUG prepares for the DISKCOMP program.

When the DEBUG program starts, the registers and flags are set to the following values for the program being debugged:

• The segment registers (CS, DS, ES, and SS) are set to the bottom of free memory; that is, the first segment after the end of the DEBUG program.

• The Instruction Pointer (IP) is set to X'0100'.

• The Stack Pointer (SP) is set to the end of the segment, or the bottom of the transient portion of the program loader, whichever is lower. The segment size at offset 6 is reduced by hex 100 to allow for a stack of that size.

• The remaining registers (AX, BX, CX, DX, BP, SI, and DI) are set to zero. However, if you start the DEBUG program with a filespec, the CS register contains the length of the file in bytes. If the file is greater than 64K, the length is contained in registers BX and CX (the high portion in BX).

• The flags are set to their cleared values. (Refer to the Register command.)

• The default disk transfer address is set to X'80' in the code segment.

Debug

All of available memory is allocated; therefore, any attempt by the loaded program to allocate memory will fail.

Notes:

1. If a file loaded by DEBUG has an extension of .EXE, DEBUG does the necessary relocation and sets the segment registers, stack pointer, and Instruction Pointer to the values defined in the file. The DS and ES registers, however, point to the Program Segment Prefix at the lowest available segment. The BX and CX registers contain the size of the program (smaller than the file size).

    The program is loaded at the high end of memory if the appropriate parameter was specified when the linker created the file. Refer to ".EXE File Structure and Loading" in Appendix H for more information about loading .EXE files.

2. If a file loaded by DEBUG has an extension of .HEX, the file is assumed to contain ASCII representation of hexadecimal characters, and is converted to binary while being loaded.

The DEBUG Command Parameters

Parameter	Definition
address	Enter a one- or two-part designation in one of the following formats: • An alphabetic segment register designation, plus an offset value, such as: **CS:0100** • A segment address, plus an offset value, such as: **4BA:0100** • An offset value only, such as: **100** (In this case, each command uses a default segment.)

Debug

Parameter	Definition
address *(cont.)*	Notes: 1. In the first two formats, the colon is required to separate the values. 2. All numeric values are *hexadecimal* and may be entered as 1-4 characters. 3. The memory locations specified in address must be valid; that is, they must actually exist. Unpredictable results will occur if an attempt is made to access a nonexistent memory location.
byte	Enter a one or two character *hexadecimal* value.
drive	Enter a single digit (for example, 0 for drive A or 1 for drive B) to indicate which drive data is to be loaded from or written to. (Refer to the Load and Write commands.)
filespec	Enter a one- to three-part file specification consisting of a drive designation, filename, and filename extension. All three fields are optional. However, for the Name command to be meaningful, you should at least specify a drive designator or a filename. (Refer to the Name command.)

Parameter	Definition
list	Enter one or more byte and/or string values. For example, **E CS:100 F3 'XYZ' 8D 4 "abcd"** has five items in the list (that is, three byte entries and two string entries having a total of 10 bytes).
portaddress	Enter a 1-4 character *hexadecimal* value to specify an 8- or 16-bit port address. (Refer to the Input and Output commands.)
range	Enter either of the following formats to specify the lower and upper addresses of a range: • *address address* For example: **CS:100 110** **Note:** Only an offset value is allowed in the second address. The addresses must be separated by a space or comma.

Debug

Parameter	Definition
range	• *address* L *value* where *value* is the number of bytes in *hexadecimal* to be processed by the command. For example: **CS:100 L 11** **Notes:** 1. The limit for *range* is hex 10000. To specify that *value* within four *hexadecimal* characters, enter 0000 (or 0). 2. The memory locations specified in *range* must be valid; that is, they must actually exist. Unpredictable results will occur if an attempt is made to access a non-existent memory location.
registername	Refer to the Register command.

Parameter	Definition
sector sector	Enter 1-3 character *hexadecimal* values to specify:
	1. The starting relative sector number
	2. The number of sector numbers to be loaded or written
	In DEBUG, relative sectors are obtained by counting the sectors on the disk surface. The sector at track 0, sector 1, head 0 (the first sector on the disk) is relative sector 0. The numbering continues for each sector on that track and head, then continues with the first sector on the next head of the same track. When all sectors on all heads of the track have been counted, numbering continues with the first sector on head 0 of the next track.
	Note: This is a change from the sector mapping used by DOS Version 1.10.
	The maximum number of sectors that can be loaded or written with a single command is hex 80. A sector contains 512 bytes.
	(Refer to the Load and Write commands.)

Debug

Parameter	Definition
string	Enter characters enclosed in quotation marks. The quotation marks can be either single (') or double (").
	The ASCII values of the characters in the string are used as a list of byte values.
	Within a string, the *opposite* set of quotation marks can be used freely as characters. However, if the *same* set of quotation marks (as the delimiters) must be used within the string, then the quotation marks must be doubled. The doubling does not appear in memory. For example:
	1. 'This "literal" is correct'
	2. 'This ' 'literal' ' is correct'
	3. 'This 'literal' is not correct'
	4. 'This " "literal" " is not correct'
	5. "This 'literal' is correct"
	6. "This " "literal" " is correct"
	7. "This "literal" is not correct"
	8. "This ' 'literal' ' is not correct"

Parameter	Definition
string	In the second and sixth cases above, the word *literal* is enclosed in one set of quotation marks in memory. In the fourth and eighth cases above, the word *literal* is not correct unless you really want it enclosed in two sets of quotation marks in memory.
value	Enter a 1-4 character *hexadecimal* value to specify: • The numbers to be added and subtracted (refer to the Hexarithmetic command), or • The number of instructions to be executed by the Trace command, or • The number of bytes a command should operate on. (Refer to the Dump, Fill, Move, Search, and Unassemble commands.)

Debug

The DEBUG Commands

This section presents a detailed description of how to use the commands to the DEBUG program. The commands appear in alphabetical order; each with its format and purpose. Examples are provided where appropriate.

Information Common to All DEBUG Commands

The following information applies to the DEBUG commands:

- A command is a single letter, usually followed by one or more parameters.

- Commands and parameters can be entered in uppercase or lowercase, or a combination of both.

- Commands and parameters may be separated by delimiters. Delimiters are only required, however, between two consecutive hexadecimal values. Thus, these commands are equivalent:

  dcs:100 110
  d cs:100 110
  d,cs:100,110

- Press Ctrl-Break to end commands.

- Commands become effective only after you press the Enter key.

- For commands producing a large amount of output, you can press Ctrl-NumLock to suspend the display to read it before it scrolls away. Press any other character to restart the display.

- You can use the control keys and the DOS editing keys, described in Chapter 3, while using the DEBUG program.

- If a syntax error is encountered, the line is displayed with the error pointed out as follows:

  d cs:100 CS:110
  error

  In this case, the Dump command is expecting the second address to contain only a hexadecimal offset value. It finds the S, which is not a valid hexadecimal character.

- The prompt from the DEBUG program is a hyphen (-).

- The DEBUG program resides on your DOS Supplemental Program Diskette.

Debug

Summary of DEBUG Commands

The following chart is provided for quick reference.

The section called "Format Notation" in Chapter 4 explains the notation used in the format of the following commands.

Command	Purpose	Format
Assemble	Assembles statements	A [*address*]
Compare	Compares memory	C *range address*
Dump	Displays memory	D [*address*] or D [*range*]
Enter	Changes memory	E *address* [*list*]
Fill	Changes memory blocks	F *range list*
Go	Executes with optional breakpoints	G [=*address*] [*address* [*address*...]]
Hexarithmetic	Hexadecimal add-subtract	H *value value*

Figure 8 (Part 1 of 2). DEBUG Commands

Command	Purpose	Format
Input	Reads/displays input byte	I *portaddress*
Load	Loads file or absolute diskette sectors	L [*address* [*drive sector sector*]]
Move	Moves memory block	M *range address*
Name	Defines files and parameters	N *filespec* [*filespec...*]
Output	Sends output byte	O *portaddress byte*
Quit	Ends DEBUG program	Q
Register	Displays registers/flags	R [*registername*]
Search	Searches for characters	S *range list*
Trace	Executes and displays	T [*=address*][*value*]
Unassemble	Unassembles instructions	U [*address*] or U [*range*]
Write	Writes file or absolute diskette sectors	W [*address* [*drive sector sector*]]

Figure 8 (Part 2 of 2). DEBUG Commands

APPENDIX 5 System Memory Map

Figure A5-1

IBM PC system memory map. (Reprinted by permission of IBM Corporation, Boca Raton, FL).

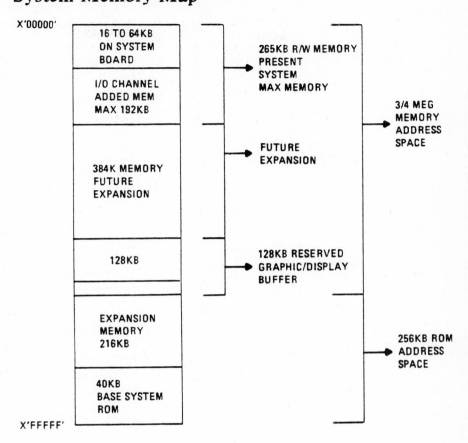

Table A5-1

IBM PC Interrupt
Vectors (0-7F).
(Reprinted by
permission of IBM
Corporation, Boca
Raton, FL)

ADDRESS HEX	INTERRUPT HEX	FUNCTION
0–3	0	Divide by Zero
4–7	1	Single step
8–B	2	Non-Maskable Interrupt (NMI)
C–F	3	Break Point Instruction ('CC'x)
10–13	4	Overflow
14–17	5	Print Screen
18–1F	6,7	Reserved
20–23	8	Timer (18.2 per second)
24–27	9	Keyboard Interrupt
28–37	A,B,C,D	Reserved
38–3B	E	Diskette Interrupt
3C–3F	F	Reserved
40–43	10	Video I/O Call
44–47	11	Equipment Check Call
48–4B	12	Memory Check Call
4C–4F	13	Diskette I/O Call
50–53	14	RS232 I/O Call
54–57	15	Cassette I/O Call
58–5B	16	Keyboard I/O Call
5C–5F	17	Printer I/O Call
60–63	18	ROM Basic Entry Code
64–67	19	Boot Strap Loader
68–6B	1A	Time of Day Call
6C–6F	1B	Get Control on Keyboard Break: Note 1
70–73	1C	Get Control on timer interrupt: Note 1
74–77	1D	Pointer to video initialization table: Note 2
78–7B	1E	Pointer to diskette parameter table: Note 2
7C–7F	1F	Pointer to table (1KB) for graphics character Generator for ASCII 128–255. Defaults to 0:0

Notes: (1) Initialized at power up to point to an IRET Instruction.
(2) Initialized at power up to point to tables in ROM.

I/O Address Map

HEX RANGE	9	8	7	6	5	4	3	2	1	0	DEVICE
00–0F	0	0	0	0	0	Z	A3	A2	A1	A0	DMA CHIP 8237–2
20–21	0	0	0	0	1	Z	Z	Z	Z	A0	INTERRUPT 8259A
40–43	0	0	0	1	0	Z	Z	Z	A1	A0	TIMER 8253–5
60–63	0	0	0	1	1	Z	Z	Z	A1	A0	PPI 8255A–5
80–83	0	0	1	0	0	Z	Z	Z	A1	A0	DMA PAGE REGS
* AX	0	0	1	0	1						NMI MASK REG
CX	0	0	1	1	0						RESERVED
EX	0	0	1	1	1						RESERVED
3F8–3FF	1	1	1	1	1	1	1	A2	A1	A0	TP RS–232–C CD
3F0–3F7	1	1	1	1	1	1	0	A2	A1	A0	5 1/4" DRV ADAPTER
2F8–2FF	1	0	1	1	1	1	1	A2	A1	A0	RESERVED
378–37F	1	1	0	1	1	1	1	Z	A1	A0	PARALLEL PRTR PRT
3D0–3DF	1	1	1	1	0	1	A3	A2	A1	A0	COLOR/GRAPHICS ADAPTER
278–27F	1	0	0	1	1	1	1	Z	A1	A0	RESERVED
200–20F	1	0	0	0	0	0	A3	A2	A1	A0	GAME I/O ADAPTER
3B0–3BF	1	1	1	0	1	1	A3	A2	A1	A0	IBM MONOCHROME DISPLAY PARALLEL PRINTER ADAPTER

Z = Don't Care, i.e., Not in Decode

* At power on time, the Non Mask Interrupt NMI into the 8088 is masked off. This mask bit can be set and reset via system software as follows:

Set mask: write X'80' to I/O Address X'A0' (enable NMI)

Clear mask: write X'00' to I/O Address X'A0' (disable NMI)

Table A5-3

IBM PC Interrupt
Vectors. (Reprinted
by permission of
IBM Corporation,
Boca Raton, FL)

Interrupt Vector Listing

Interrupt Number		Name	BIOS Initialization
0		Divide by Zero	None
1		Single Step	None
2		Non Maskable	NMI_INT (F000:E2C3)
3		Breakpoint	None
4		Overflow	None
5		Print Screen	PRINT_SCREEN (F000:FF54)
6		Unused	
7		Unused	
8		Time of Day	TIMER_INT (F000:FEA5)
9		Keyboard	KB_INT (F000:E987)
A	8259	Unused	
B	Interrupt	Unused	
C	Vectors	Unused (Reserved Communications)	
D		Unused	
E		Diskette	DISK_INT (F000:EF57)
F		Unused (Reserved Printer)	
10		Video	VIDEO_I O (F000:F065)
11		Equipment Check	EQUIPMENT (F000:F84D)
12		Memory	MEMORY_SIZE_DETERMINE (F000:F841)
13		Diskette	DISKETTE_I O (F000:EC59)
14	BIOS	Communications	RS232_I O (F000:E739)
15	Entry	Cassette	CASSETTE_I O (F000:F859)
16	Points	Keyboard	KEYBOARD_I O (F000:E82E)
17		Printer	PRINTER_I O (F000:EF02)
18		Cassette BASIC	(F600:0000)
19		Bootstrap	BOOT_STRAP (F000:E6F2)
1A		Time of Day	TIME_OF_DAY (F000:FE6E)
1B	User Supplied	Keyboard Break	DUMMY_RETURN (F000:FF53)
1C	Routines	Timer Tick	DUMMY_RETURN (F000:FF53)
1D	BIOS	Video Initialization	VIDEO_PARMS (F000:F0A4)
1E	Parameters	Diskette Parameters	DISK_BASE (F000:EFC7)
1F		Video Graphics Chars	None

Table A5-4

IBM PC BASIC
and DOS Reserved
Interrupts.
(Reprinted by
permission of IBM
Corporation, Boca
Raton, FL)

ADDRESS HEX	INTERRUPT HEX	FUNCTION
80–83	20	DOS Program Terminate
84–87	21	DOS Function Call
88–8B	22	DOS Terminate Address
8C–8F	23	DOS CTRL–BRK Exit Address
90–93	24	DOS Fatal Error Vector
94–97	25	DOS Absolute Disk read
98–9B	26	DOS Absolute Disk write
9C–9F	27	DOS Terminate, Fix in Storage
A0–FF	28–3F	Reserved for DOS
100–1FF	40–7F	Not Used
200–217	80–85	Reserved By BASIC
218–3C3	86–F0	Used by BASIC Interpreter while BASIC is Running.
3C4–3FF	F1–FF	Not Used

Index

INT 10H instruction, 84–86,
  118–119
INT 16H instruction, 68, 77–81
INT 1AH instruction, 281
INT 20H instruction, 3, 9–10
  registers, effects on, 28
  vector, 248
INT 21H instruction, 249, 281
  interrupt vectors, 249
  time of day, 281
Invalid BCD digits, 176
Inverting bits, 62–63
Inverting decision logic, 163, 170
I/O addresses, 36, 54, 217, 433
  IBM PC, 433
  on-board 8255 PPI, 217
I/O address map, 433
I/O channel connector (IBM PC
  bus), 323, 325–328, 409
I/O device table, 140–144
I/O drivers, 140
I/O instructions, 36
IO/$\overline{\text{M}}$ signal, 339
I/O pin connections, 33, 53, 214
$\overline{\text{I/OR}}$ signal, 339
$\overline{\text{I/OW}}$ signal, 339
IRET, 245, 247
Isolated input/output, 36

J

JA, 100, 112
JB, 35, 39, 112
JBE, 100, 112
JC, 35, 39, 42, 112
JE, 36
JMP, 68
  effect on pipeline, 332
  execution, 331–333
  indexed addressing, 141, 210
JNB, 112
JNBE, 112
JNS, 36, 39, 42
JNZ, 36, 47
JPE, 295
JPO, 295, 316
JS, 36, 39, 42
Jump table, 140–144, 210–212
Jump-to-self (endless loop)
  instruction, 329
  execution, 331–333

K

K (kilobit or kilobyte), 2
Keyboard, 4, 77–82
  arrangement, 4

codes, 373–375
control, ensuring of, 50
encoder, 77
entry, 135
input port, 250
interrupts, 249–250
invalid key combinations, 79
repeat feature, 49, 250
scan codes, 68, 250, 375
services, 68, 77
vector, 249

L

L (load) command, 30, 419
L (length) option in commands,
  108, 117, 423
Label, 39–40
Laboratory setup, 414–416
Latch, 215, 232, 330
Lending zeros, omission of, 7, 8
Least significant bit (bit 0), 38
LED (light-emitting diode), 53, 54
Length of data transfers, 19, 137
Limit checking, 111–114
Linear select addressing, 340–341
Linearization, 173
Line-oriented input, 261
Loading disk files, 30–31
LODSB, 100, 110–111, 124
Logic analyzer, 321
Logical device, 140
Logical functions, 25–27, 62–63,
  223–224
  clearing Carry flag, 170
  truth tables, 26, 62
Logical shift, 24–25
Logical sum, 106
Lookup tables, 85, 92–98, 190–193
  advantages and disadvantages,
    85, 97–98
  arithmetic applications,
    190–193
  code conversion, 92–98
  interpolation, 193
  subroutines, 210–212
  timing applications, 286–287, 291
LOOP, 101, 107, 187
Lost (runaway) program, 50
Low-volume applications, 81–82

M

M (megabyte), 2, 10
M (move) command, 167–168, 430
Machine language, 19
Macro Assembler, 17, 18

Mail drop analogy, 258
Mailbox, 258
Maintenance of programs, 147
Majority logic, 312–315
Manual translation, 19
Maskable (INTR) interrupt, 247, 391
Masking bits, 40, 62
Maximum, 152
Mechanical components, 82
Memory:
  accessing, 329–331, 334–335
  access time, 330
  addresses, 6, 336, 431
  capacity, 10, 338
  changing, 8–9
  examining, 5–8
  interface, 335–338
  nonvolatile, 14
  RAM, 3, 4, 7, 14
  refresh, 58, 333
  reserved, 247, 385
  ROM, 3, 4, 11, 14, 158
  segmentation, 6, 10–12, 385
  stack, 199
  stack transfers, 204
  time, tradeoffs with, 85, 193
  volatile, 7, 14, 124
Memory capacity, 10, 338
Memory enable signal, 337
Memory map, 336, 431
Memory-mapped input/output, 36
Memory/time tradeoffs, 85, 193
$\overline{\text{MEMR}}$ signal, 331, 333, 335, 339
$\overline{\text{MEMW}}$ signal, 335, 339
Microcomputer, 2
Microprocessor, 2, 4
Millisecond delay program, 71
Minus key, 8
Minute delay, 289–290
Misinterpreting data as instructions, 49
Mnemonics, 19, 125
Mod 60 arithmetic, 287
Modular programming, 146
Module, 146
Monitor program (DEBUG), 2, 5,
  12–13, 417–430
  command summary, 429–430
  startup, 5, 12–13, 417–418
Monitor segment (F000), 11
Monitoring system example, 292
Most significant bit (bit 7 or bit
  15), 38, 42
MOV, 19, 20
  flags, effect on (none), 45,
    108, 170
  order of operands, 162, 170
Moving (newspanel) display, 118–119
Moving programs, 167–168
Moving the cursor, 86
MOVSB, 122, 127
MS-DOS, 2

PUSHF, 196, 199–200
Push operations (on stack), 196, 197–200

Q

Q (quit) command, 5, 29
Queue of instructions, 331–333
??? (invalid operation code), 163
Quotation marks (around ASCII characters), 117, 425–426

R

R (register) command, 27–29
  all registers, 27
  8-bit registers, 28
  flags, 43–45
  register names, 27
  single registers, 27, 28–29
R F (display flags) command, 43–45
  keyboard control, 50
RAM, 3, 4, 7, 14
  IBM PC addresses, 336, 431
  initialization, 124
  interface, 335–338
  volatility, 7
Random-access memory (RAM), 3, 4, 7, 14
Random starting point, 124
RCL, 295–296
RCR, 296, 297, 299, 309
Read-only memory (ROM), 3, 4, 11, 14, 158
Read/write memory (RAM), 3, 4, 7, 14
READY flag (for use with interrupts), 254–255, 258
READY FOR DATA signal, 216, 221–222, 227–229
Real-time, 272
Real-time clock, 284–291
  longer intervals, 287–291
  serial I/O, 303–306
  timekeeping, 285
Real-time constraints, 273
Real-time monitoring system example, 291–292
Real-time operating system, 291–292
Real-time requirements, 273
Redirection, 146
  input, 169
  output, 30
Reenabling interrupts, 247
Reentrant subroutines, 269
Refresh in IBM PC, 58, 333

Register display, 27–29
  automatic production, 28
  bottom line, 157
  valid names, 27
Register indirect addressing, 103
  execution, 334–335
Registers, 17–18
  changing, 28–29
  clearing, 68, 74
  display, 27–28
  8-bit, 17–18
  examination, 27–28
  initialization by DEBUG, 418
  order in interrupt response, 246
  order in stack, 204
  programming model, 18
  saving and restoring, 203–204
  segment, 11, 385
  setting flags from, 108
Relative addressing, 41–42, 199
  relocatability, 42
Relative offsets, 41
  example, 41
  16-bit, 199
  starting point, 41
Relocatability, 42
Repeated keys, 49, 250
REP prefix, 122, 126–127
  breakpoint, 157
  trace, 159
Reserved memory locations, 248, 385, 432
Reset, 50
  address, 335–336
  8088 CPU, 390
  8255 PPI, 55, 232
  interrupt system, 247
Resetting (clearing) bits, 62–63, 224–225
Resetting the computer, 50
Restoring the cursor, 118, 119
Resuming a program after a breakpoint, 157, 163, 312
RET, 196, 197, 199
Return key, 6 (*see also* Enter key)
ROL, 122
ROM (read-only memory), 3, 4, 11, 14, 158
ROR, 122
Rotating interrupt priorities, 268
Runaway commands, 50
Runaway programs, 50
Running (executing) a user program, 9–10, 12, 22

S

S (search) command, 158
S (sign) flag, 38

S register (*see* Stack pointer)
SAR, 122
Saving and restoring registers, 203–204
Saving programs on disk, 30–31
Saving user registers in the stack, 203–204
SBB (subtract with borrow), 173
Scan codes, 68, 80–81, 250, 375
SCASB, 146, 165
Scheduler program, 273
Scroll Lock key, 50
Search (S) command, 158
Searching, 151–152
Second delay program, 167
Segment, 3, 5–6
Segmented memory addresses, 10–12, 269, 420–421
Segment number, 3, 6, 10
  DEBUG's automatic selection, 6, 418
Segment registers, 11, 385, 420–421
  address lines, effects on, 333, 334–335
  initial values, 418
  location, 331
  uses, 385
Segments (of memory), 3, 5–6, 11
Semicolon (indicating comment to assembler), 18
Serial, 296
Serial data formats, 307, 309
Serial I/O, 294–318
Serial/parallel conversion, 298–300
Setting bits to 1, 62–63
  8255 PPI port C, 223–225
Setting breakpoints, 156, 160
Setting directions in 8255 PPI, 54–55
Setup (laboratory), 414–416
74154 decoder, 336–337
Shift instructions, 24–25, 42, 122, 123, 295–297
SHL, 17, 24–25, 42, 138, 141, 299
SHR, 17, 42, 74, 297
Sign extension, 121
Sign flag, 38, 42
  conditional jumps, 39
  designations in register display, 44
  flag register, position in, 44
Single-step mode, 156, 158
  continuing, 163
  definition, 156
  delay routines, 311
  examples, 163
  interrupts, 257
  REP prefix, 159
  restrictions, 159
SI (source index) register, 102, 110, 124, 127
  16-bit addresses, 5–6, 10, 36